VINCENT ROTH

A LIFE IN GUYANA

VOLUME II: THE LATER YEARS: 1923-1935

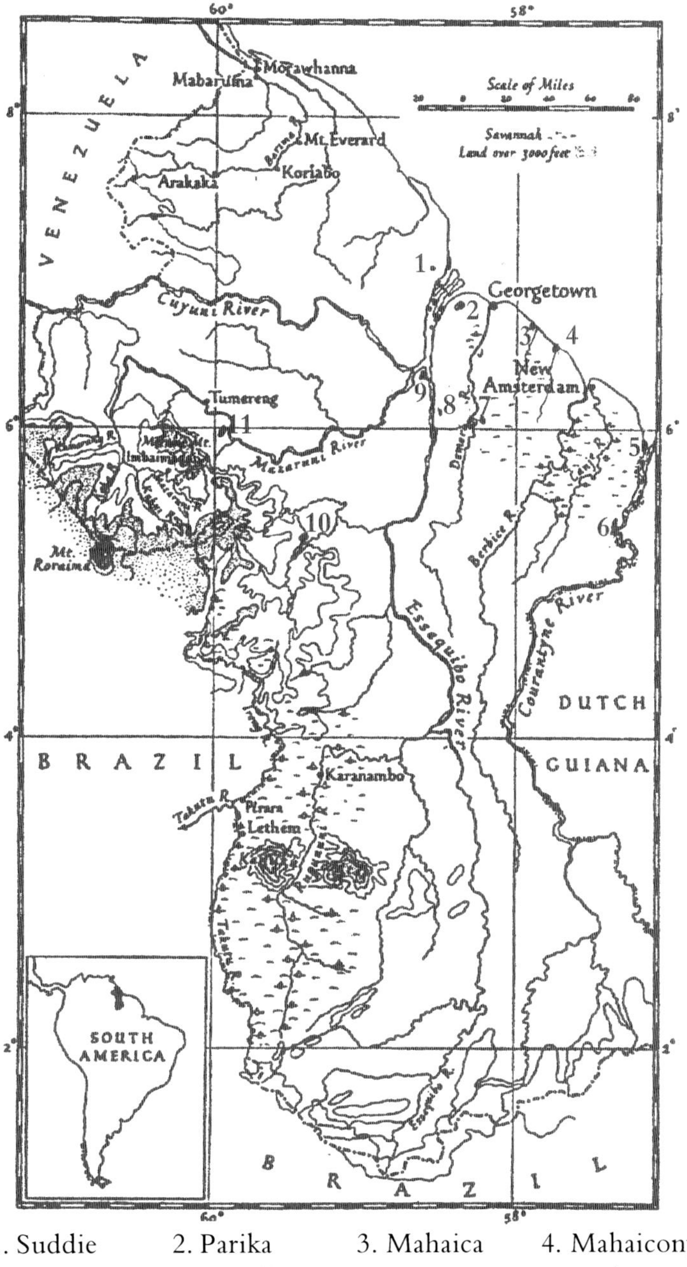

1. Suddie
2. Parika
3. Mahaica
4. Mahaicony
5. Springlands
6. Orealla
7. Wismar
8. Rockstone
9. Bartica
10. Kaietur
11. Kamakusa

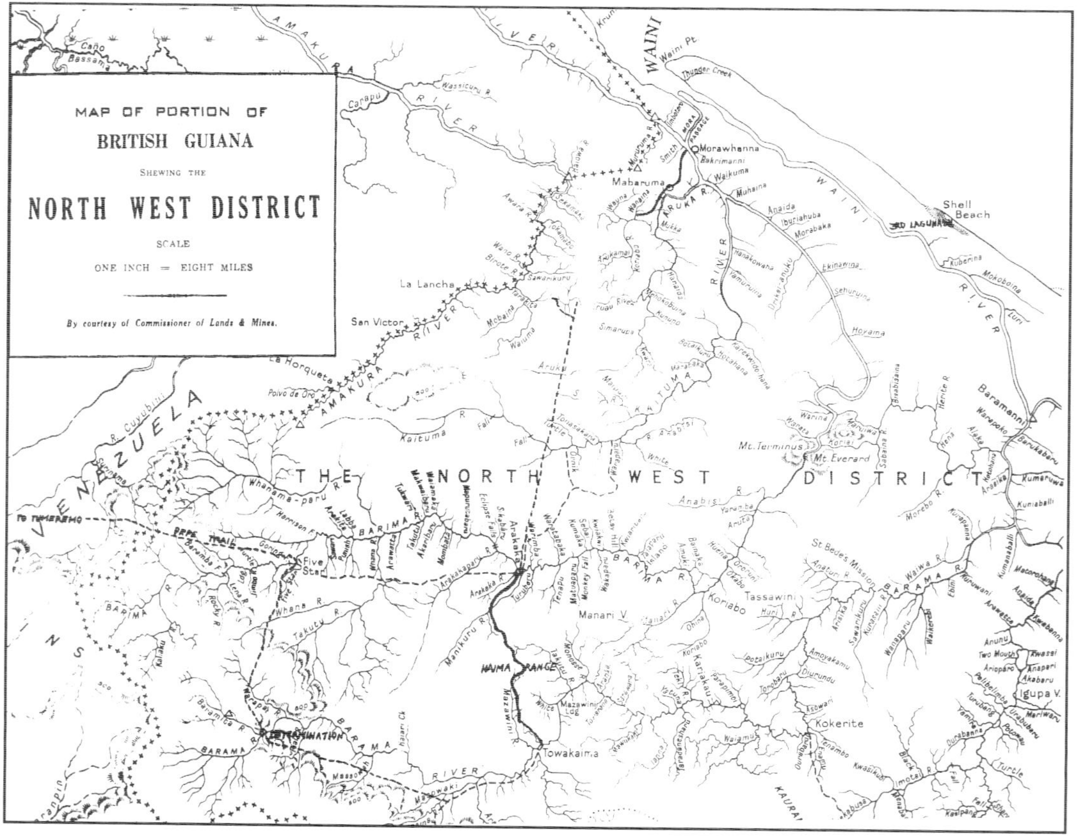
MAP OF PORTION OF
BRITISH GUIANA
SHEWING THE
NORTH WEST DISTRICT
SCALE
ONE INCH = EIGHT MILES
By courtesy of Commissioner of Lands & Mines.
THE NORTH WEST DISTRICT
VENEZUELA
WAINI
WAINI RIVER
AMAKURA RIVER
BARIMA R.
BARAMA R.
KAITUMA
Shell Beach
Morawhanna
Mabaruma
Arakaka
Five Star
Towakaima
Kokerite
Tassawini
Koriabo
Manari V.
Mt. Terminus
Mt. Everard
St Bede's Mission
La Lancha
San Victor
La Horqueta
Polvo de Oro
Baramanni
Igupa V.
HAIMA RANGE
PEPE TRAIL
TO TUMEREMO
KAURAI

VINCENT ROTH

A LIFE IN GUYANA

VOLUME II: THE LATER YEARS: 1923-1935

EDITED BY MICHAEL BENNETT

PEEPAL TREE

First published in Great Britain in 2003
Peepal Tree Press
17 King's Avenue
Leeds LS6 1QS
England

ISBN 1 900715 55 4

CONTENTS

VOLUME 2

MAPS

PHOTOGRAPHS

CHAPTER XIV

A VISIT TO THE DIAMOND FIELDS

About a week after my return to Georgetown, the Commissioner of Lands and Mines sent for me and said that the Colonial Secretary intended to go on a visit of inspection to the diamond fields on the 26th September. He proposed travelling via Wismar, Rockstone, Tew's line to the Bartica-Kaburi Road and thence along the road trace cut by Cheong, Parsley and myself to Turesi Falls, from where he would continue the journey by boat. He would be accompanied by Dr Kelly, the Surgeon General, and also, probably, by a police officer.

Bayley asked me what I thought of this scheme. I told him that Tew's line, cut in 1912, would probably require reopening and that I considered the overland journey rather too strenuous for men who had passed the prime of life and who were unaccustomed to the local conditions in the bush. Bayley agreed and proposed to advise the Colonial Secretary, the Hon R. Popham Lobb, against such an itinerary. Then, Mullin, the Assistant Commissioner, came over to the drawing office and pointed out to me that it was in our interest to encourage Mr Lobb's proposals, so that he could see the type of work we had to do. Soon he got me quite enthusiastic over the matter in spite of the fact that I would have to travel a couple of weeks ahead of the party to fix the camps, throw logs over creeks and generally overhaul the trail. He evidently persuaded the Commissioner to change his mind as well, for during the afternoon I received the official confirmation of Mullin's proposals.

I planned to leave town on the 1st September, allowing close on four weeks for the required work. However, a few days later, orders came down from the Secretariat that the party would start out on the 6th September instead of the 26th as previously arranged. The reason for the change was the fact that the wife of my old friend Mr Edward King, Commissioner of the North West District, was about to give birth. It had been intended that the Governor would visit the North West District on Mr Lobb's return from the Mazaruni and it was not until all the dates had been fixed that King discovered it would be embarrassing to have his Excellency up there simultaneously with his wife's confinement. So he wrote a frantic letter (so described by one who saw it) to the Colonial Secretary begging that the arrangements be modified to suit his convenience. As the Governor and Colonial Secretary could not be out of town together, the latter decided to make his visit earlier.

The earliest date on which I could arrange to leave Georgetown was 23rd August, allowing me only a fortnight to overhaul the seventy odd miles of trail. Fortunately I managed to pick up an Indian crew of fifteen who had come from the Moruca looking for employment.

So, after a spell of exactly three weeks in Georgetown, I set off once again for the bush. My boys accompanied me in the car to the Demerara River steamer stelling. At Sandhills, Dad and Mother, who were spending the weekend with the Sills, came out in a boat to wish me *bon voyage*, whilst Dad gave me the keys to his house so I could get his razor, which he had forgotten, and send it down by the steamer on the following day.

At Christianburg, I went ashore in the police boat and went to Dad's quarters where, getting what he wanted, I hustled off to Wismar along a very greasy path. Once there I made arrangements with Kingsland, the Superintendent, to hire a boat and tackling at Rockstone, and then checked the stores as they were transferred from the steamer to the train. Just before starting, Maggs, the Chief Engineer to Sprostons, and a party of old ladies came on the train, filling all the first class accommodation, so I stayed out on the carriage platform where Maggs joined me. What with trying to keep my balance and dodging the sparks that descended in showers from the engine, I had an exciting trip to Rockstone, where we arrived shortly before six o'clock.

At Cole Glen, where we stopped to take on water, Maggs showed me the hydraulic ram in operation, to raise water from the creek to the tank. It had only recently been installed, replacing a steam pump. Thirteen years previously I had taken the levels for this, when Thomas Dobbie had been the engineer in charge.

I was up again shortly after five o'clock next morning overseeing the loading of my boat. For the start of our journey we were tied to the powerful motor launch, *Paiana,* which at half past six set off on its thrice weekly service to Tumatumari. Captain Wood invited me up to his steering platform on the roof. The morning mist was so thick that, although we travelled within fifty feet of the bank, the trees were barely discernible and minute droplets of dew formed on the hair of my arms. But by the time we reached the main channel at the southern end of Gluck Island, the rising sun had cleared the mist sufficiently to allow us sight of the western bank.

There the captain dropped us and our boat opposite the mouth of Tiparu Inlet, pointing out the spot where Tew's line commenced.

We soon found his initial paal though the line itself was quite obliterated by bush. Behind the river levee was a deep swamp through which we waded in search of the line until the water reached our chests, at which point I decided to turn back and go to Sprostons' old timber camp at the head of Tiparu Inlet. Close behind it, Andrew Grant, late Superintendent of Sprostons, had told me, was where the line passed.

We started up the inlet which, being several hundred feet wide, had the appearance of a river but without any perceptible current. It was now several years since Sprostons' Tiparu Camp closed down and since I had paid my only visit, so it was not surprising that I passed the place and went on up the inlet for another mile before realising my mistake. Returning, we at length found the old landing quite blocked with bush and the timber path submerged to a depth of nearly four feet. We pushed the boat along this but as we had to cut every foot of the way through a dense tangle of bush rope and thorny briars, we had barely progressed a thousand feet when approaching dusk warned us it was time to return to camp.

After a further day's of cutting through thick bush and very swampy ground I decided it would be useless to continue attempting the passage through Tew's line but would proceed through the Butukari Trail instead. We returned to camp, had breakfast, loaded the boat and set off up the Essequibo River. During the afternoon we saw several large green iguanas, one of which I shot with the little .22 rifle I carried. I had often heard it said that the flesh of this lizard was very dainty and I looked forward to trying it but later, when I asked the cook where it was, I learnt that the Indians had already cooked and eaten it!

A large troupe of quaint little sackiwinki monkeys kept our company for quite a while, leaping from tree to tree along the bank parallel with the boat. Sometimes they would come down close to the water's edge and peep at us through the leaves. All sizes of the species were represented in the troupe, from old grandfathers to little babies clinging to their mothers as they leapt among the branches. The young ones big enough to travel by themselves would occasionally miss the branch to which they sprang and screamed with fright as they fell to a lower one. The use they made of their long tails was remarkable, serving the purpose of a fifth limb in their arboreal journeys. Eventually we left the little creatures behind and, crossing the wide expanse of river below Plantain Island, sighted the Arasaru Mountain in the distance. It was now turned five o'clock so we set up camp on the west bank opposite the lowest of the three Kurtuahara Islands.

Next day we took the channel to the west of the islands and soon came out into the main stream, nearly a mile wide. After rounding a point we came to a wide timber landing. A timber ballahoo was moored there and from a black boy who was baling it out we learnt that this was the new Butakari landing. The first camp was about two and three quarter miles aback, with a railway line leading to it. A locomotive and truck would arrive within the hour to take what cargo the launch had brought from Rockstone and my luggage could go up with it. This was welcome news, so, leaving the men to bring the stores up with the train, I walked towards the camp along the line. The track followed the river bank for a few hundred yards then swung inland on an embankment of white sand over half a mile of swamp. After the swamp the line ascended a long timber-covered hill at a pretty stiff gradient. Here and there were piles of wallaba wood for locomotive fuel. Suddenly I heard a shrill whistle, apparently close by, yet no engine was visible. In front of me was a dip in which I supposed the locomotive had descended, but when I saw the bottom of this depression there was no engine, though its whistle sounded again, this time much closer. The mystery was solved when I reached the bottom of the slope where a siding had been cut into the sand and here the little locomotive, *Barima,* was busy shunting ballast wagons. It was the same engine formerly at Wismar working the timber flat, and before that in use at the Barima Mine, near Arakaka.

A short time later I reached the camp which, built parallel to the track, was not visible until one actually arrived there. The camp consisted of a large shop, office and dispensary, dispenser's quarters, blacksmith's shop, manager's house and some others, all built with wallaba shingles. Behind these lay a regular village of some thirty or forty thatched huts where the labourers and their womenfolk dwelt. In the manager's quarters were two extra rooms, with spring cots and washstands for visitors.

Presently Claxton, the grant manager, came in from aback, invited me to breakfast and put his house at my disposal. He said Orella, the owner, was on the grant taking stock of the standing timber and would not be back before evening. The ballast train having come in, the engine set out for the landing, pushing an empty truck before it. I took a ride in the cab where I had to hang on for dear life as the loco rocked and swayed over the roughly laid track. It was a marvel how it stayed on the rails. At the landing we loaded the men and baggage on to the truck, though some of the men had to find room on top of the coal box at the rear of the cab. We returned to the camp about noon to find Claxton and breakfast waiting for me. Afterwards I had the loads made up for carrying and found I would have to leave quite a few packages. By the time this work was done it was three o'clock and I yielded to Claxton's persuasion that I delay my departure until the next day.

He took me along the main timber path to show me where the Butakari Trail branched off. At the beginning of the path, where the railway ended, a gang of men was building an embankment across a shallow ravine to make a siding for loading timber. Great logs were placed crossways over each other and then sand dumped over them until the desired height was obtained. By this ramp was a powerful steam winch, whose cable extended out of sight down the timber path, which ran straight as an arrow down valleys and over hills for nearly a mile to where another steam winch was located. This hauled the logs from the second mile from the railhead.

Descending the first of the shallow valleys, we crossed the little Butakari Creek that flowed behind the camp. The timber path, for some hundred yards, was covered with logs of greenheart awaiting transportation. About three quarters of a mile from camp we came to the Butakari Trail which crossed our path at right angles and ran out to the Essequibo. This last section of the trail had been allowed to grow over. The few gold diggers who had used it now passed along the railroad track and timber path. It was here that we met Orella emerging from the forest. He was very surprised to see me and pleased that I was spending the night in camp. We enjoyed a substantial dinner and spent the evening swapping bush tales. When the subject of tigers cropped up, as it invariably did, Orella told how once, returning to camp at Arawai on the lower Essequibo, he saw an immense jaguar stalking majestically about a hundred yards in front of him. Orella had a .22 rifle and, without stopping to think, fired at the beast. The tiger leapt in the air and when it landed on its feet again, made a complete turn and was now facing him with its fangs exposed in a vicious snarl. Orella did not wait to see what happened next but ran as he had never run before, not slowing down until he reached camp by a roundabout route.

Shortly after seven o'clock next morning I left camp with my string of fifteen droghers and Orella who volunteered to accompany me as far as the last crossing of the Butakari Creek, where I proposed to fix my first day's camp. I found that the Butakari Trail was still in fair condition, though blocked in a few places by fallen trees. Orella promised to have that portion of the trail running through Sprostons concession cleared before the Colonial Secretary arrived. The first two miles were pretty rough going as the trail crossed some seven or eight tributaries of the Butakari, all of which ran in deep and narrow gullies. So I was glad to reach Butakari Creek beyond which, Orella told me, the country was much less rugged. I used an old site of Orella's as the camp. We had to wait two hours for the majority of the droghers to arrive. At this rate of progress I realised we would not get through in time so I arranged for Orella to send on five more droghers with the balance of the provisions I had left. After breakfast I sent Correia with a few men to brush up the trail ahead whilst I supervised the building of the camp with the others.

Moving on next day in a general westerly direction over fairly level and forest-covered country, I had to wait for prolonged periods for the wretchedly slow droghers. We crossed a wide old line running north and south, and which I erroneously took to be Tew's line. A short distance beyond this we came to a small creek where stood several old lean-tos and benabs used by the gold diggers at the time of the Kaburi rush. By mid afternoon I came out on the Bartica-Kaburi Road at the 58th Milepost from Bartica. On this road I headed north, coming across a couple of turtles which I turned on their backs for the men to bring along. Near the 55th Milepost I came across the same old line I had crossed in the morning and, from a signboard, discovered it was the Government trail to Tumatumari and Tiboku Falls cut by Cheong some years previously. Had I taken this trail in the morning I would have saved several miles walk. An old lean-to stood by the road and I decided to camp there. It was five o'clock before the first of the droghers arrived and began cutting fresh palm leaves to re-thatch the shed. Before this work was completed a heavy shower of rain came on and soaked us thoroughly. It was dark by the time the last drogher arrived. The rain continued and because the new leaves had not set, it dripped through onto our hammocks giving us a most miserable night.

I sent Correia on next morning with the slowest of the droghers; I stayed with the others finishing off the camp and putting a greater pitch on the roof. I caught up with the forward party shortly before eleven o'clock at the 48th Mile, where I had to wait two hours for the men carrying the food box. The Bartica-Kaburi Road is a monotonous twelve foot swathe running through the forest with only a few and widely separated bends. On the whole it was fairly clear except for one section around the 45th Mile where the path was completely obliterated by fallen trees.

I wanted to camp by a small creek that ran in a gully some few hundred yards south of the road, but there were no palm trees there, and as we had left our tarpaulin at Butakari, there was nothing we could do but carry on. Near the 42nd Mile we passed a small stream and here I decided to camp, as it was close on six o'clock, even though there were no palms in the vicinity. Fortunately there was no rain that night.

Next morning I soon reached the beginning of my line to Kaburi and turned along the path towards the Parker River (also called Ikuribisi). This river was very much lower than when I last saw it, now barely two feet deep. We spent two days here rebuilding the camp and clearing the trail ahead which, from Cunningham River to the road, had not been cleared as a footpath.

The droghers Orella had promised to send me had not turned up, so I sent Correia back to Butakari with six men to bring up the balance of the rations and to act as guide to Mr Lobb's party. With the remaining nine I continued westwards along a fairly good trail that required little or no clearing, though we found all last year's camps had fallen down. In almost every case one of the forks supporting the ridge pole had rotted and broken away, letting the roof fall. We stopped at Sunshine Camp at the head of McTurk's River for breakfast.

During the afternoon heavy rain fell but ceased by the time we reached No 3 Camp at Mullin's Creek where, clearing away the debris of the old camp, we built two camps of the pigeon-trap type. The advantage of this type of camp is the ease and speed with which it can be built. The palm leaves, not being split as in the superior type of camp, last longer as they do not dry and shrivel up so quickly. Having built a third pigeon-trap camp, (their disadvantage is that constructions of this type are restricted in size), we headed for the Kaburi River, arriving at noon.

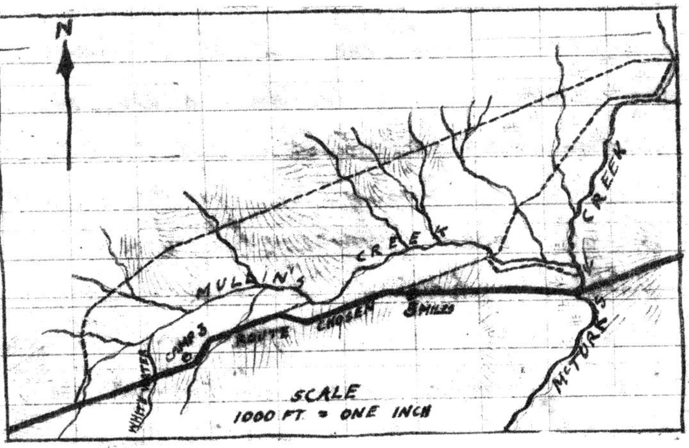

After breakfast we set about fixing a handrail to the large mora tree Cheong and I had felled to form a bridge. This job presented several difficulties. The river bottom was rocky and the force of the current gave us much trouble in fixing the three or four uprights holding the rail. Eventually, by fixing the uprights in notches cut in the side of the tacouba, and bracing them with long forks, we got them to remain in position, although the current oscillated them continuously. I had grave doubts as to their permanence, but better could not be done in the circumstances. Then we crossed some fairly steep ironstone hills until we descended to a beautifully clear creek where we found the remains of Cheong's first camp, which

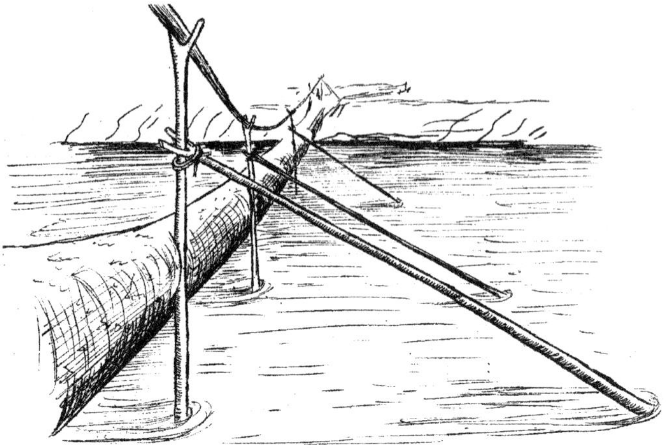

we set about making habitable. We had little sleep that night on account of the innumerable sandflies.

The section of trail we now followed ran over the northern slopes of the Ebini Hills, an ironstone formation, reaching an elevation of about five hundred feet above Kaburi. I had the misfortune to stumble on a nest of hunuhunu bees in a tacouba lying on the ground and got a very lively sting on the knee. It is a larger edition of the English bumble bee and chiefly nests on the particular wood called after it – hunuhunudani.

Five days later we reached the Mazaruni River. The going had been hard, especially the section surveyed by Parsley. This I had expected to be better, having been the most recently cut. No footpath had been cleared in the middle of the line and, in addition, the reconnaissance and false lines were all cut to the same width as the main line, so that without a map I would have gone astray on several occasions. Looking across the river, which at this point was about a quarter of mile wide, I saw a launch in front of a tarpaulin camp. Rightly guessing this to be the Warden's launch, I shouted and waved for it to come across. It was the new launch, *Control*, a small boat with a powerful Kelvin engine designed to work on the smooth upper reaches of the river above the falls. When it arrived, the captain told me that Winter, the warden, had gone to town but was expected back daily; however, I was welcome to use the camp. At this invitation I got into the boat with the first group of the droghers who had just arrived. After breakfast I got out my big tarpon hook and soon landed a couple of large perai, while the captain took a bow and arrow and shot a couple of lukunani in a small itabo nearby.

During the afternoon a couple of boats from the diamond fields passed our camp and it was a fine sight to see them run the fall. Later I walked down to the bottom of the fall and arranged with the captain of one of the launches that had just arrived from lower down the river to purchase sufficient provisions for my men to carry them back to the Ebini River. Travelling as a launch passenger was the celebrated Angel Baby, still in men's riding breeches and white silk shirt, the same lady who had been my fellow traveller on my return to town last December. She was carrying half a dozen cats in a large cage up to the various shops in the diamond fields where, she assured me, the rats were a plague.

The next day I started on the return journey with the intention of thoroughly cleaning the trail until I met the Colonial Secretary. The men worked so slowly that I had to warn them that they would not be knocked off until they reached the 32nd Milepost, which they did just as dusk was falling. Then most of them were ill the following day as a result of eating the flesh of some wild hogs we had shot a few days previously and which had turned. This quite often happened when Indians got hold of a large quantity of meat but did not get the chance of drying it properly. As a result we only covered two and a half miles. For my meals that day I ate turu palm cabbage boiled with pieces of salt pork.

We were close to the 28th Milepost when the boys working ahead shouted back, 'The gentlemen, them coming.' Mr Lobb appeared round a bush and for a moment I was nonplussed at the apparition. A tall, elderly European with large spectacles overhanging a hooked nose, wearing a disreputable old Panama hat; a khaki shirt with short sleeves, and shorts of the same colour. His knees and shins were a mass of congealed and fresh blood from the numerous bruises and insect bites he had sustained on the march. His socks sagged down over his boot tops. He was the equivalent in this country to the prime minister in England but looked most undignified and ridiculous. Then our meeting: – 'Mr Roth, I presume?' and so on. Greetings and introductions exchanged, Mr Lobb stood talking for a few minutes whilst some of his twenty-one black droghers passed, every man carrying a load on his head. The Colonial Secretary told me that the District Inspector and Dr Kelly, the Surgeon General, were coming behind – the latter suffering badly from fatigue. Their party had been seriously delayed by the slow progress of the droghers, some of whom did not come into the camp until after dark. There was considerable dissatisfaction amongst them over rations, most of which they had left behind at the 48th Mile on the Kaburi Road. Then the District Inspector, young Ashmore, appeared, looking pretty tired but refusing to admit it. He at least knew enough to wrap his legs in puttees, so he did not bear the same signs of wear and tear as Mr Lobb.

Startled as I had been at the Colonial Secretary's appearance, very much greater was my shock at seeing the Surgeon General. Imagine a bowed figure, clothed in a khaki shirt, the tail of which was worn outside khaki slacks; in his hand a long pilgrim's staff and on his feet what had once been white yachting shoes, now kept on by bands of maho bark. His face was haggard and his remarks were few. Mr Lobb went ahead with Ashmore; I accompanied Dr Kelly behind. Going down a steep clay slope I advised him to dig his heels into the soil. 'I haven't got any heels left,' was his reply. We reached Kartauri camp about four o'clock and, their rations being finished, I brought forward my last tin of bully beef and had a palm cabbage cooked.

I spent a most interesting evening with Mr Lobb discussing the possibilities of a railway to Turesi Fall. He asked me my opinion of his plan that all surveyors should take courses in geology and botany, the Government providing the necessary facilities. He thought that a lot of valuable knowledge was lost through surveyors not having the necessary expertise. I said I thought it a good scheme but that it would be rather hard on the older men to ask them to take up a fresh course of studies. 'We'll retire them then, if they are too old to learn,' was his reply. I took the opportunity to mention the disadvantages under which local surveyors were placed as compared with those in other Colonies and suggested that, in addition to the extra pay and leave we were asking for, we should have free medical attention, a benefit enjoyed by all ranks of the police force. I told him that I had already suggested this to my colleagues, but they refrained from putting it in their petition for fear of being thought of asking for too much. Both Mr Lobb and the Surgeon General considered it a very proper request.

Next morning Mr Lobb and his party, after thanking me for what I had done, set out on the last stage of their overland journey. Before leaving, Dr Kelly got one of my Indians to strap the remnants of his yachting shoes with some fresh bark. I found out why the droghers complained about their rations. They had been issued to them at Rockstone done up in loose parcels of shop paper and thrown indiscriminately into a rice bag. Now they were reduced to an extraordinary conglomeration of rice, peas, shreds of salt fish and mouldy flour.

Having seen the last of the party safely on their way, we began the return journey. Reaching the Kaburi I was surprised and gratified to see that my bridge rail was still in position, though oscillating violently in the current. During the day my trousers had begun to chafe me so I decided to take them off and was surprised at the great increase in comfort their absence afforded. I regretted it later when I inadvertently disturbed a nest of very small but very hot stinging marabuntas. Five days after leaving the Colonial Secretary and his party I was back at Sprostons camp at Butakari. Whilst on the Butakari trail I met a nice fat maam trotting along the path before me and soon had her transferred to my haversack (and ate it later as a fine roast for my dinner). As I neared the clearing I had to make myself decent, so I altered my style, wearing my pants as a loin cloth rather than an apron and, in this guise, my shirt-tail flying in the afternoon breeze, I staggered into the main camp.

I was surprised to see the new embankment had collapsed, the twisted rails indicating an accident of some sort. I learnt that the engine bringing in trucks of sand to make the embankment had failed to respond to the brakes and, running onto the unfinished section, caused the latter to collapse. Fortunately no one was hurt, the driver and fireman saving themselves by jumping, but the engine itself was pretty badly damaged. Dey, the engineer from Wismar, was still at Butakari, looking after its repair.

After spending a quiet morning in camp, I boarded a railway truck with my men and all our baggage and set off on the long grade to the waterside. At first the truck rumbled along slowly, but soon increased its speed until, as it rounded the curves near the bottom, I feared she would not stay on the rails, but the train foreman assured me there was no danger of an accident. We arrived at the landing a few minutes before the Potaro-Rockstone launch appeared in sight, a mere speck beneath a feather of blue smoke. I loaded my boat and went out to meet it. I was pleasantly surprised to find Dad on board returning from his periodic visit to Potaro, and spent the rest of the trip looking over the proofs of his large volume on the Arts and Crafts of the Guiana Indians.

As it was Friday I spent the weekend at Christianburg with Mother and Dad, returning to Georgetown on the Monday.

For some time, Winter, warden of the Mazaruni, had stoutly maintained that the only suitable route to the district was one that started from Kartabo Point, at the junction of the Mazaruni and Cuyuni Rivers, followed the old Kartabo-Puruni Road for some twenty miles, then swung south west, heading for the Puruni River at Stop Off Fall, there running south to Turesi Falls on the Mazaruni. He maintained that the richest section of the Mazaruni District as regards minerals lay in the Puruni basin and the line would naturally tap this area, which it would do were it to reach Stop Off Fall, the last serious obstacle to navigation on that river.

Winter had apparently convinced the Colonial Secretary, for as soon as Lobb returned to town the order went forth that the Winter Line was to be reconnoitred with the utmost dispatch. Although the year was drawing to a close, it was proposed to start the work at once and, together with Cheong and Lord, I received instructions to this effect.

We decided to work together from Kartabo Point and go westwards; Cheong would do the main traverse with trigonometrical heights whilst

Lord and I would do the reconnaissance with compass and aneroid. We also managed to get the Commissioner's approval for Belmonte, a young surveyor's assistant in the Department, to accompany us. Fortunately a gang of Moruca Indians were in town in search of work and these I engaged as well as five more from the Demerara River. In all, the expedition numbered twenty-eight men.

So five weeks after my return from the Bartica-Kaburi Road found me back on the steamer to Bartica. At Kartabo Point we set up our first camp in the house formerly used by the manager of Peters Mine, which stood in a beautiful grove of bamboos at the beginning of the Kartabo-Puruni Road. That afternoon we walked along the road which ascends gently from the river. It had been abandoned for some years, but a well trodden footpath showed where the diamond diggers still travelled to and from Puruni. About half a mile from the start the road suddenly changed into a railway cutting, beautifully graded but left unfinished. This was the work of the Mara Mara Mining Company, the proprietors of the Peters Mine and the builders of the road. After the closure of the mine, they proposed working the extensive greenheart forests that border the road, obtained a large concession and actually constructed the first three miles of the railroad, along which they intended getting the timber out. But, like many ventures in this unfortunate colony, after many thousands of dollars were spent, the scheme went bankrupt.

Returning to camp, Lord and I went in the boat to the picturesque little island of Kyk-over-al, keen to see the ruins of the old Dutch fort. It is the site of almost the oldest European settlement in the Colony, having been built by the Dutch near or on, according to Hartsinck, the ruins of yet an older structure built by the Portuguese. The little island on which it stands is well named 'See-over-all', as it commands a fine view of the confluence of the Mazaruni and Cuyuni Rivers. It is cared for by the Penal Settlement, the bush cut down, leaving only a few palm and mango trees. Amidst them rises the old red brick archway, the steps leading to it of a smaller yellowish-coloured brick. The keystone of the arch is yellowish-grey with an ill-defined and much weathered design on its face like a double cross. This stone was removed and sent to England where it was examined by the arbitrators of the British Guiana-Venezuelan boundary dispute in order to prove that it was of Dutch origin, though how this was done I don't know. The stone was returned to the colony and put back in its original place. The archway is about three feet thick with a clearance of about seven feet, suggesting that the rest of the building must have been a very substantial structure. I found the old rusty ends of hinges firmly embedded in the brick with cement, whilst on the opposite side of the opening were great boltholes nearly two inches in diameter.

The door must have been about three inches thick, judging from the position of the boltholes. The gateway, which is on the north side of the island facing the Cuyuni, was evidently built at one corner of the fort, judging from the position of the foundations which I was unsuccessful in tracing in their entirety, but apparently they were built in the shape of an irregular star. Towards the south east was what looked like a cannon embrasure, whilst towards the west and north west, facing the Mazaruni, the glacis was in a fine state of preservation, smooth faces of cemented stone some ten feet high, sloping from the water up to the foot of the brick wall.

As I stood on the remains of the age-old ramparts and watched the sun go down, I could not help imagining the stolid Dutch sentry of three hundred years ago, leaning on his long musket and gazing up the river that, to him, flowed from the unknown whence at any moment might appear a flotilla of canoes manned by naked, painted Caribs. Now, when he was long dead and forgotten, the boats are propelled by engines, manned by sophisticated Negroes, and bear precious cargoes of gold and diamonds. In this country of so few relics, the ruins of Fort Kyk-over-al, even though modern compared to ruins in Europe, inspire me to as great a sense of awe and interest.

The next day we began the survey in earnest, generally following the old Puruni Road. By the beginning of December we had reached the Blackwater River some twenty miles from Kartabo Point, where we decided to terminate the work for the year and return to town. I stayed back at Kartabo Point for a couple of days to look after the final transportation and some further reconnaissance in its vicinity, whilst the three others returned to town. I arrived back in town on 13th December.

On 29th January 1924 I returned to complete the survey. Lord was unable, through illness, to accompany us, but planned to join us as soon as he recovered. Instead of walking along the Puruni Road with all the stores, we sailed up the Mazaruni to a point on the left bank from which we could cut a path to reach the Puruni Road near the Blackwater River.

Going up river through the Kuapau Falls, our captain reckoned we could get through without unloading so he set his warp ahead and outside a large boat that was being unloaded. Her captain, a burly Negro by the name of Spencer, a member of the Board of Examiners for Steersmen at Bartica and, as events proved, a regular river bully, got into a heated argument with our captain and threatened to chop our warp if we tried to pass him. He added that he, 'wished to God an accident would happen to us and he wouldn't do a thing to save us.' The couple of hundred Negroes who were present took their cue from him and became very truculent. Even when Spencer learnt that we were Government officers he still continued to bluster and maintain he was justified. This meant we couldn't clear the falls that afternoon so we camped a short distance above the disputed passage. As a result of my report of the incident to the Commissioner, Spencer was severely reprimanded, struck off the Board of Examiners and threatened with the cancellation of his captain's certificate on the next complaint against him.

Yarning after dinner, the subject of tooth extraction came up and Belmonte swore that, when he was on the Cattle Trail survey, he witnessed the following: A boat hand was suffering badly with a rotten tooth and would not allow anyone to take it out. Eventually the boat captain got him to agree to its extraction on the assurance that he would not know when it came out. Unknown to his victim he had tied the end of the cord to the boat anchor and then persuaded him to allow the tooth to be encircled by a loop at the other end. On a signal, another man suddenly heaved the anchor overboard. The tooth followed half a second later.

Shortly after we established ourselves on the line again I went down with conjunctivitis, which laid me up for almost a week. Then some of the men were off sick, which slowed down the work. When we reached the point where the Puruni Road crossed the Blackwater River, we set our faces to the west south west, in which direction, we judged from the available maps, lay Stop Off Fall. It was at this point we were instructed to cross the Puruni before heading south for Turesi on the Mazaruni.

Just before we reached the Takatu River we came across a fine brown water creek some twenty feet wide and not more than two feet deep, flowing over a yellow sandy bottom towards the south. We named this Stingray Creek because as one of the men was stooping down washing his saucepan, a stingray, about eighteen inches in diameter, sidled swiftly towards him. Fortunately, before it reached him, another man saw the brute and killed it with his cutlass. I had never seen such a large ray in these small creeks before, the largest being at most only eight inches in diameter. This incident made us all keep a wary eye on the creek bed whenever we bathed during our stay at this camp. Then, as I walked along the trail from this camp, my eye was arrested by a peculiar-looking thin, dry stick that lay across the path. I touched it with the ferrule of my umbrella. The twig came to life, instantly transformed into a young labaria snake. The camouflage of its colouring was absolutely perfect.

As I sat in Camp No 18 under a large silk cotton tree close by the Watabaru River, making up the accounts at the end of March, I was suddenly aware of the men approaching our tent, led by the Spanish Arawak, Tellemann. This man had worked so well as an ordinary labourer on the fifth journey that on this occasion he had been promoted to a foreman's position, but unfortunately did not warrant the trust placed in him. He had influence over most of the Indians and by no means did he always exert it in the interests of the expedition. He now stood forward and said that the men wanted to understand how they were being paid. They were contracted on a sliding scale from 72 to 96 cents a day with their food, and every evening each man's work for the day was assessed and his price entered in the account book. Only when a man deliberately slacked, and this rarely occurred, was his price fixed at the minimum rate. Most of them drew more than the minimum. Because Tellemann imagined that he was worth more than a dollar a day, he got the others to believe they were being underpaid. Of course, I could have sacked him on the spot, but I feared the effect of such action on the welfare of the expedition. Accordingly I reasoned with him to such purpose that the other Indians, who are really quick-witted and have a keen sense of humour, were, in spite of their alleged solidarity, soon laughing at their companion and returned to their camp quite satisfied. From then onwards there was no more talk about pay.

After following the Watabaru right to its source, a thin trickle of water flowing from beneath a rock and increasing in volume every few yards, we set out to find a main tributary of the Mazaruni between the Takatu and Puruni, having its mouth somewhere between Makari and Kusawe Falls. So when Cheong and Lord returned to camp with jubilant faces I knew they had found it. Vanderheyden, our captain, later confirmed the existence of this stream, having at one time prospected along its banks. We therefore named it Vanderheyden River.

Pushing on up a creek, a tributary of Vanderheyden's River, we came to a ridge running roughly east to west. Some half a mile further on we started a steep descent into a depression many miles wide, so wide indeed that the further slopes showed blue in the distant haze. This was the basin of the Puriari, one of the largest tributaries of the Puruni, which it joins a couple of miles above its mouth. I felt like Moses looking at a Promised Land I was not destined to reach. It had been decided that I would leave the main expedition at the Puriari valley and go round by river to the Puruni, then work eastward until I rejoined the others.

Three days walking brought me back to the river where we had landed ten weeks earlier. The camp, however, was infested with dog and jigger fleas, to such an extent that Vanderheyden and the bowman had been driven to living in the boat. In addition to the swarms of fleas that immediately covered one's lower extremities, a plague of sharp biting mosquitoes made matters unpleasant elsewhere. Hastily loading the remainder of the stores into the boat, we moved across the Kuipari Channel to the opposite shore where a temporary camp was soon erected. Even so, hundreds of tiny bête rouge kept me awake throughout the night with their maddening irritation. Shortly before dawn I managed to doze off, only to be awakened at daylight by the noisy rattle of a motor boat travelling up river. Rising, I lathered my whole skin with germicidal soap and allowed it to dry before washing it off. This effectively dealt with the bête rouge.

Breaking camp we soon entered the main channel and passed Kusawe Rock, a large peculiar-shaped boulder which river custom demands the passer-by must salute by bowing the head. Not far from this was Carrion Crow Fall, sometimes called Kusawe, a mere rapid. Thence on to Karawarambo Still Water where, to the south east, could be seen the long range of the Ebini Hills. In order to reach the mouth of the Puruni we left the main up-river channel and turned northwards. This section of the river was very shallow and many large sand banks were exposed. The mouth was well hidden behind some large islands. Here, little more than two hundred feet in width, the river now flowed over a bed of large pebbles over which the men had to drag the boat, wading knee deep in the water. In this shallow stretch a school of paku were feeding and the great fish darted ahead of us in great pink coloured flashes. In a trice Vanderheyden had left the boat and was after them with his bow and long fish arrow. Splashing ahead through the shallow water with bow bent almost in a half circle, he let the shaft fly at the first fish he saw. There was a plunge and the arrow fastened by a long string to his hand was retrieved with a fine six pounder struggling gamely on the barbed end. When we reached the mouth of the Puriari River it was almost dry and covered with a dense tangle of vines and fallen trees. Here we camped for the night. After dark some of the men went out in the shallows chopping fish and returned about midnight with quite a fair catch.

Going on up the abnormally shallow Puriari, we were compelled to unload the boat and drag her over the gravel on several occasions. I travelled with Robert, the huntsman, in the corial for a few miles and tried my hand at shooting fish with a bow and arrow. So clear was the water that the perai and mullet could be seen swimming about six feet below us. The former had a habit of floating motionless in the slow moving stream, waiting to make a lightning dart at any unsuspecting prey. The refractive action of the water soon taught me to aim my arrow at a point well below the fish and, after a few unsuccessful attempts, I managed to secure a small specimen of this incorrectly named fresh water shark.

At Big Fall, where a rock bar effectively blocks the river, the boat was again unloaded and hauled across to the still water above, and the journey resumed for half a mile to the foot of Long Fall. Here we camped for the night, the men being very tired from their day's exertions.

Next day started with an hour and a half of steady hauling, shoving and levering the boat up the half mile stretch of Long Fall, which well deserves its name. At one point the only available channel passed beneath the trunk of an immense fallen tree, leaving only a couple of feet clearance between its lower surface and the water. This meant unloading the boat again. In the shallows above this fall and Tiger Creek we came across numerous paku, whose brilliant colour brightened the water. The boat abandoned for a moment, bows and arrows, paddles, cutlasses and sticks were immediately put into operation. Some of the arrows were free and not attached by cord to the archer. When one of these penetrated a fish it would go careering down the stream for a few yards, disappear for a few moments, and then protrude above the surface once more, at a point many yards distant. The men then had to chase the truant arrow and retrieve it with its attached fish.

Having secured some dozen large fish we resumed our journey and soon arrived at Stop Off Fall. There a weir stretched in an irregular arc from bank to bank. A gap in the centre acted as a spillway and allowed the passage of the boat. If Long Fall is well named, very much more so is Stop Off Fall. The weir consisted of separate boulders, none too large that it could not be moved by three or four men. This fact, together with extraordinary level character of the top of the weir, made me doubt strongly its origin was natural – it looked very much like the work of man. I was told later by Captain Jones, one of the oldest inhabitants of the district, that this weir, as well as several others, were the handiwork of the Indians who built them to serve as fish traps in the dry season.

Immediately above the fall the river bank rose steeply for some thirty feet and on this elevation we built our camp. After breakfast, leaving the men to make the clearing and erect the tents, I climbed a nearby hill and blew some lusty blasts on my bugle, hoping the main party would hear them. We had arranged a number of signals in the hope of maintaining contact. In the day time, at convenient places, such as the top of hills I was to blow my bugle and set fire to suitable hollow trees. Each night, at seven o'clock, after firing two heavy loads with the gun, I was to run the boat's engine for five minutes with the silencer off. These signals were to be sent out every evening until we met. As it happened, the other party neither saw or heard any of them.

As soon as the camp was established I carried out a survey in the vicinity on both banks of the river, as well as a time and compass survey down the river. When this was completed we cut a number of paths radiating out from the camp for a distance of about two miles so that the main party could hardly fail to run into one of them and thus find our camp. On one of these paths we came across an old prospecting line near which we found a quantity of haiari vine, used for fish poisoning.

We cut a few bundles and took them back to camp. On our homeward journey we saw the prone trunk of a dead locust tree, absolutely encrusted with gum, a valuable article of commerce that is the base of many varnishes. In appearance the raw product is encrusted with a whitish coloured powder but, when broken, it is like amber. We took a fair quantity back to camp where, at night, it made a fine torch, burning with a crackling flame.

Close to our camp, on the opposite side of the river, a fairly large creek flows into the Puruni which, for reasons explained later, I marked on the map as Fraser Creek. With half a dozen men and the bundles of haiari we set out in the corial for this creek. Near its mouth a very large haimoralli snake was observed in the shallow water. This reptile, which sometimes exceeds six feet, is very gaudily marked with rings of red, white and black, with a wicked looking head. It appears to be a true aquatic serpent and is not to be confused with the much smaller and handsome token snake that inhabits dry land.

Entering Fraser Creek we soon had to leave the corial because of the dried-up condition of the stream and the old tree trunks that obstructed its course. Scrambling over these we came to an isolated pool some fifty feet long and ten wide, into and from which the water trickled in an inch-deep stream. Ranging ourselves round the upper end of this pool we beat the sticks of haiari into pulp, washing it into the water every couple of minutes. As the powerful poison permeated the pool, a few small fish darted to the surface and began to swim round in erratic circles. Presently a larger fish appeared, to be promptly clubbed by one of the waiting men. We were soon all soaking wet from the splashing of the clubs, and the pile of fish on the bank gradually increased. It was undoubtedly cold-blooded murder, but then we considered it legitimate; we were pot hunting, not fishing. By breakfast time either the potency of the poison had weakened or we had secured all the fish in the pool, as no more appeared. Our catch included three medium sized haimara, a large quantity of dog fish and innumerable smaller species, some of these being of extraordinary shape and colour. One species, averaging four inches in length, had alternating streamline stripes of black and red, whilst its mouth was right on top of its head, like an upturned nozzle. Another of weird shape had the ventral fin beginning near the mouth and extending right to the tail. This fish was deep indigo in colour with a broad band of salmon pink near the tail. Then there were fish shaped like a patua, but much more gaudily marked, with patches of brilliant blue.

Returning to camp for a late breakfast I spent the afternoon making watercolour sketches of the more remarkable of our morning's catch until the advent of a shot of fever sent me to my hammock. Tellemann and Robert spent the day in an unsuccessful quest of some hogs, the traces of which had been seen the previous day. They had struck extensive old diamond workings on the upper course of Fraser Creek. It was on the location boards there that they saw the name of Dr Fraser, a Negro with an American medical degree, after whom I named the stream.

I then started pushing ahead with the main line southward towards the Mazaruni River. On the way back to camp on the second day, I had just reached the waterside and glanced across at the camp. There was Cheong waving a greeting. With two Indians and a bag full of biscuits he had left the 26th Camp that morning with the goal of not returning until he struck the Puruni. He had come upon the bank of the river about half a mile below the extremity of my lower riverside line and was just on the point of turning back when he heard voices and saw the corial that was returning from Thomas Fall. This picked him up and brought him to our camp No. 28. He had already fixed up a babricot, and I provided him with some dry clothes.

Naturally we spent the greater part of the night exchanging our experiences and we decided that as soon as he had brought the traverse up to the point where I had started, he would go round to Turesi Fall in the boat and work down the bank of the Mazaruni until I, with Lord, who was to join us shortly, met him with our south line from the Puruni.

Cheong returned next morning to Camp 28, taking six of my men to assist in bringing the balance of the stores out to the riverside. With the remaining men I straightened out the riverside line from the camp downwards, so that Cheong could bring up the traverse speedily. Continuing again with the line, I sent some men in the corial to transport the main party's stores up to Big Fall where they erected Camp 27.

As soon as Lord arrived, we packed up and moved on to Camp 29, which was at the southern extremity of the main survey line. We had barely started out when one of those sudden and violent squalls common at the beginning of the rainy season came on. Overhead the wind roared through the foliage and the air was thick with falling twigs and leaves, whilst now and again some heavily swaying tree would give an ominous crack. Lord, who was immediately in front of me, suddenly stopped in a listening attitude; I did likewise. A second later he yelled, 'Run!' and as I leapt forward after him, there was a terrific thud on the ground right behind my heels. A piece of rotten tree, three feet long and close on a foot thick, lay half buried in the soft ground where I had been standing but two seconds earlier. A feeling like trickling ice water ran down my spine. Torrential rain then set in. We spent the evening playing chess.

Two weeks after leaving Camp 28 on the Puruni, we met up with Cheong working towards us from Turesi Fall, close by the point where our line crossed the Kunuballi River. The day before I'd had a rather nasty accident. We had been crossing some almost flat country covered with high forest, having little or no underbush. Some hogs were seen by the men grubbing about on the muddy banks of a small stream. I was standing close to Tellemann who cut a liana that brought down a small dead branch right on top of my uncovered head. The trees spun around me in bewildering fashion and for a moment I thought I was going to faint. However, I managed to keep to my feet and, beyond a temporary bump on my cranium, soon felt little the worse for the blow. Whilst sitting in camp that evening we observed a large tortoise ambling calmly in from the surrounding bush, only to be appropriated by the men as an addition to their evening meal.

The actual line surveyed from Kartabo Point to Turesi Fall was eighty-two miles. In addition, we had done some two hundred miles of reconnoitring since beginning the work the previous October. The work completed, we despatched Robert and two men in the corial for Bartica and then shared out the small remainder of the stores amongst the men and made final preparations for our departure down river. Of our own stores, thanks to the abundance of fish and game, we took over $150 worth back to town.

Back in Bartica, we were met by the new Sub-Warden, Pip Bunbury, from whom I learnt of my appointment as Warden of Mazaruni. We reached Georgetown on 31st May after an absence of 124 days.

CHAPTER XV

THE MAZARUNI

It was in 1902 that I first began to keep a personal journal and, with a few gaps, kept it up until June 1924 when I was first appointed Warden Magistrate of the Mazaruni diamond fields. The duties of this post I found so onerous that I was compelled to give this up. Except for a detailed account of three months spent early in 1929 on the North West District Colonisation Survey, I made no further journal entries until 1930. I resumed then because I had many times regretted giving up the journal, particularly during my three years at Kamakusa which were so interesting and unique. My parents, too, had pressed me to resume, considering my journal to be of no little value as a personal life record. So, in 1930, when I was reappointed to my old post at Kamakusa, I decided to start it again and, if circumstances and strength of will permitted, to keep it up.

To assist me in my good intention I had a special leather-bound book made up for me with my name engraved in gold letters on the front cover, the idea being that I should be ashamed, having once started, to abandon the writing of such a magnificent volume. I still had in my possession the twenty or so previous volumes but they were getting somewhat motheaten. They ranged in size from a black pocket notebook to large account books. The very first, dating from 1902, dealt, in childlike writing and illustrated by very crude sketches and cruder maps, with my last outward journey from Scotland to Australia. Then followed a series of exercise books, written in pure diary form, which dealt with my schooldays at Brisbane and Maryborough in South Queensland, and a small volume dealing with my journey to Tasmania in 1906. This contained pencil sketches of the dark-eyed wide-winged albatrosses that hovered about and over the little red-funnelled steamer as she ploughed her way across the grey wastes of the Bass Straits. It was when I arrived in British Guiana early the following year that the books became bulkier and larger. The journal began with my Demerara River days, but it was not until 1922 when I was on the Mazaruni reconnaissance surveys that, in my own opinion, the journal reached its potential as a journal. When I typed out my father's manuscript translation of Richard Schomburgh's *Travels in British Guiana* I found a style which greatly appealed to me and imitated it in my own journals.

Now I consider that whilst ideally a personal journal should contain a true record of all the writer's doings, it is obvious that, unless he be a saint, this is inadvisable for two very good reasons. The first is that it would necessitate recording the names of persons who, in some cases, would certainly not care to have their names recorded in connection with the incidents in question. This objection might be surmounted by using fictitious names, but this I always felt detracted from the interest of the narrative. The second reason against total revelation is that, not being myself a saint, there are certain incidents in my life which would give pain to certain loved ones. Since one of my rules in life has been to try not to wittingly give pain to anyone, I did not intend to write any 'confessions' *a la* Jean Jacques Rousseau, even though I must admit that there have been times when I was sorely tempted so to do – to procure a heavily bound volume, fitted with a clasp and lock, and labelled *The Tale of a Misspent Life* or something to that effect! Perhaps one day, if my cynicism increases and I find myself in the miserable situation of being alone and friendless in the world, I may set about such a task.

I will now try and give a rough resumé of my doings between 1924 when the journals ceased and 1930 when I restarted them. In June 1924 I travelled to Kamakusa with G.D. Bayley, the then Commissioner of Lands and Mines, and Dr Kelly, the Surgeon General. Travelling from Georgetown, we spent the night at Colony House at the Penal Settlement from whence we started the next day in a great five ton cargo boat fitted up as a tent boat with easy chairs. She was driven by two outboard motors and, as far as I can remember we made the journey in well under a week.

At that time Kamakusa, which had only recently been acquired by Government from La Varre, consisted of a great hundred foot long barrack, an unfinished warden's house, a wireless station, operator's house and police officers quarters. We were met by N.B.W. Smith, the sub-warden and D. Harvey Read, the acting sub-inspector of Police. We spent the next day, Sunday, at Kamakusa where, on Bayley's instructions, I made a survey of the settlement.

On Monday we went up river on an inspection of the diamond fields. The first place we stopped at was Oranapai where the numerous trading shops at the foot of and on top of the sixty foot high hill adjoining the river made a fine show. We spent an hour ashore discussing matters with various traders and diamond diggers, had breakfast at the little police station at the bottom of the hill and in the afternoon went on up river past Evan Wong's shop at the then undeveloped Buck Cannister Sands to Enachu. Here we stopped for an hour and met Kosser, Krakowsky's manager, and I remember the poor fellow looked half dead from fever.

That night we camped just inside the mouth of the Eping River and next morning went up that stream to the police station which at that time was located just above Perenong mouth. From there we went into the Kurupung where we stopped at the police station just below Tacouba Creek mouth, before returning to Kamakusa where Bayley and Kelly spent another day before setting off back to Bartica.

When I first went up there the forest began forty feet from the warden's house, behind and below it, whilst a fringe of forest grew on the riverbank in front of the house. My first task was to get this cut down and let some breeze into the house. My attempts at cultivation, however, came to nought as the barren white sand on which the settlement stood would support nothing but bush, cashew trees and pineapples. My next job was to install a shower bath and water closet. This was done by the engineer of my launch, Meyers, a brown, bespectacled lead swinger of the first water. As the fresh water vat was too small to be used for other than culinary purposes, we ran a pipe from the river right up to the head tank, a forty gallon gasoline drum, raising the water by means of a small semi-rotary pump. Our system of sewage disposal was simple – the waste pipe ran into a great square pit some twelve feet deep in the hard sand. No means of ventilation was provided but the system worked without trouble for the three years I was there.

Regular as clockwork, Smith, the sub-warden, used to get a sharp attack of malaria every fortnight, so he was removed from the district and appointed warden at Potaro. His place at Kamakusa was taken by Robert Young and it was he who assisted me in painting our quarters, we being domiciled together. We generally spent the hour after breakfast and Sunday mornings wielding the paint brushes until the interior was completed. The outside of the house was done by the prisoners as part of their hard labour.

I had not been long at Kamakusa when the Public Works Department sent up a master carpenter and a gang of convicts from the Penal Settlement to proceed with the building of the hospital, doctor's and sub-warden's quarters. The master carpenter was a long, thin sportsman by the name of Forde and the convicts were a hand-picked lot of the biggest ruffians in the Settlement, and included the notorious Doanes. He had been convicted on a charge of bestiality and at his trial threw an inkpot at the judge's head. Subsequently he headed a revolt at the Penal Settlement and, along with several other prisoners, managed to escape. He was recaptured and sentenced to a further period of imprisonment. I well remember the day of his second trial. When he was placed in the black Maria he behaved like a caged lion, rocking the heavy vehicle to and fro in his frantic efforts to get out. The superintendent of the Penal Settlement undoubtedly placed him in the Kamakusa gang in order to get rid of him. He was a medium-sized, thickset Negro with a very brutish looking face. The rest of the gang, and even the warder in charge, had a great respect for him. The latter actually addressed him as Mr Doanes. He managed to put the wind up little Harvey Read so much he put the whole of his police force under arms and issued ball ammunition with orders to shoot the first convict who batted an eye. Indeed, things got to such a pass that we had to get Doanes and one or two of the others back to the Penal Settlement.

Harvey Read used to travel about with me in my launch, *Control,* and it was during one of our journeys that he developed an attack of bilious fever which nearly killed him. I got him back to Kamakusa and took him over to my quarters and from that time he, I and the sub-warden lived together in one house until Read was transferred to town. His successor was a lowland Scot named Nicole who professed friendship with me but, as I subsequently learnt, sent reports to his department to the effect that I was unable to maintain discipline. He and I were both fond of crossword puzzles and would occasionally spend Sunday mornings constructing puzzles which we would exchange at breakfast time and spend the afternoon solving.

It was during Nicole's regime as sub-inpector of police that the first district doctor arrived, a young and wild Irishman by the name of McCarthy. He arrived along with Young, who had been on a short holiday in town. I went with McGillivary, a Canadian miner, in the launch to Tiboku Fall to meet them. Back in Kamakusa we sat down to a dinner of welcome. Towards dessert we had to manhandle the little doctor and remove an automatic pistol from his pocket and, sometime later, put him to bed. He was under the sincere impression that he was coming to a hot bed of desperadoes and sat down to dinner armed. He became too fond of whisky, though the resulting illnesses he put down to fever, and finally left the colony. He was succeeded by a quiet little Portuguese, Dr Gomes, who did not appear to appreciate life in Kamakusa, who in turn gave place to Dr Coia to whom I owed my life when the blackwater fever got me.

Nicole was succeeded as head of the local police by Whittingham, a quiet young fellow, and he by Bovell Jones, with whom I got on very well. Then came Macnie, whom we shocked by our antics, and finally young Harris whom I left there. Young I was forced to send back to town on account of malarial convulsions, and he was succeeded by young Belmonte who did not make a great success of things, being a little too fond of his leisure. After him came in succession Rohee, Burrowes and Greene, the latter of whom I left there when I was forced to return to town in 1927.

Towards the end of October that year I was not at all well and Dr Coia soon diagnosed my complaint as blackwater fever. Without delay he arranged to get me down to town as quickly as possible. He put me on board the first available mail boat to the Penal Settlement where a Fairey Nichol seaplane was waiting with a doctor on board to take me on to Georgetown. The plane was a small one and after the pilot, Captain Trace, the doctor, myself and my luggage were on board, the mechanic got the engine started and climbed into his seat. We taxied up and down several times in front of the Settlement but because of its weight the pilot could not get the machine to lift off the water so we had to return to the stelling and put the mechanic ashore with instructions for him to return to town by steamer. The plane, thus lightened, soon rose off the water and we soared away down river, over the numerous islands and rocks that studded its surface. When the mail boat had run alongside the plane, a sort of rubber stretcher was put on board and I was placed in it. A portable crane was erected on the side of the plane's fuselage, the stretcher was hooked to the crane rope and I was bodily hoisted aboard, still recumbent. The stretcher was so fixed in the plane that, with the aid of some pillows placed under my head, I was able to look over the side of the plane and enjoy the wonderful scenery below.

Dr Bayley kept feeding me every five minutes with alternate doses of orange juice and medicine. The view coming down the river was exceedingly interesting. The Bonisika Creek looked like a narrow silver ribbon winding through the forest which here and there was broken by the patches of cultivation or wood cutting grants. Areas over which the bush fires had passed were very noticeable, the dead trees lying prone across each other in all directions.

The mouth of the Essequibo lay spread out below like a great map, every island perfectly distinct. Swinging eastwards we flew along the west coast just south of the railway line at a height of two thousand feet, though Trace afterwards told me that at Parika he had begun to lose height so that I would not feel any ill effects from the sudden descent. As I was lying with my head towards the nose of the plane I could not see ahead, only below and astern. The sugar estates and rice fields on the west coast showed up very clearly. Then I believe I must have fainted or fallen asleep for there was a blank until I felt the sudden jolt as the plane hit the waves of the Demerara River. Then some more taxiing to the slipway, and the grating noise of wheels as the plane, having been strapped onto the slipway cradle, was hauled ashore. The little derrick was again fixed up and I was hoisted, still in my stretcher, up into the air and then down again into the motor ambulance that was waiting alongside. The doctor got in and we then lumbered off along the very rough streets of Georgetown whilst little black boys ran behind and tried to jump up and peep through the window to see who was inside.

At the hospital I was taken to the Lady Thompson Ward and only then removed from the stretcher and placed in a comfortable bed where they kept me for some thirty days. The first day I was allowed to get up I almost collapsed and the nurses came running with saline injections, hot water bottles and all sorts of emergency fixings. When I finally left hospital, Philly had moved from George Street, after the death of her sister Alice, to a house in Church Street near Camp Street. I continued to be more or less laid up right to February 1928, but was finally declared fit enough to go on a two months' survey trip to the North West District in September and October of that year.

That trip to the North West was very enjoyable as I had the opportunity of seeing all the changes that had taken place since my departure and which I'd had a fair share in planning. I was glad to see many of my old friends, though others had gone to join the majority. My son Walter came with me on the trip and acted as cook and general caretaker. The new station at Mabaruma I now saw for the first time, as well as the finished road. We had a very pleasant week staying with Edgar Beckett and his wife at Hosororo, the while I did some surveying in the vicinity.

In February 1929 I went on the North West Colonisation Survey. On my return to town in May I worked in the drawing office where I was engaged on sorting out records and tidying up things generally. This was a sweet job which took me close on four months. Then in November we heard the sad news that Pip Bunbury, who was warden at Kamakusa, had contracted blackwater fever and died at Bartica on his way down to Georgetown. With the vacancy thus caused at Kamakusa I applied for the job and got it.

In the meantime Dad had retired from Government service and taken the job of Curator of the Georgetown Museum. Young Walter left school and took a job in Krakowsky's town office but did not stick it for more than a couple of months, after which he was knocking about from pillar to post. He went with me on both my trips to the North West and then at the end of 1929 he went on a trip to the lower Demerara River with Oscar Manson Hing, the surveyor.

Then just after Christmas of 1929 I ran into my old friend Edward Sill of Sandhills who told me he was going home that weekend along with Nat Smith of Curtis Campbell's and invited me to join them. I readily accepted. As Sill's boat was heavy and open, I suggested we used the Land and Mines tent boat. With the 10 H.P. Johnson outboard motor on the stern we made fast time up the river with the washing tide. Passing Hyde Park I could scarcely recognise the mouth of the Kamuni River opposite, as the former low bush had shot up into high forest.

Darkness caught us just before we reached Sill's landing at Sandhills. He telephoned for the lorry to come and fetch us. Whilst waiting Sill took me to the top of the river bank and showed me the sixty-foot deep cutting he was making to enable him to bring his railway line right down to the water's edge, as at the present time it stopped at the top of the bank and the wood was carted by mules to the landing.

Presently the lorry was alongside us and I was surprised to discover that it was being driven by our hostess. The road was only a rough track and the clearance between the lorry and the trees of the forest appeared minimal and with the night so dark and the light of the lorry giving very little illumination, I cannot deny having felt a certain amount of nervousness as we rattled and roared through the forest. The tall, fair woman at my side holding the jolting wheel in her capable hands reminded me somewhat of one of those Norse goddesses of old. Before too long we ran into a clearing in which I could discern the dark forms of various buildings. We entered a large building which was the grant store, one end of which was being used as a temporary dining room by the Sills. The place was brilliantly lit by electricity, as indeed were most of the buildings in the camp.

After a welcome glass of beer I was taken over to the Sill's private house, a very nicely appointed place with glass windows and electric ceiling lights and all mod cons. After a wash we went back to the store and sat down to a sumptuous meal. During the evening we were shown over the stables, which were built off the ground, bat proof and lit by electric light. Here, each in its own roomy stall, were two cows and six fine mules. Eventually we were shown to our rooms, two little guest houses set on their own near the main house. Each house consisted of a single room fitted up very comfortably as a bedroom with a nice spring bed and all conveniences.

Next morning we were shown round the camp, in a clearing of several acres in the midst of the wallaba forest. Sill had a concession of several thousand acres which he claimed would keep him busy for the rest of his life, hence his efforts in making himself comfortable here. His railway line then terminated at the main camp and was fed by cart paths but he intended to extend it. There was a large fence some ten feet high which enclosed an area of some one and a half acres, forming a vast poultry run. It had been built to prevent the havoc that tiger cats had been causing among his fowls.

At the spot where the cart tracks converged on the railhead, Sill showed us a large weigh bridge he had installed under the roadway. He explained that he paid his woodcutters by weight and not cubic quantity as was the custom on other grants. Next we came to the engine shed in which was housed a little steam locomotive with a great inverted cone of a smoke stack, one of the old fashioned spark-arrester types, which I had seen last in Australia in 1906.

The main attraction of the whole camp was Sill's new house which he had built for his wife who, he said, was always complaining that she had no decent place to which to invite her friends. It was a lovely house, fully screened with mosquito mesh, high ceilings and a great feeling of spaciousness. The kitchen was as large as a church and in the bathroom was a large English bath which Sill had got from the old *S.S. Mazaruni* when the ship was being dismantled.

When we had completed our tour we went for a ride in the lorry to Waratilla Creek where Smith and Mrs Sill had a bathe whilst Sill and I looked on. After lunch we sat chatting and then it was time for us to take our leave and return to Georgetown.

Shortly before I went up to Kamakusa we moved house once again to the corner of Laluni and Rose Streets in Queenstown, and on the night before my departure we had a sort of housewarming and farewell party. There was quite a crowd there including Charlie Cole, Arthur Greene, E.S. Parker, W.T. Lord and Harry Christiani. Later in the evening Togo Low and W.I. Gomes turned up. We had a bunch of swizzles and a very enjoyable time. Many speeches were made and everybody thought everyone the best of good fellows. I don't know how or when the party finally broke up but I seem to remember that one of Wong's cars turned up in which Phil and I and some of the others went down to the Ice House Hotel to take Togo home. Somehow I got separated from the others as my next recollection is of arriving home at four o'clock in a taxi. I had to be on the five o'clock boat to Bartica, so I changed into my travelling clothes, said good bye to the family and jumped back into the taxi and shot off to the stelling where I was just in time to hop aboard the steamer.

The journey to Bartica was quite uneventful. At the Penal Settlement Dr Payne was on the stelling and recognised me even though the only time he had seen me before was when I was being transferred from the mail boat to the seaplane over two years before. The Settlement itself looked deserted since the removal of the majority of the convicts to town.

At Bartica I had a drink and a chat with Belmonte who was now its Sub warden and then went to the Hotel Moderne where I had tea with Lucas, the assistant resident manager of the Bartica Company Ltd. Later he took me on a tour of his company's shops and I was surprised how neat and clean they were.

Next morning I left Bartica on the last mail boat being run by Krakowsky Bros, as their contract with the Government was then expiring. Among my fellow passengers was David Bornstein, one of two Jewish brothers who had recently gone into the diamond business. The captain was my old friend Manoel Pequeno with whom I had travelled up and down the river in the past. The mail boat itself, unlike the former tent boat propelled by an outboard motor that used to run the service, was a two and a half ton cargo boat with a tent amidships and driven by a 25 H.P. inboard engine, working on a movable propeller with the 'Smith Device', named after its patentee of Bookers' garage. The propeller shaft had a universal joint and lay in a groove in the stern of the boat. Attached to the shaft and extending beneath the propeller were two guards which, if struck by any obstruction, threw the propeller out of the water. This device had proved so successful on the Mazaruni River that during the past two years the majority of boats had been fitted with it. The great advantage was that a much more powerful engine could be used and the crew no longer had to paddle and were then only used to warp the boat up those falls which she could not negotiate under her own power.

The journey was one of the worst I experienced and it was aggravated by the fact that I suffered considerably with toothache or neuralgia, I was not sure which, as I could not exactly locate any particular tooth as the offender. The pain was in both jaws on the left side of my face. As I staggered round one of the stopping-off camps ankle deep in mud, I was suddenly struck by the thought that for $25 the steamship companies could take a passenger to Trinidad with every comfort and yet here, for $30, the mail boat contractor took you to Kamakusa in a loaded and congested cargo boat, dumped you out in a wet and filthy camp, which would probably collapse before the night was out, roused you whilst it was still dark and had no opportunity of performing the necessary functions of nature except at the risk of treading in some unseen filth and on top of all this you had to feed yourself. Never was I more glad to get off a boat.

As we sailed into Kamakusa, the first thing I noticed was a new Indian house just below the sub-warden's. This I learnt was the residence of Michael, one of my boat-hands, who had taken a wife. I was met by

E.S. Burrowes, the sub-warden and took over the station from him right away as his father was particularly anxious that he returned to town as soon as possible.

After a day of settling in, I got aboard the old tent boat, *Arawana,* and set off up river for a tour of the district. Whilst sorting out my quarters I found in the house my old ice machine in good working order and a set of bow and arrows and blowpipe I had left there in 1927. At Oranapai I put up with my old friend, 'Uncle Charlie' Farrier, the general manager of the New Diamond Venture Company's shop there. He gave me his usual courteous hospitality and it was not long before we were sitting down to a sumptuous dinner of soup, fresh fried basha, roast peccari and bread and butter pudding. We had a long discussion about conditions in the district and I gathered that the present depression in the fields was not due alone to the slump in the diamond market but to the excessive competition between the traders. There were too many shops for the amount of business that was being done, so prices had been reduced to a level of absurdity. This was all very well for the porkknocker, but the poor traders would eventually become bankrupt and forced to close if things continued as they were.

Next morning I travelled up to the Oranapai police station and then up the high hill at River View to the old bungalow where I used to stay in the old days and which Mr Tom, the general manager of U.D.F. (United Diamond Fields of British Guiana Ltd.), had kindly put at my disposal. Then to the Magistrate's Court, where the corporal in charge made a little speech on behalf of the police welcoming me back to the district. He was followed by my old friend, Arthur Husbands, Mark-a-Book, who welcomed me on behalf of the public. I think the Magistrate replied suitably.

The only case I had to deal with was one of disorderly behaviour brought by the police against young Walter Cappell and his wife who, on New Year's Eve, celebrated too well but not too wisely. I reprimanded them – being no doubt guided in my decision by a fellow feeling. Young Cappell was the son of my old friend of Arakaka days, Bismark Cappell, who used to drogh for Ho-a-Shoo from waterside to the Mazawini shop.

When I arrived at Enachu the next day I found my old friend Beckman in charge of Krakowsky's shop as general manager. The shop itself was much the same but for the installation of electric light generated by a Delco plant. The old cricket pitch had been converted into a tennis court on which a cow was placidly grazing. I went over to the wireless station where the mast was in a very dangerous state and looked liable to collapse at any moment, being riddled by wood ants and several of the stays no longer functioning.

After having breakfast with Beckman I proceeded to hold Court. There was but one case in the Criminal and one in the Civil Court, the plaintiff and defendant being identical in each. Neither putting in an appearance, I struck out both matters and opened office for the issue of mining licences etc. An hour later the litigant arrived saying his watch was slow. The neuralgia was worrying me again so I retired early but spent a very restless night.

Going up the Eping River I saw a new innovation in Tiam Fook's shop, the entire roof and walls now consisting of corrugated iron sheet. As we were passing this shop, a black gentleman clad in khaki hailed us frantically. As we neared the landing he smiled, his pearly white teeth appeared against his dark face and I recognised my old walking partner, Duncan McGregor Stuart, the African gentleman with the Scottish name, and the finest pair of calves in the Colony, acquired whilst training for and winning the Colonial Cycling Championship. He asked me to give him a passage into Perenong, which I gladly did, and we discussed old times on the way up. Passing the Good Hope Syndicate shop I saw a large crowd gathered to welcome me. As I passed, several guns were fired. It reminded me of the advent of a new prostitute in a mining camp in the old days.

Arriving at the U.D.F. Warrior shop we went ashore and, after crossing the cricket ground and passing through the forest behind, we came to Eugene Correia's shop, which at the time was being run by his brother-in-law, Maurice Gomes. His house, a nice little shingle cottage, stood just behind the shop within a fenced enclosure outside of which a cow and a small flock of sheep were grazing. I met Mrs Gomes, the first resident lady of the district. After spending the afternoon yarning and drinking gin I returned to the U.D.F. store where I put up in my old shingle house which Mortley had built for my use some three years before.

Next morning I held court and when that was finished I had a busy couple of hours issuing licences and collecting rentals, the take being in excess of $650.00. On closing the office about three o'clock, I was inveigled into going over to Maurice Gomes' house where I found that they had laid on a luncheon to welcome me back to the district. Duncan Stuart opened the proceedings with a long speech in which he said that while the people of Perenong appreciated all the officers who had been there in my absence, yet they were very glad indeed to have their old friend back, even though he was the severest magistrate they had had. Harry Williams followed with a similar speech in which he said that I was popular because I was approachable. After several more speeches my turn came to reply and I thanked them all very much for their very kind and unexpected welcome. I said I was more than glad to be back in my old district, but that gladness was tinged with a shade of sorrow, for my reappointment was due to the very sad death of Pip Bunbury, the late Warden. I told them that I had noticed many changes, most of them for the better: firstly, the advent of electric light at Enachu, secondly, the successful introduction of cows and sheep into the district and, thirdly, most important of all, the advent of the first resident lady, in the charming person of my hostess.

As the festivities went on well into the night, it was quite a bleary crowd that saw me off next morning. Dropping down the creek and into the Eping River we stopped to cook breakfast at Tiam Fook's corrugated iron store, which was managed by a middle-aged man called Chin with whom I had half an hour's yarn. Returning to the Mazaruni we headed upstream and just beyond Kubenang met one of Ginder's 'Tiger' launches coming down with Desmond Pierre, their general manager, aboard. The two boats came alongside and then slowly drifted downstream together for ten minutes whilst we discussed news and brandy. He apologised that he had to go down river on some urgent business but that I was to make myself at home in his house and he would return the following afternoon.

Moving on into the Kurupung River I noticed that several of the old shops were now broken down and abandoned. At five o'clock I reached Ginder's landing and moved into Pierre's house. It was much as I remembered it, except that it had been painted inside and out and now contained a harmonium. After establishing myself I went over to Triefus and met Bertie Matthews who had taken over the management of that firm's business. The two of us then went over to Krakowsky's shop where we found the manager, Algie Grimshaw, in bed with fever. We cheered him up by drinking some of his vermouth. On our return we passed along the upper path through the village.

This consisted of some eight to ten houses mostly occupied by black ladies of easy virtue. Whatever one may think of their way of life, if these women kept their persons as clean as their houses, there could not be much the matter with them. In each one the floors were scrupulously clean and showed signs of constant scrubbing, whilst the furniture, some of it being of the rough and ready kind, was also equally clean and dusted. My friends had, however, reserved the show place until last. Situated on U.D.F. land was an attractive bungalow which was approached by a path of pebbles lined with ale jug borders, and little pots of flowers. Outside the front door rustic benches were set around a table under the shade of a mora tree. Over the door was a sign: 'Kurupung Villa la Dancy'. Inside everything appeared to be painted in varying shades of green. There was a lot of lattice work and the drawing room, a fairly large place, was crowded with easy chairs, sofas and other bric-a-brac, very much like a palatial town house. The walls were covered with pictures and photographs, some of a pornographic nature. The occupants of two of the easy chairs were a couple of black ladies, old acquaintances of mine from the Magistrate's Court. After listening to some gramophone records and a couple of drinks, we left the house and, as I was not feeling well, I went back to Pierre's house where I had a light dinner, after which I went to bed, the neuralgia again giving me some trouble.

After several more days in the district, I started back for Kamakusa. At Red Hill I stopped for a moment at Lester McGillivary's headquarters where I learnt from his manager of the loss of his boat, *Grizzly Bear,* the previous day at Tiboku Fall together with three lives. As I passed down river the clouds still hid the turrets of Tapazing which I had been unable to see since my return.

By the time I arrived at Oranapai it was raining quite heavily and we had to climb carefully up the rough steps cut in the face of the fifty-foot high hill on which the Triefus shop stood, trying to avoid as much as possible the cascade of water that was using the stairway as a channel. Upstairs I found some more acquaintances, including young Smith, a former wireless operator at Kamakusa and now in the employ of Triefus, and a tall elderly Negro by the name of Stephens, who was one of the survivors of the ill-fated *Grizzly Bear*. Also present was one of the Oselmo boys who was on the *Leopard Self,* Yhip's boat which was only some two hundred feet ahead of the *Grizzly Bear* when she foundered. From the two men I was able to obtain a fairly comprehensive account of what had happened. At first someone had suggested that the two boats were racing to the falls to see who could get through first, but both men denied this. In the end I concluded that with the river being high and the boat overloaded the crew had been unable to control it as they passed through the narrow section of the falls and it had been swept back down onto the rocks.

My first night back in Kamakusa was one of the best night's rest I had had for some time, the abeyance of my neuralgia allowing me a completely undisturbed night. One great improvement I noticed was how silent the boats were as they passed the house, at least those fitted with inboard engines. In the old days the rattle and roar of the outboard motors as they passed almost under my window in the early morning was most disturbing. However, when I woke, the rain was again pouring in torrents. I began to be heartily sick of the incessant rain since my departure from Bartica. Kamakusa at its best was not a very cheerful place, but the perpetual rain and dull skies made it just about the limit.

Having solemnly made up my mind not to overwork myself here this time, as I had done on my previous sojourn, especially in view of the 40% cut in the emoluments attached to the post, I dressed leisurely and then brought my journal up to date before setting about making up the cash account for the month. During the morning I heard the tolling of the bell bird, the campanero. It persisted for about half an hour, the first time I have heard this bird up here. I then wrote a long report to the Commissioner on the wreck of the *Grizzly Bear*. I expressed my views quite forcibly on the inadequacy of the present Navigation Regulations to cope with conditions brought about by the new high-powered boats with inboard engines. The regulations controlled the length, beam and depth of a boat, but did not control its actual capacity. In 1923 few boats could carry more than 10,000 lbs.; now by building them broader both fore and aft they could carry some 6,000 lbs. more and yet still comply with the law.

A few days later my neuralgia returned and I decided I would have to do something about it, so I went to see Joseph the senior dispenser who located the trouble in the back tooth of the lower left side jaw. He said it had an old break and the gum was growing over it, and offered to extract it there and then. I decided to defer the operation until the following day.

I was about to retire that evening when Fernandes, the bush manager of the Bartica Co. or U.D.F. as it was still referred to, dropped in with General Crespo for some advice about a robbery they had had in one of their shops. When they left, I was just dozing off in my hammock when I heard a commotion outside and my bedroom door was pushed open and a powerful torch shone onto my face. It was Lester McGillivary who had just arrived with Eugene Correia, Kosser, W. Brassington and R.G. Humphrey. As my house, despite its size, had hooks for only four hammocks, McGillivary and Correia took my bed, when we finally retired for the night. Talk about babes in the woods, they looked so comical as they lay side by side with expressions of perfect innocence on their faces.

The travellers left next morning, but General Crespo, having heard that I was going to have a tooth out, decided to join me and have one extracted as well. We both adjourned to the dispenser's house where the instruments were being sterilised on a primus stove, and other preparations in the shape of cotton wool, mouth wash, cocaine and a kidney-shaped basin lay on the gallery railing. Never having experienced any painless dentistry I was undoubtedly nervous, as on both previous occasions when I had had teeth extracted chloroform had been used. However, Joseph filled the little glass syringe and proceeded to inject the gum all round the offending tooth. After waiting some minutes for the cocaine to take effect he used a small knife to cut away the gum from the tooth, none of which I could feel whatsoever. Finally he took a wicked looking pair of forceps and gave just three tugs. Only as the roots finally broke away from the jaw did I feel a momentary sense of pain, and immediately the tooth came out, a deep dull pain was experienced but immediately ceased as soon as Joseph squeezed the gum together with his fingers.

Crespo had been standing beside me during the operation, but immediately the tooth was out he was down the path like a shot, saying his tooth did not hurt any more. However, we persuaded him to come back and have it out, which for very shame he had to do. A couple of shots of whisky put us to rights again and then we sat down to a game of bridge. Crespo and I were partners against the two dispensers. After the game, which we won, Crespo told to us his adventures as a revolutionary in Venezuela.

When I had at last finished typing my annual report and clearing the remainder of my office work, I set off once again for a three-week trip round the district. At Buck Cannister Sands I went over to Markum's Mart where, it being Saturday, preparations were in progress for the usual weekly ball that was held in the saloon at the back of the shop. The place was already packed with porkknockers sitting on benches all round the walls, whilst a string orchestra of sorts was tuning up. Markum was busy writing placards in blue pencil and pasting them up to indicate where seating accommodation was reserved for the ladies, that the price of diamonds would be raised etc. Presently the ladies began to arrive, black ones, dressed in neat dance frocks, their legs clad in silk stockings. Markum opened the proceedings by dancing a stately waltz with a girl in red, and after that the dancing became general.

A large fat woman came in with a dish of black puddings which Moore, the other local shopkeeper, promptly bought in toto, but I found them too peppery. As the presence of the Magistrate somewhat embarrassed the dancers we cleared off to Moore's shop, where we listened to his radio and drank beer until well after midnight.

The next day being Sunday, I was in no hurry to get up and as Moore had to go out to one of his other shops to collect some diamonds, I took him at his word and made myself at home. When four o'clock came and he had not returned, I packed up and left as I had an invitation to dinner with Uncle Charlie Farrier. Such an invitation meant that the guest was expected to stay at least until coffee next morning. It turned out that I was not the only guest, as when I got there I found Henry Bornstein, young Wishart and a young Austrian, Einhorn, the newly appointed field manager of the U.D.F already installed. After dinner we played a couple of rubbers of bridge.

Sometime during the early hours of the morning I was awakened by a terrific yell and looking over towards Uncle Charlie, saw him poking about under his bed.

'What the devil are you doing, man?' I asked.

'There's a couple of cats making love under my bed,' he replied.

Muttering something about letting copulating cats lie I turned over and went back to sleep again.

After coffee I went over to the Bungalow on River View Hill and held Court. After dealing with two cases brought by the police, I then held a Civil Court. Having completed the judicial work for the day I was kept busy issuing licences, collecting general revenue and examining and adjusting scales and weights sent in for that purpose by the local shops. At four o'clock I went over to the U.D.F. shop where I found Einhorn and his assistant Victor Hill sorting out the week's purchases of diamonds. It was always hard to believe that the little heaps of glistening stones represented so much money and that they were the cause of so many crimes and dastardly deeds by those who sought their possession.

I spent the next few days checking the various claims in the area as I had received several complaints of location boards being moved and interfered with. When I had finished I returned to my office at the back of Markum's shop where I again checked scales and weights and collected general revenue. Finally closing shop at five o'clock, I had a bottle of strong ale with Markum, Carter and little Wilfred Gomes and then went for a stroll around the settlement. After dinner with Markum, I climbed the hill to Alfred Clark's shop where I found Wilfred, who was manager, dining with two ladies. I had not been there long when three more arrived and it began to look as if it would be a hot night.

After some dancing to a gramophone, we all adjourned to Carter's and Lampkin's. The path lay across an intervening gully and for close on half its distance ran along recumbent tacoubas, some of which were a considerable height above the ground. However, it was moonlight and we had electric torches so we negotiated the bad places safely, though I did find some bruises on my knees and legs the next morning. Arriving over the next hill we knocked up Carter and proceeded to drink gin. By three o'clock next morning it struck me as advisable to start on the return journey towards my temporary headquarters and accordingly set off across the ravine. Twice near the start I took the wrong turning and ended up at an al fresco latrine. Eventually finding the right path I negotiated the series of mantraps that carried it over the gully without breaking a limb.

Back at Clark's shop I felt the necessity of rest and knocked up Gomes. Rubbing the sleep out of his eyes and glancing up at the moon and remarking that dawn was at hand, he knocked up his cook and ordered coffee. His temporary companion now appeared, clad in pyjama trousers of red stripes and a jacket of blue stripes, which despite the clash of colour, showed off her figure very admirably. Coffee over and the dawn not yet arriving, we peeled a bottle of whisky and discussed the realities of life for a couple of hours until the dawn finally began to break. A second pot of coffee was then ordered together with ham and eggs.

By seven o'clock I had returned to Markum's, picked up my orderly and begun my inspection of the shops in the vicinity. At the first shop, everything appeared in order, the diamonds produced as being on hand corresponding exactly with the balance called for by the diamond register. However, since my experience with the manager in 1927, when I seized 120 carats of diamonds from him in the Issineru River, and the subsequent revelations he made to me in the Magistrate's Court of the capability of some human beings to lie without a quiver of the face, I had certain doubts as to the integrity of the manager, and his attitude of semi-defiant truculence towards me had done nothing to mitigate this feeling. Consequently, I asked for the keys to the safe and, being quite within my very wide authority as warden, proceeded to search within.

Right at the back I found a parcel of some 15 carats of diamonds and another of eight ounces of gold, none of which was accounted for in the registers. The manager of the shop, explained that the diamonds had been bought by his brother at the Oranapai shop and were entered up in the book there. I assured him that they were not, as I had inspected that book only two days before; he said his brother should have shown me the 'private' book. For not entering up the gold he had no explanation beyond the statement that it was not his custom to do so. Now I would have been perfectly in my rights to seize all the gold and diamonds and to arrest him on the spot but I considered the question carefully and thought that if I did so, it might be said I was motivated by spite in view of the last big seizure I had made from the firm, so I gave him a very serious warning and then accepted his offer of a drink. Nevertheless I did not subsequently forget to send a very full report on the matter to the Commissioner. Just as I was about to leave the shop I noticed several small bags of BB shot on one of the shelves. Now this item came under the heading of 'Arms and Ammunition' and required a special licence for its sale. He admitted he didn't have one, but claimed he thought it was covered by the Omnibus Licence, a statement I doubted as during my previous trip up here I had warned all the shops on this question.

A few days later, just as I was sitting down to breakfast with Kosser at Enachu, the corporal from Eping police station came in and reported a suicide at Correia's shop in Perenong, the victim being a young lad of twenty-two, called Gravesande. I fixed the inquest for the following Friday and made out the necessary papers. With the corporal was young Correia, from whom I obtained some further details of the tragedy.

It appeared that Maurice Gomes, the manager of the shop, had discovered some serious defalcations in the books for which Gravesande seemed to be responsible. He had accordingly taxed the lad with them the previous night and some hot words had ensued between them. Shortly before six o'clock the next morning the report of a gun was heard in the shop. Gomes found Gravesande with his head blown off. He appeared to have put the gun in his mouth and pulled the trigger. After this grisly discourse I sat down to a belated breakfast.

The following day Correia came back in a very excited state to say that the East Indian shopman who was also implicated in the defalcations leading to Gravesande's suicide had that morning run away and should be arrested. I asked him to give me a sworn statement but this he said he was unable to do as he only had a vague idea as to the amount stolen and the date of the theft. He then told me that Gravesande's relatives were 'talking a lot of stupidness', and trying to make out that he, Correia, was directly concerned in the lad's death. He finally decided to go to Oranapai and see if he could find the shopman there.

When I got to bed that night I could not sleep for thinking about the events that had led to the alleged suicide. Suddenly I had a hunch. Getting out of bed I sent a radio message to the Sergeant Major at Kamakusa advising him to come up and take charge of the investigations himself and giving him the names of several persons to be detained should they attempt to pass Kamakusa before the inquest.

When it was time to go up the Perenong I took with me a corporal and constable from Eping station so that they could act as witnesses at the scene of the suicide. After establishing my headquarters in my house behind the U.D.F. shop, I went over to Correia's shop. The police, who were already there, took me into the diamond department where the walls and floor still bore the signs of the disinfectant that had been used to clean the place down, whilst a pile of bills hanging by a hook on the wall had dark red bloodstains on it.

After seeing Celestine Gomes at the New Diamond Venture shop I went over to the Good Hope Syndicate shop where I found the manager, Jack Luthers, suffering from a sore throat. We discussed some whisky and presently Brownie, one of the local ladies, came along to attend to his throat, she also being the local nurse. She was followed by Bertha Martindale, the Perenong Popsy. She complained that during her recent absence in town nearly all her fowls had been stolen, so she was going to make an end of the remainder and invited us to eat her last guinea fowl the following night.

Most of the next day was taken up with the Court, and when I finally cleared the last case I went over to Gomes where I was given a glass of milk, which he was encouraging everyone to drink now that cows were in the district. Whilst I was there, De Groote came in and also had a glass. Then we set off for Luther's. There at the Good Hope shop we found his throat worse but it did not prevent him from helping us to discuss a bottle of whisky until Bertha arrived with her bird. Well, we talked and talked and still the level of the whisky would not go down past the bulge in the bottle. About nine o'clock Bertha arrived, a gas lamp in her hand and a great wooden tray covered with a cloth on her head. From this she produced a very nice tureen of soup, a plate of vegetables and another of rice, and, finally, the *piece de resistance*, a roast guinea fowl. Celestine Gomes, who had come along with her, joined us at the whisky and with her assistance the tide fell rapidly within the bottle. I had never tasted guinea fowl before but I decided that if I ever went in for keeping poultry again it would be guinea fowl. It was very nicely cooked with sausage stuffing, though the gravy was a little too peppery.

The next day being Friday, I held the inquest on the death of Gravesande. Just prior to this I gave a decision on the ownership of a claim in the Mining Court. Sergeant Major Campbell had arrived the previous morning in answer to my radio and had spent the whole day investigating and interviewing various people. By the late afternoon he had produced about a dozen lengthy statements for me to choose those I thought necessary to put before the jury. He told me that there were a number of rumours that the deceased had not died by his own hand but that he had been murdered. There was, however, no evidence to support these rumours, which were being spread by a few fellow villagers of Gravesande's from Mahaica.

I decided to have five witnesses examined before the jury, which consisted of De Groote, Charlie Gardiner and Manoel Harris, the present manager of the U.D.F. shop. The statements made were identical with the story related to me on the previous Sunday, except the detail that Gravesande, during the investigation on the Saturday night, got annoyed and tried to escape whereupon Gomes hit him twice with a whip. They finally parted, apparently without any ill feelings, at two o'clock on the Sunday morning and about half an hour afterwards Correia and three others left for Wembley Hill, some half a mile away, where they all slept at the house of a woman called Lorraine Daniels.

Of this there was not the slightest doubt, yet one of the witnesses, a truculent old man named Jas Barlow, a fellow villager of the deceased, swore that he was in a camp not twenty roods from the shop and that, after hearing the report of a gun, he had seen Correia and the three others come out of the shop and walk towards the creek. This, according to him, was at half past five in the morning and he swore he could recognise them even though they had their backs to him. The verdict brought in was death from gunshot wounds, self-inflicted whilst temporarily of unsound mind, with no one being criminally responsible.

Later that day De Groote passed some people who had a bottle covered with grey paint. He asked them what it was for, and was told that they were taking some of the paint with which the coffin had been painted to show the deceased's mother. They added: 'Look at you, they kill the man and you say he kill heself'. I also heard that after the body had been placed in the coffin, his friends had placed a knife in the dead man's hand so that when he rose he could avenge himself on his murderer. There was undoubtedly a feeling that there had been foul play. At the end of the proceedings, Gravesande's uncle asked for a copy of the evidence. I referred him to the Attorney General.

The inquest over, I then held a Magistrate's Court. The first person brought before me was my friend Bertha Martindale who was charged with disorderly conduct. However, as Inspector de Bretton, who had made the charge, had since left the Colony, the police withdrew the case. After two other cases, both of theft, I closed the Court and packed up ready to move back down the river.

Back at Enachu, I found a radio message waiting for me from Dispenser Joseph advising me to send my boatman Michael back as his wife was seriously ill. It subsequently turned out that she was already dead, leaving a very live baby behind. So leaving Michael and his baggage behind we set off up the Mazaruni.

We had not been going long when we saw a snake swimming across the river. The captain tried, unsuccessfully, to steer the boat to prevent the serpent crossing our bows, this being considered unlucky by all river men. Griffith said that this happened just before the late Captain Carter died and again before my predecessor Bunbury passed on and he wondered what was going to happen next. Well, shortly after this, there was a terrific roar from the engine and we discovered that the propeller key had broken. Fortunately we had a spare with us and in about five minutes we were on our way again and at about five o'clock we turned into the Kurupung River. The afternoon had been hot and sunny but as soon as we turned into the smaller stream there was a noticeable drop in the temperature and I soon felt so chilly that I had to put on my raincoat. We arrived at Rosman's Landing just before six and I climbed the hill to the shop of Rodriques, Choong and Lam, where I found Choong and Dos Santos.

As soon as I sat down, a fit of ague came on, so I immediately got into my hammock and Choong insisted on my trying what he claimed was a sure cure for ague. He got his East Indian cook to tie a piece of cloth round each of my big toes and brought me a glass of hot ginger ale. Between the two remedies the ague eventually stopped, but was followed by a strong fever for which I took a strong dose of aspirin, my own remedy, and knew nothing more until I woke up next morning. Not that I was much better. Although the fever had gone, I felt like a piece of chewed string, pains all over my body and a dull headache. My thoughts flashed back to the snake crossing our bows and I wondered if I was the next intended victim. I spent the day either in a deck chair or my hammock.

My mind was taken off my ailment by the arrival during the morning of two demimondaines from Rock Point, one of whom was the famous Sweet Mama. She had enough jewellery on her to stock a pawnshop and she told me that she and her friend had just come to spend the day. This meant just to meet their clients who assembled at the shop to sell their diamonds, buy goods, drink rum and purchase the favours of such ladies as might be present. For this last purpose the firm had provided quarters in a building at the back of the shop. Sweet Mama, the story went, not being satisfied with the way the good Lord had made her, had imported some rubber contraption with which to improve her charms, but a diamond digger discovered her 'gay deceivers' and though she had given him a substantial bribe to keep quiet, the wretch exposed her secret with the result that she figured as the theme of an ultra lewd song that was sung throughout the Kurupung when the rum flowed and no respectable ears were within hearing.

Choong's house was situated about four feet away from his shop and the door of the house and that leading to the back of the shop, including the back store and drinking parlour, were all opposite each other. Now the room in which I was resting also faced onto the front of the house, and when I say 'room' I should add that the walls consisted of wire mesh. The result was that I was like a prize exhibit in a cage for the entertainment of the several hundred diggers who passed before me during the day, either going in and out of the shop or passing between the shop and the house to enjoy other pleasures in the back premises.

During the day an orchestra of sorts, consisting of a violin, guitar, accordion and, from the sound of it, a very large Indian rattle or shack-shack, started up in the drinking parlour. This, with my headache, just about drove me crazy, but there was little I could do as I was the guest and it was the recognised thing for the diggers to so enjoy themselves at the shops on Sundays. The best I could do was to retire to my hammock and bury my good ear in the pillow. Now, at least, I was grateful for my deafness.

It was another week before I felt any better, though I continued on my way through the district, and it was only when I got back to Markum's at Buck Cannister Sands that I had my first really good night's sleep. Over coffee the next morning Markum told me how Epstein had been worrying him to have his photograph taken. This had reminded him of a story he had heard concerning La Varre when he first came to the district. He had arrived at an Indian settlement and wished to take a picture of the Indians in their paint and feathers and, to this end, he ordered them all to get dolled up. One old savage looked at him calmly and said, 'You go pay?'. The great La Varre nearly had a fit to think that any naked heathen should dare to think of requiring payment for the great honour of having his picture taken by the discoverer of diamonds in British Guiana. It was preposterous, absurd, goddamn foolishness. The old Indian was not impressed, merely remarking, 'Me not want – you want – you pay.' Which after all seemed to contain the basic foundation of commercial principles – a necessary commodity makes its own market.

Back at Kamakusa I sent a radio message to the Commissioner requesting permission to make a trip to the Puruni gold fields, to which he assented. One of the first things I did was to go over to see Michael's baby. Since the death of his wife he had moved to the back part of the vacant sub-warden's house. It was a pathetic sight I saw as I pushed open the door. There was poor Michael in his hammock clasping the babe against his naked chest whilst he held a piece of white cloth folded around its back to keep it warm. The child had an extraordinarily white skin, almost too white for a full blooded Indian. The face and chest were covered with what looked like syphilitic sores. How he and his brother managed to keep the child alive without a woman's assistance I did not know. Michael said he had decided to take the baby down to the Indian village of Asara, above Tiboku Fall, where he would get a woman to look after it.

Whilst I was at breakfast, my cook, Spencer, a decent young black man, came and in an embarrassed manner asked, 'Chief, if a man love a bad woman and marry her, is it a crime?' I replied that to cads and snobs it would be a crime but decent gentlemen would take their hats off to such a man, if he were sincere. This pleased him very much and he said, 'So long as you say that, chief. I don't care what they say.' He told me that he was madly in love with one of the Perenong girls and wanted to marry her, but he had no money at the present time. In the meantime, he wanted to take her out of the district and send her home and send her what he could afford each month. The funny thing was that whilst I was in the Perenong, this very same girl, Olive Lord, had come to me and said that she was thinking of getting married and what did I think of the idea. Naturally I said I could not offer much advice unless I knew who the gentleman was. She said she would give me his name on my next visit – little did I guess that the lucky man was my own cook.

Joseph the Dispenser had a different problem. He and I were discussing the rotten treatment we were receiving financially. My emoluments had been cut by forty percent from when I was up here previously, following the recommendation of the Allowance Committee. What hurt me most was that they had recommended that if a separate Magistrate were appointed he should receive a station allowance of $720, but if the warden performed the magisterial duties his allowance should be $600. Poor old Joseph was worse off than me as his salary was actually less than that of his own boat captain. I did not believe that Government appreciated these problems and I decided to bring my case before the Governor-in-Council by way of a petition.

As the time for my visit to Puruni drew near, I made the usual requisition to Campbell for a police orderly and suggested that it would be a good opportunity to send a police patrol into the newly opened district. This must have put the wind up the Sergeant and prompted him to contact the Inspector in charge of Kamakusa, who had not been near the place in many months. A day later he showed me the reply he had received saying that no police could be spared. I immediately sent a radio message to the Commissioner explaining the necessity of at least an orderly accompanying me and asked that he speak with the Inspector General of the Police. The reply, when it came, was in the usual autocratic police style: 'I.G.P. says impossible to detail orderly visit Puruni. Boat hands may be sworn in as rural constables.' The second sentence was, of course, as ridiculous as it was impracticable and once again showed the complete lack of knowledge of local conditions exhibited by those in authority. Could they imagine little Indian Henry or Michael, standing little more than four feet in height, trying to arrest a great big six foot gold digger? The lack of co-operation between the Lands and Mines Department and the police had always been very noticeable and stemmed from the time when Adjutant Nicole was first in the district, yet they had no qualms about borrowing spares for their boats and making as much a convenience of us as they could.

CHAPTER XVI

A VISIT TO PURUNI

I had not been feeling at all well for at least ten days and did not relish the trip up the Puruni, but I reckoned no place could be worse than Kamakusa and the change of scenery might assist my recovery. Two days before I was due to depart, Harry William's boat, *Local Enterprise,* arrived at Kamakusa. Captain Bellamy came in and reported that when his engine had broken down, five of the crew had refused to paddle. This was a breach of the River Navigation regulations which specifically provide for such an eventuality, so he had charged them all and put a second charge against one of them who had threatened to fight him. Fortunately for them they gave no trouble and all pleaded guilty, so, after delivering a little homily on the necessity of obeying the captain, I fined them each $5 or fourteen days and an extra fine and sentence of similar amount on the pugnacious gentleman. In order to make up my crew I chose two of the prisoners and offered to advance them the balance of their fines if they would act as my boat hands for the balance of the month at $1.40 a day inclusive of rations; to this they agreed.

On the first day out, the U.D.F. Express passed and we hailed her to borrow a stern line. This boat was packed like sardines in a tin, five on each side of the tent and their baggage between them. Amongst the passengers was Sub-Inspector Carruthers. To such conditions of travel had Government officers descended, who five years before had travelled to and from Bartica in their own tent boat. This was the result of another breach of faith with wardens by the government. In those former days I had a 'falls' tent boat, a certified steersman, bowman, engineer and a crew of six boat-hands. The inspector and sub-warden had the use of this boat when coming to or leaving, the district. Then when the first regular mail service was started, a clause in the contract provided that senior Government officers had the right to travel in the mail boat. This, of course, permitted government to abolish the expensive posts of steersman, bowman, engineer and boat-hands. When the second contract was made, the exclusive right to travel was modified so that any representative of the contractor could travel with the government officers if necessary. In the present contract no such provision was made, so officers had to take their chance and travel like ordinary porkknockers in open cargo boats.

Carruthers asked if I could take a summons and serve it in the Puruni for him. I told him that I had no policeman with me, whereupon he remembered that the U.D.F. was sending a boat up there and he would send a man by her. So, in spite of the 'shortage', it was not impossible to detail a policeman to serve a summons, though it was quite impossible to detail an orderly to accompany me there. We stopped at Asara to pick up Michael, who said the baby was getting on fine with its foster mother. We made our first night's camp just after we entered the Puruni River.

Shortly after breakfast on the following day we passed the landing of the old Peter's Mine, which was distinguishable by the bare and weatherworn posts of the Puruni bridge that used to carry the road from Kartabu across the river to the mine. Now the posts rose, black and forlorn, out of the silent grey-green water – the usual commentary on all deep mining enterprises in this bewitched country. This was all that was left of the substantial structure across which used to rumble great drays drawn by teams of twelve mules, carrying supplies to the then busy mine. The landing itself was overgrown with low forest through which no trace of any building could be seen.

After another night's camp we finally reached Allicock's landing, in charge of which was a young fellow named McBurnie, a son of old Captain McBurnie of my Barima days. Also here was Captain George Vanderheyden who told me that Allicock's claims were three hours' walk aback. During the evening Captain Griffiths came over from Monkey Creek mouth to see his son Alec who was my engineer, and the old chap had half an hour's yarn with me. He told me that the trail aback ran for some miles up the valley of Monkey Creek and then crossed a high and very steep hill before reaching the diggings. In wet weather the trail was almost impossible owing to the sticky clay of which most of it was composed, but at the present time it was not too bad.

I felt a little better next morning and thinking that a little light exercise might do both Walter (who had come with me on this trip) and I good, I decided to set off and survey the route as we went along, leaving five men to follow with the tarpaulin and baggage as soon as they had packed it up. Michael, who had developed an abscess on his stomach, stayed behind with Captain Fiedtkow at the magazine. Using Walter as a front sight I surveyed the winding trail with a prismatic compass, estimating the distances by pacing. At first I found the walk very distressing, but as my blood warmed up, the going became less fatiguing. By ten o'clock we reached a small stream some two miles from the river and here we prepared breakfast once the droghers caught us up. Whilst here, Jardine and his crew from Bartica passed us on their way to the river. He said Allicock had turned him off the position he had given him on his claim because he, Jardine, was making too much gold. Several other porkknockers passed on their way out and they too complained that Allicock had located all the lands and refused to give any of them positions on his claims. They frankly admitted that they had come to the district in the hopes of getting positions, which they seemed to consider their right. The trouble up here was that the tributor or porkknocker had fast developed into a parasite. He waited until a man with will and determination came along to prospect and as soon as he found payable land, they jumped down on him and demanded, as a right, the privilege of working on the lands and enjoying the fruits of the claimholder's work. When I pointed this out, one or two grudgingly admitted that this was true, 'But how else must we get a living?' they asked.

One old chap named McDonald Wright was very amusing in describing the trail. 'Boss,' he said, 'Me work a gold diggings in Barima, in Potaro, in Mazaruni, all about, but never the day I see a mountain like what they got on this line. When you think you dere a' top, you no meet yet. And when you scramble the top for true, Boss, you then near Heaven, true, me tell you.' In spite of his awesome description of what lay ahead of us, he admitted that he knew the hill, What-is-Man, on the Five Stars Trail and that this one here was not as bad. This was some consolation.

On the trail I noticed a peculiar rustling noise, like the sound of gentle rain in the forest. It was caused by the continual droppings of countless caterpillars feeding on the leaves of the mora trees. In places they covered the forest floor with a thin film. We also kept a sharp lookout for bushmasters which were plentiful in this area. I noticed that the trail formed a boundary line for a string of claims located by Alexander Thomas. The first one, as I paced it out, came to over 5500 feet in length; the maximum length of a claim as allowed by the Mining Regulations was 1500 feet.

By two o'clock we reached the first crossing of the Monkey Creek, and as I felt exhausted I decided to camp here. Whilst the site was being cleared and the tent set up, I was surprised to see a police constable, Roberts, from Kamakusa, come marching into camp, covered in perspiration. He reported that Inspector Carruthers had ordered him to join me as an orderly and that he had travelled up with the U.D.F. boat. The shortage of policemen at Kamakusa was evidently not so serious after all. The sandflies in the camp were so bad that we all spent a very restless night. The only relief possible was to cover one's head with a blanket and I, at least, could not remain long in such a position.

We passed several more porkknockers on their way out of the district, one of them giving me a letter which turned out to be from Alexander Thomas. After expressing a wish that I was in good health, he naively went on to say that he had heard I was in the district measuring the line and if I found his Monkey Creek claims excessively large he would pay for the excess as he wanted to retain them, his prospections having been very favourable.

Old Wright was right by nature as well as name. Ascending a long rock-strewn slope the trail ran for a hundred yards on the level, then another long slope, and then another flat, and so on for nearly half an hour. Finally we left the rocks and ascended a very steep ridge of red clay, which was dangerously slippery. At the top we met a party of porkknockers resting after their ascent. They said they did not think the hill had a name but it should be called Congrove because one slip could break your neck quite as effectively as the late lamented hangman. When my droghers arrived at the summit panting, one man threw down his load and lying flat on his back gasped out, 'God, but the sun look more near in trut.' The opposite slope was very similar except that there were no intervening flats, the trail following a long ridge between two ravines. We finally reached Allicock's camp just after three.

The camp was situated in a three-acre clearing on the slope of a hill on which grew sugar cane, cassava, water melons and peppers, whilst two or three hundred fowls of all descriptions and sizes scratched about the place. The main building consisted of a long thatched house with baramali bark walls, strips of the same material being laid on the bare earth to form a floor. One end of the building was used as a provision store whilst the other served as living quarters. A sharp shower of rain came on just as we got in and the roof leaked like a sieve. Allicock now appeared, a messenger having been sent to say I had arrived, and he told me to make myself comfortable, which I proceeded to do whilst the men built their camp at the edge of the forest on top of the hill. Shortly after four o'clock I went with Allicock to the work place to see the daily wash down.

Descending the hill we entered the forest where we crossed the little Sanari Creek and presently arrived at a large clearing where, in a pit some fifty feet square, ten men were shovelling gravel into an elevated sluice, some sixty-odd feet in length. At intervals along the sluice men were forking the gravel and breaking it up, throwing the larger pieces on to the coleh heap at one side of the pit. Knocking off the majority of the men, Allicock and three others began the wash down. This consisted in removing all the riffles from the sluice, these being a series of wooden rods nailed a few inches apart on cross pieces. They lay in the bottom of the sluice and protected the bottom from being worn away too quickly by larger stones which cannot pass between the rods. The thick sediment that lay beneath the riffles was then well broken up with forks, the flow of the water carrying the detritus towards the lower end of the sluice. The flow of the water was then reduced by means of a board at the upper end of the sluice where Allicock carefully brushed the bottom and sides with a scrubbing brush. As he came to each check, a little strip of wood about two inches high fitting snugly across the bottom of the sluice, he would remove this, and all the heavy sediment and quicksilver placed there to catch the gold would be washed on to the next one where the operation was repeated.

Nearing the bottom end of the sluice the quicksilver could be seen quite plainly bubbling along amongst the small gravel and black sand that was left. Having placed a battel beneath the lower end of the sluice, he then took out the last check and all that was left in the sluice was washed into the battel (the local name for a gold pan, a circular shallow cone-shaped iron dish about two feet in diameter). He then took the battel, twisting it this way and that and at the same time giving it a rocking motion. Then he poured out the loose quicksilver (that not amalgamated with the gold) into a baler, and proceeded with the twisting and rocking of the battel. This brought the lighter material to the edge where it was washed off by the water in which the battel was kept floating.

Presently all that was left was the heavy black sand always found with alluvial gold. As this was gradually washed out, the gold came into sight. Being mixed with the quicksilver it did not look like gold, but like freshly cut lead. When nothing but this was left in the battel, about five ounces of it, Allicock took off his yellow salloo waist cloth that served as a belt and putting the amalgam in it, squeezed it into a ball, forcing the quicksilver out through the texture of the cloth. The gold, still mixed with some of the quicksilver, was taken back to the camp, weighed, and put in a jam jar with the rest of the week's production and left for the weekly retorting that was usually done on a Sunday.

After dinner I examined his books and we discussed the question of tributors. Under the Mining Regulations, a tributor could not take his gold or diamonds out of the district, but at that time there was no licensed trader in the Puruni and I learned that some of the tributors went up to Arabagai in Krakowsky's boat and sold to the shops there. The few tributors that Allicock allowed to work on his claims, friends and relatives, passed their gold through his books and got a working sheet from him when they were ready to leave, a situation which, to me, did not appear satisfactory.

I woke up after a glorious sleep untroubled by mosquitoes, sandflies or the shaking of the tent as someone turned over in his hammock to scratch himself. Walter and I both felt very much better, the two days walking having done us a lot of good. Getting into my shirt, I found I had put it on inside out and as I was changing it, Captain Colin Williams, an elderly Boviander friend of Allicock's who was working with them, remarked, 'Don't change it, Sir. The old people say that if you put on a piece of clothes inside out you must let it remain so, and your business will go well for the day.' I did not listen to the old man's advice and, by coincidence, my business that day did not go well.

With Allicock and Walter I set off to verify the five claims of his that lay in a continuous string along the Sanari Creek. A verification of a claim consisted of a rough survey to ascertain its position and to see that its dimensions did not exceed the 1500 feet length and 800 feet breadth as laid down in the regulations. The first obstacle came about two hundred yards from the starting point where the line was completely obliterated by a whole forest of trees that had been felled across it in the making of a small clearing adjoining the claim.

Nearby was a camp that Allicock said belonged to James Mansfield, an elderly prospector whom I had known some years previously in the Rumong-Rumong. I sent my orderly to call him but he returned to say the camp was empty but had evidently been occupied that morning. Circling the clearing through the dense bush we came to what Allicock thought was his boundary line, but after some ten minutes he decided that it was not so, and it was only after climbing over a fairly steep ridge that we found the line we were looking for. Fortunately, the line here formed the trail that led to the camps of Robello and Vanderheyden and it was along this stretch that the breakfast bearers found us with the meal they had prepared in camp. After this the going was easier until we reached the western sideline of the claims and headed back to camp. Then our troubles really began. Not only was the terrain cut up by innumerable little ravines running at right angles to the boundary, but the forest was of the type known as rope bush, innumerable vines, creepers and lianas hanging festooned from the trees and lying on the ground like mantraps. Much of our time was spent climbing up and slithering down the slippery clay slopes of the ravine sides and by the time we reached camp I was absolutely exhausted and fell into my hammock and slept until called for dinner.

The next day being Sunday, I remained in camp and brought my journal up to date. Allicock performed his usual Sunday task of retorting the week's production of gold. Gathered together for a drink before breakfast, our conversation turned to the subject of searching diggers for smuggled gold and I mentioned that I had heard there used to be an old African sergeant at Bethany station on the Essequibo who had some occult powers for detecting anyone trying to smuggle gold past the station. Colin Williams confirmed this, but said my facts were not strictly correct. The man in question was not a sergeant nor was he old, but in fact a young corporal. Once he caught five men in Williams' boat. The suspects would be lined up at the station and the corporal would walk slowly down the line looking into each man's face. Suddenly he would stop and turn on one and exclaim, 'Come boy, give me that eight ounces of gold you have got hidden', and sure enough that would be the exact amount found on the man when searched, if he did not produce it of his own free will.

During the afternoon my old acquaintance, Mansfield, turned up with a long rigmarole about someone called Rodriques having jumped his claim. I promised to interview Rodriques the next day and sent Mansfield on his way. After he had gone, Allicock and Thomas told me that Mansfield was a perpetual nuisance to the legitimate claim holders in the area as he was always hanging about their camps and stealing whatever he could lay his hands on. He had arrived in the district at Christmas when everyone had gone to town, travelling down the Puruni from Arabagai in a ballahoo he had stolen from Krakowsky. He turned up again in the camp early on Monday morning and the orderly asked him to produce his prospecting licence. He stammered and stuttered and asked why he wanted it. Then seeing me coming, he turned away muttering that he would go and get it.

We set off to verify Accouri, Allicock's claim most distant from the camp and lying on a tributary of Falls Creek. On the way we were overtaken by Mansfield who told us someone had broken into his canister and stolen his prospecting licence. We eventually reached the claim and whilst going round the boundary met Robello, another claim-holder in the vicinity who had been out hunting. Having completed this verification we crossed a ridge and checked another claim. We noticed that Mansfield was following us all the way. Tied to his belt were some location boards and a hammer. What his intention was I had not the faintest idea, as he was not accompanied by the two witnesses necessary to a lawful location of a claim. I left the cook to prepare breakfast and went on to check some more boundary lines. The going was not only difficult but dangerous as the line ran along some very steep slopes covered with surface roots. A slip on any of these meant getting impaled on the sharp points of the stumps of the bushes cut to open the boundary. However, we got round safely and soon came in sight of the blue smoke of the breakfast fire. Mansfield sat in the line about a hundred yards away watching us like a hungry dog as we took our meal. After a while I could not bear to see him sitting there so I told the cook to take him a plate of rice.

The meal consumed and a pipe smoked, we set off once again to continue with the claim verification and afterwards went to Charlie William's camp where we met Williams, Thomas, Robello and Rodriques, the claim holder against whom Mansfield had complained. Rodriques, as soon as I told him the reason for my visit, told me he wanted a warrant for Mansfield's arrest, as he had stolen his tom and all his tools and hidden them. Questioning him further I found that although there was no doubt Mansfield had taken these articles, Rodriques had not sufficient evidence to secure a conviction so I advised him to bring an action in the Mining Court that I was to hold on the following day in Allicock's camp.

Something told me to look behind me and there was the ubiquitous Mansfield quietly sitting at the other end of the camp. The man seemed to appear everywhere and apparently from nowhere. I later learnt that this was his habit, to suddenly appear at a camp out of the bush and give no account of himself. The other claimholders dared not leave their camps unguarded for a moment in the daytime. Calling him over, I told him to appear before me at Allicock's camp the next morning, adding that this was an order, not a request. He said, 'All right, Sir', and disappeared as quietly as he had come. After he had gone, Thomas told me that during his absence at Christmas, Mansfield had come into his camp and stolen forty baking tins he had made out of biscuit barrels. I decided to hold a Magistrate's as well as a Warden's Court on the following day.

I awoke next morning to find all the neighbouring claim holders assembled for Court. The Warden's Court was first constituted and the arrangements were very much *al fresco*, the President's chair being a milk-box and his desk a rustic bench. Everybody else had to stand. The matter of Rodriques versus Mansfield was dealt with and, the plaintiff having closed his case, I called on Mansfield for his defence. This was such a palpable tissue of lies that I began to think that he had a screw loose. Decision was given in favour of Rodriques.

The Magistrate's Court was held next with the same furniture. Mansfield was first charged by the policeman with failing to produce his prospecting licence. From the story he gave, I was inclined to believe he had one, so I reprimanded him. Allicock then charged him with felling trees across the boundary line of his claim and failing to remove same within twelve hours. Fined $5.00 or fourteen days. Mansfield was then charged by Thomas with the larceny of forty baking tins. To my surprise he pleaded guilty, so, after giving him a lecture on the sacredness of gold digging camps during the absence of their owners, I fined him $25.00 or one month in order to discourage him from this sort of thing.

The Court over, I set off with Robello for his camp, leaving the men to follow on behind with my camp gear. The orderly decided to leave Mansfield in the custody of Allicock, who was a rural constable and promised to keep him supplied with prison rations. At Robello's camp,

I met Harry Hall, an American working in the gold field, who hearing of Mansfield's convictions told us that some weeks previously Mansfield had told him that he owned nothing but his good name which he would not lose for worlds. Mansfield had then taken charge of the burial of one of Hall's labourers who had died suddenly. He had started off by persuading Hall that the man could not be buried without two bottles of whisky to sprinkle the dead. By two o'clock in the afternoon the body was still above ground and before the funeral was completed, Hall had had to supply seven bottles of whisky and one of rum.

When I had completed verifying Robello's claims, I moved on to Henry Vanderheyden's and Charlie William's camps and likewise checked their claims. It was whilst at one of these camps that I ran out of reading matter, having failed to bring sufficient books with me from the boat. As I always read in my hammock before sleeping, I asked around to see what I could borrow and all that anyone could raise was a Bible. I completed the books of Genesis, Exodus and Leviticus before I left the district.

On the subject of reading matter, when I was Land Officer on the Demerara River, I organised and ran, not unsuccessfully, the R.P.C.L. which, to the initiated, stood for Roth's Private Circulating Library. I had observed that the inhabitants of Christianburg and Wismar were fond of reading but had difficulty in obtaining books. So I fell on the plan of starting a lending library. With the foundation of between forty and fifty books of my own, I sold the idea to the other Government officials and Sproston's people in the district, begged their assistance and was soon able to start with a couple of hundred volumes. Membership cost four pence a month and I soon had forty people on the roll. When I left the district in 1916, the library contained well over a thousand volumes.

Having completed my work in the gold fields I returned to Allicock's camp where we picked up Mansfield and, with Allicock accompanying us, set off back to the river. Instead of turning off along the trail to Allicock's landing, we continued straight on to Monkey Creek landing where I wished to investigate a report that Vanderheyden had made to me concerning certain tributors having obtained rations from the keeper of his magazine by threats and intimidation.

The magazine was of a temporary nature and consisted of two tarpaulin tents in the charge of a young man named Pilgrim. I learned that only one man had intimidated him, though in the presence of three others. The man was still at the landing. I sent Allicock, who was a rural constable, to fetch him and constituted a Magistrate's Court with Allicock as prosecutor, using a milk-box as the bench; a larger packing case as a desk.

Pilgrim's story was that James Greenway, the defendant, an elderly black man of quiet demeanour, came and told him he was hungry and had nothing to eat and would Pilgrim give him some rations. Pilgrim, sorry for the man, did so. Three days later, however, he returned with the others and asked for more rations. Pilgrim told him he could not give him any more as he had helped him already and he himself would have to pay for the goods. Then Greenway asked him if he had ever heard of what happened in the Wenamu gold field when hungry tributors were refused rations by the magazine keeper? They chopped him up and helped themselves to what they wanted. Taking this as a threat, Pilgrim became frightened and gave them what they wanted and then reported the matter by letter to Vanderheyden. Greenway admitted saying this, but assured me that he did not mean it as a threat. I told him that had he said this in Bartica, no one would have taken any notice, but using such a remark up here was a different matter altogether. Here were several stranded tributors and a supply of food that belonged to someone else, in charge of only one man. A single spark could cause a conflagration which would be difficult to extinguish, and therefore I considered the case to be a very serious one and fined him $25.00 or one month.

With the prisoner, Allicock and I proceeded back to the junction and then went to his landing where we found the others had already arrived. At dusk the temperature dropped suddenly, and dreading another cold night I had a fire built close to my hammock and kept up throughout the night. As a result I had an enjoyable sleep, only awakening once or twice when fresh wood was added to the fire and flames leapt up and illuminated the whole camp. I finally woke up at six o'clock to find Walter, the orderly and another man had left, in accordance with plans we had made the previous afternoon. They were to start at four o'clock with Allicock and paddle quietly down the river for some six miles to a small farm where, it was understood, one of Allicock's labourers, who had absconded, was taking refuge. His name was Simon Alley, an old acquaintance of mine, having been convicted for a similar offence at Kamakusa some years before. The party were to wait down river for me until I arrived to try the prisoner if they caught him.

Whilst dressing I saw one of those great black, hairy, bird-eating spiders, locally misnamed tarantulas, come strolling into camp and head for my prospecting bag. The creature was killed by Mansfield who happened to be nearby. When I mentioned the incident to Walter later in the day he told me of an unpleasant experience he had had that same morning. Lying awake in his hammock, waiting for the orderly to call him, he had passed his hand outside his hammock and felt something very smooth and soft which, unthinkingly, he began to stroke. Then something made him look at the object which to his horror he found to be another great tarantula. I could not understand how the creature had not bitten him.

Shortly after this, Frank Spencer, the cook, found one in his hammock. I think the heat of the fire must have attracted them into the camp.

We left camp at seven and about an hour later caught up with Allicock and Walter who had been unsuccessful in their quest, the bird evidently having flown some days previously. Due to this delay we did not arrive at Axe Camp near the upper end of the Morabissi reach of the Mazaruni until five o'clock, only to find it overgrown with grass, even the tent frames having disappeared. As it was too late to go on to the next camp I ordered the men to cut a new frame.

An hour later, just before dusk, I remarked to Captain Fiedtkow that I could only hear one cutlass at work and asked him if he was sure all hands were at work building the camp. Fiedtkow, who had been sitting in the stern of the boat fishing, assured me that everything was in hand and the camp would soon be finished. By seven o'clock, two hours after we had arrived, and still nothing finished, I let fly at Fiedtkow and asked whether he thought this was a cargo boat where his duties ended the moment the boat was tied up to the camp landing, and why the devil wasn't he ashore supervising the men; that the hour's available daylight should have been ample time for the eight men who had gone ashore to cut three tent frames, and if he wanted to call himself a captain he should take some lessons from those old timers, who made it their prime business to look after the comfort of their passengers.

At this he ran ashore but was soon back to say that there was no wood. Now this was the porkknocker's usual cry when he found that there was no tent frame ready for the tarpaulin to be thrown on, and he had to cut the frame himself. To think that anyone could say, 'There is no wood', in one of the densest forests in the world! I went ashore myself and met Wilson, one of the men, who said there were only three men working and he did not know what the others were doing. At this I went for Fiedtkow and gave him some more of my tongue, and seeing the orderly in the gloom I gave him a piece of my mind, too, asking whether he realised he was in charge of two prisoners under sentence of hard labour and whether he thought the government boat-hands were paid to build a tent for them.

It was not long after this that the camp was completed and I got into my hammock and everything was as quiet as a grave. When Walter came up he said I had quite frightened the men with my outburst, one remarking to the other, 'God, but the old man bad tonight.' This was the first occasion any of them had heard me go off the deep end and it not only surprised them but did some good.

On my arrival back in Kamakusa I found a letter waiting for me from Aunt Mary in Scotland, whom I had not seen since I left Strathpeffer in

1902. It was a long interesting letter giving me all the family news and asking me to drop her a line whenever I could find a moment to spare.

When I saw Sub-Inspector Carruthers he told me the real reason for the resentment shown by Gravesande's relatives at the jury's verdict of suicide. It appeared that Gravesande had been insured for less than two years and under the provisions of the policy, no payment was made by the Insurance Company should the insured commit suicide during the first two years of the policy.

I was kept pretty busy for the next ten days catching up on my office work, making sketch plans of the various claims I had verified whilst up the Puruni and in the evenings drafting a story out of the trip. Not having any water-colour brushes for my maps, I got Walter to make quite a serviceable one out of a lock of his hair. I also made a notice for the garden bearing the legend: *Pick no pines without permission,* as I wanted to eat one or two of them myself and I did not see the point of planting them for the exclusive use of the boat-hands and police. One morning, not feeling too well, I got Dispenser Abrams to examine me and he reported that I was once more suffering from haemorrhoids, and after two operations, D——!

Carruthers decided that he would accompany me on my next trip up river. He had gone up by himself whilst I was up the Puruni but found that there were a number of things that he was not too happy about and would welcome my knowledge of the area. Whilst up the Eping I met my old friend, Ralph Rice, a young Londoner whom I had not seen since 1927. He had just returned from leave in England and was already down with fever. He said he had been living exclusively on soda water and ginger ale for the past week, being unable to keep any solid food down, so I got his cook to kill a fowl and make some chicken tea.

Whilst in the district we heard rumours that confirmed a feeling that I'd had for some time that my friend Mark-a-Book was running very near the fringe of the law, including spreading the story that he had been appointed the warden's deputy, which, of course, was quite untrue. So, as we passed back by Oranapai police station, Carruthers told the constable there to pick up Markum and bring him down to Kamakusa. When he finally came before the Court I told him he had been in the district quite long enough to know the law and that he must learn to live within it. I fined him $2.50 or seven days.

It was on this same day that the death of Sir Gordon Guggisberg, the Governor, whilst on sick leave in England, was announced over the radio. I had the flag placed at half mast for the remainder of the day.

At the end of April it was time for a month back in Georgetown. The trip down was uneventful although the weather was very wet. Whilst in Bartica I heard of the death of my old friend, Philibert Pierre of Aruka. After writing letters of condolence to his brother Desmond, his father and widow, I did a short appreciation of him for the *Daily Chronicle*. Whilst sailing between Bartica and Parika on the little steamer *Pirai*, we stopped at Ithaca to pick up passengers, amongst whom was a tough, elderly white man with a real Creole brogue, who turned out to be called Wilkie, with his very attractive daughter, a fair young girl with yellow flaxen hair and blue eyes.

Finally arriving home I was pleasantly surprised to find Phil looking better than I had seen her for years. The sight of my beard, however, was a little too much for her. She said it made her feel shy, as though I were a stranger, and as soon as my baggage had been brought in she unpacked my shaving brush and razor and begged me to return to my old clean shaven chin. After a leisurely tea I made an inspection of the family, two-footed, four-footed and feathered. Old Gooding had not changed and greeted me with a mighty hug and a kiss. The maid, a new one, did not.

The mongoose, now almost full size, having been caught stealing hen's eggs and the odd chicken, was now confined to a cage where he snarled, hissed and spat at all who approached him. Seeing him in this mood one could understand his ability to do battle with snakes as his movements were like lightning. Poor old peccari had been confined to the garage because he had acquired a liking for fowls and generally made a nuisance of himself. Robert the macaw was dead, evidently through going on a hunger strike in protest against Phil's adoption of a green screecher parrot Henry had given her, and Uncle Joe the tom cat had given everybody a shock by producing a coop of kittens and was now known as Josephine. The inspection over, I got on my bicycle and went over to 69 Croal Street to see Mother and Dad.

Mother was in a rather distressed state as it appeared that there was a possibility that Dad might lose his post as Curator of the Museum due to the lack of funds brought about by the reduction of the Government subsidy. Later, when we were alone, Dad showed me the letter he had received. It had been written by young Cleare, one of the directors of the Royal Agricultural and Commercial Society, and outlined a scheme for the more economical running of the museum. After two paragraphs of thinly veiled sneers at Dad's work of improving the museum during the past two years, it went on to suggest the abolition of the post of full time Curator and the appointment of several honorary curators to look after each branch of the institution. The whole letter was an attack on Dad under the guise of economy. It was undoubtedly Cleare's retaliation on Dad for certain unintentionally indiscreet remarks Dad had made when he first took up his appointment and which had undoubtedly reflected on Cleare's work at the museum when he had been a part time curator there. Dad did not say whether he had definitely been given notice, although that was the impression he gave me.

When I got to the office the following morning, I discovered that my travelling allowance accounts had been held up due to a new, foolish, futile and unfair subsistence allowance regulation, by which, without the special sanction of the Governor, no officer was entitled to such an allowance whilst within the limits of his district. As mine began at Boerasierie Creek and extended along the coast to the mouth of the Moruca River and embraced the whole of the basins of the Mazaruni and Cuyuni Rivers, constituting at least one sixth of the total area of the Colony, and that the nearest settlement to my station was eighteen miles away, this regulation seemed extraordinary to say the least and drawn up by those who were absolutely ignorant of conditions in the interior.

During a long interview with Hohenkirk, the Acting Commissioner of Lands and Mines, he told me that he was retiring on doctor's orders to live in a cold climate owing to the filaria he had contracted a few years previously. He then referred to the article 'Puruni Gold' I had submitted for permission to publish. Having read it through several times, he suggested that I deleted all reference to the manner in which Government Officers were compelled to travel on the Mazaruni; all reference to the excessive size of gold claims; all reference to the partaking of liquid refreshment; all reference to Mansfield (described in the article as M-) and several other points. I concluded that I might as well give up any thought of publishing the article if that was going to be his attitude. I suppose I might have overstepped the mark in one or two instances, considering I was still a serving public servant. He then changed the subject, saying he wanted me to attend a meeting with him and Wood, the Conservator of Forests, with a view to regularising the spelling of native place names in the Colony.

Then I went over to the office of the Postmaster General, Mr Birkett, with whom I had a long discussion on the Mazaruni mail service. From there I went to the Audit Office and delivered the key of the canister of magisterial books I had brought down to be audited, and then went next door to the Attorney General's Office to report my arrival in town.

On seeing a report in the paper, I wrote a note to the Commissioner suggesting the necessity of holding an enquiry into the wreck of Mr McGillivary's boat, *Grizzly Bear No 3*. This was the boat he had built to replace the one lost in Tiboku in February, and was lost on her first trip up river. Discussing the matter with Jim Eytle, a captain of thirty years service, he expressed the view very strongly that no boats should be used in the falls that exceeded a length of thirty-eight feet and that the cargo capacity should not exceed 10,000lbs.

A letter from Cousin Lula arrived in which she told me that Aunt Mary had died on 18th February, so my letter from Kamakusa was of no avail. Also enclosed was an old photograph of my mother which she had found amongst Aunt Mary's effects.

I had arrived in town just in time to attend the regular meeting of Mount Olive Lodge. Old C.J. Maggs gave a very interesting and constructive lecture on the history of Freemasonry. Retiring downstairs we had a very pleasant social hour, Maggs being in good form with his stories, one of which I have always remembered: A young man, wishing to marry, approached the girls father. He, after some deliberations, replied that he did not know how the young man expected to keep a wife on his salary of £150 a year. 'Oh, we'll manage alright,' he replied. 'That's all very well,' said the father, 'but what about when the babies start to arrive?' 'Ah,' replied the youth, 'we'll just have to risk that. We've been lucky so far!'

Whilst in the office I held a Warden's Court to hear a dispute between Dr W.H. Wharton, V.B. Humphrey and A.P. Camisuli in connection with some gold claims on the Wynamu Creek in the upper Puruni. I had just got over the formal objections when Togo Low came in and, bowing to the court, approached me. At first I thought he was going to kiss me but discovered that he was endeavouring to whisper into my sound ear an invitation to breakfast.

I started to make an index of all the place names on the Colony map of 1913, giving alternative spellings, ready for the meeting with the Commissioner and Conservator. Most of the spelling had been done phonetically, as picked up from the Creole Indians by surveyors as they passed through a district, and no doubt some of the spellings I have used in my journals will not agree with those shown on the modern maps of the country. When the meeting did finally take place, Wood, the Conservator, tried to play the fool with me as though I were a mere junior clerk, while his rabbit teeth clicked together as he spoke exclusively to Hohenkirk and referred to 'Denham' as though he were a stall mate of the Governor Elect.

On receiving a note from the Commissioner to hold an enquiry into the loss of the *Grizzly Bear,* I issued thirteen summons to witnesses to appear before a Court to be held at Bartica on 22nd May.

The rains which were usually expected at the beginning of May were on time this year and I got one or two soakings during my various trips round town. Things were not made any easier as the Demerara Electric Company were taking up the old tram lines and did not appear to be very particular as to the condition in which they left the roads. When I saw Duke, the Registrar, he told me of the row the Town Council was having with the Electric Company. The Council maintained that the roads where the trams used to run were their property whereas the Company denied this. The Town Council Ordinance was not at all clear on this and a great deal of research was going to be needed before the matter could be resolved.

A letter in the daily papers written by Ginder, concerning the need for more medical facilities in the Mazaruni, brought Dr Kelly, the Surgeon General, to seek my advice on the subject. I pointed out that the presence of a doctor in the district could not prevent conditions such as those described by Ginder from arising, as the district was a large one and the doctor could not be in more than one place at a time. It was agreed that in order to allay the feelings that might have been caused by Ginder's letter, Kelly would arrange a meeting with the Mining Committee of the Chamber of Commerce and explain the Government's intentions in the area. Kelly then told me he would try and arrange for Dr B.V. Bailey to go back with me to the district when I returned at the end of the month and asked that I take him on a tour of inspection.

A day or so later I received an invitation to tea at Dr Bailey's house in Camp Street. Arriving there, I was taken by the maid into a large drawing room, beautifully furnished with easy chairs and a large sofa, out of which rose a most attractive woman who introduced herself as Mrs Bailey. I joined her on the sofa, which was one of the most comfortable I had ever sat in, and waited for the doctor to join us, which he did shortly afterwards. After a sumptuous high tea I was shown over the garden which was quite large for a Camp Street house. Returning indoors we went upstairs where I was introduced to their family of guinea pigs who lived free in one of the back rooms. I learned that they never missed an opportunity for escaping, usually finding their way under the kitchen stove where they would gnaw the wood and coals.

At the top of the house was a large, well equipped workshop and here I learned the secret of the luxurious sofa. The frame had been made by the doctor out of an old door and a piece of string mattress for the seating and the fine upholstering had all been done by Mrs Bailey and her sister. They then showed me some lampshades they were making in the style of a Chinese pagoda, out of wire frames and covered with silk.

Mrs Bailey then excused herself, saying she had to take her dogs out for exercise so the doctor and I returned to the lounge where we discussed whisky, dry sherry and colonial life in general. I then discovered that the doctor was a stamp collector, and he modestly admitted that he had about a quarter of a million, which I hardly doubted when he showed me cupboards, boxes, trunks and valises full of stamps. When Mrs Bailey returned she insisted I stayed to dinner; I could hardly refuse such a charming hostess and it was well after ten o'clock when I climbed on my bike and made for home after one of the most enjoyable visits I had made for many a long day.

As we were together as a family for once, as a birthday treat for Phil I bought tickets for the much advertised 'talkie', *Rio Rita*. I can't say I enjoyed the outing but the others appeared to do so, so I said nothing. The music was neither very audible or clear, like that emanating from a third-rate gramophone. When the film itself came on it was so unnatural as to be almost a joke, although I gradually became accustomed to it. The movements of the mouths and the actual voices did not always synchronise; a character from whose appearance one would expect a deep bass voice would speak with a high falsetto and vice versa. The play itself was a musical 'comedy' with very little plot. Of course, the fact that I could not always hear the words, but only caught a phrase here and there may have biased me against the whole performance, which I considered poor. The chorus girls did not dance in unison and on one or two occasions were decidedly vulgar in their movements. The second part of the show was better in that it was in colour and the gorgeous dresses of the women made a fine display, but this was the best I could say for a show which, to me at least, was very overrated. I decided I would wait for the 'talkies' to improve before I went to see them again.

One morning I was called to see the Detective Inspector at Brickdam police station. When I got there, having no idea what it could be about, I was asked to identify a Venezuelan named Bonifacio Marquez who had been arrested on a warrant applied for by me in 1916 when I was a Land Officer at Barima. I remembered that he had been suspected of smuggling balata into Venezuela, as I had found hidden in a small creek on British territory a corial which was identified as his. Naturally, after a lapse of fourteen years, it was impossible to proceed with the case so I arranged for the withdrawal of the warrant and the release of Marquez who had been arrested at Bartica. It did bear out the saying that the police will eventually get their man.

I went to Bartica for the *Grizzly Bear* enquiry. Long joined the train at Leonora where he was the acting Magistrate of the Essequibo Judicial District and we travelled the remainder of the way together. At Bartica, Long went off to hold his Court whilst I went over to book in at the Hotel Moderne. As I entered the building the first person I saw was old 'Daddy' Davenport pouring over figures and plans in the gallery at the foot of the stairs. He was one of the three forestry officers engaged in that colossally stupid waste of money, the reopening of the Kaburi road and its extension to Butakari. I had not seen him since our return from the North West Colonisation survey where we had worked together a year before and the old boy greeted me most effusively. Although he was only forty-six his hair was quite white and he looked to be over sixty. He had been a lime planter in Dominica until 1916 when a hurricane destroyed his estate and killed his brother. He had then joined King Edward's Horse and had gone to the war. I had tea with him, or to be precise, I had tea and he a glass of rum. He told me he was going on leave at the end of the month, the first he had had since he joined the service five years ago.

At nine o'clock next morning I opened the enquiry in the Warden's office, the Court room still being occupied by the Magistrate. The captains of the two boats concerned, Nathaniel Nedd of the *Bear* and Joseph Lewis of the *Joan C*, were duly warned that they were in the position of defendants and that they could cross examine such witnesses as they chose. Ten witnesses were examined and it became apparent that those from one boat were trying to lay the blame for the accident on the other craft and vice versa.

Briefly, it transpired that both boats had been travelling up the Mazaruni, the *Bear* on the starboard side of the *Joan C* and, as they neared Karawarambo Stream, the *Joan C* pulled over to port to sail up the left hand channel, whilst the *Bear* continued straight on up to the right. The *Bear* had not gone far when a turn tide (one of those peculiar places in the cataracts where a portion of the water runs in a direction directly opposite to that of the main current) caught her and pushed her ahead to a position level with the *Joan C* which, at that very moment was struck by the bursting of a suck tide and thrown right across the channel on to the *Bear* which she struck with her bow on the after quarter and holed her, upon which she promptly sank. The crews were unable to avert the crash due to the strong currents acting on the boats. I came to the conclusion that both captains were to blame in that they were both sailing too close to each other where such contra-currents could be expected.

On our return to town, as Long and I passed Ampa Quarry, where there had been a fatal explosion some months previously, he gave me an account of the inquest he had held on the victim of the accident. The manager of the quarry, one Griffith, a very large and tough white man, was a material witness and in the course of his evidence he casually pulled a couple of sticks of gelignite out of his pocket and dumped them on the clerk's table, explaining to the jurors that this was the kind of dynamite used at the quarry. The three jurors began to fidget nervously. Next he pulled out from another pocket a short length of fuse to which he attached a clay model of a stick of dynamite. As he explained the procedure he nonchalantly swung the thing about, tapping it on the rail of the witness box. Then, suddenly pulling the fuse out of the clay stick, he exposed a live detonator fastened to the end. 'This,' he remarked, 'would blow us all to hell if it went off.' This was too much for a Portuguese juror who was sitting next to the door, through which he promptly vanished, whilst the Coroner asked the witness to hand over the detonator to him.

When I got back to the office, Hohenkirk told me that E.G. Woolford had told him that Mansfield had complained to him about my treatment of him in the Puruni and that he was going to take up the matter with the Attorney General and the Governor.

When I called at the Audit Office to see about the return of my magisterial books to Kamakusa, it appeared that they wanted to put the responsibility on my shoulders for taking them back to the district. This I was not prepared to do, as I had posted them by steamer from Bartica and they had taken delivery of them at the steamer stelling in Georgetown. When I mentioned it to Long, he pointed that under the Magistrates Court Regulations, books cannot leave the district to which they belong, it being the auditors' duty to inspect them in the district. I said that I'd had great difficulty in getting an auditor into my district, as none of them liked going to Kamakusa and it was with great reluctance that I had brought them down with me, fearing the loss of them in the falls. The Audit Office was not overpleased when I pointed out that if the Court archives were lost they could not be replaced, whereas if an auditor was lost........

Dr Kelly's meeting with the Mining Committee of the Chamber of Commerce was held in his office the day before I returned to Kamakusa. Ginder, Cooper, Kosser, Houston and Tom, the managers of the leading trading firms, attended. The doctor gave a résumé of medical conditions in the district and convinced the meeting that whilst a resident doctor was desirable, it was not an economical proposition. Ginder, who did most of the talking, insisted on bringing my name into the discussion, telling Kelly how often and how seriously ill I was up there, whilst I argued that I'd had no more fever than was to be expected in a district such as the Mazaruni. The Surgeon General promised that if the Bartica Company was prepared to dispose of their Tumareng station at a reasonable figure he would gladly recommend to Government that the Kamakusa hospital be moved to that point. He also stated that a more elaborate system of travelling dispensers had recently been put into operation.

My last day in Georgetown was hectic to say the least, with the result that I finally got to bed just before one o'clock. It seemed I had just fallen asleep when Gooding was shaking me to say the car was waiting to take me to the stelling. Hurriedly dressing and saying good-bye to a half-awake family, I left the house and made my way to the steamer stelling where I boarded the *Basra*. Just behind me were the Baileys; Mrs Bailey was coming as far as Bartica with us.

The boat left a few minutes after five, and we retired to our respective cabins to try and complete the remainder of our night's sleep. At Fort Island we all went ashore to have a look at the old Dutch building that used to house the Court of Policy, but unfortunately the door was locked and we had no time to get the key.

At Bartica, the Sergeant Major on duty at the stelling told me that Harry Williams had come down sick and was at the Houston Hotel and would like to see me. So, after booking in at the Moderne, I went over to see Williams who was recovering from an attack of fever. In the same hotel I found Hart, the Rupununi rancher, who had come down the Essequibo a few days before in a Boundary Commission boat. He had with him a whole valise full of Rupununi tobacco, cut into half sticks, each about thirty-six inches long. He gave me one, and I invited him over to the Moderne for a drink.

Hart was a big man with a shrewd, kindly face. He had come into the colony from Brazil in 1913 with a partner called James. They started prospecting for gold on the upper Rupununi, where they found some claims of fair value. One day they got word from Melville, the District Commissioner, that Ocean Shark, the real bad man of the colony, was on their track and that they had better watch out for him. James, who was a bigger man than Hart, took the warning seriously as he knew the Shark and what he was capable of. It annoyed Hart that his partner should admit fear of this Negro and he vowed that when he met the Shark he would whip him as a matter of principle.

For reasons which do not concern this story, James left the colony whilst Hart found himself trekking with a two-wheeled bullock cart up towards Pirara, where he intended to start a ranch. In that neighbourhood, a Scotsman named MacDonald had recently died, leaving his little ranch, a few head of cattle and other livestock and some well cultivated fields to his Macusi wife. Ocean Shark had marched in on the widow and taken possession of her and her property. Every day a fat fowl had to be killed and once a week a fatted calf slaughtered for this bully who spent his days in luxurious ease in the dead man's hammock.

Hart, hearing about this, decided he would call on the Shark and fulfil his vow. When he arrived at the place he found a number of Indians and a Negro youth standing talking some hundred yards from the house. Hart asked the young Negro what he was doing there. The fellow replied rather arrogantly that he was, 'Mr Thomas' secretary.' 'And who the hell is Mr Thomas?' demanded Hart, who did not know the Shark's real name. 'And where is he?' The boy pointed to the house and Hart realised that he was to meet the Ocean Shark at last.

Approaching the house he saw a huge black man lying in a hammock. 'Are you Ocean Shark?' he asked.

'Yes, is what you want?' came the reply.

'If you're not off this ranch in five seconds I'll fill you full of lead,' retorted Hart, his right hand moving towards his gun. Like a shot the burly Shark jumped out of his hammock and rushed at Hart with outstretched hands towards his throat. Before he realised what was happening, Hart had pulled out his revolver and struck the Shark a smashing blow to the side of his head, splitting an ear almost in half. To an ordinary man this blow would have been fatal but it only dazed the Shark sufficiently long enough to enable Hart to strike the Shark again until he fell to the ground unconscious. Meanwhile the Indians stood and looked on without moving.

When the Shark recovered enough to regain his feet, Hart pointed to the north and told him to get out, and that if he ever found him back on the MacDonald ranch he would complete what he had started that day. The bully's spirit was apparently broken by the beating and he never returned. Shortly after this he met his death at the hands of two Macusi Indians whose mother and sisters he had ravished.

When Dad, who was acting Commissioner of the District at the time, next met Hart, he asked him why he had not finished off the job there and then. Hart had replied, 'Not for Hell'. He had seen too much of the slow but in the end sure working of justice in countries controlled by the British. Ocean Shark must have been a wonderful bushman as he was said to have arrived in the Rupununi on foot from the upper Mazaruni. He was originally a gold digger, but being a very powerful man and a bully he found it easier to raid the claims of weaker men and drive them away with the threat of his gun than to prospect himself. Dad had an unpleasant experience with him once in the Rupununi. Finding him in his hammock cleaning his gun, Dad asked to see his gun licence. He pointed the gun straight at Dad and told him to come and get it. Dad, being unarmed and unaccompanied by any police, could do nothing. Yet there must have been some good in Ocean Shark. Jimmy Stuart Jones, who knew him well, once told me that if the Shark was in funds, he would always give money to any of his hard-up friends.

As I listened to Hart's stories the time slipped by very quickly and it was again very late by the time I got to bed. I was still asleep when Dr Bailey came into my room to say it was ten to seven. Hastily throwing on my clothes I hurried down to the stelling just in time to say good-bye to Mrs Bailey as the *Basra* cast off. A little later, Bailey and I embarked on the boat *B.C.L.Express*.

Before we set off, the boat pushed off from the wharf so that the policeman could see whether her load-line was clear of the water. A couple of men were told to shift their positions so as to bring the load line out of the water on the side nearest the stelling. Then the boat was swung round so that the policeman could see the other side. He was not satisfied, so we had to return to the wharf where a bag of flour was unloaded. What a farce! Finally moving off, we settled down to a four day journey up to Kamakusa. As I sat thinking about what lay ahead and Hart's story of Ocean Shark, my mind went back to a conversation I'd had with Dummett, a clerk at the Treasury, who came up to me and said, 'Ah, Mr Roth, when are you going back to the Rupununi?'.

'I'm damned if I know.'

'But didn't you make a requisition for a magisterial book recently? We don't know how to send it and thought perhaps you could take it up with you when you returned there.'

'But I'm not going to the Rupununi and I've never been there.'

'But aren't you stationed at Kamakusa in the Rupununi?'

'My God, Dummett, aren't you ashamed of yourself?'

'Why, what do you mean, Mr Roth?'

'Here you are, born and bred in the country, been in Government service for some twenty years in a department that has dealings with the various districts and yet you don't know the difference between the Mazaruni and the Rupununi.'

'But Mr Roth, I'm not a surveyor!'

We reached Kamakusa at seven o'clock on the Sunday evening. On the following morning, whilst Dispenser Joseph took Bailey round the compound, I took over from Greene who had been standing in for me whilst I was in town. Then, just after midday, the Doctor, Joseph and I left Kamakusa in the dispenser's boat and proceeded up river. My boat, the *Arawana-Sanuka,* caught us up below Rumong-Rumong and we tied the two boats together.

Arriving at Oranapai at four o'clock we put up at Uncle Charlie's. After a beer with him we inspected his shop as well as that of Henry Bornstein and J.G. Stephen. The latter was very hot under the collar because the presence of a young girl on the hill was encouraging his manager to neglect his duties and steal from the shop. This was often the trouble with young men employed as shop managers.

At Merriwai we inspected the shops of Choong and Lam and Alfred Clark, the latter being established in one half of T.B. Mapp's dance hall. At Mapp's house we saw some squash vines growing on arbours, on one of which was stuck a black bottle with spots of white paint all over it. I thought this was meant to frighten off the birds but was amused to learn that its object was to attract the eye away from the blossoms lest any covetous glances be cast towards them and the blossoms drop off. This superstition, I learnt, was common along the coast and was supposed to have been brought to the colony by the East Indians.

At Enachu we found Weiss in charge of Krakowsky's. The cow having gone on strike, we had to drink beer. I was surprised to see aback the cricket field a newly-built corrugated iron house divided into three rooms, each having a female occupant. Previously Krakowsky's had been very much against this sort of thing and would not allow such women to reside on any of their lands. Now, said Weiss, as all their competitors were doing it, they felt compelled to follow suit. We went on to Tumareng where we spent the night.

As I had received a large number of registered letters by the mailboat which needed attention because they contained fees for Government, I decided to stay at Einhorn's and deal with them while the doctor and Joseph went up the Eping and Perenong. They had planned to stay overnight there but because of a tacouba in the Perenong which they had only just managed to clear, they decided not to risk staying up there in case the river level dropped and they could not get out.

In the evening the doctor showed us some very clever card tricks and then we played a couple of rubbers of bridge. The bête rouge had got the doctor in the Perenong and he sat on his cot in his shirt tails vigorously scratching both ankles and wishing someone would invent an automatic scratching machine.

After inspecting Tumareng as to its suitability as a site for a station in place of Kamakusa, we went to Kurupung where we inspected the shops. At the Bartica Company shop we condemned some ten pounds of beef as being unfit for human consumption. We spent the night there with Pierre.

We decided that we would spend the next day visiting the Makreba Falls, which lay some twelve miles above Pierre's. He suggested we used his boat, the *Tiger Queen*, a very comfortable craft some thirty feet long, fitted with an inboard engine and a tent running its whole length.

As we passed the police station I noticed a new clearing with several Indian camps and small groups of Arecunas going about their business. Pierre said that these people had accompanied Roderick Forbes down from his home in the upper Mazaruni. Passing the mouth of the Saganang Creek we got our first glimpse of the western ramparts of Mount Watabaru, a sheer face of pinkish-brown cliff deeply indented with vertical rifts. Then we got glimpses of the two peaks which stand as sentinels at the mouth of the precipitous gorge between which the Kurupung runs.

Seeing a woodskin moored at a stelling we went ashore and, climbing a hill some two hundred feet above the river, arrived at a clearing in which stood an Indian house of peculiar shape, being a compromise between a round house and an octagonal one. The eaves came down to within three feet of the ground and the surrounding wall was pierced by two doors diametrically opposite each other. In the gloom of the interior we saw a sick Indian in his hammock, several women and more children, the latter being naked but for their diminutive loincloths of red saloo. The usual number of half-starved dogs slouched away with low growls as we entered. I pointed out to Bailey one of the cassava graters made with pieces of quartz stuck in the wood and he endeavoured to purchase it. As soon as the women understood his intention they gave vent to loud *kanes* and it was explained that the implement belonged to one John, who was out hunting. I also noticed a bead queya, or lady's apron, being manufactured on a frame of bent sticks.

Returning to our boat we went on upstream and soon passed between the two peaks, which towered a couple of thousand feet above our heads. The age-long weathering of the cliff face had left great overhanging portions of pinkish-red conglomerate beneath which the high sun cast deep shadows. Pierre told us that especially at this time of year, during the rainy season, the deep rumbling of detached pieces of rock, some weighing hundreds of tons, could be heard as they crashed through the forest on the lower slopes. I was glad none came loose whilst we passed beneath them.

Now the black surface of the water became coated with a thin film of foam and some larger lumps which indicated our approach to the fall. We passed the mouth of the Seroun River and the old landing of the balata companies where the trail across the mountains to the upper Mazaruni begins, then swung sharply to the left and a minute later came in sight of the Makreba Fall. The river, constricted in the narrow groove of the ravine, tumbled down in a series of cascades between immense boulders. The upper portion of the falls was invisible behind the overhanging trees, and a cloud of misty spray cast a haze over the scene.

We could not approach nearer the falls with the boat than some three hundred yards, because of the stream's turbulence and the rocks which lay scattered about its course. We had breakfast in the boat and along with the food must have consumed quite an appreciable amount of dried froth which floated about in the air like snowflakes.

After, we set off to get some close-up pictures of the falls. Although the rock consisted of coarse conglomerate, it was frightfully slippery, necessitating in places, progress on all fours. Although I had on rubber-soled shoes I more than once just avoided a bad fall so that, after scrambling crab-fashion for a few hundred feet I decided that discretion was the better part of valour. I left the others to go on ahead and returned to the boat and read a magazine.

They came back in about an hour, having successfully scrambled up to the first visible fall and beyond to two others above. It appeared that the river descended from the mountain by a giant staircase of which the last step is the Makreba Fall. Dr Bailey was very excited over the discovery in a waterhole in the rock of mosquito larvae which he had never seen before. He and Joseph had spent some time scratching about in the rock crevices looking for diamonds! Truly the optimism of the novice is marvellous.

We set off on our return journey at about two o'clock. Some of the mountain tops previously hidden in cloud were now visible in all their silent grandeur. We played bridge to while away the time, but I could not really concentrate on pieces of cardboard whilst speeding down a black and silent river amidst tropical jungle above which sections of the great mountain wall occasionally peeped thousands of feet above us.

Back at Pierre's, Roderick Forbes came over with his Arecuna wife and little stepdaughter. He began giving the doctor his idea of the statistics of the Indian population on the upper river across the mountains and Bailey was very interested in his account of the epidemic that had almost halved the tribes during the drought of 1926.

I went over to Matthews at Triefus where I found the entire waterside and backdam managerial staffs of the Bartica Company, Triefus and Krakowsky playing bridge and drinking whisky. I was told that business was so bad that they had got together to escape the boredom of their own company. After spending an hour with them, they all decided to come back with me to Pierre's, where we found our host with a long suffering expression listening to Bailey and Forbes discussing anthropology. With the greatly increased size of the party, the doctor gave us a toast with Highland honours, quite unaware that Pierre was at the time carving off a chunk of his rubber toecap with a table knife. It was a merry evening. After dinner I have a faint recollection of joining the gang over a fowl curry at Krakowsky's and then escorting Maurice Nascemento home to his temporary quarters at the Bartica Company's premises.

Next day we returned down the river to Oranapai where we put up at the New Diamond Venture where the manager Bob Semple entertained us. Uncle Charlie was away in town. After dinner we played bridge with Bornstein until Moore arrived, when I handed my place over to him so that I could write some letters to the family for Bailey to take down with him when he returned to town. I must have fallen asleep as the next thing I remember was being awakened about midnight by a great deal of laughing and shouting.

I saw a most peculiar sight. Standing in the middle of the room was Miller, the barrister, grasping a broom, the upper end of which was holding a glass of water up against the ceiling, whilst everyone stood around laughing as someone suggested that they should play bridge whilst Miller studied the rainbow. This was known as the rainbow trick. A victim was chosen, then someone asks the company if they have ever noticed the peculiar rainbow-like effect observed in the bottom of a glass of water on the ceiling. Everyone expresses surprise and a glass of water is obtained. Placing a chair on a table, someone climbs up on to it and, with a lot of small talk holds the glass against the ceiling. Then he calls for a broom and making great play with it, puts the end of the broom handle up to the bottom of the glass. The victim is then asked to hold it for a moment. As he does so the table and chair are removed and it is then suggested that everyone goes off for a walk. It then dawns on the victim that he has been had. I once saw this trick played on Mark-a-Book, who actually let go of the broom and caught the glass in his hands.

Most of the next day was spent in holding Court. Ten of the cases were between a black girl from Trinidad called Irene Phil and the whole of the Cappell family who lived on Chicago Hill. The old lady, who must have weighed about eighteen stone, charged the girl with calling her a '— old Basra', in reference to her size and that of the largest of the Colony's steamers. It cost her ten dollars.

After Court I adjourned for dinner and a final drink with Bailey before seeing him off on Ginder's boat. On this went two policemen who had in their charge a lunatic, whom Bailey had certified. He was guaranteed not to have a dull journey down to town. The boat having finally disappeared into the night, Miller, Bob Semple, Henry Bornstein and I made a tour of the settlement and ended up at J.G. Stephen's shop where we proceeded to initiate him in the mysteries of the rainbow trick.

Whilst this was going on Irene Phil came in to consult Miller about another case of hers that was to be heard in Court the following day. Suddenly a loud bang and a cry echoed round the room and I saw a man running out of the house with what looked like a woman in his arms. Apparently, whilst the girl was talking to Miller, Fiedtkow, her lover, (who had piloted me in the Puruni), had come in, knocked her down with a blow on the head, picked her up in his arms and dashed off to their house with her. I immediately sent over to the police station and in five minutes the whole force arrived and a short while later arrested Fiedtkow and marched him off to the station.

The doctor having left, the place seemed like a hot and stagnant room through which a fresh breeze had been blowing for a week and is then suddenly cut off. When Fiedtkow came before me in Court, I sentenced him to a fine of $50 or two months in prison. The foolish girl wanted to pay his fine for him but, in her own interest, I strongly advised her against doing so, he being a despicable parasite who lived off a woman's immoral earnings.

There were further cases between Phil and the Cappells, some of which Miller advised Phil to drop, and when she refused Miller asked permission to withdraw from the proceedings. Eventually, when she saw that things were going against her, she withdrew the remainder of the cases, which should never have been brought in the first place. As she had been giving a lot of trouble in the district I ordered her to leave Oranapai within two weeks.

After breakfast, Mark-a-Book brought to my office a youth who was suffering from a very bad case of VD which he alleged he had contracted from a girl, Florence Wason, living in Buck Cannister Sands. As her authority to be in the district had long since expired, I made an order that she remove herself from all claims in No.3 Mining District within the next five days. Because of the trouble that the women of the fields were causing, chiefly at Oranapai and Buck Cannister Sands, I drafted a notice to all the shops in the district to the effect that, 'Every woman other than a bona fide claim-holder or a married woman living with her husband who was found residing away from the actual premises of her employer would be prosecuted and deported from the district.'

Originally these women had come into the district by the simple expedient of buying mining privileges. In 1925, when there were over 140 of them in the district, there was agitation from the traders, amongst them Ginder and Houston, asking that some form of control be exercised over them. They alleged that the women got hold of their shop clerks and encouraged them to steal from their employer's stock.

The Commissioner then decided that no more privileges would be issued to women, but if a man wanted a domestic servant he might, subject to the Commissioner's approval, register her as such under the Mining Regulations. At first the system worked quite well, but eventually it became the custom for a girl, for a consideration in most cases, to get a claim holder to register her as his domestic servant though he never had the slightest intention of employing her, nor she of working as such. This then developed into a regular practice.

A lady of easy virtue wishing to come up to the district to practise her profession would go to a 'plantain water' lawyer to whom she would pay five dollars and ask to be registered with Mr John Thomas. The lawyer would write to the Commissioner on behalf of Mr Thomas and eventually get permission to register the girl, who thus got into the district. She would never go near Mr Thomas but settled wherever she thought would be most profitable. One day I received an official notice which stated, 'On the application of Mr J.A. Vaughan, a claim holder in the Mazaruni, I have allowed Millicent Hunt to be registered to work for him as a domestic servant etc.'. When I mentioned this to Vaughan when I was up the Perenong he denied all knowledge of the matter. He did not know the woman, had never applied for her to be registered nor authorised anyone to register any woman on his behalf!

I also instructed the police to prosecute every woman found away from her employer's place as, under the Mining Regulations, every person in a Mining District was required to produce, on demand, some document showing their entitlment to work on a claim in that district. The Mining Regulations, fearful and wonderful as they were, did seem to cover all the facets of life in the districts to which they applied.

In the *Argosy* I read an account of an attack made on me by certain members in the Legislative Council. A.V. Cranehead brought Government's attention to the undesirability of having unqualified magistrates who had had no legal training, and he referred specifically to the post of Warden Magistrate, Mazaruni. He did, however, point out that it was the post he was criticising and 'not the amiable gentleman who filled it'. Woolford, however, followed with a distinctly personal attack, by stating that owing to some criticisms he had made about my appointment some years previously in the Combined Court, I had refused to speak to him. The fact was that I had never been introduced to the Honourable Member, who was a complete stranger to me. He said he had spoken to the Attorney General about my unsatisfactory performance of my duties as a magistrate, although he admitted I was a very capable warden. According to Woolford I would not listen to criticisms etc. I felt the attack to be personal as no mention was made of Long, the acting Commissioner of the North West District or of Harvey Read, Land Officer, Rupununi, neither of whom had had any legal training, yet acted in a magisterial capacity. Shortly after reading this report in the paper I saw Eugene Correia who said he had seen Woolford the last time he had been in town and Woolford had told him that Mansfield had been to him and told him that I had sent a policeman to arrest him and had then tried him without serving him with a summons and had fined him $20 or a month for stealing four pieces of tin, and that I had conspired with the Puruni claim holders to chase him out of the district. Correia said he had asked Woolford if he knew what sort of man Mansfield was. Woolford had replied, 'Why, yes, he's so docile he wouldn't hurt a fly.'

I had found Eugene busy sorting out his week's purchase of diamonds. I asked him to show me the famous diamond that had been to town three times and paid royalty as often. He said he was waiting to palm it off on a new buyer, as every trader in the district knew the stone by this time, it being a six carat naat – two crystals together. It was of a grey cloudy colour and had the appearance of being thoroughly shattered. I decided I must get the full story of this gem when I had more time.

The Eping, a few hundred yards above Perenong mouth, breaks up into a series of parallel channels or itabos which, in low water, are almost dry, tacouba-strewn stream beds, but with the flood waters they are converted into mysterious watery aisles through the forest. It was through this intricate labyrinth we had to force our careful way for some half a mile, keeping an eye below for tacoubas and another above for projecting branches that might sweep the tent off the boat. At length we cleared the itabos and continued on up the river.

After breakfast, with the water level high, we had little trouble in dodging the rocks and tacoubas which were mostly covered. Then we suddenly passed a landing inside a wide itabo where a tent boat was moored. We had actually passed Eytle's landing without recognising it, so different did the river appear at high water.

Leaving instructions for our baggage to be brought up when Einhorn's tent boat arrived (Einhorn had said he wanted to come with me on this trip), we set out for Eytle's and Houston's Band of Hope Placer, which was about a mile from the landing. Crossing a short piece of swamp the trail soon climbed an ironstone hill, descended across another small flat and once more climbed up to an elevated plateau. After some twenty minutes tramp the sky began to show through the trees and in a few minutes we came out on an opening of some hundred acres extent.

After a short walk we arrived at the house, a stoutly constructed open bungalow, with one portion divided off into a storeroom and an office. A busy scene lay below and we heard the irregular pounding of motors. Lower down the hill stood three large shingled logies, hidden more or less by plantain and banana trees. These were the labourers' houses. Beyond extended a wide forested flat, in the midst of which was a great white scar some forty acres in extent where every tree had been removed and their places taken by little black paper-covered watch houses placed on sandy knolls whilst two rambling constructions of staging with roofs of tarpaulin and palm leaves indicated the diamond-washing pans round which swarms of little figures could be seen labouring, some shovelling dirt, others running along with barrows of gravel on runways of planks that radiated in all directions from the machines.

We proceeded to the workplace where we found Eytle superintending the erection of a diaphragm pump over one of the machines. He showed us over the workings and described the machines to us. These diamond-washing machines or pans as they are called, are somewhat complicated in appearance, though very simple in principle. On a staging elevated between four or five feet from the ground the gravel is brought in barrows from the pit or 'cut'. Here it is shovelled into a cylindrical screen which, revolving very slowly with a stream of water pumped through it, sorts out the larger pebbles and stones which run to ground down a chute, whence they are removed by the coleh men. The fine gravel and sand with the diamonds and other heavy small material is washed down a smaller shute into an iron pan some five feet in circumference and about fourteen inches deep. Over this pan, on a spindle running through its centre, revolve five arms on each of which are set four or five steel knives which extend to near the bottom of the pan. The blades of these knives are set at such an angle that their continuous revolving gradually pushes everything towards the outer edge of the pan. The excess water escapes through a hole in the centre, carrying with it all the lighter sands which are washed into the tailrace.

The whole outfit is driven by a four horsepower motor set beside the pan beneath the level of the staging. So much dirt does the machine handle that a gang of shovel men have to work continuously to keep the tailrace from getting silted up. The correct number of revolutions per minute of the knife-bearing arms is seventeen and the keeping up of this constant speed, together with the maintenance of the correct consistency of the puddle in the pan, are two of the most essential requirements to the successful working of the machine. At the close of each day's work the concentrates left in the pan are taken out and jigged through sieves in the normal way.

At our host's request, we returned up the hill to his house where we made ourselves at home. He would not be able to leave the machines until work was knocked off for the day. At about four o'clock De Groote arrived in his own boat. Whilst he went down the hill to see Eytle I took the opportunity to get even with him for tying knots in the legs and arms of my pyjamas in Perenong the previous week. Getting his out of his prospecting bag we balled them up beautifully and put them back. At five o'clock the cook boy picked up a large conch shell and blew a series of deep blasts on it to knock off the men for the day. Eytle had to remain to superintend the washdown of the concentrates and did not come up until nearly dusk.

In the evening he told us how some weeks ago he had caught a man raiding a distant portion of one of his claims. He brought him to his camp and chained him up for the night preparatory to sending him down to the police station next day. When morning dawned, however, the prisoner was gone and the chain showed that it had been filed through. He suspected his engineer of having provided the file, though that gentleman swore stoutly that he knew nothing about the matter. Later, we slung our hammocks at various angles between the posts and beams of the house and soon dropped off to sleep, leaving De Groote sitting in his flannel tail untying the knots from his sleeping suit.

Next morning Einhorn, De Groote and I set off up the river, they to visit the Eping Falls, while I had several claims to visit along the banks. Getting to the falls was not easy because of exposed tacoubas and on a number of occasions we had to haul the craft over some shallow rapids. When we finally reached to within hearing distance of the falls, I felt too tired and fed up to scramble the few hundred yards through the bush to see the actual fall. I remained in the boat and ate some biscuits and cheese.

On our return, I stopped off at Matthew's Landing and went aback to visit the claims of Peter Williams and I.E. Williams, two Bovianders. The trail was very muddy but, fortunately, not long, and fifteen minutes walk through several diamond workings where some dozen pork knockers were busily at work, we reached Matthew's camp, a small open logie with palm-leaf roof. Here we had some tea and sardines and refused some high wine Matthews was anxious we should try. After a short rest and inspection of the workings we returned to the boat with a bucket full of ground provisions kindly given to us by Williams and Matthews. Down the river we stopped at a hunting camp occupied by some Indians from whom we procured some smoked venison and wild hog.

The journey back to Eytle's landing was somewhat hair-raising as our little boat showed signs of turning over at the slightest provocation. Once we were caught fair and square by a wave when the bow was high in the air and water was within an inch of the gunwale at the stern. Fortunately we saw the danger coming and were able to steady the boat and prevent her rolling over.

At his camp that evening, Eytle came up looking very pleased with himself; the day's production of diamonds had turned out well, each pan giving an average of sixteen carats.

It had been my intention to visit Eytle's and Houston's 'Strong Hope' and 'Pativa' blocks the following day, but in view of the weather and my sore legs I decided to spend the day in camp. In the afternoon I sat watching the little figures of the men working about the machines down on the flat, marvelling at their agility with the wheelbarrows as they ran up and down the board tracks bringing gravel to the machines. De Groote told me that most of these barrow-boys were Barbadian 'spider-men'. When in Barbados I had noticed peculiar contrivances consisting of a pair of large cartwheels connected by an arched axle, beneath which a large hogshead of molasses was swung, and so transported by three or four men. The contrivance, according to De Groote, was called a spider and the men who handled it spider-men.

At four o'clock Eytle sent up to invite me to see the wash-down. When all the water was drained out of the pan, a layer of sand and fine gravel some six inches thick lay exposed over the whole bottom. This concentrate was carefully shovelled into buckets and taken to the jigging pool where three or four men jigged it in the sieves. Each sieve was examined by Eytle personally and it was fascinating to watch the fine gravel being scraped away from the centre, every now and again exposing a twinkling diamond on the dark background of the wire mesh. The concentrates from one pan gave fifty-three stones and from another thirty-five. This latter had been working the ground on the hill and the concentrate contained a large percentage of brown pebbles of ironstone which, Eytle told me, prevented the diamonds from sinking to the bottom of the sieve. For this reason, after the sieve had been searched, the remaining concentrates were locked up in a large wooden chest until the morning when they would be dried by roasting on a sheet of iron, and then carefully searched by hand on the sorting table for any diamonds that had been overlooked.

I set off back down the river next morning and, on reaching the police station, got my mail but was disappointed to find it included no newspapers. I then went on to Triefus where Ralph Rice suggested I stayed over until Sunday. De Groote arrived just as we were sitting down to breakfast, having had trouble with his engine coming down the river. I spent the rest of the day doing office work and writing up my journal. After writing a letter to Delph, the manager of the *Daily Chronicle,* asking about my newspapers, I wrote another letter to Herbert Morris, engineers who specialised in conveying contrivances, explaining Eytle's requirements for feeding gravel to his diamond pans and for shifting the sand from his tailraces. I suggested they forwarded to him some specifications of machinery to replace much of the manual labour currently employed on the placer; something I had discussed with Eytle during my stay.

CHAPTER XVII

A TRIP TO THE ISSINERU

In July it was time for me to visit the shops up the Issineru River again, a long dismal journey which I occupied reading novels and bringing my journal up to date. After passing the little island of San San Kopai the river stretches out into straight reaches several miles in length, unbroken by any hill or clearing until Mark-a-Book's old camp at Annabarong Creek was reached. This was now inundated and abandoned. A couple of miles further on we passed the long and narrow Pereroombe Island and a little later on the smaller Warong Island. From this point on the character of the river changed somewhat for the better. The reaches became shorter and the two isolated hills, Dome and Arasuka Mountains, came into view close to the right bank. The former is named from its forest covered shape, whilst Arasuka rises gradually behind it to some thousand feet and then drops in a sheer precipice on the side furthest away from the river. Throughout the afternoon we experienced alternate periods of rain and sunshine so that we had to be constantly lowering and raising the boat's side curtains.

Soon we came to the mouth of the Meamu River and then could see in the distance the blue and white painted roofs of McGillivary's shop and outbuildings at Apaikua Fall. Going ashore I found Stevenson, the manager, with whom I spent the night.

After a refreshing sleep we continued our journey. The landing was at the lower end of an itabo separating an island from the bank and the stream was running so swiftly that we had to hold on to the stern of a boat moored at the landing and start the engine before letting go, otherwise we should have been swept into the swirls and cross currents of the falls. Clearing the island we got into calmer water above the fall and then, after passing several other smaller islands, reached the mouth of the Issineru River. At ordinary seasons the navigation of this river is very difficult owing to the number of large trees that fall across it. In dry weather the journey to Apakuni Fall, some twelve miles up, can be only done with much exertion in a ballahoo in two days. When the river is in flood, as it was then, a tent boat with an engine can get up in comfort in two hours.

It rained for most of the morning and by ten o'clock we arrived at the landing at the foot of the falls. On the left bank a steep hill rose up and on its lower slope stood a ramshackle shed of wattles with a black congo-roofing top. This was Carter & Lampkin's magazine where the stores for their shop aback were deposited by the boats before being carried aback by the droghers. At the landing were three boats: a speedboat of Correia, Carter & Lampkin's tent boat and a queer looking craft belonging to Break o' Day Wilson.

As breakfast was being prepared, Vincent Lampkin turned up followed by half a dozen droghers bearing bunches of plantains and bananas, baskets of provisions and pumpkins from his farm higher up the river which he was taking down to his firm's headquarters at Buck Cannister Sands. Breakfast over, we packed our bags for our journey overland to the shops, alleged to be two hours walk away. From the landing the path ran a few hundred feet alongside the fall where it came to Correia's magazine, a building even more ramshackle than Carter & Lampkin's. A heavy shower coming on, I took shelter in the building. Some half dozen droghers were sitting about having their midday rice whilst the magazine clerk, an anaemic Portuguese youth, sat dangling his legs from a swinging tarimba. (This is a bush bed consisting of two sugar sacks nailed to a rectangular frame, which is generally fixed to four posts planted in the ground, though sometimes they are suspended, as in this case, by ropes from the rafters.) Scattered round the sides of the magazine were piles of half bags of flour, rice and sugar, cases of gin and, on a board resting on two meat barrels, some fifty pounds of black and silver salt mackerel laid out to dry after a wetting. The odour from the fish did not improve the already musty and sweat-laden atmosphere and I was glad when the rain abated sufficiently for us to continue.

Immediately alongside and above the Apakuni Fall, the land on the left bank of the river rises so abruptly that the trail has to leave the bank, cross a high hill and descend to the river again at the mouth of the Apakuni Creek, across which a new bridge had been made by felling a large tree. The former bridge had mysteriously broken down the night before Greene, the sub-warden, had arrived there in May. He had been forced to retrace his steps without visiting the backdam. It was suggested that the damage to the bridge had been done on purpose, but this was denied by those who ought to have known. After crossing the creek, the trail gradually bore away from the Issineru towards the north east.

The going was very heavy, the best part of the trail on the level being ankle deep in mud, whilst the hilly portions were pure cataracts. The creeks were swollen and the tacoubas covered so that we had to wade right through them. As I was the tallest of the party, I went first to test the depth, the deepest coming up to my waist. We came to the highest hill yet encountered, forming the divide between the Issineru and Putareng Rivers. Another fifteen minutes walk and we reached a six-acre clearing cultivated with plantains and other ground provisions. There I met a man by the name of Sobers who owned the farm.

The trail now descended to a flat plain on which lay a sheet of water several hundred feet wide. We waded knee deep through this and then crossed some forested ironstone hills and eventually reached a cultivation of some dozen acres of waving plantain trees. At the far end of this stood a small village, several substantial houses and logies, the largest of which bore signboards indicating it was Correia's shop.

Inside were a couple of clerks, presided over by a gaunt grey-headed Chinese man in a red flannel jacket. His name was Yhap and he was the builder of Break o'Day Wilson's queer craft that we had seen at the landing. We learnt from him that Carter & Lampkin's shop stood on the next hill, so we crossed, waist deep, the little Kasserin Creek, a tributary of the Putareng, and after climbing its far bank came to a neproset covered building, its further end caged in with wire netting.

Here we found Carter in his pyjamas – he also having been out in the storm. He gave us some hot Ovaltine and we began to get out of our sodden clothes. So heavy and concentrated had been the rain that all the prospecting bags were soaked through, despite being labelled in large letters: *Bookers Waterproof.* A pity that such a reputable company persisted with this farce. Their prospecting bags were not and never had been proof against a real tropical shower that lasted for more than ten minutes. I had come off fairly lightly as only my pillow had got wet, but the poor old orderly's hammock was dripping with water and he had to borrow one. We sat down to a big meal of boiled vegetables and haimara.

In spite of the inaccessibility of this place no fewer than four ladies of the fields had established themselves here in a little two roomed house near the shop. One of them turned out to be Florence Wason whom I had ordered out of the district the previous month and who had instead fled up here. She took good care to stay indoors and out of my sight.

This section of the district had been known for some time as the Republic of Uraguay because, owing to its inaccessibility, it was the custom for people wanted in the district by the police to take refuge up here where they were rarely followed and, even when they were, always received sufficient warning to enable them to get over to the upper Puruni, another day and a half's walk from Kasserin Creek. Thus as soon as a boat arrived at Apakuni Fall, someone would look to see who the occupants were and, if they included a policeman or a warden, a messenger was quickly sent aback. Few tributors up here bothered to get privileges and many prospected on Crown Lands or worked on revoked claims without licences. Carter advised me to try and visit the area more often, or at least to get the police to do so as he assured me that some of the less sophisticated people really believed that the place was a republic and that the law did not operate here.

Between the Issineru and the Puruni there were about 300 men scattered over the area; in the previous year it had been twice that number. Carter told me that he had been informed of my arrival in the district quite four hours before I turned up, the news having been brought aback by a drogher who had made a special trip for the purpose. The only objection to the district from a commercial point of view was the heavy cost of transportation in all but the seasons of flood. At ordinary times the freight on goods from the mouth of the Issineru into the shops was one and a half times as much as that from Bartica to the Issineru mouth.

The next day dawned bright and clear and we soon had our things out in the sun to dry. I spent my time resting in my hammock. When it was time to make the return journey, the creeks we had crossed two days previously were unrecognisable, many having almost dried up and others reduced to their normal flow with their tacouba bridges exposed. Except for the mud in the previously flooded plains, we made the return journey almost dry shod.

We made a small diversion to call on Break o'Day Wilson, one of the oldest settlers in the district. He was an elderly Negro of tall stature, exceptionally large feet and a pleasant countenance. He had two fingers missing from his left hand. Some years previously his gun had burst and smashed them beyond repair. Being too far from medical aid he amputated them himself with his right hand. In the kitchen sat his Indian wife, a good-looking young woman with an infant at her breast, whilst playing in the yard at the back was his elder son, Byron, a bright eyed little Boviander some seven years old.

Carter, who was accompanying me, then took me to another of his farms, this managed by Phoenix, an elderly Negro who was also a rural constable. There Carter gave me a dish of golden pawpaws and lemon-yellow bananas. A gunshot was heard outside which signified the demise of a fowl and the beginning of breakfast preparations. Whilst the meal was being prepared I had a look at the farm, which was obviously one of the finest in the district. It had produced regularly a thousand pounds of provisions every week, exclusive of banana and pumpkins, one of the latter having weighed fifty-six pounds. A little tobacco and English cabbage was also grown here.

After breakfast we set out for the landing, where I opened office in Correia's magazine and issued some privileges and prospecting licences. Then I said farewell to Carter, boarded the boat and returned down to McGillivary's shop without incident.

Here Stevenson told me how he had nearly poisoned himself the previous night by drinking a spoonful of iodine in mistake for Sanderford's Liver Invigorator, the two bottles being identical in size and shape. He drank three doses of Glauber's salts as an antidote but was still feeling very sore. The same incident had happened in exactly the same way with Dad one night when he was living in Cowan Street, except in his case he was rushed off to hospital and subjected to a stomach pump.

I stopped for a few moments at Buck Cannister Sands and found Mark-a-Book in the process of writing a petition to Government on behalf of the traders, asking for a reduction in the cost of the Omnibus Licence, as the collective licence for shops in mining districts was called. In the old days, diamond buying, spirit selling, tobacco, general shop licences etc. had to be taken out separately, but in 1924 this was changed to one licence embracing everything and called an 'Omnibus Licence'. In those days it cost about $240 but since then it had risen steadily until it cost in the region of $437.

At Oranapai, at Uncle Charlie's, I found J.B. Delph arguing with my host and Henry Bornstein on the subject of religion. I think the others welcomed my arrival and used it to change the subject. Uncle Charlie brought me a copy of a letter he had written under the *nom-de-plume* of 'Fair -play' to the *Argosy* defending me against Woolford's recent attack in the Legislative Council.

After dinner that night I got Bornstein to tell me the tale of Neddy the Naat, the famous six carat diamond, naat being the term given to two crystals joined together. The pork knocker who found it sold it to Eric Read, Krakowsky's buyer in Kurupung for $300. He got frightened and palmed it off on Alfred Clarke for $268, himself standing the loss of $32. It went to Georgetown where it was declared and $3 royalty paid on it. Not being able to recover his money on it in town, Clarke shipped it back to the Mazaruni where he sent it to Yhip with some pork knockers. This part of the comedy appeared well rehearsed. The three pork knockers arrived at Yhip's shop late in the afternoon and pretended to get drunk. Two of them decided to leave but the third objected, saying he was coming on later. The two kept worrying him to go and the more they did, the more obstinate he became. Finally they left him, whereupon, after making a great play to make sure that they really had departed, he surreptitiously took his kiddy and passed it to Yhip, saying, 'Quick man, how much? Don't let them see it.'

Now it is a trait in the psychology of a certain type of diamond buyer that when a stolen stone is offered to him he is eager to buy it, thinking in his own mind that he can get it cheap. The sight of the diamond, especially if it is a large stone, somehow makes him forget to examine it carefully and, as often as not, he overpays, under the belief that it must be a valuable stone and he will surely recover his money on resale.

Yhip looked at it in the failing light, weighed it quickly and paid $283 for it. Looking at it the following morning he was horrified to find that he had overpaid its true value by several hundred percent, so he decided to cut his losses and sent it over to Correia's in Eping where Maurice Gomes bought it for $160 which was still $130 over its real worth.

With Correia's fortnightly parcel it went to town a second time and was again duly declared and another $3 royalty paid. When Correia sorted out his parcel at home and saw Neddy and the price paid for him he thought it could be good business to send it back to the district and dump it on one of his competitors at a profit. He recognised it as just the sort of stone that would fool anyone but a very good buyer. So once again Neddy passed up the river beyond Kamakusa to Maurice Gomes who managed to palm it off at Ginder's shop in Perenong for $200 making a profit of $40. Profit for someone at last. Pierre happened to be in town at the time, otherwise he would never have let Neddy be included in his parcel for shipment. Thus for the third time did this famous diamond reach Georgetown and for the third time pay royalty to Government. When Joe Ginder saw it he nearly had a fit; recovering, he promptly charged his buyer's account with the $200 paid for Neddy, which was sent back to the unfortunate gentleman as a present.

In the meantime, Correia had come up from town and early one morning a pork knocker brought Neddy to him. He must have slept badly the previous night and not recognising the stone, came to the conclusion that it was not really shattered but a good white stone with an opaque skin. He paid $180 for it so that Ginder's man was only out of pocket by $20. When Correia offered it with his other purchases to Kosser the following Monday, the latter recognised it, and then Correia himself remembered having sent it back to the district once before. As all the diamond buyers in the district knew Neddy by sight now Correia put it away in his safe until such time as a new buyer came to the district.

It was about this time that I developed a large angry red swelling over my right eye and at one stage was, for all practical purposes, blind in one eye. There developed a thin film over it through which I could only distinguish light from darkness. Fortunately, with Joseph's careful nursing, it gradually cleared up, although at one time I thought I should have to go to town for treatment. Indeed when Dad heard about it he wrote me a letter beginning, 'Damn everything else and come to town at once and get your eyes seen to.'

Whilst in Kamakusa I began drafting some new River Navigation Regulations which I proposed submitting to the Commissioner. I also wrote to the Attorney General asking that the district be proclaimed so that flogging could be ordered for praedial larceny as, although few cases were brought into Court through the difficulty in securing sufficient evidence for conviction, the offence was rampant in the district.

A cargo boat had just arrived and most of its occupants were ashore reporting their arrival at the police station when I got into my boat, which was moored alongside the newly arrived boat. Suddenly I heard a pitter patter along the gunwale (which was nearly on a level with my eyes) and a female voice exclaimed, 'Good afternoon, Mr Rat.' Turning my head I saw a pair of shapely legs clad in black silk stockings, rising from a neat pair of buckskin shoes with high heels and ending in a foam of white lingerie. The tent prevented me seeing any more. When the legs reached the end of my tent they stepped off the gunwale and slowly descended into my boat and thus was slowly revealed to me a flared skirt, a trim waist, a well-formed bosom clad in a blouse with a deep plunging collar, and finally the smiling face of a young woman known as Dearest. She asked if I could give her a passage topside so that she could 'meet quickly'. Because of the restricted limits of my boat and for some other reasons I very reluctantly had to decline what might have been a very pleasant journey.

After an uneventful trip of just over three hours we arrived at Oranapai where at Uncle Charlie's I met Henry Bornstein and J.G. Stephen, all in a more or less holiday mood. It was in fact August Bank Holiday Monday. We decided that we would visit the dance to be held that night by Mapp at Merriwai. I remembered all the extra work I'd had in the Magistrate's Court in consequence of the last dance held there, and thought it might be as well for me to grace the proceedings with my presence, thereby possibly avoiding the repetition of the fights that had occurred.

We left Oranapai about eight o'clock in Stephen's boat and, as I was boarding her, I saw standing in the moonlight a young Indian girl, dressed all in white, from shoes to hat. I recognised her as Julia, the daughter of old Chief Danny in the upper Mazaruni across the mountains. She had left her father some while ago and was knocking about the diamond fields acquiring a rather unsavoury name for herself. She said she had come to see me about some private matter and so I arranged to see her the following morning.

At Merriwai we found the two shops crowded with men drinking and celebrating the holiday. In the dance hall itself, Mapp stood behind the counter ready to supply liquor whilst his lady, Eliza Paul, in a pink silk dress, sat behind a cloth-covered table heaped with rolls of sweetbread, tough-looking pastry and a great bowl of anaemic-looking black puddings. In another corner a small string orchestra played some enticing music. As yet no dancers had arrived. They were outside waiting for the ladies who were dressing in a nearby house, while another crowd congregated outside that house waiting for their partners-to-be to emerge. Here and there, lying on the ground beside the trail or sitting despondently on wayside tacoubas with their heads in their hands, were those gentlemen for whom the day's festivities had already proved too much.

About eleven o'clock, the bevy of girls, having completed their toilet, trooped into the hall to the accompaniment of a murmur of admiration from the crowds outside. Undoubtedly no Georgetown ballroom could produce finer or more expensive dresses, evening shoes, silk stockings or theatre wraps. Because no gentleman had yet entered the hall, the girls danced amongst themselves. The majority of them were pastmasters of the art. It then struck me that my presence might be acting as a damper on the proceedings so, mentioning this to Bornstein, we left the hall and went for a stroll around outside.

On our return, we found the ball in full swing. I was at once pounced on by little Ismay Callender, who, from her resemblance to my idea of the famous character in *Uncle Tom's Cabin*, I addressed as Topsy and whirled her into the dance. Topsy did not appreciate this nickname and no one but I dared address her so. To her friends she was popularly known as 'Canadian' owing to her once having visited the Land of the Maple Leaf in the capacity of a nursemaid, but left her job, so she said, through her employer's husband having an exaggerated idea as to the duties of a nursemaid. Though no better than she should be, Topsy kept worrying me to get her appointed as a policewoman when, to use her own phrase, she would 'put these malicious whores in their place'. We danced until dawn.

Back at Oranapai, I woke at nine to find Uncle Charlie administering me a dose of Enos. After breakfast, at which Bornstein joined us, he and I went for a stroll round the village where, at the Bartica Company logie, we found some Indians, amongst whom was Julia, now no longer dressed in her gala clothes of the previous night. I asked her what she wanted to see me about, and she said she wanted me to write a letter for her to Ralph Paton, Einhorn's young cook, and tell him that she was very much in love with him and that if he would marry her she would promise to behave like a good little girl.

The rest of the day was spent holding Magistrate's Court. I had some more trouble with the aftermath of the famous ball at Merriwai early in May when various fights between the women had occurred. I had missed the direct aftermath as I had been in Georgetown, but I now had to deal with one of the cases that had been adjourned until this Court. This concerned Beryl Rodriques, a sullen-faced little vixen of mixed Portuguese and East Indian descent.

Unfortunately, she had Miller to appear for her so I was compelled to listen to yards of tripe where ordinarily I would have chased her out of Court for wasting my time. Of course, I did not blame Miller who was only doing his duty to his client. Her last case, in which she charged a lad with kicking her, fell down because her own witness swore he knew nothing about the matter and was dismissed. She flounced out of Court in a most contemptuous manner. As I was sick and tired of her, I took no notice of her conduct but I heard afterwards that when she got outside she threatened that if the Magistrate didn't give her satisfaction she would seek her own with a cutlass.

I opened the office until two when I packed up and proceeded to Buck Cannister Sands. Here, whilst the men went to Moore's for gasoline and rations, I went up to Carter & Lampkin's where an impromptu dance was in progress, the music being provided by a gramophone. Here I was told that Beryl Rodriques' troublesome disposition was because, when she was still in the womb, her mother had killed a man.

Going up the Perenong some days later, we found it a very different stream to the deep mill race down which we had rushed at full speed some three weeks earlier. The water was very low and we had to proceed at half speed and every now and again shut off the engine as we hauled the boat over the tacoubas.

I arrived at Correia's at the same time as the mail boat, Correia's being a postal agency. As soon as the bag was ashore it was taken to the goods bond where a tarpaulin was spread on the floor and the mail tipped on to it to be sorted. In a very short space of time forty or fifty men had assembled around the door of the bond waiting for their letters. Ninety percent of the district mail was addressed in care of the various shops and the preliminary sorting was made in respect of these premises. This done, the various bundles were handed over to the representatives of the shops for further distribution. Correia's clerk, having received his bundle, called out the name on each letter in a sing-song voice. Occasionally the chant would be interrupted by a remark, 'Passum here, he dere, look me here,' etc., as one of those present heard his name called. After dinner which, thanks to the refrigerator, consisted of iced galantine of chicken and ice cream, Correia, De Groote, Victor Humphrey and I played bridge, which the latter and I won by some 1600 points.

About three o'clock the next afternoon, whilst I was still in the office dealing with my official mail, Olive Lord came in crying and complained that my cook Frank was waiting on the trail to beat her with a stick. It appeared that the path of love's young dream was not running too smoothly. I sent for Frank and asked him what he meant by it. Shamefacedly, he promised that it would not happen again as he intended to have nothing more to do with the girl, who at once reiterated similar sentiments – another idyll bust.

Presently, Tiddemann, a tall German with his hair hanging over his collar and a long goatee beard, came to the door and asked whether I would give him a passage to Kurupung. He had walked across the previous afternoon but found the trail so bad that he did not want to return the same way. He was prospecting on the upper reaches of the Tacouba Creek. Being rather sorry for the man who had been knocking about the district for some years I promised to take him with me.

Next came Miller with a similar request, which I was pleased to give him. Packing up at four o'clock and with my two extra passengers, we started off down the creek. The Perenong was a little lower than when we came up with the result that we had to let the boat jump over several tacoubas that were only just submerged. This was done by driving her at them at full speed and then shutting off the engine just before she struck. The delicate part of the operation was to keep the boat balanced on an even keel as she slid over the obstruction. About half way down the creek we came to a place where a large tree had fallen right across the stream, which delayed us quite a time whilst we cut a passage through the branches. It was almost dusk when we reached the Eping and landed at Triefus where Rice was expecting us for dinner.

We spent the evening listening to Tiddemann reminiscing. He told us how this was a colony of mineral samples, as on one trip he had made from Potaro to Siparuni he had found specimens of twenty-seven different minerals, but nothing to indicate that any of them existed in commercial quantities. Round the slopes at the foot of the cliffs of Mount Watabaru in Kurupung he had found various pieces of cinnabar, but had been unable to find the ledge from which they had come.

On another occasion, when sleeping alone in the forest, he had been intimidated by a pair of luminous eyes glaring at him out of the darkness. He had picked up his gun and fired three or four rounds at them but they had remained unmoved. He had not been able to sleep for the remainder of the night and when day dawned he saw that the spots where the fiery eyes had been were in fact patches of luminous fungus on the trunk of a tree. I told him that I had had a similar experience with fungus on dead leaves on the Kaituma River. On the Tacouba Creek he had caught a small frog which had little globes between each of its toes and in the dark these glowed with a brightness similar to that of a firefly's shoulder lamps. We then got onto the subject of tobacco and he gave me a recipe for preparing ordinary black leaf tobacco in such a manner that it became superior to the finest Brazilian plug.

Continuing on down the Eping next day, the river even lower than when we had come up four days ago, we were shooting down the twisting channel of the Eping Falls with the engine cut off when there was a crash as the boat, with an ominous crack, bounced off a rock and instantly lay over on her starboard gunwale over which the water started to pour. Fortunately we were able to right her before she took in sufficient water to swamp her and a moment later we were out in the still water below the rapid. Beyond the cracking of a timber, no damage appeared to have been done. Reaching the Mazaruni, we turned upstream and, near Serenamu, passed Pierre steaming down at half speed as he fished with a spinning spoon. Entering the Kurupung River we stopped for breakfast at Fortunes Landing, where we met the down-river mail boat.

Going on after breakfast, with our own spinning spoon out at the end of a hundred foot line, we soon caught a large perai which at dinner that night turned out to be the most tasty fish of its kind I had ever eaten. Perai flesh was, as a rule, not very succulent eating, but this specimen was an exception. Finally, after a long and hot afternoon, we reached Ginder's landing and put up at Pierre's house. Miller went out to find his client, Alice Fraser, who had engaged him to defend her in an assault case brought against her by John Lacon, Ginder's manager here.

Tiddemann then approached me with a hard-luck story, begging for what assistance I could give him to carry on three weeks work when he was sure of getting diamonds. He kept on repeating 'on his word of honour', that he would repay me. At first I was not inclined to assist in that direction, but then remembered that I too was often in the same financial straits as he now found himself, so I gave him a $10 cheque whereupon he marched away with long swinging strides, his warishi on his back and his long beard swinging at each step and I wondered, as he disappeared from view, whether I should ever see my $10 again.

The only case in the Magistrate's Court was the one between Lacon and Alice Fraser. Though Miller did his best for his client, I found her guilty and fined her $5. It appeared that the two parties concerned had been on more or less intimate terms, then they had had a row and on the day in question the girl had gone into Lacon's office and asked for

Pierre. Lacon had given her a rude reply, at which she lost her temper and struck him on his head with her hand.

I had breakfast with J.G. Stephen, Dos Santos and Miller after which Miller and Stephen left for down river. When I had finished my office work I went with Maurice Nascemento over to Triefus where we picked up Gavin Bunbury and went over to Kurupung Villa La Dancy, where we were treated to some freshly baked bread and cheese. Dos Santos turned up and sold two pairs of solid gold bangles, each weighing nearly five ounces, to the girls for $70 a pair – so much for the earning capacity of the ladies of the fields. Returning to Pierre's house with the girls we proceeded to have a dance to gramophone music, but the proceedings were interrupted by Jimmy, the bulldog I was looking after for Kosser, who showed his displeasure by nipping the heels of the dancers.

Next day, with Maurice Nascemento and a police orderly, I made a tour of the Tacouba Creek area. After following the creek for some distance we struck off and climbed the famous Long Lady Hill where the discovery was first made in the district that diamonds could be found on the hilltops as well as in the valleys. Long Lady was a flat topped hill about seventy feet high and some four to five acres in extent and when I had last crossed it some years previously there was a large camp here and an aerial ropeway to carry the gravel down the hill to the large pans at the bottom, but now there was very little left of this former activity.

From the top of Long Lady Hill there was a splendid view of Watabaru Mountain which rises abruptly from its forest-covered talus not three miles away, and the grandeur of their rugged pink-coloured cliffs as they soar some four thousand feet into the air, their faces scarred and cracked with the weathering of countless centuries.

A short while after, Maurice said we were in the area where the notorious Neddy the Naat was discovered. The few shops we came to, I stopped and inspected and in nearly every one I found cartridges and shot exposed for sale, although the traders had no licence for the sale of arms and ammunition. I was left with no alternative but to seize them. Finally, we reached Krakowsky's shop, a large new airy building of shingles and wire mesh. Here, after a cup of tea, we sat down in Grimshaw's quarters and had a yarn. We had not been there more than half an hour when in trooped three ladies from the Villa La Dancy, who had decided to come and spend the evening here. After making arrangements for some curried fowl and roti for dinner, they went off to the creek to bathe.

Presently Grimshaw, Maurice and I went over to the Triefus shop, some three minutes away, on Sunshine Hill. Crossing a small stream on the way we heard shrieks and screams of laughter and, glancing to the left, saw the nude outlines of the three black Venuses bathing in the stream. At Triefus we met the manager, Benjamin Chan, a young Chinese, and were soon joined by Cecil Ross, Matthews and Lashley. We proceeded to discuss some whisky and admire the view of a rugged mountain whose castellated summit differed greatly in outline from the uniformly flat top of its neighbour, Watabaru.

The ladies, having changed their clothes, now turned up and the fun became fast and furious. Returning to Krakowsky's we had dinner, twelve of us sitting down to table, and after the meal we formed two bridge fours. There being only one table, the second was improvised out of packing cases. The game over, a dance was started to the strains of a string orchestra composed of a guitar, mandolin and razaong, as the small Portuguese guitar is called. Midnight found the festivities still in full swing and then there was a cry for more curry. Accordingly, a visit was made to the fowl house and the fire in the kitchen re-lit. The three ladies from waterside had by this time been augmented during the evening by two local residents. About one o'clock, the curry was produced and consumed, after which the dancing continued. Towards three o'clock I slung my hammock in Grimshaw's quarters and retired leaving the others to continue the celebrations.

I woke up at eight o'clock to find everyone but Grimshaw gone, the girls to bathe and the others mostly over to Triefus. Whilst we were having coffee, an elderly porkknocker came and raised some very strong objections to the fouling of his drinking water. He said that the girls had gone to bathe in the spring from which he obtained his potable supplies. He said that C.B. Nials, the Bartica Company ranger, had told them to go there. I took the matter as a joke and said that in that case Mr Nials should bale out the spring. 'All right, Sir,' he said. 'I go tell he the Warden want he.' Before Nials could arrive I went over to Triefus and, picking up Maurice, set off for Lashley's Lucky Strike claim.

We found him in a very comfortable little house on the hill beyond his old workings and spent an hour or so yarning with him. He told us of some of his early adventures in the district when he first arrived here in 1922. At that time there were only two policemen in the district with the result that 'might' was considered 'right'. One of the problems was keeping raiders off his claim. One morning he woke up to find about a hundred men at work on his patch. He tried to reason with the ringleaders but to no avail so, in case he was forced to use his revolver, he put some cartridges near one of the raider's fires to dry so that he would at least have some dry ammunition. After some further ten minutes or so arguing with the men, the cartridges became overheated and began to explode. With cries of, 'Ow me Gad', 'Me tell you dis red man bad', the whole crowd became panic-stricken and, dropping their tools, took to their heels. In two minutes the place was deserted.

Lashley said that it was owing to the strict measures I had adopted to deal with the raiders when I first came to the district in 1924 that conditions had improved and the district had become generally law-abiding. He then insisted that we took a light breakfast with him, which consisted of corned beef and bread, washed down with whisky. He had some very fine hot sauce in which oil took the place of vinegar. It was flavoured with some small black seeds called by the East Indians jeerah, which gave it a very piquant taste.

Back in Buck Cannister Sands, Henry Bornstein showed me a fine eighteen carat diamond he had just bought for $2500. It was almost perfect in shape and was undoubtedly the finest large stone yet found in the district, all large diamonds found hitherto being disfigured, cracked and discoloured. This one was supposed to be pure white inside but it had a slight tinge of pale green, although this was said to be only skin deep. It had been found in the Merume River behind Kamakusa.

From Oranapai I decided to inspect the shops along the trail that led over to the Puruni. I did not relish the trip as the going was very steep in places and, when wet, very heavy going through the mud. Some years before I had measured this trail and put up tin tablets with the mileages painted on them. Most of them now seemed to have disappeared, having either rusted away or, more probably, been taken by prospectors and used for location boards. I saw only the 8th, 9th and 18th tablets as we went along. At the 10th Mile we reached a locality known as No Mans Land where, in a clearing, we found the Bartica Company shop where I was welcomed by the manager, a Mr Sherry, a stout young bespectacled black man, who asked me to camp there, warning me at the same time that there was a big row going on which I would have to settle. Sure enough, I had not been in the shop five minutes when a middle-aged man called Henry Hamer came up with a tall grey-haired 'red' man named Walks and said he had a complaint to make about a girl called Irene Harper.

He said she was in the habit of taking money from men but not delivering the goods. She had taken $6 off him a week ago and he had only got it back that morning. Some weeks previously, the police had come to put her out of the district as her registration certificate as a domestic had expired and she therefore had no title to be in a mining district. He, feeling sorry for the girl, had got a prospecting licence in partnership with her so that she could remain and this, he reckoned, had cost him a week's work. He now claimed that she was not a fit person to be in the district and should be put out, otherwise she would cause murder to be done. Walks kept on shouting, 'Yes Chief, put her out.'

By this time quite a large crowd had gathered in the shop and, on my enquiring whether anyone had anything to say on the girl's behalf, pandemonium broke out as everyone began speaking. On several occasions I had to intervene to prevent the parties coming to blows. After sifting the evidence I discovered that the girl herself had paid half the money for the licence and that Hamer wanted to act as though the mining partnership included marital rites and even suggested that she gave him half of her immoral earnings as a prostitute. The previous Saturday he had beaten her badly with a stick and stolen all her clothes so that all she had left was what she had on.

I was satisfied that Hamer's allegations that the girl had taken money under false pretences was unfounded and directed the orderly to have him prosecuted for assault. An old rural constable named Nurse assured me that advantage was being taken of the girl, whom he had known in the district for the past five years and the allegations against her were quite untrue. In fact, he said he was quite ready to look after her himself.

A little Barbadian named Bynoe also spoke for her and made Hamer look very small when he dared him to deny that the girl had fed him when he was down on his luck. When Walks accused Bynoe of being armed with a razor, he quickly replied that as he was a barber by profession he walked with the tools of his trade, being ready to shave anyone at any time and in any place.

Having at last got the crowd to disperse, I had a bath, got into my pyjamas and wrote up my journal. In the evening, after dinner, I played cut-throat bridge with Sherry and Babb, the B.C.L. ranger.

Towards three o'clock the next day we approached Simiri Creek, a branch of the Puruni, its proximity evidenced by the whole country being covered by a sheet of brown water. By the time I had waded in up to my waist and the land looked to be submerged even deeper in front, I called a halt. I got Griffith to put his load on a tree fork and go ahead to see whether he could reach the further bank without swimming. He just managed to keep his head out of the water by feeling for the tacoubas with his feet. Accordingly, the rest of us set off with our loads on our heads. I slipped off the tacouba into water out of my depth but managed to swing into a small tree. Unfortunately, the tree held a nest of biting ants and for the next hour I was painfully reminded of the fact. The poor orderly got cramp in his feet when he was chest deep in the water and it was only through sheer will-power he did not double up and pitch his pack into the water. Captain Wong, the shortest in the party, had to swim. After inspecting a few shops we finally staggered into Krakowsky's shop where the manager, Corlette, offered me accommodation. After a bath and dinner I sat down to a rubber of bridge.

Kamakusa (see vol 2 p.27ff)

North Kaburi (see vol 2 p.163)

Arikara Falls (see vol 2 p. 162)

SITTING ON THE COUNTER, AN EBONY SYREN IN SCARLET BEACH PYJAMAS

"CLOTHED IN A SINGLE LEMON YELLOW GARMENT"

See vol 2, p. 178ff

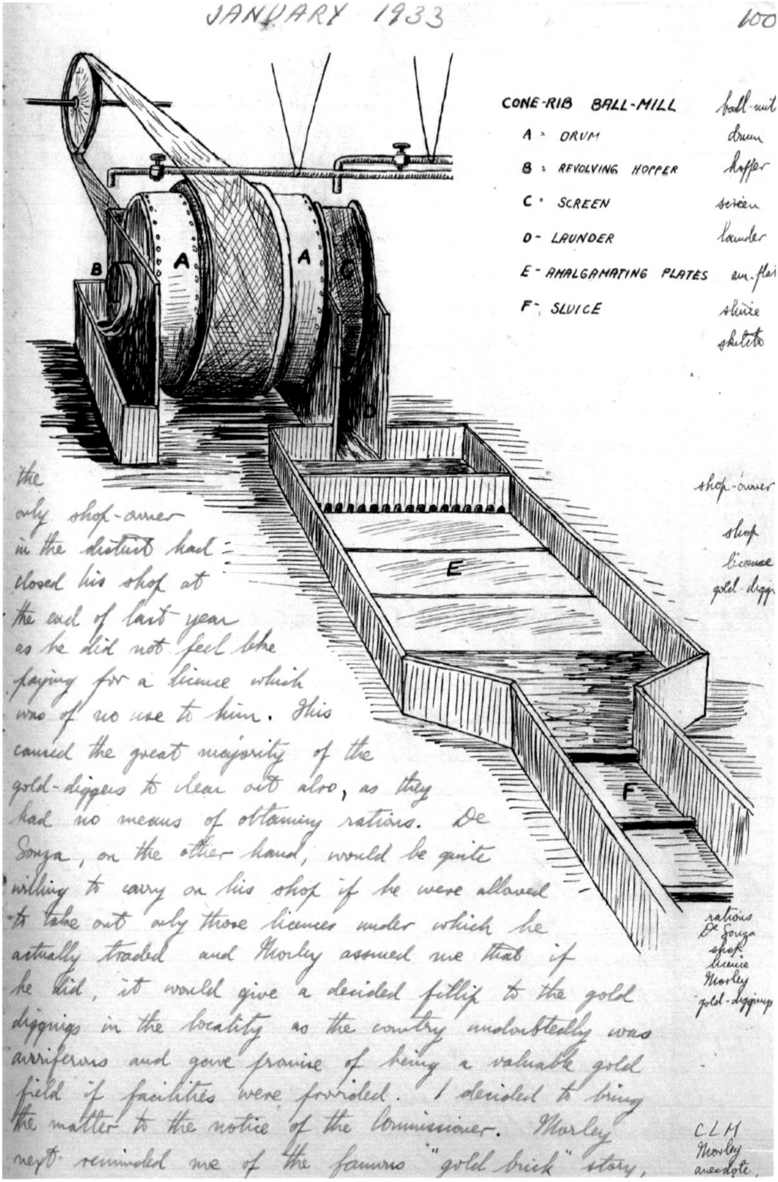

JANUARY 1933 — 100

CONE-RIB BALL-MILL

A = DRUM

B = REVOLVING HOPPER

C = SCREEN

D = LAUNDER

E = AMALGAMATING PLATES

F = SLUICE

ball-mill · drum · hopper · screen · launder · am.-plates · sluice · sketch

the only shop-owner in the district had closed his shop at the end of last year as he did not feel like paying for a licence which was of no use to him. This caused the great majority of the gold-diggers to clear out also, as they had no means of obtaining rations. De Souza, on the other hand, would be quite willing to carry on his shop if he were allowed to take out only those licences under which he actually traded and Morley assured me that if he did, it would give a decided fillip to the gold diggings in the locality as the country undoubtedly was auriferous and gave promise of being a valuable gold field if facilities were provided. I decided to bring the matter to the notice of the Commissioner. Morley next reminded me of the famous "gold brick" story,

shop-owner · shop · licence · gold-diggers · rations · De Souza · shop · licence · Morley · gold-diggings · CLM · Morley · anecdote.

Ball Mill (see vol 2 p.187 ff)

Vincent and his father

Vincent Roth c. 1950

I had intended to carry on a further two miles to Arabagai Landing but, after seeing the state of the Simiri Creek, I decided to return straightaway fearing that if the water level rose any further we would be stranded. When I got back to Oranapai and discussed my trip with J.G. Stephen, he told me that Henry Hamer was a bad egg altogether, having spent some years in his youth at the Onderneeming Reformatory.

During the Court I held there, the police charged Hamer with beating Irene Harper. As he pleaded guilty I fined him $20. Another old man, who was trying to protect the girl and who also got beaten, charged him with assault. Harper herself charged him with stealing her clothes. Although I was morally certain of his guilt in both cases, I was compelled to dismiss them because of some glaring discrepancies in the evidence.

Whilst spending the night with Mark-a-Book, he told me a couple of amusing stories about an ex-Governor here, Sir Alexander Swettenham. It appeared that he did not believe in too much pomp and ceremony and when he travelled about the country would wear a planter's hat and bush jacket. On a visit to Berbice he went by car, crossing from Blairmont to New Amsterdam. Accompanied only by his private secretary, he went to the stelling where he found two youths loading a boat with grass to sell on the other side of the water. When he asked how much they would charge to carry them over, the boys, thinking they were a couple of overseers from the estate, stated their price, but added that they must pay in advance as they had already been swindled in the past by overseers promising to pay them after they had got across.

The Governor, signalling to his secretary not to reveal their identity, paid the fare and got into the boat. As they drew near the town stelling the boys saw a squad of policemen who were to act as the Governor's guard of honour. One remarked, 'Eh, Eh, boy, is what all them polis doin over dere – is a fire? Me no see no smoke.' 'Nah,' remarked his friend, 'Is de Gubna been expect but he no been come by de train. He must a stand home an drink he whisky!' As they drew nearer, an officer called out: 'General Salute, Present Arms', and as the guard did so, the Governor bowed. The terrible truth dawned on the boys who this 'overseer' was whom they had cheeked. With cries of, 'Ow me gad, is de Gubna heself,' they promptly dived overboard and swam ashore leaving his Excellency and his secretary alone in the boat, drifting slowly down river.

The other story also concerned Berbice, but whether they happened at the same time I knew not. The Sub-Controller of Customs was sitting in his office at New Amsterdam one hot afternoon leaning back in his chair with his feet on the desk, a cigar between his lips, reading a newspaper, waiting to close up for the day.

Presently a 'down-and-out' looking character strolled up to the counter and gently exclaimed, 'Good afternoon.' The officer, annoyed at the interruption, grunted a reply without looking up from his paper.

'What place is this?' asked the tramp.

'This is the New Amsterdam Customs House.' snapped the officer into his newspaper.

'And who are you?' asked the stranger.

The officer, now very annoyed at these questions, put the paper down, got to his feet and barked, 'I am the Sub-Controller of customs and who the dickens are you?'

'Me?' replied the visitor, 'Oh, I'm only the Governor.'

Now to a process mentioned repeatedly in past pages – shop inspection. As warden it was my duty to see that the register of diamonds purchased and shipped was kept properly written up and to date and to see that the weight of diamonds actually in the possession of the shopkeeper corresponded with the balance called for by the register. I had to see that the sanitary requirements of the Mining Regulations were complied with, that the immediate surroundings of the shop were kept free from bush and rubbish, that the latrine was in good order and in a suitable position, that the quarter acre of land held for business purposes and on which the shop stood was properly defined and marked by noticeboards, that the current year's rental on this quarter acre had been paid. As Commissary of Taxation I had to see that the shop was duly licensed and that the licence was on view 'in a conspicuous position therein', that no articles not covered by the licence were exposed for sale, that the scales and weights were in order and stamped, that the notice board required by the Spirits Ordinance was up on the exterior of the building. As an Officer of the Local Government Board I had to see that the foodstuff exposed for sale was fit for human consumption. This last duty, one of the most unpleasant of all, involved sniffing at barrels of salt beef, pork and mackerel, examining the canned goods for bulging tins and opening the occasional packet of tea to find out whether it was mouldy or not, and the examining of peas, rice and flour.

Naturally, a complete inspection took some considerable time and therefore was rarely carried out in its entirety. What I generally did after a general cursory examination was to select some particular item each month. Thus one month I might count and weigh every parcel of diamonds found in the shops, another month I might carefully go through the stock of tinned foods etc. All the information obtained was noted down in a counterfoil book, a page to each shop, one copy being forwarded to town with my other monthly returns.

My four months in the bush passed quickly and it was soon time for my month's break in Georgetown. I arrived home just before midnight and was surprised to find the family still up. The reason for this I soon discovered was that a house guest had become quite ill and the doctor had been called in. Next morning the patient did not appear to be any better so I called the doctor again, who, after examining the patient very carefully, advised that an operation was necessary. As our guest was still a minor, parental consent was required. So, hiring a car from Wong, I went up the East Coast to obtain the necessary permission.

At the office I was given orders to prepare a stand at the exhibition to be held by the B.G. Workers League in the Promenade Gardens. I made up a 'gold' nugget out of a piece of granite and some gold paint and an ingot of 'bullion' out of a lead bar similarly painted. I also collected a lot of photographs of diamonds and a specimen of bauxite with an assortment of aluminium articles borrowed from the Demerara Bauxite Company. By getting all the fellows in the office to help me set up the stand, print placards etc., I just managed to get it all finished in time.

Large crowds soon gathered and my 'gold' ingot and bar attracted a lot of attention. When the Commissioner came along he appeared to be well pleased with the exhibit and indeed wrote me a note highly complementing me for stepping into the breach. Later, the Governor arrived and I was introduced to him and Lady Denham by Mullin. As they moved off, the A.D.C., Commander Rushbrooke, came up to me and asked me how long I would be in town and then said I was to come to lunch at Government House later that week.

Leaving the exhibition at half past six, I went home to dinner, after which I changed into evening dress and went down to the Masonic Hall in Carmichael Street where I attended the monthly meeting of St Andrew's Royal Arch Chapter. It was the annual election of officers. Dad, myself and Pat Barlow were all given posts in the Chapter. It was explained to me that they had to give me a subordinate position because of my absence from town. During the evening I was presented with a miniature R.A. jewel as a token of appreciation for 'work done voluntarily for the Chapter', a reference to a set of banners I had made the previous year.

On the day I was invited to Government House for lunch, I arrived simultaneously with Henderson, General Manager of the Demerara Bauxite Company, my fellow guest. We were received by Commander Rushbrooke and taken upstairs to the drawing room where martinis were served. Presently His excellency and Lady Denham arrived, accompanied by Miss Craig, Lady Denham's private secretary. After a short chat we all adjourned to the dining room where we sat down at a round table, I being given the place of honour at Sir Edward's right. The Governor was very charming and humorous in his conversation, touching lightly now and again upon official matters. He teased me about members of the Legislative Council not liking me, adding, 'Never mind, Mr Roth, as long as you don't hang anybody, I'll back you up!'

The lunch itself was a treat, consisting of hors d'oeuvres, soup, boiled fish with corn cream sauce, lobster salad and jelly followed by fruit. Sir Edward asked me if I did any writing and when I replied that I did said I must send all my articles and official diaries direct to him, and not through the official channels. I was also to prepare a memorandum embodying my views for improving the district as he believed in 'encouraging the man on the spot'. After lunch, the ladies having retired, we adjourned to the drawing room for coffee and cigars and a further half hour's chat. We took our leave close on two o'clock, His Excellency telling me I was to see him again before returning to my district.

Whilst in town, I continued with the hearing of the mining dispute between Dr Wharton, Humphreys and Camisuli. I also attended one or two meetings concerned with the projected removal of the Kamakusa station to Tumareng, but nothing transpired. Mullin repeatedly made the point that Government had no money for such an operation, and with the recent shift in the fields following the diamond shout at Rumong Rumong and the gold find at Karanang, it was all left in abeyance.

Back in Kamakusa again and having a beer with Harry Williams at his place in Towaikru, a tall elderly black man came in. He said his name was Alexander Thomas, a claim holder in the area, and that he was the brother of Kaburi Thomas. When I remarked that it was rather strange for both of them to have the same Christian name, he said his father was very fond of the name Alexander and therefore had given it to both his sons. What surprised me even more was when he told me that he was a brother of Ocean Shark. It appeared that this fellow knew me many years before when I was in the North West and presently, when Harry left the room, he offered me a fine diamond, 'for my son' as he put it, and seemed rather hurt when I refused it.

It was on this trip that I met Crawford, a young American Negro pork knocker, who some years before had had a thrilling Crusoe-like adventure on the Essequibo River. He and four other men were returning from a prospecting trip and were streaking their corial down an itabo when it got away from them, leaving them stranded on a small island. They set to and built a raft, but when it was completed, it was not large enough for all of them, so three of them set off on this frail craft, but only one managed to reach civilisation, the other two being drowned on the way.

Crawford and his companion spent a month on the island making another craft, but Crawford refused to risk himself on it, saying that he preferred to die on land. His companion set off alone and was never heard of again. For three months Crawford remained on the island, keeping himself alive by eating raw lizards and gnawing palm seeds. At the end of that period, the only other survivor of the five was on his way back up river to the claim that they had been prospecting. He persuaded the boat captain to travel in the channel alongside the island where they had been marooned. Expecting to find the decomposed body of Crawford and the other member of the party who had remained behind, whom he naturally assumed had died long since from starvation, he took a lot of disinfectant with him. One can imagine his surprise on stepping ashore and being greeted by a living skeleton whom he recognised as Crawford.

When I next saw McGillivary, he complained to me about the illicit store that the Correias were carrying on at Issineru Mouth, buying diamonds and selling goods cheaper than he could with his legitimate shop. He assured me that the business was being run quite openly and that I could catch them any time I went there. So that my boat should not be recognised, he told me to take his from his Kurupung shop. This I did.

My original plan was to camp near Warong Island and await darkness before proceeding to McGillivary's shop at Apaikua Fall so that there would be no chance of Correia's spies carrying a warning of my arrival. James Hodge, who was with me, one of McGillivary's staunch supporters, advised that there was no danger of this, but that I should go straight on and, on arrival at McGillivary's, he would send one of his labourers up to Correia's to sell a diamond and thus obtain definite proof of illicit trading. As events turned out I should have stuck to my original intentions. However, I followed Hodge's advice and resumed my journey.

At Apaikua Fall, Stevenson, McGillivary's manager, who was also with us, advised me to let the police boat, which was with me, drop down below the fall so that it would not be seen when Correia's boat approached. A few minutes later and Correia's boat swung into the landing with two boys aboard. One then called to Stevenson and asked if he had any currants. Now I knew that Correia's boat had just come up river a few days previously so it immediately struck me that this request was merely an excuse to come down river and see what boat had just arrived. I knew that in a few minutes they would push off with the news that the Warden and police boat were in the area, so I did some quick thinking. I asked why their boat had no licence number, and ordered it to be detained and the engine to be taken up to the shop.

Meanwhile, unknown to them, Stevenson had sent a man overland with three marked diamonds to sell at Correia's with instructions to take whatever goods he liked in exchange. About an hour later he returned with the news that they refused to buy the stones. Evidently they must have smelt a rat.

Taking the sergeant and Stevenson in the boat, we proceeded at once up river to where, in a newly-made clearing opposite the mouth of the Issineru River, a large building was under construction. Beneath the half-finished roof was a quantity of barrels and boxes. A freshly painted board indicated that it was Correia's shop, but I had reason to believe that it was really his brother who owned it. It was very well located so that all the boats approaching from down river could be scrutinised before they reached the landing.

By the time we arrived, I was not feeling at all well so I sent the sergeant and my orderly ashore. They searched the men in charge, as well as their canisters, but found no diamonds. Correia, the clerk in charge, told the sergeant that I had been expected. I subsequently learned that Correia's woman, Lorraine Daniels, had the diamonds, knowing that we could not search her.

When we got back to McGillivray's shop I got straight into my hammock and asked for some tinned fruit, whereupon Stevenson told me that it was an old Creole belief that when a sick person asked for fruit it was a sign of their early demise! Not feeling at all well, I packed up next morning and went straight back to Kamakusa where I spent the next seven days in bed with a high temperature.

When I was sufficiently recovered I held a Magistrate's Court, at which the police charged a young man called Clifton Aaron with hitting another on the head with a stick without any real provocation. I gave him five months hard labour as I intended to put down the use of sticks which was becoming rather prevalent in the district.

After Court I found Wilfred Gomes waiting for me to report the bad conduct of his domestic, Justina Fredericks, for whom he said he was no longer responsible. I ordered her off all claims in the district, which was the nearest approach the law allowed me to eject undesirables. Just prior to this I had made similar orders against Mary Hutson and Caroline Harding who, according to the police and Pierre, were a menace to the district.

I feel a description of Kamakusa is in order here. Approaching from down river, after passing the tiny tree-covered islet close to the right bank of the river, euphemistically termed Kamakusa Island, one suddenly comes to a high bank, rising steeply from the river and covered with a dense growth of low bushes, the tops of which barely project above the level of the ground on top of the bank. A small leaf-covered Indian house is passed and then the high forest gives way to a clearing in which two rather pretty and cool looking white cottages appear. These are the quarters of the sub-warden and medical officer, but since the withdrawal of these officers from the district they have been abandoned to the bats. Beyond these, and showing its end gable on to the traveller, is what appears to be a small closed-in house but which, seen from the front, turns out to be a building twice the size of the two former, with a wide gallery with shutters and windows extending along the front of the building. At the top of the front steps the flying of the Union Jack on a short mast indicated whether the warden magistrate was in residence or not.

Immediately in front of the warden's house was a projection of land which narrowed the river to its minimum width in these parts. Just beyond this, and so close to the bank that it appeared ready to topple into the water at the slightest provocation, was the old post office and wireless station, a small unpainted wooden structure squatting on the ground. In those days of long wave wireless, the building was crammed full of electrical machinery to which current was supplied by a dynamo driven by a Ford engine that once propelled the car of a former government electrical engineer. With the introduction of short wave radio, all this machinery was scrapped and the whole receiving and transmitting apparatus housed in a corner of the wireless operator's quarters. The old building was then used for charging batteries, which was usually done on Sunday afternoons when the irregular explosions of a little toy motor relieved the monotony of the day.

Around the point of land and just back from the landing was a great hundred foot long wooden building with a red roof. It housed the warden's office, court room, police office and barracks, dispensary, quarters for the N.C.O., bailiff and boat-hands. Here by law every craft had to stop whilst its occupants produced the documents entitling them to be in a mining district. Those on downward bound boats had to bring ashore their baggage to be searched for illicitly held diamonds. These searches were of such a perfunctory nature as to be almost farcical.

Standing at the landing and looking upstream, a row of three small cottages could be seen and in the far distance a larger building with an apse-like addition towards the river. This last structure was the hospital, the apse being the operating theatre, added to the main building at the request of the first Medical Officer to be appointed. As far as I can recollect, he only had occasion to perform one major operation here, when he removed the leg of a man after it had been crushed by a falling tree whilst the man was sleeping in a logie at Buck Cannister Sands. The intervening buildings were the wireless operator's quarters and post office, the Police Inspector's quarters and dispenser's quarters. Set back from the river and behind the open space between the large station building and the wireless operator's quarters was a long narrow building of zinc with seven doors and no windows which many travellers at first sight imagined was used for sanitary purposes. They were mistaken – this was Kamakusa prison. Beyond the hospital was a little farm run by various members of the station, bounded on the west side by a little stream, the Kamakusa Creek, at the mouth of which stood the river gauge where the fluctuations of the water level were read twice a day.

The history of the origin of Kamakusa is not without interest. In about 1920 a young American, La Varre, came out to the colony and, on the strength of discovering diamonds here, persuaded some wealthy New York capitalists to back him in working the Mazaruni fields. His story of how he discovered diamonds has a decided Munchhausen flavour. In the remoter parts of the interior it was still the custom of the Indians to use a cassava grater which consisted of a slab of wood in which were sunk countless little pieces of sharp-edged stones. La Varre swore that on looking carefully at one of these graters he found many of the stones to be diamonds. Although the story is just possible, its improbability is evidenced by the fact that the edges of the local alluvial rough diamonds are rarely if ever sharp. Anyway, diamonds were being worked in the colony at least 30 years previous to this alleged discovery.

Returning with a couple of million dollars or so, La Varre looked round for a spot at which to fix his headquarters and decided on the site of the almost abandoned Indian village of Kamakusa which, incidentally, owing to the spiral course of the river, happened to be the nearest point in a straight line to the source of the Mazaruni, which lies only eighteen miles across the four thousand foot escarpment that runs parallel to and south of this section of the river.

Here he proceeded to build logies, erect the present station building and prepare the materials for his own residence. In the meantime, he was buying diamonds at such extraordinarily high prices that there is little doubt he was mainly responsible for the boom year of 1923 when Tom, Dick and Harry, hearing of the easily acquired money, flocked to the district and sold low quality diamonds for high prices. It was even rumoured that one trader imported cheap diamonds from South Africa and sold them at a profit at Kamakusa.

Naturally, this state of affairs could not continue indefinitely. About this time Government had finally decided to establish a station in the district and the warden was commissioned to find a suitable site. He had practically decided on Buck Cannister Sands when the crash came and Kamakusa went into liquidation. As a result, the warden recommended its purchase by Government. The materials for La Varre's residence were then erected under the warden's supervision as quarters for himself.

I spent Christmas with the folks up the Perenong and, on my way back to Kamakusa, called in at Buck Cannister Sands where I had breakfast with Mark-a-Book, whom I found in a very contented frame of mind, having earlier that morning, acted as midwife at the birth of a baby to Maud Britton, one of the most famous ladies of the fields.

At Oranapai I found a group of about sixty pork knockers waiting to appeal to me for Government assistance. They were hungry and could not afford the cost of a passage to town. During the past few months things had been rapidly deteriorating due to the slump in diamond prices, and even though the men had some diamonds, they could not sell them for enough to buy a week's rations, reckoned to be about $3. Uncle Charlie and the Bornsteins told me that they had been giving free rations to the destitute men, but that they would have to stop as they could not afford such philanthropic gestures.

Holding a Magistrate's Court here, I heard a very interesting case in which a man called J. Joseph was charged with practising obeah for money or reward. The evidence was that he went to J.G. Stephen's shopkeeper and told him he could give him something which would ensure his getting a better position with higher wages. The shopkeeper told him to come back in the evening and, in the meantime, reported the matter to the police, who gave him a marked dollar note. When Joseph returned in the evening he got from his client three needles, a tallow candle, a bottle of white rum, a three-inch nail and a piece of white cloth and told him to be ready to accompany him to the burial ground at midnight. This was agreed to and the police duly informed. Towards the appointed hour, the police hid themselves in the burial ground and presently the obeah man and his client arrived. Stripping off all his clothes, the obeah man put on a loincloth and, after sprinkling a grave with the rum, spoke some form of gibberish, then put three nails on the grave, one at the head, the second in the middle and the third at the foot. After more incantations, he picked up a few pebbles and bits of stick which he wrapped in some newspaper. He put his clothes back on and returned to the shop with his client who was handed the newspaper parcel for which he paid with the marked note. The next moment the obeah man was seized by the corporal who had followed the men from the cemetery. The sergeant reported that he had been convicted in Georgetown on a similar charge and, on hearing this, I deemed him to be a rogue and a vagabond and sentenced him to four months imprisonment and twelve lashes of the cat.

When the time came to leave, the crowd of destitute pork knockers had risen to about a hundred and, realising that something drastic had to be done, I sent a radio to the Commissioner of Lands and Mines explaining the position to him. I was not feeling at all well, having a severe attack of fever and sore throat, so went straight back to Kamakusa and to bed.

And so 1930 ended on rather a despondent note, and 1931 began no better. I spent the first couple of days of the New Year in bed with a temperature of 103° and on the afternoon of the second day, the Enachu dispenser arrived up with Roberts, a young wireless operator, in an unconscious state with blackwater fever, who by eleven o'clock the following morning was dead. As I still had a high temperature, a bad attack of bronchitis and was spitting blood, the dispenser would not let me attend the funeral so I sat and watched it from my bedroom window. First came the sergeant marching with arms reversed, a stick taking the place of a rifle; then came the coffin borne by the dispensers, Joseph and Lewis, a couple of policemen and two prisoners. Kingsland and Clinkett, the Magistrate's clerks, acted as mourners, walking immediately behind the coffin on which, for lack of flowers, two palm leaves were placed crosswise. It was a dull cloudy afternoon as the poor chap was taken to his last resting place, and as I watched the pathetic little procession I could not help thinking that it might easily have been me instead of poor young Roberts as the occupant of the rough and hastily constructed coffin.

As I did not seem to get any better, and fearing a return of blackwater fever, I radioed the Commissioner asking that an officer be sent up to relieve me as soon as possible. A day or so later I began to feel better, when Mullin and Inspector Ashmore arrived to decide what could be done to relieve the plight of the destitute pork knockers. Because of my state of health, Mullin said I was to return to town and radioed for Hastings to come up and take over the district. He decided, too, that all the destitute men were to be brought down to Kamakusa where a relief camp was to be established until transportation could be organised to evacuate them down river. Those who were well and willing to work were put to work on various projects on the station.

Soon the men started arriving by the boatload. We accommodated some in the large house Michael built just before his wife died and others in the bottom parts of all the residential buildings. The sick were placed in or near the hospital. We requisitioned food from the upward bound cargo boats and a receipt was given to each captain for the goods taken. Boats were commandeered to commence the evacuation of the men, who at the peak numbered over three hundred.

With Hastings came Dr Subryan who went methodically through the whole camp and found one hundred and sixty men reporting sick. He then went to each in turn and asked them if they were fit to travel and thus reduced the number to sixty. Thinking the question had to do with their immediate evacuation, all the malingerers at once brightened up and assured the doctor that they were quite fit and well.

As soon as I had handed over to Hastings I packed up and returned to town. I had not been long in the house when Wilfred Gomes came and interviewed me on behalf of the *Daily Chronicle* concerning the true state of affairs in the Mazaruni, because all sorts of wild stories were beginning to circulate as the pork knockers began to arrive back in the city.

When I went into the office next morning, Christiani expressed horror at my alleged *faux pas* in granting an interview to the press. When I saw Mullin he made no reference to it; he presumably had not seen the press report – yet. Amongst other things he asked me whether I thought there was another possible route to the diamond fields other than by river. I brought out my old scheme of extending the Kartabo Road westwards, which appeared to satisfy him. He then told me to apply for two weeks leave, which I promptly did.

During my period of sick leave I continued to transcribe my journals and happened to mention to Dad an entry I had made in June 1908, referring to an outbreak of yellow fever in Suddie. He told me that it was quite true, having been discovered by Dr Ozzard by means of microscopic studies and that one of the first victims had been S.H. Bayley's first wife. To save the colony's reputation, the senior medical authorities denied it and made out that Dr Ozzard was mistaken. Dad, however, assured me that there had been yellow fever in Suddie in June of 1908.

One Sunday morning, young Walter Camacho came and told us about a big fire in the house of his brother-in-law, Cregan, in the early hours of the morning. He had been there at the time and escaped dressed only in shirt and pants. Shortly after lunch, Outridge arrived to tell me that Cregan had perished in the fire and was to have a Masonic funeral at three o'clock, starting from Roraima Lodge. Arriving at the Lodge just before three I found most of the brethren assembled in evening dress. After opening the Lodge we adjourned in our cars to Christ Church. The hearse bearing the coffin with the charred remains of Cregan was waiting outside the Lodge and followed us to the church where an impressive service was conducted by Archdeacon Kissack. We left afterwards to the solemn strains of the Dead March played on the organ; then the procession formed up and proceeded to La Repentir cemetery where the Archdeacon concluded the burial service, after which the masons, some seventy of us, took charge of the proceedings. The white gloves thrown on the coffin were so numerous as almost to cover the wreaths.

The day after the funeral I received a letter from Mullin demanding an explanation as to why I had granted an interview to the press concerning conditions in the Mazaruni. The outcome of this was that I received an official letter from Mullin warning not to give any more such interviews and informing me that the Governor had expressed his displeasure at my indiscretion. It transpired that Mullin himself had raised the question and reported the matter, together with my explanation, to the Colonial Secretary. It was certainly not the sort of thing his predecessors would have done but he had apparently sworn to get even with me for Dad's remarks about his integrity some years previously, and this he must have considered an opportunity too good to lose.

At the same time I received a letter from the Attorney General asking me to comment on a petition sent to the Governor by Joseph, the obeah man, praying that that part of his sentence ordering him twelve lashes of the cat-o-nine-tails be remitted. I replied that I saw no reason for such remission.

When I finally returned to the office at the end of February, one of the tasks I was given was that of diamond valuing. After the economic troubles in the diamond fields, Government had changed the export tax on diamonds from fifty cents per carat to six percent of the market value. This value was assessed by the Department of Lands and Mines with the assistance of the Amsterdam quotations supplied periodically by the Crown Agents. Mullin had been doing this himself, but when I returned to the office he was on the Kaburi Road with the Governor so Christiani asked me to take over the duty.

Some time after this I saw a minute of the Governor's on the subject in which he said, 'I have not the slightest confidence in Mr Roth as an expert diamond valuer, though no doubt he does his best.' Of course, I had never professed to be an expert and was merely carrying out the instructions of the head of my department. If one gives an order to a carpenter for pair of shoes one should not grumble if the shoes are not well fitting. I eventually handed the job over to Marie Wong, of whom Krakowsky told me the following yarn:

Greenberg, a diamond buyer, declared a parcel of diamonds he wanted to export at $2600. The Controller of Customs challenged his figures and Marie Wong was asked to value them. This she did at $4600. Greenberg, hearing this, offered to sell them to her for $3600, a thousand dollars less than what she declared them worth. 'Oh, but I have not got a licence,' declared Miss Wong. 'Never mind,' said Greenberg, 'I'll buy you a licence for $240 so that you can buy my diamonds and I will still be satisfied with the profit I make'. This put the wind up Miss Wong who even refused them at $3200 plus a licence, to which figure Greenberg had descended. Of course he objected to her valuation and eventually Cooper was called in as arbitrator and he assessed the parcel at $2519, a figure below Greenberg's declared valuation. To such a farce did Government's system of *ad valorem* export duty on diamonds come.

I usually went to see Mother either on my way to the office or on my return journey in the afternoon. Telling her one day about a parcel of diamonds I had valued, she asked me to whom they belonged. I told her they were Ginder's, who, rumour had it, was leaving the Colony for good to settle in the south of France, he obviously having made enough money to be able to do so. Mother remarked that it was a pity that Dad and I had not done the same thing, but she supposed it would have been no use, as none of the Roths, with the exception of Uncle Bernard, who left £85,000, had been able to accumulate money. At most they managed to amass just sufficient to get along by.

Of the lot, Uncle Felix was the most impecunious as, until the death of his second wife, he rarely had sixpence to rattle on a tombstone. After his first wife had left him, he was travelling in France where he met a woman with whom he had been in love before his first marriage. She was well-to-do and told him that if he got a divorce she would marry him. Apparently, like the majority of the family, Uncle Felix was no better than he should be, but by keeping very quiet for six months he secured his divorce and married his first love, who gave him an allowance of £300 a year and, in addition, paid all his bills. Being a wise man he banked his allowance so that when the lady, after making him give up his medical practice and keeping him under her thumb for several years, died of alcoholism, Uncle Felix found himself with a little money in the bank. For the third time he embarked on the matrimonial sea, this time with an admiral's daughter who eventually buried him of cancer and inherited the major portion of her predecessor's money.

I was still not feeling very well during this period and suffered a great deal from dyspepsia. Mentioning this to someone one day, they said it might be due to a condition known to the Portuguese as *boosh* and to the East Indians as *nara* and that I should see a nara doctor This I did. He was a young fellow called Lazarus. Stripping me to the waist he made me lie down on a bed and, after examining the relative position of the navel and breasts, said that I had it 'bad'. He then proceeded to massage my stomach towards the navel, which, he said, was out of its correct position, which he had checked by placing a string between it and each nipple and finding a difference of half an inch between the two measurements. He then placed me face down on the floor and placing his foot in the small of my back raised my left arm and right leg and jerked them together, then repeated the operation with the right arm and left leg. When he had finished he tied a bandage tightly round my abdomen, telling me to leave it on until he saw me again.

I saw him again for three consecutive days, when he would massage my stomach and back, but all I seemed to gain from this treatment was a fever at night and severe muscular pains in the back. My faith in Mr Lazarus as a panacea for nara wilted, with the result that I called in to see Dr Edmonds who diagnosed my complaint as acid stomach and sent me for some X rays which revealed that I had a duodenal ulcer. I was put on a strict milk diet, told to cut out smoking and remain quiet and given a medical certificate for three weeks leave. Phil, too, was not well, for which her doctor, Nichols, recommended a course of injections. He said she was suffering from chronic dysentery.

It was towards the end of May that I heard that Eddie Parker had got orders to proceed to Kamakusa to relieve Hastings. When I saw Mullin I told him that I was very surprised as I had understood that I was to return to the district. Mullin said that he did not think that I should go back just yet. I asked him if it was only a question of my health or whether he was dissatisfied with the manner in which I had carried out my duties there. He said it was solely the matter of my health. Talking to Eddie Parker on the subject, he told me that he was objecting to the posting on the grounds that he had had two attacks of blackwater fever and, having seen the Surgeon General, had been advised not to return to Kamakusa.

Parker and I were, at the time, preparing an estimate for a chain and compass survey of a tract of land some twenty four thousand acres in extent, lying between the Demerara and Berbice Rivers, applied for as an exclusive permission for bauxite prospecting by the Demerara Bauxite Company. The survey would involve over ninety miles of line cutting and in places access would be very difficult. We arrived at an estimate of $35,000, being less than 1.04 cents per acre and about $38 per mile.

C.P. de Freitas, one of the surveyors who had been surveying parcels of land up the Demerara River for the British and Colonial Bauxite Company, told me that it was reckoned that in the old rubber fields behind the saw mill at Christianburg there was enough ore to provide work for eighty years, the average depth of the deposit being about eight feet.

When I first went to the Mazaruni in 1924 I met a mining engineer by the name of Bissel Thomas who had a very nice folding armchair amongst his camp furniture which, when he came to leave the colony, he gave to me as a souvenir. When I came down to town in October 1927 with blackwater fever I had to leave the chair behind. Hastings, who relieved me up there, coolly told me that he liked this chair so much that he was taking it over and asked how much I wanted for it. I told him I did not wish to dispose of it as it had been given to me as a souvenir. Hastings did not return the chair but on my return to town this time I found it standing in the corner of the drawing office. Then one morning I missed it and, on making enquires, was told that Miss Gonsalves, Hastings' fiancee as he called her, (though how a married man could have a fiancee I don't know) had sent for 'Mr Hastings' chair', and Cole, not knowing it was mine, had given it to the messenger. As soon as I heard this I sent the lady a little note asking her to be good enough to return the chair which had been given to her in error.

Eddie Parker eventually succeeded in his objection to going to Kamakusa and Stanley Burrowes was sent instead as sub-warden, and thus was Hastings relieved. When he was back in the office I tackled him on the subject of my chair. He took my breath away by stating that I had agreed to let him have it in settlement of car hire amounting to at least $15 I owed him. I had not the slightest recollection of this and Cole, who looked after the car at the time, said he was sure my bill did not exceed $5 at the most. Naturally, one could not argue under such circumstances so I let the matter drop, but what a wonderful lawyer was lost when Hastings became a government surveyor.

One day towards the end of June, Christiani told me it was tentatively proposed that I should go up to the North West District at the end of the rainy season and carry out some routine surveys. He did not think it was the Commissioner's intention that I should return to the Mazaruni on account of my health. Later, this was confirmed and so I immediately wrote off to Phang in Morawhanna asking him if I could hire his tent boat.

Tuesday 21st July was declared a public holiday to celebrate the union of the Colonies of Essequibo, Demerara and Berbice into the single colony of British Guiana. The official celebrations were to be held later in the year and the Commissioner asked me to organise a stand on behalf of the Lands and Mines Department for the exhibition that was to be held. I reminded him that I would, by then, be up in the North West District and suggested that Cleare take charge of the arrangements.

Calling on Delph, the manager of the *Daily Chronicle*, about my journals, I asked him how the edges of bound books were marked as they were in a variety of colours. He said originally the edges of the books were dipped in a specially prepared bath which resembled oil floating on water and then cold water was run over the resulting colours. This method was laborious and expensive, though the results were more lasting than those of the cheaper method now used, which was to paste a transfer paper on the edges and, when nearly dry, pull it off, the marbled effect of the paper remaining on the book edge.

He then took me on a tour of the printing and binding works. The most interesting machine was the old original hand-press on which the *Royal Gazette* had been printed more than a century before, and on which the most valuable stamp in the world, the famous *1856 B.G.* first saw the light of day. It was a most archaic looking piece of machinery and it was obvious that it had been made before the days of mass production. The great sliding counterweight on the top was in the shape of an eagle. It had been made in Edinburgh by a firm that had ceased to exist many years ago. It is now an exhibit in the National Museum.

Shortly before I went to the North West District, Mullin and I had a meeting with the Governor. After reporting to Commander Rushbrooke we were ushered into the Governor's office, a large airy room. At a desk at the farther end of it sat Sir Edward Denham, a short bull-necked gentleman with smooth shaven face and hair a colour between 'carrots' and 'sandy'. He greeted us and, after enquiring after my present state of health, told us to sit down.

Sir Edward outlined what he wanted me to do on my forthcoming trip. He said that there was a great area of Crown Land lying uncultivated and as the people had no money to pay the cost of surveys and rental he wanted the land to be given out for peppercorn rents, as long as the people cultivated it. He then called in a stenographer and dictated a letter to Long, the Commissioner up there, outlining his plans and said that the Agricultural Superintendent and I were to work along with Long in the selection and distributing of the land.

When the interview was over, we returned to Commander Rushbrooke's office where he asked me to return at twelve thirty for lunch, Dad having also been invited. The other guests turned out to be Dr and Mrs Mann. In the dining room was a collection of pictures of all the past Governors of the Colony which Sir Edward had put together and on a radio cabinet in the entrance hall I noticed the carved and painted box given to the Governor by my parents in appreciation of his kindness to them. When the party broke up after a very enjoyable meal, the Governor's last words to me were, 'Now, Mr Roth, you understand what I told you this morning. I want you to help the people of the North West. You help me to do that and I will help you to get what you want.'

CHAPTER XVIII

THE NORTH WEST DISTRICT REVISITED

On the 11th August I sailed on the *Tarpon* for the North West District. One of my fellow passengers was O.R. Bennett of Garnett & Co. who was on his way up to the firm's estate at Aruka. He told me the firm was very worried over the lack of sufficient fresh water at their coffee factory, as the brackish water interfered with the preparation of the coffee and caused the production of an inferior quality.

At Morawhanna I met W.A. Phang at his shop where, waiting for me, were my old crew whom I had asked him to collect together: Pablo Beria, Elias Oselmo, Rose Smith and Ambrosio Jacintho. Pablo told me that his father, Pedro, my old captain was presently at Wansa on the Amakura in Venezuela. The Government chauffeur then arrived with a note from Long asking me to come up to Mabaruma in the car and have breakfast with him so, crossing the river to the eastern end of the town, I set off in the very rickety old Ford along the very rough road to Mabaruma. As we climbed the foothills the road improved somewhat and soon we were racing down the avenue of rubber trees that lead to the station compound.

Just outside the compound gate stood a large troolie house which had not been there when I visited the area in 1929. It had been built for Sir Gordon Guggisberg who was to occupy it during the extended visits he proposed to make to the district in connection with his colonisation plan. When His Excellency died, so did, I am afraid, his colonisation schemes.

On my way to Long's office I saw his clerk, Harry Solomon, poor old Sealy's successor. During breakfast, Long and I discussed the Governor's land scheme. Long was very much against it, saying the farmers had as much land as they could cope with already and people did not value things they did not have to pay for. However, he would go along with the Governor's instructions and hold meetings and explain the land scheme to the farmers.

Just as we were getting up from the table I received a radio from Duke asking me to send his sister to town as she was urgently needed at home. She was the same hospital nurse who had travelled to the district with Parsley and I in 1929 when we came to do the Colonisation Survey. I showed the radio to Long; his face fell as he told me he understood she was on leave and was supposed to have gone to town on the last steamer. He said he had heard that her charms had got her into trouble and he advised me to check with Dr Ho-a-Kai before answering the radio. This I did and the doctor said that Nurse Duke had been given fourteen days leave which expired that day. She had not turned up for duty and he knew that she had not travelled to town and was almost sure that she had gone into retreat on one of the nearby farms. He said he would make some enquiries as to her whereabouts for me.

I then used the ambulance to move my luggage up to the rest house, the government lorry being out of commission. During the evening I received a note from the doctor saying he had received a letter from Nurse Duke applying for an extension of leave and the address she gave was Wansa Mission on the Amakura River in Venezuela. I sent a radio to Duke giving him this information.

Having trouble with my stomach, I went over to the hospital to get some medicine from old Glasgow, the dispenser. On my way I met Gillespie, the agricultural superintendant, who had been acting for Beckett during that gentleman's leave. As we walked along he told me the following amusing anecdote. He requisitioned from his department for six dozen bunches of budding tape, a broad white tape which, specially treated with resin, is used to bind the buds to the stocks, when grafting. They sent him six dozen bunches of office red tape!

Talking to Glasgow, I learned some of the details of Sealy's end. Apparently his child became ill which affected him to such an extent that he could not sleep at night and had been seen walking up and down the compound in the early hours of the morning. Then his child died and this broke him up completely and he had to be sent to hospital. When Sealy returned to the office, Long told him to return to the hospital until he felt completely better. This he did. Next morning Sealy was missing from the hospital and an immediate search was made. Someone like Sealy had been seen at about two o'clock that morning walking along the road towards Morawhanna and several people said they thought they had heard someone shouting for a boat just before dawn at the stelling. Two days later some Indians reported seeing a body floating in the Mora Passage.

The farmers, once they heard of Government's proposals with regard to the distribution of Crown lands, quickly put in their applications and I was soon busy setting out their respective lots. One of the lines the men cut passed alongside the Hosororo burial ground where graves of varying ages were indicated by wooden crosses or borders of ironstone boulders and planted with crotons and other flowering plants, including frangipanis. Forest grew all about the graves, there being a space of only some thirty feet by twenty which was weeded and swept absolutely clean of all leaves and sticks. Within this clearing was a large concrete tomb surmounted by a wooden cross on which was painted the pious request, 'Of your charity pray for the soul of the Reverend Mother Margaret Mary, Foundress of the Missionary Sisters of Mercy, who died 24th May 1928, R.I.P.' This was the grave of the good Englishwoman, Emily Sarah Swyer who devoted many years of her life in teaching the Indians of this colony. I first met her at Rockstone in 1910 when she was on her way to her missionary convent on the Takatu, on the Brazilian border. Six years later she was at Morawhanna convent when young Walter first went to school there. Now her bones lay with those of her beloved Indians beneath the red clay of this forest glade on the hill slope behind the convent she founded.

One day, going down to the stelling at Morawhanna, I met Phang who had just returned from a visit to town. He told me that he had visited some farming areas on the East Coast where he was surprised to find that the Department of Agriculture was held in as much disfavour as it was in the North West District, where, with a few exceptions, it was completely ignored. The farmers felt that the department had repeatedly given them advice which turned out to be disastrous, as in the famous instance when large areas were planted with the *sapium jenmari* rubber tree until it was discovered that *hevea* was the variety that produced the best quality rubber; and then there was the cockle pest for which the department had been unable to find a remedy.

Nearly every evening I would have a game of chess with Long and yarn about our various experiences. We got onto the subject of the economic situation in the North West District since the bottom had fallen out of the coffee market. Over 90% of the farmers had depended on coffee as their permanent crop and now that it no longer paid they did not know to which crop they should turn their attention. The Agricultural Department could only suggest the planting of limes as being suitable for the pegass soil of the hills up the Aruka and Koriabo Rivers on which the great majority of the farms were located. But, as Long pointed out, the hills were quite a distance from the existing farms and if the farmers had to spend all their time travelling between their ground provision farms on the swamp and their citrus orchards in the hills, then one or the other must suffer from want of attention.

During another of our evening discussions, Long mentioned something that I had often wondered about. He said he was under the impression that a certain diamond buyer made a good thing in smuggling diamonds out of the colony, though how he did it he had not the faintest idea. Some time ago, when Long was Magistrate of the Mazaruni, this dealer left for England on one of his periodic visits. He declared 700 carats of diamonds at Kamakusa and in due course paid royalty on them. He then showed them to several firms in Georgetown, but no sale was forthcoming and so he left the colony with them. Some time later Messrs Triefus in London wrote back to Cooper here asking him how much he had offered on their behalf for the 2500 carats which the dealer was now offering them in London.

At the beginning of September, Long took me some three miles up the Koriabo to show me some free grants he had given out, which he wanted me to include in a survey of that area. We went ashore at the newly empoldered tract of a young East Indian named Debedin. Next to his lot was a likewise newly empoldered grant of a woman named Lali, whose son, a handsome East Indian, Mohabir Singh, I recognised as the youth I had caught on the Amakura River in 1919 carrying an unlicensed gun. He was now running a small saw-pit here and kindly put a logie at my disposal.

Whilst here, I met an elderly East Indian labourer named Barossa who was in a very comatose condition, on a rough bedstead of boards and sugar bags after an orgy of drinking Bay rum. He was supposed to be doing some trench digging for Mohabir Singh and it took him all of three days to come round and start to take an interest in life again. Government had recently raised the duty on Bay rum to prevent it being used as a beverage, mainly by the East Indians, but this had not proved very effective as the people still bought it, claiming they needed it for medicinal purposes. One night Barossa told me of the circumstances in which he had come to this colony. His parents were well-to-do peasants somewhere in Central India, his father owning a rice field, some cows and a small shop. Barossa and his child-wife (he was married when he was about six years old) and his two elder brothers and their wives and his sister all lived together in their father's house, whose word was law. The brothers helped the father manage the shop and plough and sow the rice field whilst little Barossa's job was that of cowherd.

One day, when he was about eighteen, his mother was taken ill and, his father, brothers and their wives being away from home, Barossa, being the only child near at hand, was sent for. His mother clasped him to her breast and told him where her money was hidden and that he must take it. Then she gave up the ghost. When the brothers learned that Barossa had been left their mother's sole heir they naturally were not at all satisfied and the seeds of discord were sown in the hitherto happy house. The womenfolk were no better than the men. Barossa stood it for a long time until one day he returned home to find his wife in tears. She told him that her sister-in-law had cursed her very badly. Barossa decided to put an end to the unpleasantness once and for all.

He told his wife not to say a word but to pack her clothes and jewellery. They went to bed as normal but at midnight stole out of the house without waking the others. He had the equivalent of $700 in cash and the pair caught the early morning train for the nearest big city where they went to the emigration department and indentured themselves for five years in British Guiana. After they had been at the department for several days, Barossa spotteded his brothers looking for them, but with the help of an official, he and his wife were able to hide in an upper room whilst their relatives hunted in vain. Next day, along with a batch of other emigrants, they were sent to Calcutta where they remained 16 days before embarking on the immigrant ship *Ganges* which brought them to the Colony in just over 40 days.

Barossa was allocated to Plantation Anna Regina where his child was born and died. When they had been there three years, his wife died and then he became reckless and lost all his money. His indenture over, he left the sugar estate and worked in the balata bush and diamond fields and eventually ended up as a labourer in the North West.

About this time, I received a formal letter typed on best quality paper and signed by the Commissioner himself. Such letters presaged matters of importance, generally informing the recipient either of promotion or that he was on the mat. Unfortunately, this missive came under the latter category as it informed me that in the matter of a claim made by one Williams at Enachu, I as warden had mistakenly treated it as vacant, when in fact it was already held by Krakowsky. This had been brought to the Governor's notice by the President of the B.G. Workers League and that my carelessness had met with the Governor's censure.

This matter had been dealt with before I left town, but as I was not given the opportunity of seeing Williams' original application for the claim, I was not inclined to feel that I was guilty of any carelessness. It was always my practice to examine the claim registers most carefully before issuing any information as to whether a claim licence was available or not, but I could not defend myself on this charge without comparing the original letter of enquiry and the claim register at Kamakusa. I decided to reopen this matter when I got back to town. How Mullin must have enjoyed signing this letter! And yet, when I saw him just before I left town, he was more charming than ever. Such was the character of the man.

Having run out of reading matter, I borrowed some books from Phang. One was *Octavia* by Margot Oxford. It dealt with the life of a young society girl. It contained some good descriptions of fox hunting; these pages being the best part of the book. There were one or two surprisingly explicit accounts of love passages between the girl and the man she marries. No stickler myself, I just like an allegedly decent book to be decent. Fancy the wife of a famous British Premier writing and publishing a passage like this: 'Her night-gown slipped off, leaving her throat and shoulders bare. Seized with an intense fire, he stretched himself on the bed beside her and buried his head in the coldness of her breasts. She lay resistless, while his fingers pulled away all that was left of her night-dress...her naked body looked very white against the coloured coverlet.'

When I first arrived in the district, Gillespie was acting as Agricultural Superintendent whilst Edgar Beckett was away on leave, but at the end of August, Beckett was back in the district with his charming wife and five year old son. Shortly after they had settled into their quarters, they were burgled whilst away on a trip to Moruca. Close on $300 worth of jewellery, clothing and provisions were stolen. Eventually the culprit, an East Indian by the name of Khan, was caught and most of the stolen articles were recovered. Beckett was convinced that Khan had been helped by one of the East Indian girls who had worked in the house and whom they had dismissed for dishonesty. Beckett used to expound at length on the general worthlessness of the local girls, especially those from Hosororo. He had warned one of the girls working in the house against the intentions of a certain young man. The young lady coolly replied that she could take care of herself as she knew what bush to drink. So much for the 'poor unsophisticated Indian maiden'.

The British Guiana Centenary celebrations at Morawhanna took the form of a regatta and sports meeting under the aegis of the North West 4H Club. I was appointed judge and took up my post on the stelling at the police station at ten o'clock when the regatta started. This was the finishing post for the boat events. The first was a handicap motorboat race from the mouth of Washikuru Creek to Morawhanna. Phang was the starter and as he could not swim he encircled himself in a great cork lifebelt which by no means decreased his already healthy girth. The starting point was out of sight from the stelling so I had a long monotonous wait before half a dozen black dots appeared on the river far in the distance. Gradually boats of all shapes and sizes ranging from little corials to fair-sized bateaux appeared. The winner was Francis Gerome's corial, driven by a small Johnson engine, which won by several lengths. Poon would have been second in his bateau but for the fact that he turned round before reaching the winning post, but his second entry, a corial, gained second place. The other craft did not finish.

Another long delay ensued before the next race took place, one for corials with five pullers. I entered the police corial with my crew and it was a fine sight to see the four craft flashing down the river, all the paddles of each boat dipping and rising in perfect unison as the sun sparkled on the wet blades. My crew won by about four lengths.

Dispenser Glasgow then came up and invited me to have a drink. From the knowing look he gave me I gathered that the invitation was to partake of some smuggled Venezuelan rum. I followed him to D'Andrade's old billiard saloon which, divided into three or four rooms, was now occupied by Dorcas Hutson and her two daughters. In the front room they ran a bubb shop. Passing through this and the sitting room we were conducted into the ladies' bedroom where, from behind the mirror on the dressing table, the liquor was produced.

It was then close on one o'clock and though only the first two races had been held, it was decided to abandon the remaining aquatic events and proceed with the flat races. We all adjourned to the cricket pavilion which, decorated with flags and bunting, was screened off from the road by a temporary wall of trooli leaves erected earlier in the day. The races were so arranged that they began at various points in the town and finished on the cricket field in front of the pavilion. Long arrived shortly after one o'clock and was accommodated in a specially erected tarpaulin tent alongside the pavilion.

An amusing item on the programme was the flourwater dip. In a tub of water well mixed with several pounds of flour were thrown several coins of various denominations. Competitors had to dip their heads into this opaque fluid and pick up the coins with their mouths. It was amusing to see the competitors' faces as they emerged from the floury liquid and the look of disgust when the coin proved to be a half penny instead of the hoped-for shilling. At Long's suggestion a particular coin was marked and whoever picked it up would receive a special prize of $5 presented by the Commissioner.

Another amusing event was the girls' candle and needle race. Seven girls sat on as many barrels placed sideways, with their feet off the ground and, balancing thus, each girl had to light a candle and hand it to an attendant, then race fifty yards to a table from which she picked up a needle and a piece of thread. Having threaded the needle and handed it to another attendant she ran another fifty yards to the winning post. I was one of the attendants at the table and in her excitement one of the young ladies almost transfixed my hand with her threaded needle. An extra event was put in – a race for men over forty. This was great fun. I entered but, whilst looking to see that my rivals were toeing the line properly, got left at the post.

The events were brought to a close with a tug o' war and Miss Horsham concluded the day by delivering the prizes, which the old warrior did with all the grace of a first lady of the land. Long left and with Glasgow, and Nicholas Hutson I adjourned to Dorcas Hutson's speakeasy where we had an *al fresco* supper of smuggled rum, fried morocot and bread.

A dance was held that night in the Anglican schoolroom, but Elias Oselmo had invited me and the other boys to his house where he had some cassiri. I left Walter to go to the dance and went with Nicholas Hutson in his corial up Bakrimani Creek. My large torch gave us ample light to see our way up the dark and winding stream. After about half an hour's paddling we heard the noise of fiddles and presently arrived at a landing where half a dozen corials were moored.

In the house half a dozen couples were dancing to the strains of an orchestra composed of violins and quatros. On the benches running round the four sides of a large room were seated some two dozen men. Elias introduced me to his wife, a sister of Rose Smith, who immediately brought me a calabash of mixed cassiri and warrap.

After several dances and drinks Nicholas and I started our return journey down the creek at about two o'clock in the morning. At Morawhanna the schoolroom was still lit up and we heard the strains of music issuing from it. We found half a dozen couples still dancing, although the majority of the people had gone home. Walter was still there and appeared to be enjoying himself with Florrie D'Andrade sitting on his knee. After a dance or two with Mary Boyer and Beryldina Gomes we finally left the building at close on four o'clock.

As we passed the pavilion we saw the recumbent forms of half a dozen people sleeping off the effects of the festivities. I spent the remaining couple of hours till daybreak in Zeno's empty house on Third Street and then adjourned to Claudina Gomes for coffee. Whilst with Claudina, she and her daughter Conception anointed the ringworm on my legs with raw garlic, which they said was a cure for this disease.

I returned to my quarters and had a bath and a shave and then went round to Dorcas Hutson's where I met her brother Nicholas; we spent the morning masquerading in ladies' dresses. There was a cricket match during the afternoon which I looked in at for half an hour or so then went to Claudina's for coffee. I was by this time beginning to feel the effects of the past thirty-six hours festivities and as soon as dusk fell I had my supper and retired to my hammock where I slept like a log.

The festivities over, it was time to resume work again. My first job was to survey twenty-five acres immediately opposite Hosororo landing for John Ferreira, a tall, thin elderly, tough-looking country Portuguese with a square chin. With him were three of his half-Indian children, the eldest a very shapely young girl of about fifteen. Referring to her I suggested that he would soon have prospective sons-in-law knocking around. 'Oh no, Sir,' he replied. 'There's no market for that these days.'

Whilst on this same survey, we saw several tapir tracks where the animals had come out of the forest to bathe and defecate in the trench. An extraordinary trait of these peculiar animals, the largest South American mammal, is that apparently they can only defecate in water. This was amusingly instanced in the case of a young specimen which Inspector Whittingham had when he was stationed at Mabaruma. There being no water there except in vats, the animal had to be drenched with a watering can regularly every morning.

As I travelled around in the falca with my gang, I used to sit on the bench immediately in front of the steersman and immediately behind that on which the Holder brothers sat side by side. The natural consequence was that my gaze rested on the backs of these two men. Now it may sound foolish, but nevertheless it was a fact that the continued sight of even their backs made me despondent and low spirited. There seemed to be some aura emanating from them that went against my spirit. In little Willie's case it must have been his general air of awkwardness, combined with a certain smugness, whilst in his brother's case it was undoubtedly his general discontented and sullen disposition. This latter had been growing steadily worse during the past weeks but as the poor fellow was shortly due for retirement I tried hard not to have any parting unpleasantness with him, if only for the sake of the long months we had spent together in the forest in years past when he was more active and in better disposition. Then one day I changed my position in the boat so that I had my 'betes noires' behind me. The result was very gratifying as I disembarked in the same good spirits in which I started.

A wet Saturday morning whilst up the Kaituma River at the beginning of December prevented me from going out to work so I stayed and watched some coffee pulping operations. My interest was in a special machine designed by a local man which obviated the need for double pulping. The pulper was set up with a long shallow tray whose bottom consisted of a half inch wire mesh fixed at its open end. Two men caught hold of the handles with which they turned the drum, a wooden cylinder covered with numerous metal studs. A hopper immediately over it was kept full of water by means of buckets and the coffee berries fed in gradually through another hopper at the side. The crushed berries slid down an incline onto the sieve against which they were rubbed by three or four Indians standing on each side. This forced the beans through the wire mesh, leaving the skins on the sieve whence they were swept out on to the dump pile outside.

Whilst at a party given just before I returned to town in mid December, Reverend Cossou gave us some amusing reminiscences of his days in Christianburg. It was his custom to baptise illegitimate children on Wednesdays and legitimates on Sundays. One Wednesday he asked an Indian woman what name she desired her child baptised. She replied, 'Duet, Sir.' 'Duet. Duet!' exclaimed Cossou, 'Why don't you call it Mary or Jane?' 'No, Sir, Duet is the name the father does want.' Well the child was so christened and as Cossou was about to write up the baptismal register the father arrived. Cossou said to him, 'That's an extraordinary name you have had your child christened, Duet.' 'No, Sir,' replied the father, 'it is not Duet, Sir, it's De Witt, after the pills.'

On an other occasion, he had arranged to marry a couple at eleven o'clock on New Years Day. Eleven o'clock came and the parson was ready but none of the contracting partners had appeared. At length after a long delay the bridegroom arrived, flustered and alone. 'Where is the bride?' asked Cossou. 'Parson, she done got twins,' was the reply.

Back in town Dad gave me his current joke. A young man had been away from home for three or four years and during his absence, and unknown to him, his parents had undergone a rejuvenating treatment at the hands of a Dr Voronoff. When the young man returned home he was surprised to find no one to meet him. Walking along the road towards his home he overtook a young woman pushing a pram with a baby in it. As soon as she saw him, the young woman released the pram and casting her arms around his neck exclaimed, 'Why, Jack, don't you recognise your mother?'. Very taken aback and much embarrassed the young fellow explained that his mother was an elderly lady. After a long talk, the young lady, having explained the doctor's treatment, half convinced him that she was his mother. At length, pointing to the baby in the pram, he asked, 'Well, whose baby is that then?' 'Ah,' sighed the mother, 'that's your poor father. He took an overdose!'

Early in the New Year, Wilfred Gomes approached me on behalf of P.C. Wight, the proprietor of the *Daily Chronicle*, on the subject of my accepting the editorship of the paper in succession to the late Herman Phillips. I said I would consider it at a salary of £500 a year with a five year guarantee and on condition that I was responsible to no one but the proprietor. As these terms were hardly likely to be acceptable I forgot all about it.

About the same time Mullin called me in to his office and showed me the annual confidential report he was sending to the Governor on me. I got the shock of my life. According to him my worst feature was that my administrative capabilities were fair. I was loyal, zealous, hardworking, had a good eye for country, was a good descriptive writer, was willing and did much work for government out of office hours.

Most weeks during my stay in town I went round to the Victory Lodge and in the absence of the substantive holder of the post, I acted in my old capacity as Secretary and during the course of one proceedings I was invested as Senior Warden of the Lodge for the current year. On another occasion, Allan Outridge asked me to give the third R.A. Lecture, which I managed without breaking down.

When I went to see the Governor he appeared to be in a very good mood and expressed surprise at the great improvement in my appearance. Indeed I had put on so much weight that I'd had to buy a cummerbund to hide the fact that I could no longer do up the top button of my trousers. Still I could hardly tell Sir Edward that. He asked me many questions about conditions in the North West District and enquired after Long and Phang. Speaking of the latter he said he liked 'the old boy', although in the early days they had not always seen eye to eye. Sir Edward then spoke of Dad and told me he was very fond of him and he had a very deep regard for him and would do all he could for him. At that time he had Dad delving among the archives and *Royal Gazettes* of the period 1831–51 extracting from them all items of interest which he, the governor, intended to have published in book form.

After leaving Government House I went to the Public Buildings where I gave Dad a resume of the interview, after which I invited him to Bookers for an ice cream. In Fogarty's new store was a show window fixed up as a bachelor's bedroom with a dummy of the occupant standing beside the bed garbed in a dressing gown. Dad went in and suggested to the manager that he put one of his lady clerks, attired in a dainty nightie, in the bed. The small addition, Dad assured him, would attract large crowds and custom.

That evening after a Lodge meeting I went on to the King George Hotel where things were very bright due to a warship being in port. There I met several of my old Mazaruni acquaintances including Duncan McGregor Stuart whom I had not seen since Christmas Eve of 1930.

One afternoon, Jim Eytle rang me up and asked me to go round to his office under his home, Overton House in Brickdam, to discuss his Tacouba Creek concession. I advised him that there was no need to have it resurveyed so long as he had the original boundaries open. Our business over, we adjourned upstairs where we were soon joined by Tommy Houston and had tea and yarned and discussed whisky until seven o'clock. During this time we got talking about local juries and Tommy told us his experience as a juror in a murder trial at the Supreme Court in town.

The twelve had been locked up for several hours in the jury room where the ventilation was none of the best. The furniture consisted of a long table with a bench on either side. At one end of the room was a washstand and a basin of water and at the other a nuisance bucket. Houston and two other jurors were for entering a plea of not guilty whilst the remaining nine were for guilty. After being taken back into court and having told the Judge that they were not agreed, His Honour decided that they should consider the matter a little more and see whether they could not arrive at a unanimous verdict. When the foreman told Houston and the latter realised that he was to be locked up in that hot and insanitary room once again, he exclaimed, 'Well, he's guilty then.' It is on such irrelevant threads that a man's life hangs under our much vaunted jury system where a man is tried by his peers.

CHAPTER XIX

DEMERARA BAUXITE SURVEY 1932-

In mid January, Mullin told me I was to complete a survey for the Demerara Bauxite Company of 400,000 acres between the Demerara and Berbice Rivers which Parker had started the previous year but had been unable to finish due to a breakdown in his health. On the way home I called in to see Parker and discovered that he had completed only about a quarter of the work and I realised that I should be away again for the next three or four months.

At the end of January, Philly and I went on an outing down the East Coast. At five o'clock on the day in question, Togo Low and Alma Forde came for us in a car and we set off down the East Coast road. Reaching Mahaica we turned up the road running along the left bank of the river until we came to Pln La Bonne Mare where the proprietor, Azeez Rohaman, was expecting us. He was at the time living in the house formerly occupied by the deputy manager because the manager's house, a large two-storeyed house, had caught fire and burned down in a mysterious manner on the night when Rohaman and his wife had been away in Georgetown. Rohaman introduced us to his wife and sister-in-law, then took Togo and me to show us the large rice factory he had erected behind the house. At the time the estate was planted in rice and coconuts but, as a result of an agreement he had reached with Pln Cane Grove, the neighbouring sugar estate, he was seriously thinking of planting it back in sugar cane and getting Cane Grove to grind it for him.

Back at the house we sat down to a fine East Indian dinner of both wet and dry curries. The Rohamans were Mohammedans and this being the month of Ramadan they fasted during the hours of sunlight but, judging by the groaning table to which we sat down, they certainly made up for it at sundown. We ate dholl and rice in the approved eastern fashion with our fingers. The meal was brought to a close with baked sweet cassava. Adjourning to the drawing room we danced to the strains of a gramophone until eleven o'clock when we started on our twenty six mile journey home which we reached fifteen minutes after midnight.

I finally left for the Demerara Bauxite Company's survey on Saturday 13th February 1932. It had been agreed that I would take Walter and Henry with me and, following a plea from my neighbour Mrs Juister, her son Martin. Mrs Juister and her niece, Alma, wanted to give Martin a send-off but because of the small size of their house, Phil and I decided that it should be held at ours. The party started at six o'clock and when we came to sit down to table at eight there were fourteen of us and an hour later the party had grown to twenty. At midnight we had an extra dinner of sauerkraut and souse.

At two o'clock the party began to break up and soon only Basil Parrett and Vivian Woolford were left. I knocked up Charlie Cole and got him to drop us at the Ice House where Togo, who had left our house less than fifteen minutes before was pretending to be asleep. Eventually we managed to convince him, after making certain threats, that discretion was the better part of valour and he opened his door and regaled us with two jugs of strong ale. When he told us he had no more we expressed our disapproval by dismantling his bedstead and heaving it through the window; he told us in a few well chosen words his candid opinion of us.

I had arranged with the Public Works Department for us to travel up the Demerara to Christianburg on board their tug *Seba* which went up twice weekly with her string of barges to the Seba quarry. The only snag was that Captain Matheson had declared his intention of departing at three o'clock in the morning. After making sure that the boys were aboard by nine o'clock the previous evening, I went round to Croal Street and said good-bye to Mother and Dad and then to Regent Road to see Mrs Juister and Alma and so to Trent House where I picked up Bertie Williams and Henry Bornstein, who had just come down from the Mazaruni. With Jimmy Wong, who was driving the car, we went to the King George Hotel where we had some beers and yarned.

We had a final drink at the Mariners Club where we arrived at midnight. Here we consumed several more beers, a plate of sandwiches and watched some dozen of the club members deeply engrossed in a game of pepper for coppers. Finally at two o'clock we set off for the Public Works Department up by the lighthouse. Here my companions bade me farewell and returned home to their warm beds whilst I made myself as comfortable as I could on a tarpaulin-covered pile of luggage until Captain Matheson arrived.

We got under way an hour later than originally intended and, once clear of the stelling and the barges in line astern, I joined Matheson on the bridge where we yarned about the old days on the Demerara River, he telling me the whereabouts of those of my old acquaintances who were still alive. When the eastern sky began to lighten, he suggested we should have a rest and placed his cabin at my disposal, while he slung his hammock in the adjoining passage. When I awoke some four hours later we were just passing Sill's landing at Sandhills. Basil Parrett then produced some cold roast chicken and potato salad, the last of the delights of town we expected to taste for many a long day.

I spent the day alternately reading Edgar Allan Poe's *Tales of Mystery*, dozing and watching the scenery, which had not changed much since I used to patrol the river sixteen years before. At some points, houses I remembered had disappeared, at others their number had increased. The most remarkable change to me, however, was the absence of timber punts drifting downstream laden with their outslung cargo of greenheart timbers, or empty ones returning upriver. Not a single one did I see during the course of the day; the only sign of present activity in this former chief timber-producing district of the colony was a couple of rafts of light wood floating down river.

Just below Hurudaia, the *R.H.Carr* overtook us, taking care to give the string of punts a wide berth. Matheson told me she always did this since her owners had had to pay damages for running into the *Seba's* tow some time ago. Towards six o'clock we came into view of the 'Christianburg Lighthouse', the two famous cabbage palms that towered above the forest on the east bank of the river just below the corner from which Christianburg can be seen. A few minutes later the old Christianburg House came into sight and we were soon tied up to the wharf, where I was met by van Sertima, the Land Officer, and Meigon the representative of the Demerara Bauxite Company. Forming a human chain and passing the baggage and stores from hand to hand, my men soon had all our impedimenta unloaded and packed beneath the house where they themselves slung their hammocks, whilst I and the boys settled down in the Government Officers Quarters upstairs.

Sight of the various rooms of the ancient house brought back many old memories. This was the Commissary's room occupied by Legge and Low until their office was abolished and the duties handed over to me as Land Officer in 1911. That one was old Spence's, the manager of the sawmill, and later occupied by poor old Sharples and where he died. The big bedroom in the south east corner used to be the Public Officers' dining room, which had now been changed to the one nearest the head of the stairs. The next room was where Kim Mansfield, then Agricultural Instructor, fell asleep with a candle burning next to his mosquito net and all but burnt himself and the whole building had it not been for the sharp nose of the watchman, old Black Jones, now long in his grave. Downstairs, only the large courtroom was still used for its original purpose, the great sitting room next door being stripped of all its furniture and lying empty as a barn. The offices used by Spence, Sharples and myself were locked so I could not see their present condition. In the rear wing of the house the police were still stationed as they were in my day.

The garden was neglected and there was no sign of Spence's famous grapevine beneath which he regularly buried the remains of his hunting dogs saved from tigers. Behind the kitchen, the graves of the old Pattersons, feudal lords of the river, the original builders and owners of the house, were overgrown and dank, their occupants forgotten. Their massive oaken furniture and heavy gilt-framed pictures, brought from their ancestral home in Scotland, had been removed; their mill had been dismantled and their water conservancy destroyed to provide the bauxite of which its dams consisted. Truly was the glory of Christianburg departed.

After a makeshift dinner I went to see van Sertima at his quarters, the Land Officer's house and my former home for seven years where both Walter and Henry were born. Externally the house was much as I had left it but inside were some slight alterations and improvements. Leaving him after a short yarn I went next door to the former magistrate's house, now occupied by Meigon, whom I found on the point of setting out for a walk to Wismar. He asked me to accompany him which I did.

The walk along the narrow path was a surprise to me. In inverse proportion to the abandoned air of Christianburg proper, the Red Camp to Hooboodie section had prospered. For every single shop in the old days there now seemed to be three, indeed, every fourth or fifth building seemed to be a shop, owned mostly by Chinese, though the original and oldest shop in the locality, owned by Ho-a-Shoo, had just been closed and was about to be rented to another Chinese shopkeeper.

As we walked along the road we could see the numerous electric lights of Kokataru across the river, what the Americans were pleased to call the 'coloured section' of MacKenzie. It was said the colour bar was more strictly observed at MacKenzie than anywhere else in the Colony. Passing Hooboodie we reached Wismar where signs of abandonment were again evident. The railway was closed and the permanent way in places overgrown with bush. In a small cottage near the gloomy and empty station, old Belford, the former superintendent, had his residence and we dropped in and had a beer with the old boy who seemed genuinely glad to see me again. We talked over the old Rockstone days for half an hour and then returned to Christianburg where Meigon insisted on me having a final beer with him. I finally got back to my quarters shortly before eleven o'clock and went to bed with the hope of making up two nights sleep, in which anticipation I was not disappointed.

Next morning, after arranging with Fraser, my chain bearer, to issue a week's rations to the men, I went over to van Sertima's and got him to take me in the launch *Control*, which I used to have at Kamakusa, up to MacKenzie. If the glory of Christianburg had departed, it certainly had not gone far. Where, sixteen years before, a line of forest extended along the east bank of the river, broken by an occasional small clearing surrounding a woodcutter's thatched house, now extended the ultra-modern industrial plant of the Demerara Bauxite Company and its adjacent residential areas, together with a fine concrete recreation hall and cinema.

Rounding the bend above Wismar, we came to a large wharf alongside which was moored an immense barge, *Klondyke*, with a great tower-like mechanical loader on it. Before the river had been thoroughly surveyed, the larger bauxite boats could not take on a full cargo of ore at the wharf but had to drop some miles down river where the loading was completed from this barge. Behind the wharf was an immense storage shed for the bauxite, connected by a covered conveyor with the drying and crushing plant which lay behind. Near the store was a large water tank raised close on a hundred feet in the air on thin spider-like legs of steel. Beyond the wharf was the power house with its battery of five stout iron smokestacks. Shortly after passing this last structure we came to a stelling at which we disembarked and made our way to the office of the manager, Mr Rucker, a large, typically clean-shaven American.

After arranging to return on the following morning to discuss the survey with the Company's Chief Engineer, Crabtree, we returned to Christianburg, where we joined Meigon and sat down to swizzles. Whilst thus yarning and imbibing, old William Gilkes of Lucky Spot passed by and we asked him in. The old man was in his seventy-second year and getting very shaky. Still, he was by no means the oldest inhabitant in the district, an honour claimed by Mrs van Lange of Christianburg who, if she lived another month would celebrate her hundred and first birthday. Meigon told me that she was still very active, going to church every Sunday and insisting on doing her share of the housework.

In the late afternoon, Charlie Fiedtkow arrived with four local men, thus completing my complement for the trip, fourteen men and a chain bearer. After dinner, when I had finished writing up my journal and dropping a note to Phil, I sat talking to the caretaker, a buxom young Negro woman with an attractive appearance who kept me comfortably entertained until eleven o'clock when I retired to bed.

Next morning I sent Parrett and eight men up the Karabara Creek, a stream flowing into the Demerara River from the east a couple of miles north of Christianburg, with instructions to make a camp at the first savannah whilst I went with Fraser and the others to MacKenzie to pick up the Company Surveyor, Fung-a-Ling, who was to show me our starting point. Whilst in MacKenzie I left a note at the office for the Gigliolis, who were then living in the township, informing them that I was in the district and apologising for not having had time to call and see them.

Having shown me the paal that marked the north east corner of Pln Noitgedacht, the northernmost point of the company's private properties, Fung-a-Ling returned to MacKenzie and I set up the theodolite and gave the men the bearing on which to cut the line which I believed would bring us out on the Karabara Creek, hopefully somewhere near where Basil was setting up our first camp.

Sailing up a tributary of the Karabara Creek a day or two later, looking for a suitable site for our second camp, we came to a landing at which a whole fleet of corials were moored. At the water's edge a woman was busily engaged in cleaning the carcass of a labba, whilst a plump young Indian girl was washing a small baby. This place was called Limona and was the home of old man Stellingburg and his numerous offspring.

I went ashore and up to the house where I found old Mrs Stellingburg supervising two of her granddaughters who were preparing cassava for bread making, one peeling the tubers whilst the other grated them. As I sat watching them, it made me wonder whether the violent oscillations of their breasts did not harm Indian women when they were thus occupied. Old man Stellingburg was out hunting, but his wife said two of her grandsons would show me a suitable place for our camp. It would have been much more pleasant had she suggested her granddaughters instead.

At the proposed camp site we sat down to breakfast and whilst eating we could hear the peculiar deep drumming sound that the Indian women made whilst bathing, to warn approaching strangers so that they would not be caught unawares at their ablutions. The sound is made by a peculiar slapping motion on the water with cupped hands, one hand striking the surface a fraction of a second before the other. The resultant deep boom, produced by an expert, was audible a long distance away. Then, glancing up the creek, we saw two brown faces, capped with shocks of jet black hair, gliding down the water. It seemed out of keeping with their natural modesty for Indian girls to approach strangers in this manner whilst bathing, but the phenomenon was explained when the faces proved to be those of two little boys who had come down to investigate the surveyor. Asked if they were not afraid of water boas they replied, 'Camudi there, sah, but they no trouble we.'

I noticed, set beside the creek, numerous fish traps consisting of cylindrical tubes made of baramali bark or bamboo and called kwiama.

They are fixed between two sticks planted parallel to each other and operate by means of a weight released by a trigger connected to the bait inside. As soon as the fish enters the cylinder from the bottom and nibbles the bait the whole contraption falls and imprisons it against the mud bottom. Old Stellingburg told me that occasionally snakes were caught in them and on such occasions the owner of the trap had a lively time when he emptied it into his corial. Fish caught in them were invariably found to be suffocated when removed.

It had been my intention to get our stores for the latter part of the trip along the Hariwa trail above Malali, but Stellingburg assured me that this and all other Demerara–Berbice trails had been obliterated completely by the forest fires of 1912 and 1926. He suggested that my best course would be to get them up the Karabara Creek and down the eastern boundary line behind me. In Stellingburg's opinion the great fire of 1912, that had destroyed thousands of acres of fine wallaba forest, was by no means the first of such catastrophes. He remembered seeing many moss-covered heaps of charcoal in the high forest previous to its destruction in 1912.

He told me he had lost most of his sons and daughters during the blackwater fever epidemic of 1926, so that only two of his younger sons and several grandchildren were left to him and his old wife. Discussing the decline of Indian inhabitants on the Karabara, I remarked that all his grandsons would have to seek wives in another part of the district, there being practically no Indian girls left in the neighbourhood. Stellingburg replied that he did not know where they could go to find wives from amongst their own people as 'the pullawalla at Wismar had taken all the Indian girls'. Pullawalla was the local name for the West Indian Negroes who had settled in and around Wismar since the opening up of MacKenzie where they worked. He said government no longer seemed to worry about black men taking Indian girls. It had been very different in the past when a man who took an Indian girl either had to marry her, be heavily fined or go to jail. He admitted, however, that more often than not the women themselves were to blame.

Before we finally moved on, Stellingburg warned me to be careful of rattlesnakes which, since the last fire, had appeared on the sandhills, where hitherto they were unknown. They had long been found on the coast savannahs on the Mahaica and Mahaicony Rivers and it appeared that with the destruction of the forests to the south they had extended their habitat to the newly created wastes of low muri bush and exposed tracts of bare sand. However, during the trip we did not see or hear any rattlesnakes, though we did come across quite a few labarias – three on one particular day. Whilst waiting by a creek for the boat to take us back to Camp No.2, the men caught one alive by means of a running noose tied to the end of a stick. It was a yellowtail labaria and, although no more than ten inches in length, it was fully developed and quite as venomous, if not more so, than the common big labaria. It was similar in markings to the big labaria, with the exception of the last inch and a half of tail which was of a uniform pale yellow colour and devoid of any markings. Henry wanted to take it in the boat with him but I insisted that it was killed first. He had been assiduously collecting the heads of the labarias we killed and extracting the yellow poison from their fangs, in the hope it could be used in the manufacture of a snake serum, and at dinner that night he handed me the vial containing the poison and all but dropped it in my soup. Later he asked me to let him have some high wine in which to preserve the yellowtail labaria. At this there was a roar of protest from the occupants of the Ritz next door who, hearing the request, objected strongly to such a waste of good liquor in the wilderness.

From Camp No.3 we reached the beginning of the eastern boundary. This was at a point six and a half miles due east of our starting point. As we were measuring the last tally (one thousand feet) Martin, who was acting as follower on the chain, said that a black snake had followed him for several hundred feet through the line, stopping when he did and going on as soon as he proceeded. This seemed to confirm a statement once made to me by Pedro Beria, my former chain bearer in the North West District, that if certain snakes hear anything being dragged through the bush, such as a surveying chain, they will come up to investigate. If this be a fact, then the belief that snakes are deaf must be a fallacy.

On the evening of nearly having snake poison added to my soup, I mentioned to Parrett the story I had heard of a drunken overseer somewhere on the West Bank falling asleep and waking to find that one of his legs had been swallowed by a camoodi. Parrett assured me of the authenticity of a similar case on the Mahaicony River when a sleeping Indian had a leg swallowed by a camoodi and the leg had to be amputated, as mortification had set in before he was released from his predicament.

Returning to Camp No.3 from up the line, I found Walter down with fever and Martin in a rather serious condition. It appeared that he had been ill before coming up with me and the hard work of the past couple of weeks, to which he was quite unaccustomed, had caused a serious relapse. I explained to him the necessity of his going at once to the doctor and gave him a letter to Dr Giglioli explaining the position. The next morning, Charlie Fiedtkow and an Indian left for MacKenzie with mail, so I sent Martin along with them. The rest of us set off for Camp No.4.

There were two dogs on the expedition: Pluto belonging to Caesar Cunha and Buddha, our puppy. Never having been out of town before, he found bush conditions very strange. What seemed to frighten him most was water, because whenever camp was broken and he knew he would be taken in the boat, he cowered, shivered like an aspen and hid in the bush from which he had to be forcibly removed. In the end, we found that by pretending to ignore him he learned to overcome his fear and he would follow at my heels without any trouble.

At Camp No.4 I was surprised to see several vanilla vines growing on the dead, upstanding trunks of burned trees on the sandhills. I had always believed that this plant grew only alongside water, where so much of it is seen on the rivers of the North West District. Also scattered through the burned bush were those most graceful plants called travellers palm, though they seem to belong to the plantain rather than the palm family. A slash with a cutlass on the fleshy flat stem produces a regular shower of water; indeed, a few days before, we could get no other water and it was from these well named plants that the men slaked their thirsts.

My daily system now was to take six men and proceed with the line due south for ten miles whilst the remainder were left to drogh stores to the head of the line. This moving of stores became more and more of a problem as the distance from our point of departure increased. The terrain we crossed was generally undulating, interlaced with streams, burned forest and dry bracken. The days were without shade and very hot whilst the nights were cold. On several occasions the thermometer dropped to 57° F overnight. Parrett, who felt the cold, used to line his hammock with old newspapers which became known as Basil's blankets. He was always complaining that he had great trouble hiding them from the boys who used them for toilet purposes.

As we were clearing a section of the line through some thin muri bush south of Camp No.5, there was suddenly a yell from one of the Indians: 'Get back, look a hell of a kunukuse', this being the native name for the bushmaster, the most feared of all snakes. At this warning, those ahead dashed back and we all peered into the brambles beside the line, where against a rotten log lying prone on the ground could be seen the glistening coils of an immense snake which lay quite motionless. One man swore it was a bushmaster, another that it was a rattlesnake, but when we calmed down sufficiently to look at it more closely we found it was a beautifully marked land camoodi or boa constrictor. It was evidently asleep as it gave not the slightest sign of being disturbed by all the noise around it.

The men armed themselves with sticks and Basil approached carefully and chopped at its head with his cutlass. The serpent gave a feeble wriggle and immediately had its back broken by the sticks. We pulled it out of the bushes and found that Parrett's slash had almost bisected the brain and apart from the reflex action of its mighty muscles the animal was dead. It measured exactly nine feet in length with a girth of fifteen inches. Although it proved to have nothing in its stomach it was extraordinarily fat in proportion to its length. Its beauty lay in the wonderful markings and colouring of its skin which, towards the tail, exactly resembled the bed of russet red dakuma leaves on which it lay. Forcing open its mouth we found that on each jaw it had two rows of teeth, an ordinary set for gripping its prey in the first instance on the jaw bones, and a subsidiary set of smaller teeth on the inside of the lips. When the snake starts to swallow prey of greater diameter than its mouth, the jaw bones come apart and the serpent really pulls itself onto its food in the same way that one pulls on a glove, pulling first one side then the other. By extending the lips on one side of its mouth and hooking them on with the subsidiary teeth it gets a greater purchase for pulling the lips on the other side up to and beyond those already hooked, when the process is repeated until the whole animal passes into the snake's mouth.

Leaving Henry and Fiedtkow to skin the animal, we pushed on with the line. Parrett told me of the case of an Indian boy who, easing his bowels at the creek side on the Mahaicony, was seized by the rump by a water camoodi. Fortunately he held on to the branches and yelled for assistance which fortunately was at hand. Many years later, as a man, he still bore the marks of the snake's teeth on his backside.

When we came to leave Camp No.5, Buddha, as usual, ran off into the bush and refused to come in answer to my calls. I left him, thinking that he would follow the droghers when he found the camp abandoned. However, he did not turn up with them when they returned on their second trip, and when they finally left Camp No.5 they said he ran further into the bush when they went to catch him. Two days later Buddha had still not reappeared and we gave up hope of ever seeing the craven-spirited little beast again. But, returning to Camp No.7 after a tiring day, I was pleasantly surprised to find the prodigal Buddha tied up near my tent. He had turned up about noon, full of ticks, but otherwise apparently none the worse for his five days' starvation.

Caesar Cunha, who had for the past week been suffering with diarrhoea, tried some Indian medicine prepared for him by Correia. It consisted of the gum and bark of the kakatoa tree boiled together and sweetened to a syrupy consistency; this was also used as a cure for coughs.

I spent Sunday in Camp No.10 and, after writing up my journal and writing several letters, took my rifle and the dogs and went for a stroll in the savannah just north of the camp in the hope of finding some game. In the sand I found the tracks of a large deer, probably the same animal that had been heard walking round the camp in the early hours of the morning. Suddenly from the depths of the forest I heard the shrill notes of a bugle which, from its high pitch, sounded suspiciously like my own, which I had left in town. Hastening back, I reached the line just in time to meet Charlie Fiedtkow and Martin Juister as they emerged from the forest. The latter, indeed, had my bugle which he had brought up from town where he had gone after spending nine days in the hospital in MacKenzie.

Just south of Camp No.11 we reached the limit of our southing, having covered sixteen and a half miles, and I turned the line so that we would proceed due east for a further five miles. We soon ran into extensive muri savannah, consisting mainly of dakuma bushes. On the way Fiedtkow killed a very deadly looking snake close on four feet long with a tremendous triangular shaped head exactly like that of a bushmaster, though from its markings the serpent evidently was not of that species, as it did not have a barb on its tail. We came to the conclusion that it was a morabanna, and we did in fact see and kill several more during the trip.

Pushing on eastward along the line, after covering some three and a half miles I still had not reached the Wiruni River which, according to my rough plan, I should have crossed after approximately two miles. So, I returned to Camp No.11 and sent six of the men back to Camp No.8 to bring up the stores whilst the rest of the men went a couple of miles north of the camp up the line to cut a droghing trail or sirahi in a south-easterly direction until they cut the boundary line where we were to set up Camp No.12. In this way the droghers would save themselves a few miles walk with their loads.

Caesar, who was on the sirahi cutting work, brought in a baby haka tiger which he had caught on the trail. It was about the size of a half-grown kitten and in shape resembled a weasel. The body generally was jet black, the head and neck being a light grey, the muzzle shading off to black. Under its throat was a patch of very pale orange. The little beast seemed quite tame and let itself be handled without showing any objection. However, when Caesar gave it some jam, the snap it made at the toothsome titbit included his finger. As time passed he became quite tame, spending most of his time sleeping in a hammock but every hour or so he would wake up and start to crawl about and utter a peculiar little grunt indicting that he wanted to get out. Put on the ground he immediately started to play around the camp, climbing the posts and table legs until his little front legs got tired when he would drop to the ground.

He and Buddha, to start with, looked at each other with a certain amount of suspicion, but after a while they became the best of friends and would play together quite happily about the camp. When he was picked up he played like a kitten, boxing with his paws and trying his sharp little teeth on one's fingers, or licking them. He enjoyed eating bread and milk although he consumed only a very small quantity at a time. His hind feet were somewhat similar to a monkey's and all his paws had bare, smooth-skinned palms. His sharp claws were not retractable and he scratched himself with his hind legs like a dog. When he was asleep he covered his little rat-like eyes with his paws.

Returning to the head of the line next day we continued on our way and after a further 3,300 feet we stood on the bank of the Wiruni River, here a forty foot wide stream of black water flowing northward between narrow fingers of ite palms at a speed of about four miles an hour. From its depth and current it was quite evident that the stream could not be forded so we looked about for a tree suitable to form a bridge. Alongside the line at the edge of the water rose the stout cylindrical column of a tall ite palm which we cut down. It fell with a resounding smack right across the river but its fall broke the heavy leaf-circled top clean off, with the result that the end of the trunk sank a couple of feet short of the further bank. A couple of men scrambled across and cut another palm of similar species that grew on the opposite bank. This fell as desired but, like the first one, broke off at the head, leaving the trunk in a more unfavourable position than the first one which we decided to use.

Leaving the men to erect Camp No.13 on the west bank I returned to camp and brought my survey sheets up to date. Here I found Henry cooking a large brown monkey which he had shot earlier in the day. He had discovered a well grown foetus inside the creature, which was extraordinarily like a human one. The Indians, however, considered this no obstacle to eating the meat. The same day, Paul came in with a fine turtle tiger he had shot. It was slightly smaller than an ocelot and though possessing a fine coat, not as handsomely marked as the latter. After dinner Henry set about removing and stretching the skins of the monkey and the tiger whilst I wrote a letter to Edina Wolff and Phoebe Alstrom, the caretaker, of the Public Officers Quarters at Christianburg.

Next day we moved up to Camp No.13. Walter left with the baby haka tiger in his hand and after he had gone some distance, put it on the ground when it followed him for the rest of the way, loping along with its peculiar undulating swing. After breakfast I put the line-cutting gang on the job of fixing a handrail over the first ite palm we had felled, after first hauling the broken end of the trunk towards the further bank and bracing it with a couple of posts. It thus formed an improvised bridge, the top of which projected a couple of inches above the water and, with care, could be negotiated with comparative safety. This done we proceeded with the line to the east of the river. For close on a 1000 feet it ran through a dismal ite swamp in which the water reached halfway up my thighs and to the waists of the shorter statured Indians. It was not a pleasant job cutting through this section. After a while we once more found ourselves on dry land and proceeded to climb a hill covered with high forest and a few small greenheart trees. Dropping down into and climbing out of a steep gully we eventually reached the end of the twenty-first mile on a high plateau from which we returned to camp.

Back at the river I crossed the slippery surface of the bridge. Buddha, who had so far got over his fear of the water as to swim across the river and join me, now tried the return trip on the bridge behind me. Tired from his exertions, he slipped off the palm trunk into the water and after some difficulty managed to scramble back. His efforts must have tired him still more, for a moment later he slipped off for a second time, but this time, to my horror, he was caught in the powerful swirl of the current against the palm and immediately swept down below it. Now, I noticed that a large mass of foliage was jammed against the lower side of the trunk and I realised that he was tangled up in this foliage. I probed with my stick but could not feel the dog, so I yelled frantically to Walter that Buddha was drowning. He fortunately was clad only in a singlet and pants. Looking downstream, I saw two things simultaneously: four little brown legs pointing skywards and waving feebly, and Walter's body plunge into the rescue. He caught the dog just as he drifted past the camp, his head submerged, and swam to shore with it. Back at the camp I found Walter holding the dog by his hind legs and trying to shake the water out of him. The poor little beast appeared dead, its tongue hanging out from between clenched teeth and its eyes already getting glassy. We rolled it and squeezed its chest and I held open its tightly clenched jaws whilst Walter thrust his hand down its throat and pulled out masses of twigs and leaves that the poor beast must have swallowed in its death agony beneath the water. Sidney Fiedtkow then came up and declared the dog to be dead. However, Walter, who was almost crying, and I continued to apply artificial respiration and after about a quarter of an hour's hard work we saw signs of returning animation. The eyes began to move, the chest to heave and the heart to beat. Eventually we got the animal sufficiently revived to take an interest in life, though it was evident that it was still in pain from the water in its lungs. After holding it in his lap for a while Walter got it to drink some milk and by evening we reckoned it was out of danger.

The incident gave me a great shock to see how quickly the lively little animal had changed into almost a lifeless corpse. Anyhow poor Buddha certainly owed his life to Walter's presence of mind and pluck in jumping into the black, swiftly flowing river. After seeing what happened to the dog, I realised that a man slipping off the bridge with a load on his back would stand a very poor chance of freeing himself from his shoulder straps in time to save himself. Accordingly I ordered that no one was to carry a backpack across, but that a small raft was to be made and all the stores ferried across the river

Continuing with the line and crossing several more gullies we reached its east end at twenty-one and a half miles. Here we bent the line once more to the south and, climbing up a very steep slope, emerged on a high plateau covered with tall forest. After the forest we emerged into a muri savannah, where Caesar climbed a tree and excitedly reported that approximately two hundred yards ahead was 'pure grass to the horizon without any bush'. Pushing on we found he spoke the truth. As far as the eye could see, the land to the east rolled away in gentle undulations clothed with thick grass and only occasional little clumps of bush. About a mile away from us, in the crease of a hollow, a row of ite palms indicated a stream, whilst to the south, ahead of us, a faint blue haze on the horizon showed the forest marking the distant boundary of this extensive savannah. Despite the tremendous distance across the savannah, the comparative proximity of the palms cheered us up as we knew where water could be found. But it seemed odd to be able to gaze at some fifty square miles of grassland without seeing a single cow. What were our ranchers doing? Here was an immense natural savannah within easy distance of the Berbice River with not an animal on it.

As there was nothing for the line-cutters to cut, their only task was to trample down the grass and form a trail. Owing to the absence of bushes to provide line sticks, Fraser planted the few he had several hundred feet apart, lining them up with a pair of field glasses which he always carried. Henry, with his shirt tied to a pole and fluttering in the breeze like a flag, led the line and kept us in the right direction without having to look back at the sticks every moment. On the way back to camp I fired the grass to improve the walking conditions for the droghers.

Back in camp I learned that Walter had gone out hunting up the creek and had not yet returned. I began firing my rifle at half hour intervals, convinced that he had lost his way. When the men came in, Cunha and Barasalte set off up the creek in search of him. However they had not gone beyond hailing distance when he strolled in from the opposite direction. It appeared that he had followed the camp creek up to its source and, crossing a low hill, found, not two hundred feet away, a large black water creek which I had expected to meet on the line. He followed this down for some distance until he came to some falls about six feet high. Retracing his steps up the creek southward, he missed the place where he had crossed over from the camp creek and went on for a couple of miles until he smelled the smoke from the burning savannah. He then left the stream and followed his nose and reached the edge of the savannah, knowing that the fire could only have been started by us. He looked for and found the line sticks and used these to find the camp. His straying had solved the mystery of the missing Arauma. His only hunting success was to find a maam's nest on the ground with a single greenish blue egg in it. The presence of only one egg instead of the usual full clutch indicated its probable freshness, which was subsequently proved when he used it to make a very tasty pancake.

My mail included news that poor Phil was down with an attack of shingle pox; a letter from A.J. Cheong described his experiences on top of Roraima with the Boundary Commission and a letter from Commander Rushbrooke enclosed some correspondence from Wood, the Conservator of Forests relative to the incidence of muri bush. Concerning the latter, it appeared the Governor had sent him my description of the various types of dakuma forest that I had sent to Sir Edward, for his comments. Wood appeared to consider muri to be a type of tree whereas from my own observations, extending over twenty years, the term muri as used by the Aboriginals appeared to mean any open scrub country irrespective of the flora.

As I was resting in my hammock one Sunday in mid April at Camp No.15 at twenty and a half miles, I saw in the distance a black man on a little grey horse, with a rifle slung over his shoulder. I sent Fraser down to see who he was and he brought the stranger back with him. He turned out to be the manager of the Rupununi Development Company's ranch at Waranana on the cattle trail ten miles from its terminal at Takama on the Berbice River. He said he was boundary riding and seeing my line sticks was following them up to the camp. Whilst he drank a cup of tea I got all the topographical information I could from him. He told me that the forest about a mile and a half beyond the head of my line hid the Bada Creek, a branch of the Ituni River and that my line appeared to be heading straight for the Dukalika mouth, my objective.

The savannahs in this vicinity were, apparently, good for cattle grazing but not for breeding purposes as the calves could not thrive. The company had about a thousand head of cattle here, of which we saw a few a little later on, and some horses. After staying about an hour he cantered off up the grassy slope and disappeared over the horizon.

At thirty and a half miles we crossed the Bada Creek, a clear stream some fourteen feet wide and eighteen inches deep running west of south. I regretted leaving the savannah where there was always a stiff breeze to keep away the small flies. As soon as we dropped in the hollows they were a dreadful nuisance. Just short of thirty six and a half miles we struck the Arauma Creek, a tributary on the left bank of the Ituni. The line as laid down on the map should have struck the mouth of the creek; we hit it just thirty feet above. Considering the rough nature of the survey this seemed almost too good to be true but nevertheless it was a fact, and without any cooking!

We crossed the Ituni, again by felling a tree across to the opposite bank, and proceeded up its southern bank for a couple of hundred feet until we came to the Dukalika Creek which was to form part of the eastern boundary of the area under survey. The long hard trek was beginning to tell on us. I was suffering from a couple of painful boils on the underpart of my right forearm and ringworm. Poor Martin had a nasty boil on his ankle, and, to add to our troubles, the haka tiger was starting to become vicious, especially when he did something for which he had to be reprimanded. Martin's boil brought out a waxen kernel on his groin which forced him to use a stick. It was a pitiful sight to see him hobbling along the line, yet his German doggedness came to his rescue and he was still able to force a smile when he reached a new camp. But the kernel gradually got worse and turned into a flat abscess the size of a saucer. It was very worrying and obviously quite out of the question for him to think of undertaking a forty mile walk back along the line. All I could think of was for him to hang on and struggle from camp to camp until we could get him to the ballahoo on the Kamakabra Creek.

Then Caesar and Fraser suggested that we get a ballahoo from a grant on the Bada Creek and send him down the Ituni to Paradise where he could catch the Berbice steamer. This seemed a very sensible idea so next day I sent Caesar and Peterman off to the grant with a letter explaining the situation and requesting the loan of a craft. At midday they arrived up with the craft and a note from the manager. He turned out to be a man called Nelson whom I had known in the Mazaruni as one of Ginder's diamond buyers. He told the men that had he known that I was the surveyor in the district he would have come over to see me.

So, bidding adieu to Martin, I sent him off with the two men and gave him my mail to post on the river steamer. Five days later Caesar and Peterman returned. Leaving our Camp No.19 on a Monday afternoon they had dropped down the Dukalika Creek and Ituni River to the mouth of the Bada Creek where they put up for the night at an abandoned Indian camp. On the Tuesday they went on down the Ituni, which in places was bordered by the savannah on which they saw large numbers of cattle. They managed to exchange their large ballahoo for a smaller corial but even with this craft they did not reach the Berbice River until six o'clock that evening. At Paradise they found no fewer than five shops where everybody seemed to have a high old time, there being no representative of law and order in the district. By this time Martin was unable to walk so they stayed with him until the steamer arrived at eleven o'clock on the Wednesday night when they put him aboard. After the steamer left for New Amsterdam at five thirty the following morning, Caesar and Peterman started back up the Ituni, slept at an Indian settlement and on the Friday reached the grant where they returned the boat and walked back to camp.

Henry persuaded me to try some of his ringworm cure which he had concocted with some urasaru seed. He had dried it, pulverised it and mixed it with Vaseline and iodine to form an ointment. The irritation being so bad I was glad to try anything.

Finally on Saturday 14th May from Camp No.25 we found the source of the Dukalika Creek, the limit of our travels south. That evening we broached a bottle of high wine in celebration. Basil, in a reminiscing mood, entertained us with stories about Edgar Hicken, the Berbice Croesus.

Hicken had been left the wealth of an old planter called Patoir, the last of the resident sugar kings, whom he had served as secretary. Hicken settled down as a wealthy country gentleman on the three properties at Drill, East Lothian and Cape Clear. As a stout, middle-aged coloured man Hicken was inordinately fond of boasting about his riches, declaring that he could produce more actual cash at short notice than any other man in the country. One day Parrett had remarked to Hicken that if he, Parrett, were to strike it rich in the diamond fields to the extent of a $100,000 he would consider himself rich. '$100,000 dollars?' scoffed Hicken, 'What is that? I keep that much in the house.' This might have been true as he always had a revolver by him and was terribly nervous. He was a very sickly man, always a-tremble, due no doubt to the quantity of gin he consumed. Whenever he lent money to anyone he would always boast about it. 'You know, I lent Percy Wight $72,000 the other day. I don't suppose I shall ever see it again.'

He kept two secretaries, sisters, one of whom he decided to marry, and to this end sent both of them to England to buy the trousseau. When he went over to join them he said he did not like the place: 'Everywhere was too small, not even big enough for his boots'. When Rolls Royce, according to their custom of not selling any of their cars to countries where they were not already established, refused to sell him one, he left England in high dudgeon. His main hobby, besides gloating over his wealth, was the study of Madame Blavatsky and her works in which he had implicit faith.

The survey was now virtually finished. I sent a party back down the line to MacKenzie with mail and instructions that they were to get the Government launch *Control* and tow the big tent boat up to Friendship. There they were to get two ballahoos and proceed up the Kamakabra Creek to the western boundary cut by Parker. There they were to set up camp at the southern end of it and extend it southward until they met our westerly line. I hoped to meet up with them in about a fortnight.

Setting off on the westerly line towards Camp No.26 I had my rifle ready as there were indications that deer were in the neighbourhood. But descending a slope towards the forest covering the Yarawaia I lost interest and got careless in my outlook. Suddenly it dawned on me that the large brown animal trotting down the line ahead of me was not Pluto (Caesar's dog) but a big deer. I was so astounded at the discovery that I seemed to lose my wits. Instead of immediately taking a shot at the animal whilst it was less than a hundred feet away and in the clear, I waited to get a good bead on it with the natural result that it trotted off out of sight behind some bushes. Although I hurried to the spot where it had left the line I could see no further sign of it. I was so ashamed of myself that when I related the incident in camp I garnished the story by asserting that just as I was about to pull the trigger a fly got in my trigger eye. No, I'm afraid I'll never make other than an armchair huntsman.

Returning to camp next day from the line I learned that the tiger had met its Waterloo. Having been let out of his box for an hour to take the air he objected to being put back, and when Caesar persisted, he went for him, biting him on his heel. Very foolishly Caesar climbed a tree and the tiger immediately followed and proceeded to bite pieces out of his rump until Henry picked up a stick and broke its back. Even thus maimed when it fell to the ground, the animal tried to attack Henry, crawling behind him with its forelegs, its hind limbs being paralysed. It gradually became weaker and I told Walter that it could never recover and out of mercy it should be destroyed. Walter at last agreed, but when it came to the point his soft heart prevented him, so he begged Henry to do it for him. Whilst somewhat more of a Spartan than his elder brother, Henry nevertheless jibbed at deliberately taking such a creature's life in cold blood so whilst they were thus arguing I picked up my rifle and put the animal out of its misery, efficiently and instantly. Poor Walter was very upset and I felt sorry for him as he had devoted a lot of time and trouble to the quaint little beast which, in its mild moments and especially the evenings, could be quite affectionate.

Exactly a fortnight later, after leaving the Dukalika Creek and travelling just over ten miles due west, we met up with the party that had gone round to evacuate us. It was with great relief when I finally sat down in the ballahoo, set off down the Kamakabra Creek for the Demerara River and thought back over the seventy miles of line that we had just completed.

As we travelled, Parrett told me a yarn about Ben Hart, the Rupununi rancher, which he vowed he got from Hart himself. Hart was travelling to the coast by boat, bringing with him his wife and children, including his eldest son, a mischievous imp of eight. Born on the ranch in the Rupununi, the boy knew all about cattle and the surgical operation of making steers, which he had often witnessed. One afternoon during the journey, Hart was asleep in the boat and the front of his trousers was open. Mrs Hart, happening to glance up, was just in time to prevent her son from castrating his father with a large knife. The boy thought it was a great joke – his father thought otherwise!

When we reached the Demerara I would certainly not have recognised the area as I knew it sixteen years before. The forest fire of 1926 had swept both banks in this section and the dead upstanding trees that rose out of the second growth had altered the appearance of the river considerably. At Malali landing, only old Sproston's shop and logie remained, the former now being run by W.R. Seon; of Knoop's house not a vestige remained. We ran down the rapids and I put up for the night at the lower landing in the parson's rest house.

During the evening, a stout, elderly coloured lady came to see me and I soon recognised her as Mrs Alfred Paul, a younger sister of my old friend, Mrs Deane of Arasaru. She told me that Mrs Deane had died some seven years ago. When she had gone I settled up with Amos Henry, A. Paul, Sidney Fiedtkow and Semichee as they were leaving the expedition the next day as we passed their respective homes.

Loading our ballahoo for the last time, we paddled off next morning down the river over which hung a thin haze of the famous Malali mist. The river having risen overnight, we made quick progress on the swift current. A lot of the old places I had known were either abandoned or replaced by new and smaller houses. Passing Seba quarry I could see great changes had been made since poor old Harvey's days. Thousands of tons of rock had been removed in the intervening years and the outline of the place was quite unrecognisable. After dropping Semichee at his home we came to the Muritaro Mission. There only the church in which I was married was recognisable. Shortly after, we arrived at Friendship, the home of Edward Fiedtkow, father of Charles and Sidney, whose mother was Phil's eldest sister. I stayed there about an hour, having a glass of fresh milk and some fresh coconuts whilst the luggage was transhipped from the ballahoo to the large tent boat. Thus refreshed, we set off again down river. On the right bank of the river at Mahaicabally there was a scene of great activity. A deep cutting extended several hundred yards inland from the river, forming a great pink gash against the dark green of the forest. This was the Trewern Mine where several steam shovels were at work digging bauxite and dumping it into trucks. Along the river bank a short squat locomotive ran snorting up and down, shunting the ore wagons. Noticing a carriage full of people, facetiously marked *Pullman*, though it would have made a poor cattle truck, I deduced that a train was about to depart for MacKenzie. Going ashore, I found that it was due to leave at five o'clock, in ten minutes time, and was told to ask at the manager's office, a small building nearby. Here I met the assistant mine manager, a young black man named Alstrom, brother of Phoebe Alstrom. He said I could certainly have a passage to MacKenzie on the train but that it would not leave until Fung-a-Ling, the mine manager, was ready. As I waited I watched the steam shovels biting up the blasted rock, swinging round and discharging their loads into the trucks alongside.

At five o'clock the whistle went and there was a mad rush up the cutting towards the train which quickly filled up with the mineworkers bound for their homes at MacKenzie. When Fung-a-Ling arrived we joined the train in the section reserved for senior staff. The sides of the Pullman were open, only the ends being covered with a fine wire mesh to protect the passengers from sparks. However, as we were sitting on the front bench of the coach next to the engine and the wire gauze at that end had a great hole in it, we were kept busy dodging the sparks that blew in on us as we rocked and swayed along the track. By the time we arrived in MacKenzie it was quite dark and as Alstrom had a corial to take him over to Christianburg I gladly accepted his offer of a passage. I was really glad to be back in a civilised place again and after three days journey in an open ballahoo I felt dirty, unkempt and unshaven.

Next day I went back to MacKenzie to thank Rucker for all his help and assistance and to collect my mail from the post office. I then paid a call on the Gigliolis. There I found the whole place was upside down with half packed cases. Presently Mrs Giglioli appeared, a young woman with very large eyes that held a worried expression. She explained that they were due to leave for England in a few days after ten years in MacKenzie, and hence the chaos. I said I would detain her no longer but she insisted on my staying to meet her husband who was just finishing off some photographs of a recent hunting trip on the Essequibo. A few minutes later the doctor arrived, and a man more unlike an Italian it is hard to conceive. Perhaps being Scottish on his mother's side accounted for his blue eyes and sandy hair. He showed me some magnificent photographs of the forest and its denizens, and then, after a glass of beer, I departed and left them to their packing.

After finally clearing up all my affairs in MacKenzie, we caught the steamer back to town. To my surprise I found the Gigliolis as fellow passengers and Canon Roberts Rea, with whom I had a reminiscent chat, reminding him of the time I took him up to the Great Falls almost twenty years before.

Reaching Georgetown at four o'clock, I found Dad on the stelling waiting to meet us. Leaving Walter to look after the baggage, Dad, Henry and I got in a car and started for home. However, Dad insisted on us accompanying him to a house in Broad Street of an old Portuguese acquaintance of his Pomeroon days, known as Jumbi Driver, whose daughter had been married that day and whose wedding was now being celebrated. After drinking the health of the happy couple, we went on to Croal Street where we were greeted by Mother. Leaving Dad there we went on home to find Phil in pyjamas. She had been obliged to call the doctor in that morning; nevertheless she was looking much better than when I had left her three months before.

Dad told me the following story which he had heard during my absence. A certain parson had entered a golf tournament, but arriving late had to play against a young lady who was a stranger to him. Wishing to be sociable he said , 'Er, my name is Peter, but er I'm no Saint.' 'Oh, that's all right,' replied the girl. 'My name's Mary, but I'm no virgin!'

A few days later, returning to the office after breakfast, I noticed a charming looking lady clothed with great chic, in a corn-coloured dress, walking the pavement. My attention was drawn by the extraordinary clearness of her white skin and as I turned my head to look at her, she turned her face straight towards me. Like a perfect little gentleman, I looked away. But being human, after a lapse of a few moments, when I assumed the lady had gone on, I looked back and met her doing the same thing. She stared with such brazenness that I assumed her to be a demi-modaine and, to make sure, got off my bicycle at the gates to the Law Courts and stood watching her. Sure enough, she looked back again and when she reached Lee's Photo Studio she pretended to study the pictures in the window, every few minutes turning round to look in my direction. Then she sauntered slowly into the studio, looking back at me once more. As I had an interview with Mullin I could wait no longer, but decided to look out for her again. In the drawing office I related the incident to Phang, who said she must be the French woman who had recently moved into a house next to the Mariner's Club in High Street.

On my desk I found the volume containing the first twelve chapters of *Morawhanna Memories* with a memo to the effect that the Governor had no objection to its publication provided Mullin was allowed to make what deletions he thought necessary. Scanning through it quickly I found he had not used the blue pencil as heavily as I had expected. I later took it round to Delph to see about getting it published, and a couple of weeks later I was pleased to see the first of the series appear in the *Daily Chronicle*.

During this period one of the books I read before going to sleep was R. Blathwayt's *Through Life and round the World* in which several pages gave an account of the author's meeting with my Uncle Felix Roth in West Africa.

One Thursday afternoon shortly after my return to town, I was on my way to the museum to see Dad, when Horace Lopes called out to me as I passed his store, The Bedstead House. He told me that it was Mrs Juister's birthday that day and he was going up there at four o'clock to pay her a surprise visit and asked me to try and turn up also for a few minutes. Whilst with Dad I bought from him a pretty Indian bead apron, or queyu, as a birthday present. On my way home I dropped in at Mrs Juister's for half an hour and surprised her with my knowing that it was her birthday. Lopes was already there with several others. After drinking the lady's health I went on home.

CHAPTER XX

THE BARTICA–POTARO ROAD

One Monday morning at the end of October 1932, Mullin, the Commissioner, came into the Drawing Office with two Frenchmen whom he introduced to me as Delaitre and Rieus. They had been sent out by their government to enquire into the development of the interior of French Guiana, especially with regard to its mineral potential. Rieus was the Chief Engineer of Public Works at the Ministry for the Colonies whilst Delaitre was an expert adviser to the Ministry on gold mining. The latter was a very big man with a pleasant expression who spoke English quite well but very slowly. Rieus, on the other hand, was a short stout man who could not speak any English at all. They were on their way back to France and at the request of the Governor of French Guiana, our Government was giving them every facility to examine conditions here for the purpose of comparing them with those in the French Colony. At Mullin's request I took them upstairs to the geological branch where I showed them the specimens we had there, in which Delaitre, in particular, showed great interest.

For the rest of the day I worked on the old records. The balance of the evening was spent working at my journals and *Morawhanna Memories*.

Next morning Mullin called me to his office, where I found Delaitre and Rieus. He told me that it was planned that the two Frenchmen should visit the Bartica-Potaro Road, but as Delaitre was suffering from toothache, Rieus would have to go alone and as he spoke no English it had been decided that I should accompany him as interpreter and guide. We were to leave town next day and return on the following Monday.

Next morning I went to Fogarty's store where I bought a French dictionary, my knowledge of the language having become somewhat rusty. From there I went to the Colonial Transport Department where I obtained a free pass for the journey from McDougall, who was acting as general manager during Andrew Grant's illness. He told me he was instructing his officials along the route to give us every facility and had notified the caterer on the steamer to expect distinguished passengers.

I then called in at the Tower Hotel to see that Rieus had a travelling pass and a letter of introduction from the Director of Public Works to John Aldie who was in charge of the bridge-building operations across the Potaro, at Garraway Stream. On my way home I called in to say good-bye to Mother. At home I packed and after dinner went to Victory Lodge where I presided over the meeting, leaving there shortly after eleven.

I picked up Rieus and Delaitre and we made our way to the steamer stelling. Dad was there to see us off. Shortly after Dad and Delaitre had gone ashore we were on our way to Vreed-en-Hoop. Isaacs, the Traffic Superintendent, was there to meet us and conducted us to a reserved compartment on the West coast train. At Parika we boarded the old *Basra* and headed up the Essequibo River. The caterer, warned of our arrival, provided the best breakfast I had yet partaken on a local steamer. I introduced Rieus to a swizzle which he would insist on drinking in sips. After breakfast the captain put the flying bridge at our disposal and sent up two Berbice chairs. In these we spent the afternoon, yarning and sleeping. I managed to get through with the assistance of my dictionary and was very pleased to note that Rieus had provided himself with one too.

We reached Bartica a few minutes before six. At the Hotel Moderne we took two of the best rooms. I saw V.A. Pires and arranged with him the food we were to take with us on the trip. After dinner and half an hour's yarn we both retired to our rooms.

Next morning, the two lorries of the Colonial Transport Department drove onto the stelling to be loaded up. The first was a great six-wheeled Albion, the second a one and a half ton Ford. It was in the latter that we were to travel, three spring seats having been fixed therein behind the cab. Shortly after eight, the Albion, piled high with cargo and some half dozen second-class passengers perched precariously on top of it, rumbled off down the street. We followed a few minutes later. In addition to about a ton of cargo, Rieus, I and Alfred Clark were the only passengers. The driver, a young Negro by the name of Harris, was accompanied by a young black boy, whilst the third member of our crew, a thin elderly man, sat on the baggage behind us and held our breakfast basket.

With a long blast on the horn we rolled off the stelling and turned south along First Street, the inhabitants waving to us as we rumbled past. Before reaching the limits of the settlement however we were delayed by the Albion which had stopped to take on more passengers – golddiggers for Potaro and labourers for the bridge-building at Garraway Stream.

The heavy Albion prevented our Ford going at its normal speed and it was only after repeated and prolonged blasts on the horn that the driver of the big vehicle drew sufficiently to one side to allow us to pass and even then we all but grazed the clay wall of the side cutting. With a clear road ahead of us, Harris let her go all out and for the first few minutes I had the wind up as we careered at some fifteen to twenty miles an hour along the narrow and winding road. But the driver knew his job: the engine roared up the hills in low gear, and rattled free on the down grades, rocking and swaying on the uneven surface and although Harris slowed down on the corduroyed sections we nevertheless were bounced about like three pills in an empty box. Occasionally, as we were bounced an extra six inches off our seats, Clark would grunt, whilst Rieus and I called on our Maker in our respective tongues.

At Seven Miles we stopped at the camp of the first of the four gangs placed permanently on the road to maintain it throughout its 122 miles. The men were cutting and laying corduroy on those sections where the sand was very loose. Harris told us we had to wait for the Albion, it being the practice for the two lorries to travel together, in case either broke down, when the passengers would be transferred to the other. Presently a distant roar was heard and the great six-wheeled vehicle rolled into sight, its enormous width blocking up the whole road.

Going on we came to the deviation that had been made to avoid the crossing of the Big Bara-Bara Creek and whilst on it we got stuck in the loose sand, the back wheels sinking in so deep that the casing of the differential gear began ploughing the sand and piling it up until we were brought to a stop. With the arrival of the Albion the combined crews and second-class passengers began cutting tree branches and twigs and laying them on the road and, with a shove, the lorry was got clear and we continued our journey.

At the Twenty Third mile we stopped for breakfast: roast chicken and cold boiled potatoes we had brought from the hotel. One of the men took a bucket and descended a nearby gully and returned with it full of good brown wallaba bush water. Rieus looked very askance and wished he had brought Delaitre's filter with him. However, I managed to persuade him that it was quite potable. Breakfast over, Harris lay down on the side of the road and went sound asleep and the other driver had great trouble waking him when it was time to be on the move again. Harris had spent the previous night until six in the morning at a dance. Every few miles he would stop and, on the excuse of waiting for the Albion to catch up, would lie down in the shade of the forest and take forty winks.

Just beyond the Forty Second mile, we passed another maintenance gang working north and for the next few miles the road was as smooth and well swept as a table top. We made fine progress through this section, which was very picturesque, the long stretch of road shining like a clean-cut swathe between the great forest trees. At the Fifty Fifth mile we left the original alignment of the old Bartica – Kaburi Road and swung more to the south along that laid out the previous year by Parsley, Lee-Own and Ridley to Garraway Stream on the Potaro.

Near Seventy mile we came to the first bridge since leaving Bartica. It was a narrow but very substantial structure built entirely of greenheart, several hundred feet long and crossing the narrow flat bordering on, and the actual branch itself, of the East Kaburi River. About a mile further on we came to the East Kaburi River itself, a stream some 30-40 feet in width and crossed by a similar wooden bridge over a 1000 feet long, this being necessary to carry the road across the narrow, riparian swamps. At Seventy Six and a half miles we came in sight of the third bridge, 400 feet in length, crossing another branch of the East Kaburi and its bordering swamps. On the slope beyond the bridge stood Pires' and Silva's substantially built rest house (of sawn lumber with a zinc roof and magazine) and the C.T.D. garage where the lorries were housed for the night.

We painfully lowered our bruised and shaken bodies to the ground and had our baggage off loaded. Clark, Rieus and I put up in the rest house, where my first job was to see my charge fixed up comfortably. Mullin had lent us his folding cot which I now erected for Rieus, who seemed delighted with it. Having washed our hands and faces in a bucket of water on the doorstep, there being practically no amenities in the building, we got into our pyjamas and adjourned to the quarters of the magazine keeper, an elderly coloured Dutchman named Verwayen. His was the only part of the building that had any sort of furniture. Here we dined off the remains of our roast fowl, a tin of roast beef, and some great big bakes that Verwayen's housekeeper, a light-skinned elderly woman with coppery hair, had cooked. The meal over, we were glad to adjourn to bed where in a few minutes I, at least, was dead to the world.

I awoke next morning feeling as though a cartload of bricks had been trundled over me, every bone in my back being stiff and sore as a result of the bouncing and jerking I had received the previous day. Rieus, however, woke up as fresh as a daisy, assuring me that he felt no ill effects. I noticed that he and Clark, both having more avoirdupois than I and very much more flesh on that portions of their anatomy that bore the brunt of the shaking, got through the journey less painfully than I did.

Next morning we resumed our journey in the Ford, leaving the Albion to follow behind. The road now consisted of a series of switch-backs, running off one hill to climb immediately up the next. It followed a watershed between two tributaries of the Potaro and at one or two points the ridge between the gully heads was so narrow that the road had been built up with timbers to afford sufficient width for the lorries to pass. At the top of an ascent we got a glimpse of Eagle Mountain beyond the Potaro. Rieus expressed surprise at learning that the distant blue mass was within the borders of the Colony and that there was the possibility of our visiting its foot the following day.

Shortly after ten o'clock we approached the present end of the road at Garraway Stream on the Potaro, its proximity being indicated by the number of tents along each side of the road occupied by the labourers engaged on building the bridge. The camp, for the most part, consisted of tarpaulin tents, with a few palm-thatched shacks interspersed between them. Before us was a great scene of activity. On the riverside of this ridge extended a temporary street of tents, before the nearest of which the Union Jack was flying from a rough flag staff indicating the police station. Beyond that were several stores of rations and materials, then the dispensary and hospital and then the office of the Resident Engineer, this being the only wooden building in sight. On the road itself, motor lorries and little tractors and trailers were hauling rock and red clay from the excavations at the end of the road, and dumping it down the gully on the left. Clouds rose from the red dust that lay six inches deep all over the place.

We stopped at the end of the road where a gang of about a hundred men were excavating and drilling down to the bed rock on which the bridge foundations were to be laid. The rat-tat-tat of jack hammers driven by a couple of motor-driven compressors drowned the lesser noise of the hand drills, whilst in the adjacent blacksmith's shop the clang of the hammers on the red hot drill bits added to the general noise.

We made our way to the Resident Engineer's office before which a crowd of men were receiving their wages. Within the stiflingly hot little office were four or five people amongst whom I at once recognised Jock Aldie, not only by his short stout figure, round red face and bushy moustache and heavy ginger eyebrows but by the broad Scots roar of his enquiry: 'What the hell air ye doin here, mon?' With him was his chief assistant Claude Craig and a young Portuguese clerk, busy attending to the paysheets and a tall old Scandinavian American, Fred Norman.

Having made the necessary introductions, Aldie asked us to excuse him whilst he got his mail ready for despatch by the returning lorries. He put Craig at our disposal to show us around and to give us all the information we wanted. Taking us back to the end of the road Craig showed us how the ridge on which the road ran here was really a rock dyke which had turned the course of the Potaro to the south until it had cut through, forming a channel little more than 300 feet in width between the two rocky hills. This was the narrowest place on this section of the Potaro and chosen for this reason as the site for the bridge. From there we descended the eastern slope, along a steep path, crossed a little ravine on a footbridge and came to a tent pitched in the shade of some tall trees. Here, sitting in a canvas chair, I found John Menzies, his face and body swollen to an abnormal size with what looked like Bright's disease. He had been here over six weeks and refused to go to town, maintaining that he wanted to be buried here in the hills and not in the mud of Georgetown. He had come up with Norman's expedition to show them some gold claims, but apparently his promises had not materialised and Norman had dispensed with his services, though for humanity's sake had arranged for his care and subsistence until he got to town. However, as Craig explained, whenever a lorry was ready to go, Menzies would make some excuse to postpone his departure.

After a short chat with Menzies I went to Aldie's bungalow, on a gentle slope near the river, a couple of hundred yards away from the construction work and separated by a strip of high forest. The wooden building contained some four or five bedrooms with a central dining and sitting room and the whole structure was covered with palm thatch.

Suddenly Aldie could be heard on the hill yelling, 'Stand clear!' the preliminary signal that the morning blast was about to take place. Twice again he shouted the warning. A couple of seconds after the third shout there was a loud ear-splitting explosion, short and sharp, but whose echoes reverberated amongst the hills for several seconds whilst rocks rained down in the river throwing up pillars of white water. One or two pieces fell uncomfortably close to the house and, on one occasion, Craig told us that a piece had come through the roof and landed on Aldie's head.

Aldie and Norman came in and all eight of us sat down to breakfast of wild hog done up in various forms. We spent the afternoon in the bungalow yarning and I interpreted Aldie's figures and costs of construction for Rieus. He explained to me that French public opinion was divided on the future of French Guiana. One party considered it should remain as it was, a dumping ground for undesirables, the other that its mineral and forest resources should be developed. As both parties were about equal in influence, the French Government had decided to send a commission out to investigate the possibilities of development. In French Guiana they found the local government very much in favour of building water-grade roads to the interior, but Rieus, after looking over the position, advised watershed routes. The local government officials laughed at his suggestion as impracticable. Imagine his delight then on finding such a road in British Guiana and, according to him, built so economically.

Colin Ridley, who was doing some survey work between Tumatumari and Kuribrong arrived shortly before six, surprised at seeing me here.

We spent a convivial evening, Aldie and I entertaining our French guest with Scottish songs and a performance of the Highland Fling.

At dawn I was awakened by Aldie's heavy hand on my shoulder and his bull voice in my ear enquiring whether I intended sleeping all day. At half past six the Minnehaha Development Company's boat arrived for us and Rieus and I, accompanied by Ridley and Craig, set off up the Potaro River. Just above Garraway Stream, and in the immediate vicinity of the road, were several small houses which had been built for the prostitutes who reckoned on good trade with the road construction gangs until Aldie, a few weeks before, had chased them all away. On the opposite bank was A.F. Silva's workings, their presence indicated by the tents and a motor pump set on a scaffolding over the river.

Half an hour's run up the river, which was very low, brought us to Potaro landing which I hardly recognised as the same place I had visited some twenty years ago. Only a couple of rotten beams remained of the stelling, but Sproston's house was still there, now occupied by R.G. Humphrey, the present owner of the Minnehaha Development Company. At the landing was what was purported to be a lorry, though such a ramshackle vehicle had I never before seen. It had but three wheels, the driver always removing the fourth when he visited Tumatumari to prevent any unauthorised use of the vehicle. The fourth wheel restored, we all climbed aboard the crazy contraption, Ricus and I squeezing ourselves in the cab beside the driver, the others squatting on a pile of goods in the body of the truck.

For the first three or four miles, the forest consisted of a second growth, as a consequence of the forest fires of 1926. A mile from the landing we came to where the forest had been cut down for the construction of the road from Garraway Stream to the old Potaro – Konawaruk Road, so that when this and the suspension bridge were completed it would be possible to drive from Bartica to Konawaruk. Some distance further on we passed the branch road leading to Kangaruma landing, higher up the Potaro, the route used by visitors to Kaieteur Fall.

Somewhere beyond Seven Mile we stopped for a few minutes at Gallienne's shop and soon had some fine views of Eagle Mountain and its opposite number, Flatteras. A little further on we stopped again by some houses from one of which a stout young Negro woman, whom I knew in Mazaruni by the name of Little Basra, came out to greet me. We passed by the government compound, (police station, hospital, and public officers quarters) and, a mile further on, at Twelve Mile, we reached our destination, the headquarters of the Minnehaha Development Syndicate.

Here Humphrey's new residence, Mahdia House, spread its ample proportions on the brow of a low hill. Descending from the lorry we walked along a short branch road where we heard the clanging and banging from the blacksmith's shop and the more distant rumbling of the dredge on the flat. At the smithy we introduced ourselves to E.H. Humphry, the manager, an elderly, quietly spoken, coloured gentleman who spoke with an air of old world refinement. He was busy superintending the smelting of the week's production of gold and its casting into an ingot.

From there Humphrey took us down to see the dredge. Following a small truck track for a couple of hundred feet we came out on the paddock, as the cleared flat on which the dredge worked was called. In the centre was a wide pond, the further shore of which consisted of yellow tailings. Floating at the nearer side of the pond was what, at first sight, looked like a small factory building on a sugar estate. This was the dredge, its ladder of great buckets then motionless, whilst at its other end, its extremity projecting over the tailings, was the long sluice. The hull consisted of a great iron pontoon, whilst the upper works and machinery were for the most part enclosed by sheets of corrugated zinc. Getting into a little ballahoo we were ferried on board where, dodging hot steam pipes and greasy engines, we climbed up various ladders and along narrow gangways to the upper portion of the structure where the bucket chain turned over the wide sluice, in which were great masses of clay and gravel. Suddenly there was a great throbbing as the powerful pumps got to work and a miniature Niagara of muddy water gushed out of various pipes and instantly filled the sluice with a foot of water that tumbled and churned the clay along its length. Next moment a heavy rumbling was heard and, as the whole structure quivered, the bucket chain started to move. It was weird to see the great buckets creep into sight one after the other, turn slowly over, and dump their contents of yellow clay into the watery chute. We returned to the floor of the dredge and, standing by the lower end of the bucket chain, watched it at work. Weirder than the sight of the buckets creeping over the upper pivot of their travel was that of them emerging slowly and relentlessly from the muddy water at the edge of the bank, some full of thick clay, others with but a half load according to the resistance offered to each bucket as it dug into the earth. Then everything came to a halt. Winches rattled and the whole bucket chain was slowly raised out of the water. Other winches rattled, wire cables slid through sheaves and the blunt nose of the dredge swung slowly forward. Again the buckets were lowered and recommenced their slow movements against the raw edge of the bank. As they ate all that came within their grasp, the winches controlling the mooring cables were put in slow motion and the dredge gradually veered sideways, to bring the buckets against fresh earth. After spending some half an hour on the dredge we were ferried ashore and returned to the blacksmith's shop where we were shown the ingot, the result of the previous week's work. It weighed fifty-two ounces. We then went to the office in which was also housed the government radio station, which in part was subsidised by the company. Rieus despatched a radio to Delaitre.

We next went up to Mahdia House, a fine large residence with mosquito-proof gauze fitted to all the windows and doors. Two large refrigerators were in evidence, and from these were produced refreshing iced drinks. Ridley told me that some golddiggers had been to see him about a disputed claim and requested that I saw them, which I promised to do.

Having resolved the golddiggers' problem with Ridley we returned to the house and, picking up Rieus, set out in an antiquated car for Prosperity Hill where Humphrey and Krakowsky were carrying out some hill mining with a Belgian mining engineer named Gaspar. After about half an hour's driving we came to an area of red clay where the forest had been cleared for the workings. We left the car beside the head of a ravine on the further slope of which a lengthy scaffolding supported a long iron trough that led water to a sluice a couple of hundred feet long, on which a dozen or so men were working. There we met Gaspar, a young man with a very keen face and pronounced chin.

He explained that at the ravine head, he had a large motor pump which lifted the water from the creek to the top of the hill where he led it where it was required along the broad iron trough. As the pump sent up a steady stream of water, the variation in quantity required by the operations was obtained by the simple expedient of stationing one man at one of the joints of the troughing where he separated the two sections in accordance with signals, thus diverting the water off the sluice down into the ravine. He told us that he had only been working back sands that had already been worked by porkknockers, and in the first three days had recovered over six ounces of gold with his long sluice. I was surprised and pleased to see old Michael as foreman of the outfit; he had carried Krakowsky's diamonds from their shop in Puruni to their Enachu headquarters.

Rieus having seen all he wanted, Gaspar invited us up to see his house where he regaled us with rum punch and chocolates and showed us a collection of photographs he had taken in the Belgian Congo.

Bidding good-bye to our host we returned to Mahdia House where, after a fine tea, we said farewell to Humphrey and set out for Potaro Landing, taking with us the company's gold canister, which he had asked me to take to town. We dropped down to Garraway Stream, reaching the bungalow shortly after six. We were all pretty tired so spent a quiet evening. Aldie was very disappointed that I joined him in only two whiskies.

Aldie had arranged for one of his trucks to take us out and return with his stores so we set off at seven o'clock in a Bedford lorry with about a ton of sand in the tray to prevent it jumping about too much. The spring seats we had used on the outward journey were dumped on the sand. Our first stop was at the maintenance gang's camp at Sixty One miles where the foreman told me how interested he was in reading my 'Morawhanna Memories' in the Sunday issues of the *Daily Chronicle* as he had worked on the construction of the road there.

The journey was quite uneventful until we reached Thirteen Miles where we hit a patch of very loose sand which brought us to a complete stop. However, the Ford caught us up and her crew helped us to get free, promising to wait for us at the next bad section ahead. We had not gone very far before we got stuck again and had to wait until they came back and rescued us. By now the light was failing so it was decided that we should continue our journey in the Ford. I had to ride on the casing of the extra fuel tank between the cab and the tray of the lorry – which I found to be the least shaken position in the vehicle. Then we saw some driving. Harris, with his head lamps full on, illuminated the forest-walled road until it was like daylight, let the lorry all out, and we leaped and swayed and rolled up and down the hills and round the bends where the centrifugal force all but threw me off my perch. We finally rolled into Bartica at eight o'clock. At the hotel we had a warm whisky and soda, the ice being finished, and then sat down to dinner.

Sailing down the Essequibo next day, Rieus and I sat on the flying bridge discussing our trip. At Parika we noticed that the flag on the Leguan ferry boat was flying at half mast and at the stelling news reached us of the death of Andrew Grant, the acting manager of the Transport and Harbours Department. We reached Georgetown at three o'clock and were met at the stelling by R.G. Humphrey's son to whom I delivered the gold canister. At the Tower Hotel I left Rieus with his colleague and, after accepting an invitation to have breakfast with them the next day, went on home where I found everything upside down in preparation for the celebration of Walter's coming of age.

As there seemed to be some doubt as to whether some guests understood their invitations, after tea I went down to Nottingham House and saw Sam Taylor. After a short yarn I went on to the Ice House to see Togo Low and Pires but unfortunately they were both out. I then went up Croal Street and reported my safe return to Mother and Dad and then returned home.

After dinner the guests arrived, including the Coles, Alma Forde, Sam Taylor and a bunch of Walter's friends, as well as Eugene Correia and Ralph Rice. We had some dancing to the electric gramophone and at ten o'clock adjourned downstairs to the ceremonial cutting of the cake. The party finally broke up at ten o'clock.

Before going to the Tower Hotel I made a map for Rieus showing the route of our trip. The meal, when I got to the hotel, lasted close on three hours and was well washed down with champagne. Leaving the hotel I saw Grant's funeral as it passed on its way from St Thomas' Church. In the evening I went to Nottingham House where I yarned with Taylor and had dinner with him there. Afterwards I went to Sandbach Parker's wharf where I boarded the *S.S. Oranje Nassau*, and said farewell to Rieus and Delaitre who were sailing on the tide.

At intervals throughout the morning of 11th November various young ladies called at the office selling Flanders poppies. The usual silence was observed at eleven o'clock, after which I went to Hutchinsons for a pair of stockings for Phil and then to Bookers for a bottle of mayonnaise for my breakfast salad. I stopped at the Cenotaph to look at the wreaths that had been placed there. During the afternoon I spent my time making tracings of Cheong's map of the Tiboku trace.

It was about a week later that a young Englishman named Chislett called on me at the office for advice about going into the bush. He had just arrived in the Colony with about £30 in his pocket and was prepared to work for a living in the bush – another case of the lure of the jungle and thirst for adventure. I told him what I could and then sent him to Sam Taylor with a note of introduction as I knew he was planning to leave for the Mazaruni in the next few days. Chislett had no sooner left me when another fellow, Bill Fleming, came along with a similar request. I told him what I had told Chislett and then gave him some copies of the new Mining brochures and advised him to study these and to come back if he wanted any further information.

During the past few days a man called Bruen had been coming into the office looking at some work Cole had been doing for him. He was a retrenched engineer of the Public Works Department and had taken up private practice as a surveyor. He had the habit of keeping his hat on in the office so I had a placard printed in black and red and placed where everybody coming into the office could not fail to see it. It read: 'GENTLEMEN having business behind the counter will kindly remove their HATS'. I noticed that it had the desired effect.

Dad gave me the following tale over tea one day: PopePius IX had enunciated the theory of the Immaculate Conception. When he died and sought admission to Heaven, St Peter refused to admit him. He appealed to God the Father without avail. He appealed to God the Son and was likewise unsuccessful. As a last resort he appealed to the Holy Ghost. 'Who?' enquired the Holy Ghost – 'Pius IX? What? Let that rascal into Heaven after he spread that scandal on Earth about me and the Virgin Mary – Not on your life!'

Shortly after I got home Sam Taylor called round, bringing with him a Mr and Mrs Thiel, some friends of his, who were going up the Mazaruni with him the following day. In the course of our conversation I learned that both Chislett and Fleming were also going up with them.

On my way to the office I dropped in at the Daily Chronicle and had a yarn with Delph who was supervising repairs to the foundations of the building which had been attacked by wood ants. I saw greenheart beams absolutely riddled by these insects. This greatly surprised me as I had always been under the impression that this wood was impervious to their attacks.

At ten o'clock I went to the steamer stelling to see Sam Taylor and his party off. Sam was clothed in trousers and a none too clean white shirt and wore no hat. He looked worried and perspiring. Thiel and Chislett were wearing khaki shirts and trousers that shouted their newness, whilst wide-brimmed cowboy hats crowned their heads. Mrs Thiel was similarly garbed and looked rather weird in slacks. Indeed, the whole group were the object of glances from the majority of the folk on the stelling who, though accustomed to seeing ladies departing for the interior in breeches, were unaccustomed to seeing female limbs enclosed in slacks. Calling me to one side, Taylor asked me what I thought of his gang. 'A proper bunch of crooks,' I replied.

CHAPTER XXI

CHRISTMAS AT KAMAKUSA

At the beginning of December 1932 the Commissioner told me that he wanted me to go up to Kamakusa to relieve Hastings as the latter was ill. He promised that I would not be there longer than six weeks. I went round to Krakowsky's office to enquire about a passage. There I found Clement Krakowsky looking pretty fed up about a trick that had been played on him. The previous evening, he had received a telephone message, purporting to come from the stationmaster at Parika to the effect that Gaspar had just arrived by boat from Bartica, very sick, and was proceeding to Vreed-en-Hoop by car and that Krakowsky should meet him there with a launch. Accordingly Clement had rushed off to the Customs and asked for their launch, but had been told that it would not be available for another hour. Then he received another message from Parika to the effect that Gaspar would not come through until morning. As soon as he got home he got a third message to the effect that Gaspar had just died at Parika. Because Gaspar was not only an employee but also a very good friend, Krakowsky naturally spent a very bad night. Next morning he rang the stationmaster at Parika to arrange to bring the body to town. Judge his surprise when the stationmaster denied all knowledge of Gaspar or of any telephone messages he had sent the previous night. No boat had arrived from Bartica nor had anyone died at Parika. Krakowsky had then gone to the police and had no sooner started to relate his story when the police inspector interrupted him, saying that he knew the culprit, an East Indian who had just come out of prison where he had been sent for playing a similar trick on someone else.

I was unable to get a passage through Krakowsky, nor from Pires & Silva's and was forced to go to J.C. Ginder Ltd and book a passage on the mail boat. This done, I went to Brodie's and Rainer's where I bought some goods for the house so that Phil and Walter at least would have their normal Christmas fare. In the evening, after a Masonic meeting at which W.E. Delph was installed as Master of Mount Olive, some of us adjourned to Mabels where a rough house dance was in progress. There I met a young fellow named Glasgow who was the captain of a rum-running schooner that was in harbour. Born in Scotland he had been taken to New South Wales where he had been brought up. He had worked as an officer with the Union Steamship Company of New Zealand until he piled one of their ships on the rocks with over 400 passengers on board. The outcome of this was his present job; the command of a schooner rum-running to the U.S.A. He said he was very uneasy as the schooner owner owed him over $500 and he couldn't get a cent and feared that the owners had gone bankrupt and left him holding the baby.

After two days preparation I was ready for the journey up to Kamakusa. Henry, who was coming along with me, and I were seen off at the stelling by Phil, Walter and Dad. At Parika we boarded the steamer *Basra* and proceeded up the Essequibo. During our stop at Fort Island I saw an East Indian with a fine sackiwinki monkey tied to a stick, which he was offering for three shillings. I could not resist the temptation of buying the comical looking creature, which promptly bit my finger in fright at its transfer of ownership. I arranged with the caterer on the boat that he would take it to town by Monday's steamer. One of the other passengers on the boat was B.R. Wood, the Conservator of Forests, and I spent the rest of the journey listening to his witty yarns about his life in India where he had spent a number of years before coming to British Guiana.

We arrived at Bartica on the stroke of seven and made our way to the Hotel Moderne where Henry and I shared a room. After dinner I went for a stroll with Arthur Greene, the sub-warden, to Austin's shop for a drink and on the way I slipped and sprained my ankle. Next morning, Sunday, I could not put any weight on my left foot so I decided to spend the day in bed resting and reading Sabatini's *Scaramouche*.

On Monday morning I went down to the post office and sent a radio to Walter telling him to meet the steamer and receive the monkey. With the mail boat from Mazaruni came C.T. Spence, the sub-warden, who was on his way to town for Christmas. We discussed conditions up at Kamakusa and Spence complained bitterly of the way he had been treated by Hastings. Back in the hotel I met Gillespie and McWatt who had come up from Parika in the police launch the previous night. They were going over to the Penal Settlement and invited Greene and me to go along with them. At the Settlement we were met by Neville Smith who took us up to his quarters.

In the living room I was surprised to see a large theodolite set up near one of the windows and was amused to hear Smith's story about it. Some time ago, when all the other officers were away, Smith had been asked to keep a watch on a gang clearing a patch of ground on the other side of the river. To avoid having to actually superintend the men personally he hit upon the idea of setting up the instrument in his room and having an occasional peep at them through the telescope. Once while watching them, he noticed that the gang was short by one man. So he quietly got in a boat, crossed the river and found the leader asleep under a little shack. When he woke him the man was so flabbergasted that he grabbed the alarm clock used to signal knocking off time, and ran up the hill with it in his hand. Smith still kept the theodolite in his room and amused himself watching the boats passing on the river. One afternoon he saw a big cargo boat coming down from the diamond fields, and another upward bound. The boats stopped and went alongside each other for a few moments, a breach of the Navigation Regulations. Later he heard that some diamonds had been lost in transit down river. They had been shipped on the very downward bound boat he had seen stop.

Shortly after nine o'clock next morning Henry and I boarded the mail boat *Gray Master*, a five ton cargo boat with a short tent immediately forward of the cargo space. Altogether there were some thirty persons on board of which about a dozen were regular boat hands. We were delayed for about an hour when one of the latter disappeared at the last moment. We saw the delinquent being dragged along by two policemen, having been found hiding behind the police station. The next delay was when Greene, in his position as Navigation Officer, ordered three half bags of rice to be taken out to leave the water line clear.

At last, we headed up the Mazaruni River but stopped at Barakara for a quarter of an hour for the captain, Leslie Vanderheyden, to get his baggage. At least that was the excuse he gave me for this breach of the Navigation Regulations. He made no excuse for the next stop, however, at Kartabo Point. We steamed up Tetruba and Marshall Falls; unloaded some cargo at the foot of Mapituri whilst we hauled up Kokobe Fall and swung back to the head of Mapituri to pick up our cargo. The river was extraordinarily dry and the journey prolonged in consequence. To add to these difficulties, the so-called first-class passage, for which $20 was charged, had few comforts. The tent, while extending the full width of the boat, was barely six feet long. A single cushion was placed on one of the narrow cross-benches and passengers sat here with their backs against biscuit drums, kerosene cases under their feet, whilst their knees barely cleared the backs of the wet and sweaty boat-hands in front. The bench immediately in front was covered with the boat-hands' baggage, so one could not put up one's feet, but had to sit straight up all the while. Immediately in front of us were some twenty fowls, in boxes and tied loosely by the legs.

Six o'clock found us at a place called Yapimoo, just above Crab Fall. The moment the bow of the boat touched the bank there was a wild scramble by the boat-hands as each man tried to mark a good position (by placing his hat at the desired spot) for slinging his hammock among the riverside trees. Any trespass on such a marked spot brought an instant and noisy row which, but for the presence of a magistrate, might have lead to blows. It being dry weather, no tent was put up ashore, but a runner was erected on two horses placed at bow and stern of the boat and over this a tarpaulin was thrown. The captain slung my hammock on this runner whilst he himself slept on the tarpaulin-covered cargo beneath me. Henry slept on the boat cushion in the tent boat.

Next morning the river was an inch higher than the previous night, and the captain predicted we would find deeper water higher up. At Maripa the cargo was unloaded except for a half dozen barrels of gasoline and beef, and carried over the rocks to the level water above. The bags of rice and flour were placed in one great pile and the cases in another. The latter, too close to the water and unstable, toppled over and two cases fell into the water. Then followed a wild scramble to rescue them before they were carried down the fall. They were retrieved just in time and the contents laid out to dry in the sun. One case consisted mostly of drugs and, in consequence did not require much attention but the other contained several dozens of drill trousers that had got thoroughly wet, so two Chinese tarpaulin passengers, (second class passengers who travel on top of the cargo) were set to dry them.

Whilst the boat was being warped up the fall, I sat on a rock and wrote up my journal. By ten o'clock we continued our journey to Arikara Fall where the boat was again lightened by the removal of some cargo. Whilst this was being done I made a water colour sketch of the fall from the upper end and, as the boat was being reloaded, I went for a walk along a wide itabo, the lower end of which debouched at the foot of the fall. Normally it was a regular river; now it was just an eighty-foot wide gash in the forest, its floor of rock and sand.

In the afternoon I suffered the stench of the sun-warmed fowl droppings in the boat bow. I finished reading *Scaramouche* and then began *The Crimson Smile*, a collection of humorous Russian short stories collected by M. Dekobra. In the late afternoon there was a short sharp thunderstorm accompanied by a little rain. We warped up Popikai Fall and its itabo and, about six o'clock, camped at the top of Amatuk Fall. After dark I was flashing my electric torch along the opposite bank when my attention was caught by two small spots of red light that glowed so intensely in the light of the torch that they were actually reflected on the surface of the water. The men told me they were the eyes of an alligator.

The river level had not changed during the night so that we were compelled to take the Kuipari Channel whence I got a glimpse of the hill from the foot of which Cheong, Lord, Belmonte and I began our trial survey in 1924. We now had several miles of still water before us, and the *Gray Master* lived up to her reputation as a fast boat.

At Topeku or Pimpler Fall the men had to unload and carry much of the cargo across the sharp rocks and warp the boat up. We got through Mary Fall, and, taking the Tamandua Channel close to the right bank, reached Sapira Fall at three o'clock. This is a low water fall, being level at high water, but was now turbulent and angry with the result that the boat again had to be unloaded and hauled up. Whilst this was in progress I made a water colour sketch of the fall from the bottom.

Going on a few hundred yards we came to the foot of Pabrakesh Itabo where the crew unloaded the boat completely and droghed the cargo across the portage. The barrels of gasoline and beef, too heavy to be lifted, were rolled across, each of the former requiring three men to trundle its 500lbs weight. I walked across to the upper end of the portage and looked across Kaburi Pool which was studded with rocks exposed by the low water. South Kaburi Fall was absolutely dry and presented a reddish brown colour on account of the withered water weeds that had died as the water receded. Returning to the lower landing I read *Wonder Stories Quarterly* while the boat was washed out. The tarpaulin had no sooner been put down when a short sharp shower of rain came on, so we took shelter in the boat.

During the night the river rose some three inches. Whilst the boat was being hauled up Pabrakesh Fall, Henry and I went across the portage and waited at the upper landing. Many cartabac were rising slowly to the surface, exposing their black backs and dorsal fins as they turned over and dived again. Looking down the Pabrakesh itabo I could see the twisted hull of a boat piled up against a water-worn rock at the top of the channel, water weeds growing in patches on the upturned bottom. This was the wreck of Ginder's boat, *Tiger Buddy*.

Our boat at length having been brought up, the cargo was reloaded and we crossed Kaburi pool to the rock at the foot of Station Itabo and that of North Kaburi, down which the water fell in two distinct ledges, each some four feet in height. Every piece of cargo again had to be taken out and droghed to the top of the fall. Whilst this was being done I made a water colour sketch of the upper portion of the North Kaburi Fall. I then walked up the Station Itabo and across South Kaburi and back, dryshod. I got back in the now empty boat, which was to be hauled up Paiarimap Fall, the only outlet between the two levels having sufficient water at present to float the boat. Steaming back into the pool we turned into the narrow shute barely twenty feet wide, down which the water poured at an angle of some twenty degrees. The boat was wedged towards the edge of the main current where an isolated rock broke its force and there the men sprang ashore and with all three lines began to haul whilst the bowman and two others stood chest deep in the current and braced the heavy boat off the rock with their shoulders, like modern Atlases.

Having at length got the boat up this ledge she was turned out of the main straight channel and hauled up a lateral one between two great boulders only a few inches wider than the craft. When this was negotiated we found ourselves on level water at the head of the fall and, crossing over, loaded the cargo again. We went on once more at about three o'clock; negotiated Haiowa and Mora Falls without unloading, until we came to Mora Boy Fall where the current necessitated taking out the cargo once again. As the cargo weighed in all about 14,000lbs, nearly seven tons, it will be realised that the constant loading and unloading was no light task. It was now that the Bartica bound mail boat passed, shooting down the fall with an easy grace, while our crew laboured on the ropes to get the *Gray Master* up into smooth water. Whilst they were thus occupied I wrote up my journal until a shower of rain compelled me to put away the book. The rain passed and we went on into the setting sun to the foot of Makari Fall where we camped at a quarter to seven.

In Bartica, Pequeno recommended an elderly East Indian by the name of Nattoo to look after my cooking on the journey up river. He was over sixty and absolutely hopeless. In my ration box I found all the tins mixed up in a mess of rice and sugar that had broken out from their parcels. Poor old Nattoo was so cold from working in the water all day that he was shivering and tumbling about all over the place. I relieved my feelings by expressing my views on Ginder's 'first class' passage.

During the evening I yarned with Vanderheyden who told me that a young cousin of his had been swimming in the river at Barakara when a perai took off one of his toes as neatly as though it had been done with an axe. Vanderheyden had immediately thrown out a fishing line and in a few moments caught a large perai. Cutting open the fish, he found the toe inside. Another story he told me concerned the voracity of the haimara. Whilst on a fishing expedition near Mary Fall he crossed a small itabo on a tacouba, the top of which was but a few inches above the water. His hunting dog, which was following him, slipped off the tacouba into the water. Leslie looked down and saw two great haimara tearing the animal in pieces as the water became reddened with its blood.

One of the boat-hands, a big burly Negro, slept on the tarpaulin close by my hammock and during the night kicked me on the head, but apart from this I had a restful sleep.

The boat was again completely unloaded and the cargo droghed to the top of Makari Fall which was roaring down at an angle of about thirty degrees. I walked on the rocks and was impressed greatly by the sight of the great river now consisting of acres upon acres of hard rock through the midst of which a single narrow channel of water had bored its way. The rocks lay in all manner of forms, here a shelf, there great boulders split by the elements, yonder they had the appearance of having been suddenly coagulated whilst boiling. One could imagine what a dead planet must be like.

The crew had a difficult time trying to haul the empty boat up the fall, but just when matters looked almost hopeless another boat arrived from up river and, her crew assisting ours, the boat was got up. Meantime I sat in the shade and wrote up my journal.

A short distance above Makari we passed yet another downward-bound boat that stopped alongside to borrow a couple of gallons of gasoline. During the afternoon I made a sketch of the crew resting in front of me, whilst the engine drove the boat along unaided in Karawarambo Still Water. About four o'clock we reached the foot of Itaki Fall and proceeded to unload all the cargo with the exception of the barrels. Whilst this was being done Vanderheyden spread a tarpaulin on the rocks and on this dumped the contents of the two great mail bags which I assisted him to sort. Significant of the changes in the district since I was last there two years ago was the fact that one of the largest bundles of mail was for Honey Camp, the new gold centre above Turesi.

Now another boat arrived at the top of the fall we were about to negotiate and her crew assisted ours on the warp, on which I counted over forty men. They tugged and strained and got the boat almost to the top when she began gradually to slip back. A second time they tried, and again the boat slipped back. Now the men on the stern line let go their firm hold with the result that the suck of the current swung the boat out into the fall and water immediately began to pour in over the quarter. Fortunately, as the result of the captain's hoarse screams, they got hold of the rope again and pulled the boat to safety.

All the beef and gasoline barrels were taken out and then the boat was finally hauled up. Our helpers then got back into their own boat which slid down the fall like an arrow and continued its downward journey. It was very exciting to watch this boat take the fall. Half way down the run was a large moss-covered rock just below the surface of the water, almost in the middle of the narrow channel, leaving but little room for the wide craft to pass. However, she cleared it safely and disappeared round a bend in the river. We noticed a most objectionable smell and the presence of a couple of carrion crows in a nearby tree directed our attention to a rock-bound pool at the edge of the forest in which lay the bloated body of a large alligator.

In the evening I listened to more of Vanderheyden's yarns. He told me about Captain Rhodius, our present bowman, bringing a boat down Itaki Fall a couple of months ago when he was in charge of a canister of gold and diamonds belonging to Krakowsky Bros. and Pires & Silva. The canister was on the stern bench and because the bend was taken too sharply a wave came over the stern and swept the canister overboard. Because of the strength of the current it was hopeless to try to dive for it, and the insurance was accordingly collected. Some time before, an similar incident happened to Captain Bellamy in Mutusi Hole but there, the water being shallow, the canister was recovered.

Scattered amongst the rocks in Itaki I saw numerous cases and barrels and learned that they had formed part of the cargo of Ginder's boat *Tiger Mail* which had been wrecked a few weeks before whilst attempting to steam up the fall. Vanderheyden told me that it was a common thing for barrels of beef to be lost at the bottom of North Kaburi as they were being unloaded from the boats. Because the rock was rather steep, the barrels sometimes got out of control of the men handling them and would roll down into deep water from where they were not always recovered. Some weeks previously a barrel had got away from Vanderheyden's crew. He dived for it and in so doing discovered two others that had been lost from previous boats.

At daybreak we continued our way up to the upper section of Itaki Fall, where once again the cargo was droghed over the portage. Whilst there Rhodius showed Vanderheyden and Henry where the canister of gold and diamonds had been lost. The water was now much lower and calmer than at the time of the accident, so, getting a long pole with which to sound, Henry and Vanderheyden took turns at diving to the bottom in search of the missing treasure but without success, as the strong current at the time must have swept it down and, in all probability, broken the canister open amongst the rocks.

Rhodius went fishing more successfully and returned with three large pacu and a lukunani. For bait he had used the seed of the water wallaba, which he called masetta. This bait pacu are very fond of, but it was the first time he had known a lukunani taking it. Unlike the pacu I had seen before, of a deep red, these fish were practically black with only a suspicion of red. Whilst waiting on the bank I made a water colour sketch of the lukunani and by the time I had finished it the boat had been hauled up and reloaded. We left the top of Itaki Fall at ten o'clock.

At Tonka Bean Camp, about a mile higher up, we stopped to issue rations to two men who had been there for thirty days guarding some cargo that had been left there by one of Ginder's boats that had broken down and had been compelled to return to Bartica.

At the little but powerful Paka-Paka Fall we once again unloaded and hauled the boat up. Rhodius was off with his fishing rod in search of more pacu. His agility in the water was marvellous. Wishing to cross over to some rocks above the fall and on the further side of the swift stream, he plunged boldly into the current, still holding his rod. He was swept down to the brink of the fall before he got his footing in chest-deep water, then began to walk up to the desired rock, using the fishing rod as a support against the powerful current that bubbled against his chest. Suddenly he lost his footing and was swept away, the rod, its butt fastened between the rocks, being left with its end quivering above the water. I was about to shout for the lifeline to be thrown when I saw him emerge safely in an eddy on the further side. Nothing daunted, he plunged back into the stream and retrieved his rod and returned to the rock where he proceeded with his fishing. When we were ready to go on again, he was too near to the fall to attempt to swim back from there, so a lifeline was thrown and he was hauled aboard like a fish.

At Kapuwera Fall, a short but very steep cataract, the cargo was unloaded again and the boat warped up. Henry and I remained on board during the process, which I found altogether too exciting for my liking. The crew had the greatest difficulty in getting the heavy craft up the steep ascent. When they had got it almost to the top it began to slip back into the boiling maelstrom and only the smartness of the man holding the end of the warp, who passed it round a stout tree limb and tied it, prevented this happening. Whilst the boat was being reloaded I noticed the river was rising perceptibly. I occupied my time in writing to Mother and Dad and bringing my journal up to date. Just before dusk we reached the foot of Kartauri Fall, where we camped for the night.

The river rose another three inches during the night, which pleased the crew as even an inch of water made a lot of difference in the navigation of the heavy cargo boats. Shortly after we started off we saw a fine powis standing at the edge of the water. The old Chinaman yelled, 'Look, a carrion crow', much to the amusement of the crew. Henry shot at it with his BSA air rifle and the smack of the slug could distinctly be heard as it struck the bird's head. The powis dropped, but, with the tenacity of life peculiar to these creatures, was up on its feet in an instant and running off into the forest. The boat was put ashore and four or five men ran into the forest but failed to find it.

Soon after it was discovered that the boat had sprung a leak. It was run onto a sand bank where, the leak having been located in the bow quarter, it was temporarily caulked with a piece of cloth.

Just below Turesi Fall we stopped at the camp of Nathaniel Charles to deliver mail and then steamed up through the fall, which was quite placid now. Shortly after ten o'clock we arrived at Honey Camp, a small settlement of some nine buildings strung along the right bank of the river at the foot of a low steep hill. It was the depot for the gold diggings some ten miles aback, and the shops of Tiam Fook, Pires & Silva and a magazine of Ginder's. In the Pires & Silva's shop I met the manager, Old Joaquim, with whom I had a glass of beer.

Leaving Honey Camp, we steamed up the great broad reach to Morabisi. I sat and listened to the bow crew yarning to themselves. The subject was R.D.L. Hill, the magistrate, and his escapades in Bartica. The previous August he had attended a dance there and, becoming exhilarated, started to throw his weight about, fought the police, knocked down Jock Aldie and hit poor Ogle in the stomach. Eventually he was overpowered, roped like a steer, and put to bed.

As the river continued to rise steadily, we were able to steam up Tiboku Fall without the assistance of the warp. Towards five o'clock we sighted Banana Landing, the depot for the Karanang gold and diamond fields. A very broad sand bank lay in front of this place and as the water over it was still too shallow to permit the loaded boat to pass, we had to stay about a quarter of a mile offshore, whilst a small boat put out for the mails. As we waited for it the wind blew us on to the sand bank and as the waves were fairly rough on the wide expanse of water, we had a little trouble getting off again. We continued travelling until half past seven when we stopped for the night at Robello's camp at Rock Point.

Here I saw a type of fish trap new to me. Vanderheyden called it a double mason and said it was commonly used by the Bovianders of the lower Mazaruni who learnt it from the Arawak Indians. It consisted of a basket-work cylinder about four feet in length and about eighteen inches in diameter, with a funnel at each end and a hinged door at the side through which the bait was inserted and the trapped fish removed. It was made of laths about three quarters of an inch wide cut from the outer skin of a palm tree.

We made an early start in the morning and by the time I had shaved and written up my journal we were in Kamakusa, most glad to bring a very uncomfortable journey to an end. How different to when, some eight years previously, the Warden travelled to and from Bartica in his own boat. Now the conditions of travel put senior government officers in extremely *infra dig* positions; the principal claim-holders did not travel up and down the rivers in cargo boats but in their own, comfortable tent boats. It was formerly the condition of the mail contract that the warden should have the exclusive use of the whole passenger accommodation of the mail boat when he travelled, but this had apparently been omitted from the contract in recent years.

I found Hastings in his house, looking by no means ill. The gallery had been converted into an office and a boat-hand was thumping away at a typewriter. Hastings informed me that he rarely used the office as it was too hot. I suspected that it was because of his desire to evade the expenditure of the energy required to move to and from it.

After breakfast I formally took over from Hastings and gave him my opinion of his pretending illness in order to get to town for Christmas. He had apparently had a touch of pleurisy a month or so previously, but he appeared to be completely recovered when I saw him. I pointed out that I had already spent two Christmases in Kamakusa, and it was up to him to take his turn. Having concluded my remarks, the truth of which he denied with a hurt dignity, Hastings proceeded there and then to get an attack of fever and, declaring he could hardly stand up, deputed Stoly, the captain, to show me the items on the inventory. By the time I had checked this I was so fed up that I went to my bed and slept.

I spent the next morning going over the papers with Hastings and found things in an awful muddle, no proper record of files having been kept, and this led to another row when I told him what a thoroughly lazy bounder I thought him to be. When he finally departed by the mail boat in the afternoon he neglected to say good-bye.

Harry Bornstein came down with the mail boat and I was pleased to have someone to talk to. Whilst we sat yarning he told me about an unpleasant experience he'd had coming up the river in February last. They had reached Kartauri Fall at three o'clock in the afternoon and run hard and fast on a rock in otherwise deep water, with a very swift current on one beam and a strong suck-tide on the other. The water was too deep for the men to wade ashore and the current too swift to permit their swimming. The captain declared that if the water rose, the boat, from the position in which she was jammed on the rock, would capsize, and if the river level dropped, the weight of the cargo would break the boat's back. So he hummed and hawed and did nothing until, just before dusk, a young Indian boy who was on board, managed to get across the current with a fishing line in his hand. Having reached an island he dragged the lifeline across and, by means of this warp, made the boat fast. Nevertheless, the rest of the crew refused to risk the passage across the maelstrom, even with the rope, and so they remained all night huddled together and wondering what was going to happen. Bornstein suggested to the captain that he jettison some of the cargo and so lighten the boat sufficiently to get her off the rocks but it was not until seven o'clock the following morning, after sixteen hours in their precarious position, that the captain agreed to throw the gasoline and beef barrels overboard. The boat, thus lightened, was got safely off the rock and the journey continued without further adventure.

Having sorted out things in the office to the best of my ability, I packed up and left Kamakusa in the tent boat, *Anarabisi,* driven by an Archimedes engine and, accompanied by Henry, a police orderly and a crew of three, headed up river. The *Anarabisi* had been acquired from my old friend Mark-a-book (A. Husbands) who had called it *Flying Fox*. It was the custom of some of his friends, whenever they got the chance, to pull the old boy's leg by changing the second 'F' of this name into a 'P'! I spent the afternoon in the boat making a new index for the Prospecting Licences Register, the one in use having been allowed to get into an awful mess through the illegible and careless writing of the boat-hand clerks and the careless insertion of oversize extra leaves.

In the vicinity of Sipari Island we picked up the police boat which had broken down with Sergeant Osbourne on board. We towed him up to Oranapai where we arrived about five o'clock. I had dinner with Henry Bornstein in his very confined living quarters (between his shop and his backstore) during which he gave me an interesting account of some orthodox Jewish customs. In the evening Henry and I adjourned to Farrier's old house where we put up for the night, the building now being used as Courthouse and Warden's quarters. After coffee I went back to Bornstein's and bought a fortnight's rations from him. I then inspected the three shops in the locality, those of Bornstein, J.G. Stephens and Pires & Silva, as well as the several tracts held under Crown Lands permissions, which were mainly in the names of women of the fields.

My work at Oranapai completed, we set off again up river, Bornstein accompanying us. Our next port of call was Buck Cannister Sands, and what a different place it was to the Sands City I had known before. Of the eight shops that two years previously had lined the river bank and the hills behind, only one remained and even this was not one of the original eight. Second growth forest had already grown to a good height on most of the business sites, and close to the blackened and charred posts of Mark-a-book's shop was a smaller building, the headquarters of Wolf Nagler. Beside it was Mark-a-book's house, much as it had been but improved by the addition of modern sanitary conveniences.

Here I found fat Bentham in charge and, walking up the hill, found Moore's old shop converted into a dwelling house at the door of which a young Negro woman was standing, clothed in a lemon-yellow dress which, until she saw me, she was holding high enough to expose the greater part of a not unshapely ebony thigh. Her name, she informed me, was Justina Fredericks, and her six months contract as a domestic with McGillivary having just expired, she wanted it renewed. She wished her new employer to be the owner of the house outside which she was standing, a young black man named Stanton who was making a brave attempt to cultivate the surroundings.

Leaving Bornstein with Bentham, we proceeded up river, stopping at Sampsons Landing for breakfast. Whilst the meal was being prepared I went for a walk along the Red Hill to Eping Trail. In very dry weather, when navigating the Eping River was very difficult, the mails were sent in by this trail, which joins the river just above Krakowsky's shop and then runs up the bank to the police station.

In the afternoon we came to McGillivary's headquarters at Red Hill. Externally the building looked the same as before with its three foot wide longitudinal stripes of alternate blue and white and the owner's six foot high initials painted on the zinc roof. Inside, however, I found the shop empty, the back store being full of goods and I learnt from the watchman that the place was now used as a magazine for the owner's shops at Kurupung and Apaikua. McGillivary was away at the latter place and was expected back in a few days time.

Moving on, we came to Enachu which at first sight looked much as I had left it. Having inspected Pillay's shop, where the owner and his son told me that they did not sell enough in a week to feed themselves, I sent the boat on to Ginder's whilst the orderly and I walked overland, through the collapsing frame of Triefus' abandoned shop to Yhip's, which I inspected. Thence to Ginder's, where the first thing I noticed was D.E. Pierre's beautiful garden, enclosed by high wire-mesh and with numerous rose bushes in tubs. Formal flower beds were separated from each other by paths of real white gravel and not broken shell, whilst the rear of the enclosure was packed with young green vegetables. Learning that Pierre was also up at Apaikua, the recently discovered diamond field, we went on to Krakowsky's headquarters.

The most noticeable feature here was the newly-replaced dispensary. The manager's quarters at Krakowsky's had also been enlarged and now consisted of an open verandah, an office, a large dining and sitting room, a bedroom and bathroom, not to mention numerous electric lights festooned all over the place and worked by a small Delco plant. Weiss, the manager, had been taken down to the hospital at Kamakusa a few days before, but young Nascemento, the shop manager, made us very comfortable and we listened to some classical music on a fair gramophone, though since getting my electric machine, my ear was spoilt for all of the old type machines.

After tea I walked across to Ries' hill, the old site of M.A. Goring's shop. I was surprised to see that the whole hill had been cleared of forest, fenced and planted with grass on which some half dozen cattle were grazing contentedly. What was more surprising was that a fair attempt had been made to level all the stumps and outcropping rocks. This I learnt subsequently was because the clearing was intended primarily as a landing strip. However, the aeroplane for which it had been made had crashed in Bartica earlier in the year. After a short chat with Ries and some Strauss music on his very good gramophone, I went for a walk some half mile aback to the house of Addie Spencer, an old and very black lady friend of mine, with whom I yarned for half an hour.

Returning to Krakowsky's, we sat down to a very fine dinner, at which the table waiting was performed by two well-dressed young black girls who lived in an electrically lit range of rooms behind the cricket field, and were registered as domestics with Krakowsky's. I found this particularly amusing, knowing that the girls were unblushing members of the oldest profession, and knowing that it was for my express benefit that they were deputed to act in accordance with the terms of their registration certificates as domestic servants.

The whole situation of women in the diamond fields had taken on a Gilbertian air, and this through the half-hearted interference of Government who had succeeded excellently in making themselves a laughing stock in the matter. In former years women bought mining privileges and came into the diamond districts with no one to say nay. Wherever they went, enough willing hands were ready to put up more or less comfortable shacks and the arrival of a new girl at any centre was the occasion of much gun-firing into the air and the consumption of many drinks. Ninety nine percent of these women were out and out prostitutes, but they numbered amongst them a few who, in addition to their ancient trade, actually went in for mining, with their own registered labourers. One of the most famous of these was the notorious but ill fated Hannah Da Silva, better known as Judge Box, who was shot by her husband, himself originally one of her own registered labourers. I knew Hannah for a couple of years before her death. In her youth she must have been a remarkably good looking girl. Her greatest weakness was drink and it was this what ultimately led to her downfall. Others of these women were harpies of the worst class who battened off the shopkeepers and assistants, encouraging them to steal their employers' goods and money and, on a few occasions, even diamonds. Things came to such a pass that Ginder and Houston, two of the leading traders, approached the Commissioner of Lands and Mines for some relief in the shape of restrictions being placed on 'loose' women coming into the diamond fields.

The press, inspired possibly from the same source, took the matter up and scarce a week would pass without some person, generally anonymous, writing a painful story about the starving wives and children on the coast, abandoned because their bread-winners could not tear themselves away from the sensuous embraces of the ladies of the fields. It struck me at the time that, if such men did exist, their wives and children were well rid of them. The type who hung round the women's houses, fetched and carried and generally acted as pimps for them, were often of the lowest sort who never did, or intended to, work to support a wife and children.

With all this outcry, Government decided they should do something, so the order went out that no further mining titles were to be issued to women. The first thing to happen was the receipt by the Commissioner of a telegram from Houston ordering him to instruct the sub-warden at Bartica to let his (Houston's) housekeeper accompany him up the Mazaruni, the latter official having refused to allow his boat to clear with the woman aboard. Then for a week Mullin was besieged by lawyers whose clients desired to take their female companions with them to the diamond fields. The legal gentlemen soon convinced the Commissioner that he had no power under the law to prevent them, so he wriggled out of the awkward position by permitting women to go who were registered as domestic servants with responsible claim-holders.

This might have worked satisfactorily if the claim-holders as a whole had backed him up, but they did not. One can hardly blame them as no serious check of such registrations was made by the Department in town where these 'permissions to register' were granted. Consequently, it became the practice for women desirous of going to the diamond fields to approach any claim-holder in town and asking him to register them. As often as not he did, with the result that they got registered for an employer whom probably they might not set eyes on again during the whole six months of their service. Thus at one time, in 1930, checking up on these permits, I found my friend Correia had no less than seven women registered for him as domestic servants, though I knew he actually employed none.

Towards the end of 1930 I began chivvying these women back to the premises of their respective nominal employers and threatening to eject them from the district if they did not stay put. But it was a hopelessly time-consuming task and I could not imagine that Government intended the warden-magistrate to occupy himself exclusively chasing prostitutes all over the district, so I gave it up and let things slide. I did, however, exercise my powers as warden in regard to four of these women. Mary Hudson and Carrie Harding I ordered out of the district after conviction for assault and on representations of the police. Mary Stanford I put out on the representations of the Chief Government Dispenser and Laletha Da Silva was similarly dealt with on the representations of Harvey William's friends who feared her continued presence would lead him to commit an assault himself. But I now saw that the Commissioner had allowed all four to return, so I did not propose worrying myself any further.

In 1929 the Department had even begun threatening claim-holders of permissions that these would not be renewed if they allowed loose women to reside on their premises. They went as far as to embody this in the conditions under which permissions were held, but it made no difference. If the threat had been carried out, the permissions of the principal diamond traders, such as Krakowsky, McGillivray, Stephen, Ries and others, would have had to be cancelled and such action would have raised more dust than Mullin would have cared to see.

Meanwhile Hastings had capped the entire comedy by warning everybody in writing to have their accounts covering the payment of registered labourers, especially of their domestic servants, ready for his inspection. This raised such a roar of laughter that it was a wonder he could not hear it as he sat telling his beloved Junks down in Cove and John what a hard time he'd had up here.

The following morning Tommy Houston passed up on his way to Eping from Ginder's where he had been recovering from an amusing shipwreck. Whilst in the middle of a spree at Krakowsky's, the mail boat arrived with the news that Rosenstraunch had arrived at Buck Cannister Sands with the girls Edina Wolf and Laletha Da Silva. Without more ado Tommy got in his boat and hustled off to the Sands whither he arrived sometime after midnight and woke up Rosenstraunch and the girls and spent the remainder of the night with them.

Rosenstraunch had come in to take over the assets of Wolf Nagler. These included two cows which he promptly sold to Tommy, who put them in his boat and, taking the two girls with him, set off up the river for Eping. When he was almost opposite Ginder's at Enachu one of the animals suddenly kicked one of the bottom boards out of the boat which immediately began to sink. The cries of the girls attracted the attention of those ashore and a couple of boats came out to their assistance. They managed to get the cows untied before the boat went down but most of the girls' baggage got well soaked before it was retrieved.

After he had gone, I heard about one of his other escapades. Some weeks previously he and Robles, one of Krakowsky's European diamond buyers, were playing poker for moderate stakes, drinking as they played. Eventually Robles insisted that the stakes should be unlimited and, after hesitating for some time, Tommy agreed, with the result that he took $700 off his opponent.

After spending an hour in the office I learnt that Pierre had returned from Apaikua so I went down to Ginder's to have a yarn with him. He told me that Hastings was a by-word for laziness in the district and that he had outstayed his welcome here. After breakfast with him I went to Ries' shop, which I inspected, and then went up to Tumareng where I inspected the magazine that served as the headquarters for Pires & Silva. I returned to Krakowsky's where, after inspecting the shop, I did some more office work until Rosenstraunch dropped in for tea. He was full of his experiences of coming up the river through the falls. He had travelled out to the colony from Miami by seaplane and vowed that this aerial journey had fewer thrills than he had experienced on the Mazaruni between Bartica and Tiboku. I assured him he would have even greater thrills on the downward journey. He said he thought he would prefer to wait up here until a seaplane service was established.

Next day I dropped down to Ginder's where, in Pierre's comfortable quarters, I held an enquiry into the wreck of the mail boat *Tiger Mail* at Itaki. The captain, Henry Grant, although warned of the enquiry, failed to turn up so I took the evidence of the bowman, engineer and several boat-hands, as well as that of Pierre, who had travelled by the same boat on the voyage immediately prior to the accident.

The story of the witnesses was that, on arriving at the foot of the lower fall, the captain had a portion of the cargo unloaded and then started to steam across the channel so as to enable the crew to haul the boat on the further side. Whilst crossing, the boat hit a rock, turned on its beam and sank. The mail canister, with a fair amount of money, was swept away and as the hinges of the cover as well as the lock were broken, both it and its contents were lost. Despite repeated official warnings, the bowman was not at his post but at the awkward paddle at the stern at the time of the accident, the bow paddle being wielded by an unqualified boat-hand. In addition, it was proved that Captain Grant took out less cargo at this spot before crossing than he did on the previous trip when he had Pierre, his employer, on board, even though the water was some eight inches lower than on the previous trip. On the evidence, I found the accident due to gross negligence on the part of the captain in that he did not unload his craft sufficiently before crossing and also to his neglect in not having his bowman at his proper post.

After taking breakfast with Pierre, I did some office work until the departure of the mail boat when I dropped down to McGillivray's where I found him and M. Correia busy with their correspondence. I went off and wrote up my journal till dinner and after the meal got into my hammock and fell asleep.

Correia's cargo boat arrived up at Red Hill the next morning, so he left us immediately after coffee and set out in it for Apaikua. McGillivray accompanied me later in my boat whilst his own was loaded up with cargo, mainly liquor, for his shop at Apaikua, following my suggestion that he would have a more comfortable trip with me. Shortly after eleven o'clock we stopped on a sand bank at San San Kopai to cook breakfast.

It was a dreary afternoon travelling up the long reaches of lonely river and the occasional showers of rain added to the dreariness. Towards six o'clock we reached Anaribisi Island where we found Correia's boat broken down and progressing at a snail's pace by means of half a dozen paddles, so we stopped and took him on board. We were now amidst the new diamond workings and at several points on the right bank could see groups of pork knockers having their evening bath at the edge of the river, as well as on the island, where wisps of blue smoke curling up into the evening air indicated the presence of camp fires.

Swinging a bend, we came in sight of the Meamu River and, a short distance below it, a newly cleared hill on the summit of which could be distinguished a couple of tarpaulin camps. At the waterside, the familiar outline of Sam Taylor could be distinguished, but as we got ashore the difference to the spick-and-span white-suited and helmeted figure familiar in town increased and I hardly recognised the disreputable, old, brown-bearded Boer who now greeted me.

At his camp we found Thiel lying in a sugar bag tarimba, weak as a child after a week's bout of fever. Mrs Thiel, still clad in khaki shirt and slacks, was hustling round superintending the camp chores. Under a nearby tarpaulin I found Chislett and Bill Fleming, the two young Englishmen who were with them. Mrs Thiel insisted on our staying to dinner, so we sent my boat on up to Apaikua with Correia who wanted to get up there as soon as possible and arranged for McGillivray's boat to return for us as soon as it had discharged its load.

We had dinner al fresco, sitting about on the sick man's tarimba, in hammocks and on boxes. Taylor had certainly got a rough and ready camp for his friends though he told me he was building a house on the actual summit of the hill, some fifty feet higher than his present location. Dinner over, McGillivray, Henry and I bade the folks goodnight and set out on the last mile of our journey. The night was pitch black and we had to thread our way between the rocks of Apaikua Fall. I had the wind up as the grey forms of rocks loomed up out of the darkness and the black current was discernible by the patches of foam that floated into the dim light shed by a single lantern slung over the bow of the boat. I gave a sigh of relief as we finally reached McGillivray's landing, a pile of jumbled rocks at the immediate top of the fall.

In McGillivray's shop a gang of men was playing cards round a long table on which was burning a single acetylene lamp. They were playing *vingt-et-un* or, as they termed it 'vinshoon'. At McGillivray's suggestion

I joined in. The chips were valued at five cents each, the maximum bet being six chips. Nevertheless, despite the moderate stakes, when the bank came to me I dropped $15 in the first two hands. Drawing an ace, I had double but found two players with five cards against me. On the next hand I drew another ace and, reckoning such bad luck couldn't repeat itself immediately, doubled again. Again two pairs of five knocked me down. We played until three o'clock and I had a loss of $10.

As McGillivray had not got round to building his residential quarters and his manager occupied the only bed, which was in the diamond buying office, he slung his hammock over one end of the counter in the shop and I mine over the other, the salt meats end. Henry had his in the space between and the front of the shop.

After completing my office work I held a Magistrate's Court at McGillivray's dining table. The police were charging a young black man with assaulting a young black woman, Mary Stanford, one of the four women I had earlier put out of the district. The sordid details, as described by the police in a matter of fact manner, were typical of one side of life here. Defendant paid his money and had a short time. When finished he was not satisfied and, demanding his money back, held on roughly to the woman who screamed for assistance. The police not pressing the case and the defendant expressing contrition, I advised him in future to take life as he found it, reprimanded him and ordered him to pay costs.

I took the boat up to Correia's but found that he had not yet finished stocking his shop although he hoped to have it ready by Christmas Eve in two days time. Sending the boat back I walked down to Krakowsky's where I found my old friend Joe Barker in charge. Also there, acting as cook, was my old house boy, Frank Spencer whom Hastings had discharged after my departure from Kamakusa in 1930. The shop, although only recently opened, was already under repair, a large tree having fallen on it and demolished the rear portion, fortunately without more loss than one flask of gin. It is extraordinary that in every accident involving damage to property it is invariably alcohol that suffers first and most.

Consuming several beers I had long yarn with Barker who agreed that the diamond trade here was crooked from top to bottom and added that he had got into the habit of doubting every man's word. When a pork knocker told him that a rival firm had offered him $150 for a diamond, he mentally decided that the offer did not really exceed $90. Barker then accompanied me to the next shop, Ginder's. We passed the site chosen by Yhip for his shop, crossed a narrow creek on a high tacouba and passed the house of Caroline Harding, a very dark and powerful limbed girl, who was at home ironing a gorgeous coloured night-dress and expressed her pleasure at seeing me again.

Ginder's shop was packed with diamond diggers who had begun their Christmas celebrations. One could scarcely move in the place. A great big mustachioed Negro, by the name of Bush, who was half tipsy, was twanging on a guitar and singing an improvised song about the beasties of the Apaikua diamond field. Those who had no money, and they appeared to be in the minority, were drinking at the expense of their friends. John English, the young Negro shop manager, was busily buying diamonds and, after I had made a perfunctory inspection of the shop, he invited me up to his quarters just below the shop where he would join me as soon as he was free. His house, yet unfinished, consisted of a board floor and palm-leaf roof and was furnished with a single table and a couple of benches. The floor being some four feet off the ground and the steps not yet erected, it required some agility to get into it.

We were no sooner installed when the jet-black features thatched with snow-white hair of old dispenser Bollers appeared. We helped the old gentleman up into the house where he literally fell on my neck with pleasure at seeing me again. English produced several bottles of beer and we had a most enjoyable time.

Presently two girls were seen approaching from the direction of Pires & Silva and as they got nearer English called them to join the party. One was Justina Fredericks, my friend of the yellow dress at Buck Cannister Sands, who in the meantime had changed her mind about being registered as a domestic for Stanton and decided to remain with the old firm of McGillivray to whom she had come up that morning. The other, Florence Mitchell, was one of the most pleasant-faced girls I had ever met and her disposition corresponded with her face. English insisted that we joined him at breakfast which was brought up forthwith from the shop kitchen and, when the meal was over, Bush arrived with his guitar and more liquor inside him and sang a ditty of welcome in my honour.

It was then close on four o'clock, so I decided to move on to Pires & Silva the next shop, the girls deciding to accompany me. Here we found a similar but bigger crowd and at the request of Dean Gouveia, the manager, we adjourned to a back room where more beer was forthcoming. Bush again turned up with his guitar and before I knew where I was, the two girls were giving a wonderful exhibition of the *dance a ventre*. The contortions with which they twisted their bodies were astounding and I am sure that they never learnt this but inherited it in their blood from their ancient African ancestors.

Henry then arrived in search of me and we all returned in the dark by the light of bottle torches to McGillivray's where we found McGillivray himself presiding over a big game of *vingt-et-un* in his back store. Not wanting to join in the game I accepted the girls' invitation to go along to their house behind the shop where we had a much needed supper of boiled pork, part of a pig that had been slaughtered that morning. Dean Gouveia soon joined us at the feast and the next thing I knew it was close on five o'clock when I left the house and returned to the shop where I climbed into my hammock above the pork and beef barrels.

After some three hours sleep I got up and went down to Taylor's and had a long yarn with him about his plans for working in the area. Leaving him, I dropped down the river to Anarabisi where I went ashore at St Rose's Landing and struck inland through a series of flat plateaux rising in a series of short steep slopes until I came to St Rose's Camp, a large clearing containing some dozen camps. St Rose was away in town, but I saw his manager, an elderly black man named Drakes, who complained bitterly about the number of men who, working on a neighbouring claim of Cox's, slept in St Rose's camps and refused to leave on being ordered to do so. Having inspected the claim registers I went to St Rose's claims, Why Worry and Elder, where I saw several crews of porkknockers at work. From there I went on to Francis Jacob's Dodo No.1 where I found that old pioneer at work with a gang of registered labourers. I noticed here that in certain spots the diamond gravel was of a pinkish colour, almost more like gold gravel. Moving on I went to Cox's claim, Look Out, where the men that Drakes had complained about were pointed out to me. I went over to them and warned them to get out of St Rose's camp within twenty four hours or face the consequences.

Someone hailed me and, glancing up the shallow gully, I saw the well known and ever youthful figure of my old friend, Duncan Stuart, standing under an umbrella and watching the jigging of a sieve. Beyond him some sixty to seventy men were working in crews at their pits, the whole floor of the forest-filled valley a scene of great activity. Duncan introduced me to Horace Cox, the owner of the claim, a youthful, short brown man in a large hat. I also met a bunch of my old acquaintances here including J. Robello, Manine Lovell, Perkins, Dan French and numerous others who had been given positions on the claim by Cox and were working their own pits. I was asked to 'bust a sieve' as it is termed, the searching of the sieve for diamonds after digging. At Cox's order, a jigger came out of a pool and brought a gravel-filled sieve to me. I began scooping the coarser gravel from the top and then with two fingers pushed aside more lightly the finer concentrates in the centre until the dark metal mesh was exposed. Fastened in the mesh I spotted two small diamonds as well as a sweetman, which I mistook for the former.

Together with Stuart and Robello, Cox took us to his little house on a nearby hill, on the way showing me a pit from which one hundred and fifty carats had been obtained. Once in the house we were all served with wine. Having examined the claim registers I returned to my boat and made my way back to Apaikua.

Christmas Eve found me going up to Le Desir Creek with McGillivray to verify his claim, Le Desir, and we had no sooner started the survey by pace and compass, when a steady rain came on and continued until we had finished. Dropping back to Apaikua we went ashore at Correia's shop, which was by then stocked and open. Much of his dry goods had got wet on the journey up river and he now had them hanging on cords to dry in the roof of the building where they presented a kaleidoscopic array of colours, being mostly female dresses and intimate garments.

A couple of whisky's and some Christmas cake with Correia warmed us up and we returned overland to McGillivray's where, sitting in the one and only chair, and clad in shirt and shorts, we found Edina Wolf awaiting us, she having arrived from lower river about half an hour beforehand. This girl had a jinx with regard to boats. Having been on board Houston's boat when the cow sank it the previous week, she had just figured in the wreck of Krakowsky's boat in which she came up from Enachu. This boat, just before entering Apaikua fall, ran onto a rock and got stove in. Fortunately the captain was able to run ashore and get the cargo transferred to Ginder's and Rosenstraunch's, which being nearby, rushed to his assistance, before she sank.

After dinner we all sat down as usual to a game of *vingt-et-un* in the back store, Rosenstraunch but not Weiss joining in the game. Out in the shop some thirty to forty men were packed, drinking and singing songs to the accompaniment of a 'foo-foo' band. Edina lay on the bed in the diamond office and occupied herself watching both parties. Having lost yet another $10 I withdrew from the game and went into the shop where I had some beers with Joe Barker, who did not gamble.

When he left I got into conversation with Florrie Mitchell who after a while invited me down to her house where she produced a bottle of whisky. Eventually she got into a pair of scarlet beach pyjamas and told me she proposed to wander round the shops in them. As she set out on her masquerade I returned to McGillivray's at what must have been about three o'clock on Christmas Day where I threw myself down on the unoccupied section of the bed, my hammock not having been slung as usual. At daybreak I was awoken by a terrific shouting and, on opening my eyes, beheld, sitting on the counter an ebony siren in scarlet beach pyjamas. It was of course Florrie Mitchell who, with big Joe Welcome, had come to wish us a Happy Christmas.

After coffee I went to Krakowsky's where, in the back store, Weiss sat in his hammock surrounded by a couple of dozen men and three or four women who were celebrating Christmas in the approved style. Duncan

Stuart soon arrived up looking very down in the mouth, as his pit had been cleared up the previous afternoon without any diamonds being found, whilst everyone around him had been more or less successful. Poor Duncan seemed to be dogged by persistent bad luck with his diamond digging though many of his friends put it down to his own carelessness in not watching his men properly. It was often said that whilst ostensibly watching his jigger he was often sitting down engrossed in a novel. There is no doubt that on several occasions claims that he had abandoned as worthless had turned up trumps for those who followed him. Opinion was that his men got the diamonds, and this through his own slackness.

About eleven o'clock we packed up the boat and with McGillivray, Duncan Stuart and Edina Wolf, set off down the river to Taylor's hill. At the landing we saw Big Sam on top of the hill firing off several rounds from a great rusty automatic pistol which he had to hold with both hands. This was his Christmas greeting to us. We found Thiel considerably better, sitting up in his hammock and smiling. We all sat down to Christmas lunch, which Edina helped Mrs Thiel to serve. We had quite a good blow out, which I rounded off with the last of the cigars Gauge Griffiths had given me for Christmas just before I left town.

At three o'clock McGillivray left on his return to Apaikua in my boat which went up to fetch Weiss who had asked me to give him a passage down to Enachu. With Duncan Stuart, Edina and Weiss, we left Taylor's hill and set off on our thirty-odd mile trip down to Enachu. Arriving shortly after eight thirty we sat down to a sumptuous dinner, at which Edina presided at the head of the table, clad now in normal female garments. Afterwards there was dancing, but feeling too tired to participate I asked Duncan Stuart to walk over to the dispensary to see Abrams but from the sounds of feminine laughter that was coming from his bedroom we guessed he was otherwise engaged so we started back to Krakowsky's.

As we descended the clay hill from the dispensary, Duncan leading, his feet suddenly shot from under him and he came down on the broad of his back. The situation was so humorous that I just sat down and laughed as Duncan, growling something inaudible, picked himself up and went on his way, while I sat on top of the hill trying to decide whether I should risk negotiating the slippery path and waiting to see whether Duncan would return. He did not, and subsequently told me that he too had sat down by a tacouba in the path for quite a while waiting for me and, as I did not come, had gone on to Krakowsky's. Meanwhile I decided to return to the dispensary where I tumbled into a hammock that was slung in the dining room.

Waking up shortly after six my first impression was the look of surprise on Abrams' face as he opened his bedroom door and found me still in his house. I explained my night's adventure and made my way to Krakowsky's for coffee. The great event of the day here was a cricket match between Apaikua and Enachu in which I and Ben Perkins had been asked to act as umpires. For gowns of office we borrowed silk dressing gowns from Prudence Bellamy, one of the women living in Krakowsky's range. After the first innings I found the sun too hot to allow me to remain in the field, so I retired and went down to Ginder's where we had some more drinks, returning to Krakowsky's for dinner.

In the evening I went to Ginder's where a dance was in progress in the large dance hall there, the orchestra being augmented by a piano, the first I had seen in the diamond fields. I stayed there until the early hours of the morning when I found my way back to Pierre's quarters where I found him, still in his clothes, spread-eagled across his bed with his head hanging over the side, dead to the world. Having succeeded in levering him into a more comfortable position and shoving a pillow under his head I flung myself down beside him and got a couple of hours sleep until daylight when, after coffee, I went down to Ginder's where the dance was still in progress. After breakfast at Abrams I boarded my boat taking with me Gewerc, Henry Bornstein's brother-in-law, as well as two pork knockers who had asked for a passage.

Going into the Eping all went well until we came to the fall which looked rather turbulent. As we tried to steam up it, the boat bounced on a rock broadside on with such force as to throw the pork knocker who was acting as bowman, with great violence into the water. The poor fellow struck his knee sharply against a submerged stone. Having got him back on board, we ran the warp ashore and hauled the boat up the fall.

At Perenong Mouth we camped with Gewerc at Bornstein's shop. Going over to Correia's shop I had a yarn with Louis Gomes whom I found in bed with his head bound up in a damp cloth, trying to recover from the effects of Christmas. John Campbell joined us at dinner at Gewerc's and told us that during the previous week an Indian named Isaiah, who was fishing in the upper Eping, had sunk with his woodskin at the very spot where, some ten years earlier, E. Brindley Babb got swamped and lost all his belongings. Whilst diving for his woodskin, Isaiah had discovered Babb's canister with his diamond scales inside.

Proceeding on up the Perenong I inspected the various shops as I came to them. At Pires & Silva's, the manager, a young coloured fellow, Henry de Souza, asked me to swear him an affidavit. He had apparently submitted a story to *True Stories Magazine* and the editor required an affidavit to the effect that the story was an original composition and not copied from any other publication. I did not spend more than a day up the Perenong as I was afraid the water level would drop and leave me stranded, so having completed my business there I hurried back down to the Mazaruni and so back to Kamakusa.

Back in the office I learnt of the loss, whilst it was being hauled up Makari Fall, of Austin's boat, *Swift No.6*. The news did not surprise me as when I had assisted Green to inspect this new boat whilst I was in Bartica I had prophesied then that she would never reach Kamakusa, so ungainly and punt-like was she. Her maximum depth of three feet six was carried fore and aft to within a few feet of bow and stern. Such were the boats now being built, and yet they complied with the regulations as to maximum length, breadth and depth. In former days, craft were considered safe for a load of 12,000lbs yet these new craft were carrying some 18,000lbs, not including the weight of the crew and their baggage and had only a freeboard of ten inches. The *Swift No.6* had travelled on her maiden voyage in company with one of her sister boats and thus had a double crew to haul her up the falls, and so was able to reach Kamakusa but, on her second trip, when she travelled alone, her crew were unable to hold her and she slipped back and was wrecked in the fall.

I began compiling a new Claim Register as the existing one as kept by Hastings and his boat hand clerks was in such a hopeless mess, but after about a week in the office it was time to set off up the river again. The day we left, Henry was feeling a little sore as he had awoken to find that vampire bats had attended to his toes during the night; his sheet and blanket were stained with blood.

Whilst in Oranapai I met Mary Nicholls, a great fat Negro woman, who had lived there for a number of years. She was originally a cook at the Ice House Hotel when Dad used to stay there. Mary then unburdened her soul to me concerning Hastings. She said he always carried Junks' photo about with him and kept it on his office table in camp, only turning it face downwards when he held Court. He canvassed all the shops to get them to take the hot sauce and preserves she had made. All the hot sauce at Stephen's shop went bad, so Hastings told Stephen to throw it away but to keep the bottles for him. This seemed a novel occupation for the warden-magistrate of the district.

Holding court at Enachu in the large dance hall behind Krakowsky's shop, I found my old acquaintance Carrie Harding up before me. Together with John English, Ginder's manager at Apaikua, and four others, she was charged with assaulting a one-eyed gentleman named Joseph Solomon. English did not appear and had the cheek to send me a letter asking that I postpone the case as this was his busy day. I promptly issued a warrant for his arrest. The other five pleaded guilty. The police story was that Carrie's canister containing $85 had been stolen from her house at Apaikua and, suspecting Solomon, an old convict, she and the others got hold of him, took him to her house and tied him to a chair and beat him until he admitted he had hidden the canister in Coelho's field at Le Desir Creek. The party then took him up there and, despite the fact that it was night, made a thorough search amongst Coelho's cassava and other crops. Not finding it there they took Solomon back and gave him another beating. I fined each of them $10 and ordered them to pay $10 to Solomon. The matter had its sequel in the Civil Court when the Coelho brothers sued English for $74.40 for damage to their crops. I gave judgement for one sixth of this amount and advised the plaintiffs to sue each of the five other defendants for a like amount.

In the evening I got yarning with Coelho and his cousin Lewis Da Silva, who insisted that Weiss, Henry and I should drink a beer with them. They were a tough bunch of Portuguese who had stayed up in the Apaikua district for years without going to town, subsisting mainly on the produce of their farm and prospecting, occasionally making quite a good haul of diamonds. They probably knew more about the district than anyone else, with the possible exception of old Francis Jacobs, of whom they told the following story.

The old man apparently let his Indian woman search his sieves for him. When done, she threw the concentrates on the ground, with the result that the whole floor of his camp was carpeted several inches deep in these concentrates. One day Coelho and Da Silva were on a spree and paid the old man a visit. As he sat on a low stool listening to his partner and Jacobs talking, Da Silva picked up a piece of short stick and began idly to stir about in the concentrates on the floor. Suddenly he spotted a diamond which he picked up without attracting the attention of his host. Continuing his apparently idle poking about, but now watching very keenly what he was doing, he soon found another diamond. On leaving Jacobs they went to a shop where they sold the two stones for $11. The talk then got on to Duncan Stuart and Coelho repeated the old story about Stuart's ill luck being due to his own carelessness, adding that, only a week before, his chief man, Buckley, sold twenty eight carats without Stuart's knowledge.

Whilst at Enachu, a tall elderly black woman, Margaret Smith, came to 'lay her grievance' before me as she called it. Taking off her hat, she began by showing me a large gash behind her ear, which looked suspiciously like the scar of a major mastoid operation. This, she said, had been done at MacKenzie Hospital and left her 'not too right in the head', with the result that when people annoyed her she got into a terrible passion and was afraid that one day she would commit herself. Down at Banana Landing where she lived, certain men took a pleasure in teasing her by calling her 'Tiger Gang Gang' and she appealed to me to give her a couple of free summonses so that a stop could be put to the annoyance. I advised her that her best course of action was to take her grievance to the police.

The day I left Enachu to go up the Kurupung River I woke up with a temperature of over 99°F which gradually rose throughout the day. I remembered very little of the journey as I was more or less in a coma as I lay huddled in the boat wrapped in my blanket. When we finally reached Ginder's at four o'clock I tumbled straight into Pierre's bed in his rest house, my temperature now being 103°F. To try a cure for my fever I started to take some quino-plasmoquin, a new anti-fever drug. But after a terrible night with severe pains in my head I remembered that it was in this same house in 1930 I had taken a single dose of plasmoquin with the same results. I decided to take no more of it and sent to the police station for some ordinary government quinine. However, what I finally received was a new alkaloid of quinine called totaquina.

Later on Alice Fraser came in and asked if there was anything she could do for me. She told me how glad all the women were that I had come back, as they could now live in peace, as when Hastings had been there, they had to run into the bush and hide, otherwise they would be prosecuted for being away from their employers' premises.

Standing outside Ginder's rest house I saw a number of naked Akawoios passing up the river in their woodskins. Wondering whether I could get them to fix up the scale lines of my hammock, I called one of them ashore. He was a burly, short-statured Indian who, on being asked his name, replied, 'Me William. You no know me? Me been a town the other day for shoot people.' I then recognised him as the Indian who, a couple of sessions before, had been acquitted of the murder of two Negro pork knockers in the upper Mazaruni. When asked whether it was two or three men he had shot, he naively replied, 'No more two me shoot'. Having examined my hammock he promised to bring one gal the following day to fix it as that day he was going further up river to shoot hog. Needless to say there was no visit from William or one gal to mend my hammock.

On the return journey, along the lower end of the long reach known as Carapia Point, we got a fine view of that great cone-shaped rock known as The Klit as well as, nearer at hand, a corner of the square table topped Mount Watabaru.

Calling in at Ginder's at Enachu to buy some rations and pay my bill, I learnt that the police sergeant was at Krakowsky's with a woman prisoner. When I got there I found Eugene Rawlins in custody on a charge of wounding her fellow Barbadian, Lorraine Daniels, with a prospecting knife. I opened Court and tried her. As usual with fights between women, a man was the bone of contention and Rawlins swore that Daniels attacked her first with her fist. Enraged, she stooped down and, picking up a prospecting knife that was lying on the ground beside her, made a swipe at her opponent with it, who barred the blow with her arm. The knife inflicted a gash eight and a half inches long and one and a half inches wide on her forearm and required eight stitches. I could do no less than sentence Rawlins to two months imprisonment. At the sergeant's request I arranged to take her down to Kamakusa along with Susan Lucas, a quiet little black woman temporarily engaged to escort her as female turnkey. After an overnight stop at Oranapai we reached Kamakusa at half past ten where I put the prisoner, the female turnkey and a police constable on a downward bound boat which would carry her to Bartica and thence to Georgetown prison.

It was at this time that I began work on a revised edition of the *Mazaruni Miners Guide* which I had first published in 1927, and in view of the revived interest in gold mining I included a section on the regulations governing the working of mines.

Going over to the hospital for some tablets, I had a yarn with Joseph who complained about the number of anopheles mosquitoes at the bottom of my compound. There was at Kamakusa a remarkable immunity from malaria; those who remained on the station rarely if ever got malaria and this was put down to the fact that the mosquito carriers had no hosts from which to get the malaria germ. Patients in the hospital with malaria slept under mosquito nets and the malaria carriers who passed up and down the river were not there at night when the anopheles feeds. This was another good argument for not allowing boats to stop at, or declare at Kamakusa after dark. The only occupant in the hospital was a young Indian woman suffering from bronchitis. A couple of her friends had come to see her and one, a young girl who could not have been more than twelve years old, was sitting on the jigger-infested sand beneath the hospital, as I thought, playing with a sturdy red baby. Approaching closer I was amazed to see that she was nursing the child. The girl's breasts, though full and well developed, were no larger than a small Gloy bottie.

I was anxious to meet Philip Morley, the manager of the placer claim, Charles F, and hearing that he was at the workings preparing to ship the fortnight's production of gold in a few days time I decided to go and visit him. Taking Henry, P.C. McCalmont as my orderly and Sergeant Osbourne, I left Kamakusa and sailed down the river to Banana Landing, stopping at Robello's place at Rock Point for breakfast. Going ashore I found the De Souza shop closed and the manager, a young Portuguese named Pereira, in bed with fever. He told me that the shop had been closed for some three or four weeks and was now used exclusively as a magazine for the Charles F. claim. This lay on the Meparu Creek, a branch of the Karanang River, and some seven miles from Banana Landing.

As Henry did not want to go to the claim I took my orderly and two of my boat-hands and set off for the claim. Through the trees behind the magazine I found a field of some three or four acres planted up with a crop of young ground provisions. A small shack stood at the nearer end of the clearing outside of which two men and a woman were working. The latter, on seeing me approach, came towards us and I recognised her as Tiger Gang Gang. She said that this was her house and farm. The trail, after skirting her farm, crossed fairly flat country for some three miles then became more hilly with several creeks to cross.

After some two hours we reached the largest of the creeks yet encountered, some twenty feet wide flowing over a shallow sandy bottom. According to my information this should have been the Meparu Creek, but I subsequently learnt that it was the Haimaraparu. Crossing this, the trail ran in a wide and well-kept boundary line on which location boards told us we were running between the claims Friends and Success of the Mazaruni Gold Workings Co., a subsidiary of Krakowsky's. Here the trail forked and taking the right hand path we soon became lost in some old workings on the edge of a creek.

As I could not trace the trail beyond this point we returned to the fork and tried the left hand path which, after running along the bank of the Haimaraparu Creek and finally crossing it, brought us to a large grass-covered clearing where we found two pork knockers who informed us that the Charles F claim was but five minutes further along the trail. Re-entering the forest and crossing a low ironstone hill we soon heard the rumbling of machinery and, crossing a narrow flat, saw through the trees a large opening on a low hill in front, with several buildings including a large zinc-roofed shed.

There we found Morley, a little brown-moustached cockney, superintending several men looking after the quartz mill, which was known as a rib cone ball mill. It consisted of a steel drum about three feet in diameter and equally deep, slung on its axis horizontally and revolved by a belt driven by a Petter motor. Inside the drum were numerous balls of manganese steel varying in size from somewhat larger than a cricket ball to that of a golf ball. The quartz, broken into pieces of about one and a half inches, was fed by hand into a sickle-shaped revolving hopper set at the end of the axle of the barrel. The revolutions of the barrel caused the steel balls inside to pound the quartz to the consistency of flour and a stream of water washed it through a circular screen that revolved with the drum at its further side. From the screen the powdered quartz and its accompanying gold was washed into a narrow box called a launder, in the bottom of which quicksilver was placed. From here it was washed over three amalgamating plates consisting of sheets of copper an eighth of an inch thick, silver-plated and with quicksilver smeared on them and finally through a sluice with five checks. What gold the amalgamating plates missed was caught by the checks in the eighteen foot long sluice. The water for the mill was thrown up by a motor pump located about a hundred yards away in a small creek that washed the base of the low hill in which the workings were situated.

Having examined the plant, Morley took me to see the workings, a great gash across the face of the hill some twenty to thirty feet deep, as many wide and a couple of hundred feet long. The gold occurred in several quartz stringers, some of which were horizontal, others dipping at an angle of forty five degrees. The original owners of the claim had cut the sides perpendicularly, and fifteen feet below the surface had undermined it. Morley showed me the spot where the face had fallen in and killed a man the previous year. He was now cutting the sides at an angle of sixty degrees to the surface.

After supper with Morley in his very rough and ready camp I listened to his yarns, and *could* he talk! He told me he knew several similar quartz formations in the vicinity and suggested that Government should remove this area from that in which the diamond diggers were compelled to take out omnibus licences. All the diamond diggers had cleared out when the original small deposit of diamonds had become exhausted. De Souza, the only shop owner in the district, had closed his shop at the end of the previous year as he did not feel like paying for a licence which was of no use to him. This caused the great majority of the gold diggers to clear out too as they had no means of obtaining rations. De Souza, I was told, was willing to carry on his shop if he were allowed to take out only those licences under which he actually traded. Morley assured me that if he did, it would give a decided fillip to the gold diggings in the locality as the country gave promise of being a valuable gold field if facilities were provided. I assured Morley that I would bring this to the attention of the Commissioner on my return to Kamakusa.

After a few more beers I was beginning to feel somewhat drowsy when Morley reminded me of the famous gold brick story which he then related to me. Some twenty years previously, an ingot of gold, allegedly shipped from what was said to be the Peters Mine, turned out on arrival in New York to be an ingot of perfectly good lead. In those days the gold was not shipped through a bank but through local shipping agents. It appeared, Morley continued, that the shipping clerk and the secretary of the Peter's Mine Company kept a duplicate of the company's seal. The two men had put their heads together and after the gold had been cleared at the Lands and Mines, substituted the lead.

The mill, not having started until four o'clock that afternoon, was operated up to midnight, and every now and then Morley would interrupt his storytelling and run down to the mill house to see that all was in order. Just after midnight the mill was stopped and the ensuing silence seemed all the more marked after its persistent dull rumbling.

The contents of the launder were then removed and placed in a small wooden tub which was placed under Morley's hammock and a small amount of cyanide thrown in. This was to make the gold settle, because it was so fine it would be washed off by the water. Morley told me how once when his supply of mobiloil had run out he had, to keep the plant running, raided the kitchen and taken all the butter, lard and cotton seed oil he could find and used the resulting syrup to lubricate the engines and bearings. Morley continued to yarn until I fell asleep, but I did not have much rest because the lamp was kept lit, and Morley's dog, which slept beneath my hammock near the tub of gold and sand, would get up and scratch itself every half an hour and in so doing knock my back, and Morley himself appeared to get up every hour or so and drink a cup of tea. I got up at half past six and watched the process of cleaning up the amalgamating plates, to get the gold off. They were first scrubbed with sand and a piece of sharp-edged wood to loosen the amalgam of quicksilver and gold it had caught, which in appearance is a dull silver paste. This was then got off the plates by squeezing over them a large rubber squeegee, similar to those used in preparing glazed photographs, but very much larger. The amalgam thus removed, it was washed down into the sluice. The final concentrate, (consisting of the heaviest sand and all the quicksilver thrown into the launder, plates and sluice since the beginning of the shift, and all the gold that had combined chemically with the quicksilver) was now washed in a battel to get rid of the sand and the surplus quicksilver that had not amalgamated. This latter ran off in its original liquid form and was bottled for re-use. The residual amalgam was then placed, along with that obtained during the past fortnight (which filled two jam jars), into a large iron retort around which an immense fire was built.

The seven-foot long pipe, leading at a downward angle from the top of the retort, was bound round with sacking on which water was continually poured to keep it cool. The heat then volatized the quicksilver from the amalgam and, in vapour form, it passed through the wet pipe where, its temperature being reduced, it returned to its original liquid form and shot out of the end of the pipe at first in spurts of separate silver blobs and then in a continuous stream that was caught in a basin of water placed below the end of the pipe. Presently the silver flow began to diminish until it finally ceased altogether. The retort was taken off the fire, opened, and a solid lump of yellow gold shaken out on to the ground. It weighed a little over forty ounces; the weight of the amalgam put into the retort had weighed just over a hundred ounces.

As soon as the gold had cooled sufficiently to be weighed, Morley packed it up in his prospecting bag and we set off for Banana Landing. On the way he pointed out to me outcrops of quartz similar to those he was working at Charles F. We passed several old pits that had been dug in the search for diamonds and Morley demonstrated to me why no diamonds could be expected there. In every case, except right out at the river, the gravel consisted of angular quartz and not water-worn pebbles as would be the case in alluvial deposits where alone the diamonds are found in this country. We reached Banana Landing just after midday, I feeling very tired after my long unaccustomed walk. Henry made us laugh when he related how the sergeant had slept in the boat the previous night and, having put on his pyjamas, was trying to unfasten the stick that kept the side flap of the tent out like an awning, when he overbalanced and fell head first into the river.

We spent the night at the landing and left next day for Kamakusa. Before leaving I held a Magistrate's Court at which I tried a man called Caesar Neil for using insulting language to Margaret Smith. As he appeared to be very contrite I made him apologise, reprimanded him and ordered payment of costs.

Two days later, Hastings arrived back in Kamakusa and I wasted no time in handing over to him and returning to town. It was now the end of January. Whilst travelling down to Bartica I learnt of the death of my old friend, Mark-a-book, Arthur Husbands.

Back in the office I found marching orders to proceed on the location survey of the new Tiboko Road. I was to lead the survey party with Ridley as my chief assistant and Lee Own as the third surveyor. I wrote to some of my old men in the North West District, Moruca and Demerara River, asking them to join me on the expedition.

One day, whilst in the office, I was shown some very interesting stamps by Mrs Lynch. They had been used on the old German battleship *Moltke* which had surrendered with the rest of the German fleet at Scapa Flow at the termination of hostilities in 1918. When the vessel was subsequently raised some ten years later the safe was opened and the stamps found inside. They were in almost perfect condition; on only two specimens were there small rust-like marks. The naval officer who had sent them to Mrs Lynch vouched for their authenticity as he had been present when the safe was opened.

CHAPTER XXII

TIBOKO ROAD SURVEY

The last Saturday in February 1933 found me on the stelling on the first stage of my journey to the Tiboko Road. There was quite a large crowd there to see me off, including Phil, Walter and Dad. I had called to say good-bye to Mother on my way through town. Among the passengers who were travelling with Henry and the rest of us were Jacques Willems, my godson, who had just returned from England where he had gained his B.Sc. in Engineering, and B.R. Wood, the Conservator of Forests. Joining the train at Vreed-en-Hoop, I shared a compartment with the latter who entertained me with some interesting information about the forests, the ecology of which, he said, would take a dozen experts fifty years to study. In Trinidad, he said, the total number of different species of forest plants was six hundred and thirty; in this Colony there were a least ten-fold that number. Wood further explained that many species which hitherto had been supposed to be identical, had been found to be not so, the difference, however, only showing in the leaves of the young saplings, the adult trees being in all appearance identical. Another interesting fact was that certain trees adapted solely to arid conditions, such as the dakuma, may also be found in stagnant swamps where the water is full of matter poisonous to vegetable life. These trees, being used to a very small quantity of water in their natural habitat, the upland sand areas, thrive in the stagnant water by using so little of it that they suffer no ill-effects. whereas another tree, used to water, would be killed by the toxic properties of the stagnant swamp.

At Parika we found the little steamer *Pirai* waiting to take us up the river instead of the commodious *Basra*, which was undergoing a general overhaul. Most of my men had come round from Georgetown in her, and by the time we first class passengers had got aboard she was fairly crowded. At Bartica just after five we were joined by Davenport, formerly of the Forestry Department, who was also coming along with us.

Next morning, shortly after six o'clock, our gear and stores were loaded onto four lorries and we drove out along the Bartica-Potaro Road to the depot at Seventy Six and a Half Miles, which we used as our first base. Here we off-loaded our provisions and personal baggage and, after issuing the men with a week's rations, we set them about making waiaries with which to drogh the loads.

Lee Own and a dozen men set off to build Camp No.1 on a branch of the Kaburi a little over three miles from the depot. They followed Pires & Silva's droghing trail that ran from the depot to their shop on West Kaburi, whilst Ridley and I went back down the road to Seventy Five Miles where the new road was to branch off the existing one. Going ahead with a compass I set out the line and at every hundred feet planted a notched and numbered peg. Ridley followed and showed Davenport how to take the cross sections. As the country was fairly flat the work did not take long and we were soon able to join the others who in the meantime had moved up to Camp No.1. A rough line for the road had been made by Cheong back in 1922 and Ridley had subsequently done some further work on it. Our survey was not to be considered one of alignment but of a strip of land some five hundred feet wide in which a suitable alignment could be made by the construction engineers.

The work, to start with, was very slow due to an outbreak of influenza amongst the men, but thanks to a quick response to my request for additional medical supplies I soon had the epidemic under control.

On one of the evenings before we left the depot, the conversation turned to ghosts and Davenport told us that when he was in Dominica there was a house in Roseau that had the reputation of being haunted by a young bride. Government eventually acquired the house and proceeded to pull it down to make room for a bond. In Roseau, all the better class houses had their bathrooms in a separate building in the yard, and the bottom of the bath in this house consisted of a large marble slab which, when the workmen removed it, was really a tombstone laid upside down. On it was an inscription, dated 1815, from which it was learnt that it had covered the body of young girl who had died on the very day she was to have been married, from a broken heart caused by the death of her fiancé the previous day.

Mansfield used to amuse us with his strong addiction to the use of Formalin which he used for every conceivable illness of the flesh and to fumigate the whole area round his hammock. We christened him Formalin Fred. He normally had a charming personality and was a very interesting conversationalist, being highly intelligent and well read. Sometimes, however, the devil in him would show itself and he appeared to take delight in attempting deliberately to shock his listeners with his obscene and pornographic remarks. I discussed him once with Edgar Beckett. He claimed that Mansfield used to state frankly that when he behaved like a gentleman his European personality was uppermost and when like a worthless fellow the African in him had the upper hand. He was quite destitute of personal modesty and in the early mornings, when doing his physical jerks, and in the evenings, when about to bathe or retire, would walk about the camp quite unconcernedly in Nature's garb.

Davenport was a very good-natured fellow and always ready with a smile at the slightest provocation. Because of his pronounced white beard he soon earned the nickname of Daddy. One day, looking in the mirror he exclaimed, 'Why, this blasted beard makes me look seventy', in which remark, truth to tell, he was not far wrong, although he was, at the time, only forty-nine.

As the work on the survey progressed we found that Cheong's trace, cut some eleven years previously, was considerably blocked with fallen trees and new growth, which necessitated us clearing the main survey line for droghing purposes. Near the Issano River, because of extensive swamps, I decided to leave the trace and swing north west a few miles to the source of the Okuwa River and then turn west again, crossing the Issano several miles lower down than did the original trace, which I hoped to rejoin near Waiamu River. This would require a lot more reconnaissance work and would slow down the work somewhat, though the cost per mile was well within the estimate, working out at $95 on the assumption that the rations cost 32 cents per man per day.

Just before I started work on this deviation to the line, on Friday 7th April, I received two radios by special messenger. The first read:

'COMMISSIONER LANDS AND MINES TO SUB WARDEN BARTICA. FOLLOWING MESSAGE TO VINCENT ROTH TO BE DISPATCHED BY SPECIAL BEARER FIRST AVAILABLE OPPORTUNITY STOP ARRANGE TO COME DOWN IMMEDIATELY TO DISCUSS URGENT MATTERS CONNECTED WITH SURVEY LET RIDLEY CARRY ON MEANWHILE'.

Now what was the meaning of this I wondered? The Commissioner could not have received my first report when he sent this message. Then I collected the second radio. I saw a memo of Greene's attached. My heart sank when I read it. 'The enclosed telegram is a message to you from C.L.M. 'I offer deepest sympathy.' The radio read:

IF TELEGRAM TO ROTH OF TODAY'S DATE NOT ALREADY GONE CONVEY TO HIM INSTEAD THAT I DEEPLY REGRET TO INFORM HIM THAT HIS FATHER PASSED PEACEFULLY AWAY TODAY AND THAT HE

CAN RETURN TO TOWN BY EARLIEST OPPORTUNITY LEAVING RIDLEY IN CHARGE STOP IF TELEGRAM HAS BEEN DISPATCHED LET THIS MESSAGE FOLLOW BY FIRST OPPORTUNITY.

And it was only by the last mail I had received a cheerful note from Dad saying he was going into hospital for about three weeks and that he wished 'I could follow in father's footsteps'. I had had the dear old chap so much in mind the previous Sunday, the 2nd April, his seventy-third birthday. From the radio I gathered that he had died on the Wednesday.

After dinner I handed control over to Ridley and made arrangements to go out on the following day on the chance of catching a lorry before Wednesday. The news of my bereavement and imminent departure having spread amongst the men, I was greatly touched the next morning at the way they showed their sympathy. Some came in person and tendered it verbally, others wrote little notes either individually or in groups.

Leaving Henry with the survey, I said good-bye to him and the others and set out from Camp No.7 with the firm intention of reaching the depot at Seventy Six and a Half Miles that afternoon, the distance to be covered being about twenty-three miles allowing for the twists and turns of the droghing trail. In the vicinity of Camp No.5 I saw no fewer than four maam, but having no gun with me there was nothing I could do about it. After almost continuous walking, except for a short break for breakfast, I reached the depot just before four, where to my delight I learnt that a lorry would be passing through at three o'clock in the morning bound for Bartica. So after an early dinner, tired and sore, I tumbled into my hammock. The lorry was on time and I reached Bartica shortly after midday.

On the Monday boat with me were Schultz, Jones and Ogilivie and their families. As we sat in the saloon yarning, one of the stories Schultz told that amused me was as follows:–

A millionaire visited a strange town and to honour him the citizens invited him to a round of golf. At the end of the game he put his hand in his pocket and brought out three pennies which he handed to the caddie. He placed them in a row on the palm of his hand, looked at them intently and then at the donor. 'What's the matter, my man?' asked the rich one, 'Aren't they good money?' 'Oh yes, Sir, yes Sir, it's quite good money,' replied the caddie. 'But you know, Sir, I'm a fortune teller, I am. I can tell you your fortune by these three pennies.' 'Oh yes,' replied the millionaire, 'that's interesting. Well, tell me my fortune young man.' Well Sir,' said the caddie, turning over the first penny, 'this one tells me you are a millionaire.' 'Yes, that's quite right, I am.' 'And this one tells me, Sir, that you are a bachelor.' 'My word, that's extraordinary, I am that too. Now what does the third one tell you?' 'The third penny', replied the caddie, 'tells me that your father was also a bachelor!'

At Makouria Creek, Ursula Willems and her son Jacques came aboard together with Evelyn Waugh, the novelist, who had been spending the weekend with them at Makouria. Stopping a little later at Ithica we picked up Miss Wilkie, a young white girl with blue eyes and flaxen hair – a sight for sore eyes. She travelled with us on the train and I teased her all the way to Vreed-en-Hoop.

On the stelling at Georgetown I was met by Christiani, Van Sertima and Cleare from the office and Schryver. Taking a car to Croal Street I found Mother and Walter awaiting my arrival. After a few words I went home to Phil and returned to Mother in the evening. I then learnt that Dad had died from uraemia. He had not been operated on as the doctors said it would have been a miracle had he survived, and if he had he would have been bed-ridden for the rest of his life. He had gone into the hospital on the Friday after telling all his friends jocularly, as they thought, good-bye. He became unconscious at midnight on the Tuesday and remained in that condition until he died at three o'clock on the Wednesday afternoon. He was given an immense Masonic funeral on Thursday, there being twenty-eight cars of Freemasons and eighty of other people.

The next two months winding up Dad's estate were very hectic. But the thing that really occupied my time was finding a suitable house for us all to live in. Phil and I had decided that Mother could no longer stay on at the house in Croal Street. However, until we found such a house, I decided to take over Dad's old room and stay with Mother. One of my first tasks was to phone up Togo Low at the Ice House and ask him to undertake the job of looking after Dad's estate. Going through Dad's dispatch box in which he kept his most intimate private papers, I found a letter addressed to me, written several years previously. The envelope was marked that it was to be handed to me after his death.

I was asked to call on the Governor, Sir Edward Denham. He appeared to have felt Dad's death very much and asked for a photograph of his old friend. He told me that within an hour of his arrival in the Colony, when he looked round the Council Chamber after he had been sworn in as Governor, there were two persons he missed, the two men he had heard of before coming to the Colony and did not see there. He had asked for them. 'One was Sir Charles Cox', he said, 'and the other was your father, Mr Roth, and now both are dead.' He told me to ask him if there was anything I wanted him to do for Mother or myself and ordered me on no account to return to the bush without going to see him again.

In April I thought I had got a house in Brickdam whose then tenants, a doctor and his wife, were about to leave the colony, but the solicitor, Carlos Gomes, changed his mind at the last minute which really annoyed me. The wife sounded to be a bit of a girl as I heard whilst up at Joe Schryver's house drinking beer, when he told me the following tale concerning her. One evening she was parked on the Sea Wall in her car with a young man who was not her husband. The doctor's car came into sight, so the lady made her escort get into the rumble seat, shutting the lid down on him until her husband had passed. This the doctor did not do, but got into the car and asked his wife to take him home. There they locked the car in the garage and went upstairs. The wife then made some excuse about having left something in the car and went downstairs to release her prisoner from the rumble seat. When she opened the lid she found her young friend unconscious and he had to be rushed to hospital to be revived! Attending the sale of the doctor's furniture, I heard another tale of her escapades. Going up to the Botanic Gardens one day alone in her car she 'happened' to meet two gentlemen in theirs. Someone, however, put the doctor wise to this and he found his wife there with the two men. The doctor pulled out a revolver and started to fire shots in their direction, presumably to frighten them. This he obviously did as they both dived into a nearby trench. Whilst they were floundering about in the water the doctor made his wife let the air out of their tyres before taking her back home.

At the end of May I was at last successful in finding a house in Waterloo Street that suited us and made things much easier for me by having Mother and Phil under the same roof. During this time I finalised my 'Morawhanna Memories' as Delph was wanting to start publishing them in the *Sunday Chronicle*. I also finished my *Mazaruni Miners Guide* which Delph told me he intended to publish as *British Guiana Miners Guide*. With these out of the way I agreed to make for Delph a very large scale map of the Colony which, at a scale of four miles to the inch, would be some fourteen feet high and seven wide.

At the beginning of June, Cole and I paid a visit to the City's Waterworks as I wished to borrow the large scale drawings of Georgetown that had been made for the Sewage Scheme to have copies made for the Lands and Mines Department. Having given me the drawings, Aitken, the Engineer in Charge, offered to show us round the works.

Firstly he showed us their wonderful system of recording and signalling, including an elaborate machine with a clock-like pendulum that drew a graph of water consumption in Georgetown during every hour of the day. Graphs from the previous weeks showed that the period of greatest consumption of water in the city was between the hours of six to eight in the morning when the city had its daily wash. Apparently we did not bathe so extensively on Sundays, but Aitken explained this by the fact that these hours on weekdays had the largest consumption for industrial purposes. The period of minimum consumption was around three in the afternoon whilst the afternoon bath between office and tennis and cricket was faithfully shown by a peak in the line between four and five o'clock. The same instrument also recorded the hourly pressure in the mains. This varied during the day and dropped at night to a regular low figure which showed a single rise on the night of the previous week's fire alarm, when the pressure was increased. We next looked at the electric automatic signalling system. Aitken told us that it had been invented and patented by himself and was built up entirely from standard parts of a telephone installation. Whenever anything went wrong at any of the twenty-four pumping stations scattered about the city, the emergency pump came into action. That was signalled by the ringing of a bell and the appearance of a light over the number of the station in question. As soon as the emergency pump finished its task, the bell rang again and the light went out.

Aitken then took us over to the pumping station proper. He showed us how its electrical power supply was brought from the power station on the other side of the city by two independent overhead lines which, following different routes, also supplied power to the sewage pumping stations on the way. The station housed four great pumps, each driven by a powerful electrical motor. At normal times only one pump was required, the others used only in emergency. Aitken then went to a large switchboard and pressed a button; a second later a second pump began to work with a deep hum. Should the electricity supply fail, there was a great crude-oil four-cylinder 250 h.p. motor in a corner of the station.

At the beginning of June I recommenced work in the office. I had in fact been to the office at Mullin's request to discuss the Tiboko Road Survey on several occasions and had spoken to Major Craig, the Director of Public Works, as to the best locations for construction camps as it was Government's intention to start the work at an early date.

Shortly after I resumed work in the office, Ridley and Lee Own returned to town, having completed the survey as far as the Issano River. A near tragedy had befallen them on their way down the Issano when their boat struck a tacouba and sank, throwing all aboard and their luggage into fifteen feet of water. Lee Own, who could not swim, almost drowned; many things were destroyed by the water and a few things, including Charlie Gonsalves' camera, were lost, as were my chessmen, which Kaufman swore I borrowed from him some ten years ago – very likely I did.

One of my office jobs at this time was to sort out parcels of diamonds for royalty assessment, a new system having just come into force whereby fifty cents per carat was charged on all diamonds except bort, rubbish and stones used for industrial purposes, on which the royalty was only fifteen cents.

One of the new innovations in Georgetown was the Demerara Meat Company's shop. Here meat could be ordered by telephone and sent up to the house twice daily. When I called in to open a monthly account, Beckett, the manager, told me that he'd had to sack all the shop girls for incompetence. Dr Fulton, the managing director, had insisted on having a shop full of attractive female assistants. Beckett had caught one girl telling a customer that the raw sausages were cooked, ready for eating, whilst another had held her nose whilst serving tripe. Obviously their brains did not match their beauty.

In mid July I was told to resume the Tiboko Road survey as soon as possible. Lee Own was not coming this time as he had been detailed for some work on the Courantyne coast. His place was to be taken by Sweetnam.

Shortly before I left for the bush, Mother gave me a ring that had once belonged to Dad. When he was on the north coast of West Australia on his Royal Commission, he came across an old Spanish priest who had worked for many years amongst the Aborigines. He had so deprived himself serving them that when Dad met him he was clothed in sacking and starving. Dad gave him food and clothes and was apparently very kind to him. When Dad was about to leave the country, the old priest told him he had nothing with which to repay all his kindness but a heavy gold ring which he insisted that Dad should take. It was made of West Australian gold. When Dad took it to a jeweller in Brisbane he assured him it was pure gold. On the inner surface of the ring were roughly scratched the priest's initials: 'S.C'.

'Daddy' Davenport, when he heard about the resumption of the survey, pleaded with me to take him along. I was reluctant but later relented. This was a mistake. The day after I had advanced the men some of their wages I was passing through Main Street when I saw Davenport come swaggering across the road, his hat at a jaunty angle and his stick swinging as though the whole town belonged to him. He was heading straight for the Tower Hotel and it was pretty obvious that he had not spent all his advance on rations and clothes. As soon as I got home I rang the hotel and asked to speak to Davenport. When he answered the phone my suspicions were confirmed. He spluttered and stuttered and made out he could not hear me and in the end he put me onto the barman. I explained the position to him and asked him not to let the old fellow have any more to drink and to ring me up if he proved obstreperous. Later, the barman phoned to say he had been unable to stop Davenport from obtaining further liquor and that he had left the hotel in a cab bound for Mabel's. I rang up Brickdam Police Station and got hold of Inspector Collins to whom I explained the position. He promised to go and take the old chap home.

After attending a meeting of the executive committee at Victory Lodge, I then went on to Croal Street where at Jacques Willems' house I found a little jollification in progress in celebration of his safe arrival back in the colony with his bride, Winnie. Phil and Henry were already there and after a very pleasant couple of hours, Jacques and his wife ran us all home in their car.

Next day I heard that Collins had picked up Davenport at Mabel's the previous night and had taken him back to Trent House outside of which he had posted a policeman to make sure Davenport did not go out again.

I left Georgetown on Saturday 12th August to resume the Tiboko Road survey. Henry had left earlier that day with the men on the Georgetown–Bartica boat. Quite a bunch of folk had come to see us off including Phil and Walter, Togo Low, Pat Contey and W.I. Gomes. Amongst the Bartica passengers were Mother (who was spending the weekend there), Ursula Willems, Jacques and Winnie Willems, Tommy Houston and his wife, Ravenor, Charlie Farrier and other Mazaruni folk, including a family, participants in a mining dispute I had been hearing just prior to my departure. On the train to Parika, Tommy Houston told me that the family had been working serious obeah to win their case and that they had brought the obeah man across the river with them so that they could win their dispute after he had given me the once over.

On the following Tuesday we embarked on the *Shining Star* and, at nine o'clock set off up the Mazaruni. There were thirty-six of us on board; myself, Ridley, Sweetnam, Parrett, Davenport, Henry and twenty-three of our men, as well as Captain Nedd, the bowman, engineer, and four boat-hands to bring the empty boat back to Bartica.

Shortly after two o'clock on the Thursday we arrived at Honey Camp where we put up at Ginder's Magazine where the clerk, R.V. Farrier, put a room at our disposal. We had to wait here for Blenman to arrive as I had arranged to hire a small boat from him. He arrived some three hours after us so we were able to leave early the following morning. With Blenman aboard we travelled on up the river to a small island, just below Issano Island, on which was a small Indian village. Here Blenman borrowed a woodskin, which we towed behind the boat on our way to a small creek on the left bank of the river near a place called Hill Foot. Here Blenman handed over his small boat to us whilst he returned down river in the woodskin.

We turned into the Semang River and travelled up a couple of miles until we came to the first island. Here we found Cheong's line on the left bank and, searching on the right bank, found its continuation there. Here we built our first camp. When all the stores had been taken out of the boat we dispatched it back to Bartica.

Next morning, we set about ferrying the men across the Semang and began the survey along Cheong's line westwards towards Tiboko. I ran the main line with Henry lining and Parrett chaining. Ridley and Davenport did the cross sections, the former initiating Sweetnam into the work. The line crossed undulating country, crossed two saddles and a small creek flowing southward to the Semang. We finished the day's work at a gully head after doing 7,000 feet.

Next day I made a reconnaissance to the north west in an attempt to avoid going round the big loop followed by Cheong's line as it approached Tiboko, but I found my way blocked by a deep gully so I had to continue along the original line. When the breakfast carriers caught us up they reported having seen a puma as they came along the line. In the afternoon we climbed onto a ridge of ironstone forming Tiboko Falls and knocked off after cutting 7,200 feet.

Next morning the line passed through an old fire burn where the growth was extraordinarily thick. As we descended towards the river we were able to distinguish the steep hill on the north side of the Tiboko gorge, whilst immediately below us the brown waters of the Mazaruni flowed on at their narrowest and deepest. We reached the river bank exactly at the end of the third mile from Semang and here I terminated the line just half-way up the gorge and well clear of the fall. It had been my original intention to carry it on into the bay just below the mouth of the Karanang River but after looking at the spot at high water I was satisfied that the present termination would do for a landing.

We planted the third mile post and a large signal post then began to open the line backwards to the point on the hill where I had left Cheong's line. We then returned to the Semang and extended the line across the river and its islands and through our camp. From bank to bank it was over 600 feet wide, the main river being over 250 feet. Now began the Semang–Issano section of the survey. Immediately behind the camp we crossed a dirty muddy swamp some 150 feet wide in which flowed a fairly deep creek, whose width I could not ascertain because water covered the entire swamp. Fortunately a large tree had fallen across it, making a suitable bridge. We then came to a rocky creek some 50 feet wide. The sky now became so overcast that Henry had great difficulty lining and the roll of thunder indicated the approach of an electric storm. Because of my two adventures with lightning whilst in the proximity of a steel chain on the Demerara River, I gave the order to knock off and we returned to camp where I brought my diary up to date.

Leaving Ridley to measure the width of the river between the two paals by the subtends method, I proceeded with the line, crossed the creek below the falls and headed in a general south-easterly direction for a couple of thousand feet, along a ridge that ran roughly parallel to the big creek. We crossed a small clay flat in which two or three small tributaries of the former creek ran, and came to the foothills of the Semang range where we once more joined Cheong's line, which was still quite discernible though cut some twelve years previously. At the forty-fourth peg we came across one of his old camps. Having run up gently along a spur for a thousand feet or so, the line suddenly bent almost at right angles to the north east and began climbing the side of the range.

We then met Peterman who had been out hunting. He had two fat peccari, the smaller species, abouya, known in the text books as the collared peccari, although on these two specimens the collar markings were almost indiscernible. I sent Allsopp to assist him in taking them back to camp and cleaning them. Each front leg was tied by the feet to the corresponding hind leg and the carriers' arms slipped into the loops so formed, so that the animal straddled across his back in a true pig-a-back fashion. They looked very comical as they set off down the trail.

The climbing now became somewhat difficult on account of the loose ironstone rocks and the numbers of tree roots that spread over the hard surface. Then the old line made a sudden turn which was not shown on the tracing I had of Cheong's line. Coming out of a gully it resumed its north easterly direction over an ironstone slope for a few hundred feet to a second rock-filled ravine in which another mountain torrent flowed. In the pools here, transparent as glass, we saw many small fish marked like iarrau but with the addition of an upright mark amidships. In shape they looked like the huri.

Having carried the line up to the ninety-fourth peg we began to clear the site of No.2 Camp. By three o'clock the line cleaners had reached us and we started back for camp. With the trail cleaned, the going was much easier though care still had to be used to avoid a slip.

For dinner that evening we had fried peccari brains. During the meal Henry related a grisly tale from Belize that he had got from Ridley. It concerned a Jekyll and Hyde character who was known as a fairly well-to-to and respected man about town whose hobby was sea fishing. Then one day, a young girl was found exhausted on the beach with a bullet wound in her body. She was taken to hospital where she told the following story. She had embarked the previous day on the sloop *Gazelle* along with three or four other passengers. They had travelled almost out of sight of land when suddenly a man appeared and, in cold blood, shot down the captain, crew and passengers. She also was shot and in spite of her wound managed to reach the shore where she was found. At once a hue and cry was raised and it was discovered that the murderer had fled to the Republic of Honduras. He was brought back to Belize and at his subsequent trial it was discovered, by his own admission, that he had been responsible for the destruction of over twenty sloops and the murder of close on two hundred souls. He would secrete himself on a vessel and then in the night take the captain and crew by surprise and shoot them down ruthlessly, throwing the bodies, after robbing them, overboard. The male passengers were treated in a like manner but the unfortunate women suffered a worse fate before being consigned to the sharks. Ridley vouched for this story on the word of his mother who, having lived in British Honduras, knew the girl concerned.

Our camps were generally established at a distance of three miles from the previous one. Usually, in the mornings, Parrett, with a gang of sixteen or seventeen men, set out to make the clearing and erect the frames for the tents. The main one, occupied by ourselves, was some forty feet long and had a proper frame for three-quarters of its length, the side runners not extending over the remaining quarter as I preferred to use hammock posts and so not be disturbed at night by the movements of the occupants of the other hammocks. Along the whole of one side of the tent was built a stout babricot to hold our baggage, some two feet above the ground.

Meanwhile Henry prepared the legs for our two tables, the tops of which carried in a specially made canvas bag from camp to camp. At the end nearest the kitchen was placed the drawing table which, covered with a piece of oilcloth, also served as a dining table. It consisted of two leaves of cedar, reinforced with end braces and held together by movable slats fitting into slots on the undersides of the leaves. When properly wedged this formed an almost perfect drawing table. At the other end was fixed my writing table which consisted of two leaves hinged together and resting on cross pieces set on four sticks with forked ends. Outside our camp a large babricot served as a washstand and here were ranged our three enamel washbasins and a bucket of water. Inside the camp, at my end, a small high babricot was built, little more than a foot square, on which I kept my toilet articles. A short sapling was set up as a hat rack, on which my hat, haversack, belt, umbrella and bugle were hung. The four hammocks were slung in the middle of the tent between the tables. Near the dining room end, about forty feet away the kitchen was built, with a roof of palm thatch and by it was a deep pit in which the kitchen refuse was thrown and covered with earth each day. Nearby was the turtle pen. The two cooks slept in the kitchen. To one side was built the ration tent, known as Rowton House, where Parrett and Davenport lived alongside the expedition's stores. The labourers built their three large tents some distance away. The digging of a latrine pit and clearing a path to it, as well as one to the nearby creek, and the erection of my bathroom, a platform of stout sticks on which I stood whilst performing my afternoon ablutions with a bucket of hot water, completed the arrangement of the camp.

One evening I got Davenport reminiscing about Dominica and he told me that it was customary for all the lime planters to have mistresses on their estates. They were known as housekeepers and were usually mulatto women. Davenport and his brother each had one, indeed for a short time they had three in the house. It appeared that Davenport's mistress had two friends in Roseau and she wanted them to come up to the estate. Davenport's brother said he would take one and they decided to share the third between them. It transpired that Davenport also knew Brooke who had travelled out with Dad and I on the *Tagus* in 1907 and whom Dad used to call the fat boy. When I went to Dominica in 1913 I found him established as a lime planter, although he seemed to spend most of his time at his town house in Roseau. Davenport said he was a great epicure and had gout by the time he was thirty.

One morning in October, Ridley told me that he had heard that Elias Oselmo and his party, who had been back to look for the June survey line at the Issano the previous week, had visited the scene of the boat accident and recovered Charlie Gonsalves' canister and had brought back its contents without reporting the matter to me. I made some enquiries amongst the men and learnt that Gonsalves' Shakespeare and another book of Henry's had been seen in the men's camp, being dried, as also the remains of his camera.

When the morning bugle blew for orders I called the gang in question to one side and, in a few choice words expressed my great disappointment at their conduct, asking those who had any of the articles to return them at once. To my great relief it turned out that John Barasalte was the only culprit, Elias and the others apparently considering it none of their business. Barasalte, taxed as to why he had not reported the find, said he thought I had been informed and that, 'as he heard the things were lost and he found them, he kept them.' I ordered him to bring everything to me whereon he went to his tent and brought the two books, some clothes, a safety razor, comb, toothbrush and the face of the camera. With the exception of the last item, which had disintegrated beyond repair, they were in wonderfully good condition despite their three months' immersion.

Davenport had, on several occasions, expressed a longing to see a hollow mora tree on fire. At our Camp No.11 there were several in the vicinity so I decided to oblige him by building a fire in a hole in the base of a tall morabuke that grew about 200 feet away from the camp. It smoked a good deal but as it did not appear to have a vent, the hole not extending far up the trunk, I reckoned the attempt a failure. The next tree I looked at seemed more promising as its trunk was hollow right up to its branches. In fact it was so large that nine of us could stand inside the base of the trunk and, looking up, see a patch of light sixty-odd feet up the great black shaft. We promptly lit a big fire inside it and then watched developments. At first, a column of greyish blue smoke rolled lazily out of the hole, but as the upward draught fanned the fire below, the smoke belched out with greater speed. The fire below began to race upwards with the steady deep roar and in about a quarter of an hour the inside of the trunk was well alight. Then from the top there shot a steady column of flame, blackening and burning the foliage above, whilst glowing embers began to shoot out and fall to the ground. Davenport came rushing up from the camp in ecstasy at the roaring inferno and I repeatedly had to warn him to keep further away in case the tree should suddenly fall. This applied to Ridley and Sweetnam too who would persist in getting too close in order to have a good view. We also lit a fire in the hollow of another much smaller mora about half way between the one already alight and our camp. This one also soon roared up in a steady flame but not as big and impressive as the first one. Back at camp I saw that the first tree I had fired was still burning at the base and roots and that there was a distinct possibility of it falling on the camp. Accordingly we got some buckets of water and apparently extinguished the fire, clouds of steam rising from the damp ashes at the foot of the tree. Whilst we were thus engaged, there was a prolonged loud crash up the line and a cloud of sparks rose from the direction of the first mora as its top collapsed and came tumbling to the ground. Meanwhile the second one afforded us a fine display of fireworks as we sat at dinner. There was a hole high up at the main fork whence a large tongue of flame issued steadily whilst an incessant shower of sparks fell all about. Presently a fiery crack appeared along the whole length of the main trunk, exposing the incandescent interior; gradually this crack widened until suddenly the burnt shell of the trunk collapsed in on itself and the branches fell straight downwards, still maintaining their upright position. Next morning we woke to find the tree near the camp was well alight again at the base. Hoping that it would fall during the day when no one but the cook was in camp (and he being duly warned), we set off to work.

Proceeding with the line over some gently undulating hills we came across a peculiar ground plant consisting of a single flower without any leaves. It appeared to grow from a bulb. The outer part was a dull red colour and it broke into five white petals in a star shape, the interior being a lemon yellow. Shortly after breakfast the line suddenly ran off the high ground and entered a large flat, where it passed beside a tree on whose trunk, some twenty feet above the ground, was the peculiarly shaped corrugated nest of the terrible quakoo marabunta. There is a popular belief that if the words 'heave out' are spoken aloud within their hearing, these insects will emerge from their nest and attack the passer-by. This may be so as it applies to any loud shouting, whatever the words. The quakoo is the most feared of all the marabuntas and, from personal experience, on the Kartabo Road in 1924, I consider their sting to be more painful than that of the munuri ant.

On the way back to camp I found some ripe sawarri nuts. As we neared the camp I saw that the mora tree had not yet fallen, although the base had burnt almost right through. Not daring to let night come with such a veritable Sword of Damocles over our heads, Ridley took a man and cut that side of the roots away from the camp and then piled more wood on that side to hasten its burning. Just as we were about to sit down to dinner the giant came down with a mighty crash on the side away from the camp, but with such speed that had it come down in the direction of the camp we should have had little chance of escaping. At the first sound of its fall we all rushed out of the tent but had not got ten feet away when it reached the ground. No more tree-burning near camps for me!

By now our survey of the Tiboko Road was almost completed and indeed on the 19th October at Peg 2395 on the Kaburi–Issano section and Peg 1201 on the Semang–Issano section I planted a stout post on which was written the name and date of completion of the survey as well as the names of the personnel of the party.

At dinner on our last night in Camp No.11 we were discussing cases of mental aberration and Ridley told us how travelling to town on the *Basra* one day he saw a man with a sakiwinki. Remembering his little sister wanted a monkey he went up to the owner and asked the price. 'Eight shillings,' replied the man. 'H'm,' said Ridley, 'that's rather a stiff price. Does it talk?' The man looked at him and then smiled as he replied, 'No, Sir, it don't talk.' 'Oh well, in that case I won't take it,' said Ridley and walked away as the man looked wonderingly at him. Later Ridley remarked casually to his sister that he had very nearly bought her a monkey that afternoon but, as it couldn't talk, he had not done so. 'What!' exclaimed his mother, 'Do monkeys talk now?' Only then did Ridley realise what a fool he had made of himself, having acted as if he was buying a parrot and not a monkey!

From Camp No.11 I took eight men and proceeded to cut a trail northwards to the Issano River, for the purposes of evacuating the expedition, and reached that river in a distance of just under four miles. From the three points at which I had seen it, the Issano was a most sinister-looking stream, its water being black and opaque.

As we were going to stay in this location for only a day or so we made the clearing only large enough to contain the tents. As the leaves were brushed away from the ground four or five large scorpions were discovered and killed. Barasalte, who claimed to be inoculated against their bite, or to have, as he called it, the 'scarpian cut', could undoubtedly pick them up with impunity and let them run about on his hand, which they did with their tails curled up close against their backs, making no attempt to sting him.

The weather was now turning wet and after the confines of the forest I was looking forward to returning to Georgetown and civilisation again. Davenport did not know what to do with himself now that the work was over. Parrett told me that the old boy was not sleeping at night but lying on his hammock, chain-smoking his cigarettes. He did not know where he would get lodgings in town as he had not settled his account at Trent House except for $10 he had sent whilst out on the survey.

From Camp No.12 we moved off along the left bank of the Issano until, a little less than half a mile from our camp, we came to its confluence with the Waiamu. Here we crossed by a tacouba bridge made by the men the previous day and carried on along the river bank until we reached Hopes Landing, from where we sailed on into the Mazaruni and so on to Honey Camp.

The place was very quiet, the only visitor being old Henry Vanderheyden whom I had not see for many years. Allan Blenman was also there and we all repaired to Cameron's quarters in Pires & Silva's shop and discussed some beer. During the afternoon I managed to get Blenman to give Davenport a position on one of his claims; he went even further and promised to get him a couple of labourers. Having concluded this business, Blenman and I adjourned to Tiam Fook's shop where we were entertained by a somewhat voluptuously built young Black woman called Beryl Cozier.

Shortly after noon on the following day, having said good-bye to Davenport and the folk at Honey Camp, we packed ourselves aboard the downward bound Pires & Silva boat. There were forty-two of us on board and, there being no tent, we were pretty crowded on top of the tarpaulin. After an overnight stop just below Kusawe Rock we reached Bartica just after three o'clock on the following afternoon. After tea at the hotel I gave the men some money to buy shirts and trousers in which to go to town. Although it was Sunday, the Pires & Silva manager very kindly opened the store to accommodate them. I had dinner with Belmonte, the sub-warden, at the Hotel Moderne and afterwards strolled round to Austin's where Lashley accompanied me on a stroll round the town. We ended up at the house of a Mrs Forde, an Indian lady, where there were several stalwart Akawoio girls with tattooed faces and ponderous breasts, the most conspicuous and unsophisticated of whom was called Ellen.

On the boat to Georgetown I spent most of the morning paying off my men from the North West so that they could catch their steamer home as soon as they arrived in the city.

In November, the Governor called me to see him about Dad's papers on old Georgetown which, he said, should be published. Mullin, when I returned to the office, seemed rather annoyed about my interview with Sir Edward, remarking that 'every time the Governor sees you, he seems to get the impression that surveyors have no work to do.'

It was at this time that I met my old friend Dr Alfred Mistowski. He had not changed much in the intervening twenty-seven years apart from the fact that his hair had turned quite white. He was over in the Colony to adjudicate on the musical examinations being held in the Town Hall. I was to have taken him to lunch with the Governor but he was unable to make it due to his musical commitments. When the Governor heard of this he invited us to tea instead where the three of us had a very pleasant couple of hours. When it was time for Mistowski to leave the colony I went down to Garnett & Co.'s wharf to see him off. The launch took us out to the float anchored close to the West Bank above Pouderoyen and we had not been there many minutes when the plane suddenly appeared over the East Bank, descending gradually to alight on the water even more gracefully than a bird. She taxied straight towards us at what seemed to be a great speed as the expanse of her great wings seemed to stretch out and widen every split second.

Within a few yards of the float the engines were shut off and the plane came almost to a dead stop, so that the attendants had no difficulty in fending it off with their long poles. Within a matter of seconds, the gangway was fixed from the float to the plane, two lines of hose were run onto the wings in which the fuel tanks were located and a noisy little motor pump started to pump the aviation spirit aboard.

Meanwhile the pilot, a youngster dressed in a neat naval-style blue uniform with gold wings on his chest, clambered out, followed by some thirteen passengers. As he saw Mistowski's two little cases he exclaimed, 'Gee, just look at all that baggage.' They all went into the cabin and presently Walcott, the local agent for Pan-American Airways, came up to Mistowski and told him he would have to leave behind twelve pounds of his luggage as the plane had a full load. I pointed out forcibly that Mistowski had booked a return ticket in Trinidad and after further discussion it was decided that he need only leave behind what he had not brought with him. This was two volumes of Dad's translation of Schomburgh's *Travels in British Guiana* which I had given him. I promised to forward them to him at the first opportunity.

Mistowski then went aboard with the other passengers, disappearing through the roof of the cabin. The plane was then pushed off from the float and then the pilot, after waving farewell from the cockpit, ran up the engines to full throttle. With a deep roar the aircraft sprang forward over the water, leaving a swirl of spray behind her. In a few moments she lifted into the air and then swung off over the West Coast and within a few seconds was out of sight.

CHAPTER XXIII

COURANTYNE ADVENTURE

A couple of days before Christmas 1933 I went to look at some new cars which had just come into the colony. In Booker's garage I was particularly struck by a 1934 Morris Ten, a beautiful little saloon car of ten horsepower with four cylinders. The manager, De Souza, agreed to bring it up to the house in the afternoon and take Mother for a drive in it. We went for a run to Beterverwagting and back and Mother was so pleased with it that she agreed on the spot to buy it, the price being $1050.

On Christmas Eve, Phil and Walter attended midnight Mass at the Cathedral returning home just before two o'clock. I was already in bed. Next morning I cycled up to the cemetery where I placed a wreath of forget-me-nots on Dad's grave and thence back to Brickdam to visit Sam Kaufman. After spending an hour with him I went on to P.J. Willems where I found most of the family at home and drank champagne with them. I finally got home to have tea with Mother and then had a short rest until five o'clock when Sam Taylor, our sole Christmas guest, arrived in state in a five-seater car. We sat down at seven to a sumptuous Christmas dinner from which we did not rise until a quarter to nine, just in time to hear the King give his Christmas message to the Empire.

After the holidays De Souza delivered the car and gave me the first of a series of driving lessons and after a week I was tested and passed.

We saw the New Year in at Winnie Willems house in Croal Street. Ursula was away at Makouria, so things were a little quieter than they might have been. However, we drank in the New Year in champagne and then Leon drove us all home. He had dark hair, so we made him enter the house first in conformity with the popular superstition.

One evening during the holidays Walter and Mother exchanged yarns about their schooldays. Walter told us one about Father Smith, one of the priests at St Stanislaus College that he had got from one of the boys at the school. Father Smith apparently had the habit of surreptitiously smoking a cigarette in the classroom, though, of course the boys watched him. One day the boys were astounded to see him haul out a lady's silk stocking from his pocket instead of matches! Mother then reminded me of an incident of my boyhood days in Brisbane. There was a young imp of a boy visiting our neighbours. He was about six and I twelve or thereabouts. Mother told me to take him home, as he had got his clothes messed up with tar. On the way he asked me, 'I say, do you always do as your mother tells you?' 'Of course,' I replied. 'What a damn fool you must be,' reposted the six year old!

One morning in January I awoke to find the whole place was flooded. The middle walk of Waterloo Street was a canal whilst half the Parade Ground was submerged. I had to jump along the parapets on my way to the office. Murray Street was a sheet of water and near Camp Street it was over a foot deep and the floods did not subside until a little after one o'clock. Cars rushed through the flooded streets, casting great showers of spray ten to twelve feet on either side. The records showed that during the previous twelve hours seven and a half inches of rain fell on Georgetown.

After work I took Mother for a drive. Three large trees had been blown down in Main Street and two in Brickdam. Turning out of Oronoque Street into Lamaha Street I narrowly missed colliding with a bus that failed to blow its horn. We went as far as Plaisance where we had to turn back because the road was flooded. The tops of the tombstones were barely visible above the water. Cattle had been driven off the pastures and were congregated on the parapets and the road itself, so driving was not easy.

The following day I received a formal demand from the Postmaster General for the telephone rent for the quarter. As I'd had no service since the wires were destroyed by the Tullock fire in Church Street two days after Christmas, I wrote back saying that I did not intend to pay the rent until the service was restored and asked what rebate was due to me for the absence of service. On the way to the office I called in at the McInroy Building (telephone exchange) and got a copy of the contract between the Postmaster General and telephone renters.

During January I was temporarily transferred to the office of the District Commissioner in Georgetown as a Commissary as they were short-handed there and I had relevant experience. The chief duty of a commissary was the issuing of licences. Having been a commissary in each of the districts in which I was stationed, the work was not strange to me though in town there appeared to be a special licence book for each individual licence, whereas in the out-districts we relied to a great extent on a blank book, filling in the details ourselves. The cash book was made up each day and the cash sent to the bank by messenger. The first day I sent $958 to the bank. The only drawback was that one day I found I was $2 short, which I had to make up out of my own pocket. Formerly commissaries received a risk allowance of $8 a month.

I stayed in this temporary post for about five weeks then returned to the Lands and Mines Department where I started checking through the old office records and destroying those that were no longer required. It was whilst I was doing this that I came across a report on the conditions in the mining camps in the North West in 1893. It described vividly their insanitary condition, a condition I saw duplicated in certain camps on the Mazaruni in 1924 and 1925. I put a minute on this file mentioning the above and sent it forward. During the afternoon Mullin appeared before me, threw down the file and remarked, 'I am surprised at you writing such a minute, Roth', and walked away. I saw he had put a sarcastic minute on the file regarding my bringing the matter up. I felt I had made the connection between past and present conditions in absolutely good faith and hoping that if the steps recommended therein were carried out now, it would prevent the reoccurrence of such conditions as existed, say, at the inception of Buck Cannister Sands. I felt very upset at his minute and drafted one in reply asking if there was anything I could do these days to satisfy him. I showed it to Messervey and he strongly advised me not to send it. I decided to follow his advice but instead to thrash the matter out verbally, so I marched straight into Mullin's office.

There I told him that he seemed to have a personal bias against me, judging from the tone of his minutes to me over the past few years, that he never or rarely acknowledged my reports, much less said thank you. Being now well worked up I told him that it was not fair to carry on with me the feud he had with my father without just cause. He said that I was looking at matters from quite the wrong point of view, that he had recently reported very favourably on me in his annual confidential report, which he offered to show me. I declined, saying I accepted his assurance, though it was certainly news to me. Then he blurted out, 'You have given me the impression, ever since you relinquished your post in the Mazaruni, that you are continually holding the Department to ridicule – and this also is the impression of your successor.' This grossly unjust charge so dumbfounded me that I did not know what to say, except to deny it. The impression he got from my minutes was that I apparently did not think before I wrote. I exclaimed, 'Very well, I shall write no more.' And with that I left his office.

After I had returned to my desk and cooled off a bit I wrote the following minute:–

Commissioner,

This afternoon you informed me that since I relinquished the post of Warden, Mazaruni, I gave you the impression that I was constantly ridiculing the Department and that this view was held by my successor. Your impression is without any actual foundation and, in fairness to me, I ask you to state your reasons for such belief, that I may refute them. I find it very hard, after twenty-six years of hard-working and loyal service to the Department to have its head take such a view of my conduct and unless such erroneous impression can be erased from your mind there is nothing left for me but to ask that you be good enough to recommend my transfer to another branch of the service when a suitable vacancy occurs.

Respectfully submitted,

Vincent Roth.

I placed the minute in an envelope, marked it confidential and left it on Mullin's desk. Next morning, as soon as I got to the office, Messervey handed me an identical envelope with the remark, 'The Chief asked me to hand you this.' I found my original minute with the following addendum:–

Mr Roth,

I cannot accept your version of what was said at an interview which you sought and conducted in a fit of temper; nor can I undertake a confidential correspondence on the subject. If you want to discuss the matter calmly you can come and see me with Mr Christiani when I am free from the Legislative Council.

J.M.

At breakfast time I went to the Public Buildings and discussed my disagreement with Mullin with Bolton Campbell. He strongly advised me not to have an interview with only Christiani present as a witness and warned me to be very careful as Mullin was said to be a very vindictive man. The same afternoon I went back to the Public Buildings and had a private interview with Niven Gilchrist over the matter. He expressed his indignation very forcibly and also advised me strongly not to accede to any interview in the presence of Christiani, who 'would side with the Commissioner of Lands and Mines and to hell with Vincent Roth'. He told me to put what I had to say in writing, officially, but to be very careful and sure of my facts, since Mullin was a 'dangerous brute'.

After tea, to get the Mullin affair out of my hair, I took Mother up to Ogle to see how Walter was getting on. Phil was unable to come with us as she was again confined to bed with her old stomach complaint and was under doctor's orders to rest. Mother had bought a plot of land at Ogle that Walter was going to run as a chicken farm. On the day of our visit, work had just started on the house foundations. Walter in the meantime was living on the site under a tarpaulin.

In the office a day or so later a bunch of the youngsters were having a hearty laugh. I asked what the joke was. They were discussing meanness and someone instanced a senior member of staff. Before his departure on a protracted stay in the Mazaruni, he had allegedly sent his wife to their married daughter in Berbice, put his car in storage, shut up the house, sacked the cook and killed the cat. Someone added that the last assertion was wrong, since he was too mean to own a cat, but used his neighbour's cat to catch his rats.

Later in the day I was instructed to proceed to the Courantyne Coast and River to undertake routine surveys there. I called in on Sam Kaufman, who was on leave at the time, to ask him about conditions in the Courantyne.

At the end of February, just prior to setting off for the Courantyne, I took Mother to Berbice to see her friends, the Gigliolis. We left home just after seven and some fifteen minutes late reached Ogle where we stopped long enough to say good morning to Walter and then went spinning off down the coast. But just beyond the bridge at Mahaica we came to one of the cuts that had been made in the road to assist the escape of flood waters. The repairs had not been completed and the gap was covered by a temporary bridge little more than six feet wide consisting of greenheart planks laid loosely and not nailed. I managed to get the car over and we passed three or four similar places before we reached De Kinderen. The countryside was in places still inundated from the January floods. Beyond De Kinderen the road was reasonably good and we were soon doing a steady forty miles an hour.

We ran through Mahaicony in great style, passed the coconut groves of Letter T, crossed the Abary and made good progress down the west coast of Berbice. This part of the country looked dismal, the dead grass of the flooded flats not yet having begun to grow again. In places I had to drive very carefully on account of the number of cattle and sheep that were grazing on the roadside parapets. One feature we noticed peculiar to Berbice was the number of bullock carts in use on the road.

Soon we saw the two great chimneys of Pln Blairmont looming ahead. Just beyond Rosignol we passed the rows of cottages of the estate labourers, next the overseers quarters, some new ones in the course of construction, and finally to Dr Giglioli's house, a large two storeyed structure standing between the road and the Berbice River. Mrs Giglioli met us and took us upstairs where we waited for the doctor to return from his visit to Pln Bath of which he had the medical care as well as of Pln Blairmont and Pln Providence across the river. All three estates belonged to S. Davson & Co., the cane from the other two being brought to Blairmont for crushing. The doctor soon arrived bringing with him Fitzmaurice, the estate accountant, and we all sat down to a breakfast of Italian food.

After breakfast Giglioli showed me some photographs he had taken during a recent visit to Italy. They were of the reclamation of the malaria-infested Pontine marshes where there had been an old medieval city, entirely abandoned, through the prevalence of malaria and of the new town of Lictoria, built by Mussolini on a section of the marshes that had been rid of the fever and reclaimed for cultivation.

Two days later was the christening of Jacques' and Winnie's boy. First I went to R.G. Humphrey for a shampoo, haircut and beard trim and then to M.V. Hings to buy a present, choosing a pretty little silver christening cup. Romiti, the other godfather, rushed in in a great state of worry and I laughingly remarked, 'I know what you've come for.'

'Yes,' he replied, 'and what the hell must I get?'

I left him trying to decide between a hairbrush and a spoon and went on to Jacques' house in Croal Street.

At Brickdam Cathedral we witnessed the christening which was performed by Father Marques. The names chosen were Pierre Jacques Anthony Vincent. The little fellow behaved remarkably well during the somewhat lengthy ceremony. He did not cry and only when turned on his tummy did he dribble out the salt that had been placed in his mouth. When the priest made the sign of the Cross the baby moved his tiny fist up to his forehead and then down to his tummy as though he too was trying to make the sacred sign. Romiti looked very comical holding the lighted candle at the latter part of the ceremony

Returning to the house we drank the baby's health in champagne and exchanged yarns. Talking of the late King Albert, old P.J. suddenly put his hand in his trouser pocket and, pulling out a black and shiny chestnut, remarked, 'King Albert gave me that in 1921.' He said that he and his sister-in-law were picking chestnuts from the ground beneath the trees in a park in Antwerp when a tall man came up and started picking up chestnuts too. His sister-in-law nudged him and whispered, 'That is the King.' Immediately P.J. took off his hat and bowed. King Albert chatted for a few minutes and then exchanged a chestnut as a souvenir; P.J. had kept his in his trouser pocket ever since.

During the evenings I continued transcribing of my journals and writing up 'Morawhanna Memoirs', and just before I set off for the Courantyne I received permission from the Governor to publish my article 'Hiking on Mahaica' in the *Daily Chronicle*.

On Monday 5th March we left for the Courantyne. I despatched the baggage to the station at seven o'clock and a few minutes later Walter and I followed on foot. I had decided to take Walter along as there was little for him to do whilst his house was being built. At the station were Basil Parrett, Fraser the chain bearer and an Indian I was taking along. Just before eight o'clock, the fifth man, Austin, turned up. Austin, a young Negro who had been studying surveying on his own, was desirous of putting in his ninety days in the field with a qualified surveyor, as required by the regulations, before he could sit his examinations.

The train left just after eight o'clock. At first I thought my only fellow passenger in the first class carriage was a young attractive dark girl dressed in a blue and white sailor-boy style suite with a similarly coloured beret, but just as the train started Mr De Abreu, the assistant traffic superintendent, came in and we carried on a more or less interesting conversation right through to Mahaica where he left the train.

From this point on I was able to devote some attention to the dark girl who sat opposite me. I could not place her as to her condition or morals, or even to her race. She wore no ring on her left hand and yet her figure did not strike me as that of a maiden. She had kicked off her fashionable shoes and sat with her brown silk stockinged feet on the vacant seat in front of her, displaying a pair of plump calves and the edge of a white lace-edged petticoat. Once she moved her legs and exposed for a moment a portion of comfortable thigh encased in a pair of tight fitting orange coloured drawers, but her attitude was by no means immodest, as she kept her gaze constantly out of the window, revealing a clean cut profile. I could not decide whether she was a mixture of Negro and East Indian or whether she was pure Negro with her hair ironed smooth. Her dark skin was smooth and well powdered with an even touch of rouge on her cheeks. Her suitcase and hatbox had labels of the Canadian National Steamship Company on them and I gathered from a conversation I'd overheard at Mahaica station that she had just returned from a holiday in Trinidad and was on her way back home to Berbice. At one point she had trouble retying the string with which her hat box was fastened so I offered to do it for her. She replied graciously in a high falsetto voice that appeared so very much put on that I decided against pursuing her acquaintance any further. Thereafter I contented myself with a casual glance at her facial profile which certainly held a certain amount of charm.

Shortly after twelve we were at Rosignol and then onto the little steamer, *Lukunani*. On our crossing the Berbice River we nearly ran aground, so silted up was the river on the townside.

Miss Cossou was there with a car to meet us and we were soon being greeted by the parson and his wife at their home in Philadelphia Street. After a very nice breakfast we walked down the Strand, the main street, to the stelling. Most of the shops looked old fashioned and the street had no continuous pavement, but consisted of individual sections of varying heights in front of each mercantile establishment. I passed a little hut-like building which I took to be a barber's shop until, glancing at the sign, I saw it was the chambers of my old friend V.D.P. Woolford, the solicitor. Stepping inside I found him engaged with some clients and Inspector Edmonds. After an exchange of greetings we went on to the stelling where we found Fraser and Basil looking very worried.

W. Nurse, the Land Officer, who was arranging transport for our party to Letter Kenny was also there and the reason for the worried expressions was that two of the promised buses had failed to turn up. Then a bus turned up driven by a little cross-eyed fellow, who told Nurse that he was afraid to take the risk of breaking police regulations by carrying passengers and goods in the same bus. I agreed about this and told him to arrange for a lorry. This was soon forthcoming and our gear was packed onto it and sent on its way. About three o'clock the rest of us set off aboard a yellow bus called Shanghai. As we approached the bridge leading out of town we found that the driver, Matthews, had been well advised with regard to the regulations, as all outgoing buses were being stopped by Inspector Edmonds. Climbing onto a platform he cast a searching eye over the interior of the bus. If a bag was spotted under a seat and identified as not personal baggage, out came his notebook and pencil. The offender noted, we were allowed to proceed.

Swinging round by the mental hospital, as the lunatic asylum is now politely called, we crossed the Canje and were soon travelling down the longest stretch of straight road in the colony, crossing the Grand Canal, a relic of Dutch days, but now almost obliterated south of the road. On the other side stretched pasture lands, dotted with the black and brown forms of cattle and sometimes almost hidden by a snow-white carpet formed by thousands of white herons, cranes and other aquatic birds. There were occasionally spots of brilliant scarlet where a few curri-curri condescended to associate with their less brilliantly plumaged relatives. In the meantime the famous Courantyne wind kept up a continuous rustle and roar against the roof of our bus, and hummed amongst the telegraph wires alongside the road.

Presently a palatial building loomed up out of the flat pasture. This was East Lothian, the mansion of Edgar Hicken, the local Croesus. At length the interminable stretch of straight road came to an end and we ran through Rose Hall Village after passing the chimney of Pln Albion factory. From there we entered Pln Port Mourant, the highway passing between the factory and the staff residences. Thence to Bloomfield and Letter Kenny which, with Auchlyne, constitute one long straggling village.

There we managed to hire the upper flat of a small cottage from Goorbharri, a shopkeeper, where we installed ourselves. As there was no kitchen we had to erect one with tarpaulins. Behind the house was a home-made windmill which drove a coconut grating machine. After an early supper I hired a small car from the landlord and, with Walter, drove back to Port Mourant where, in the overseers' quarters we found Ralph Rice and spent an hour with him before driving back to Letter Kenny. The wind was so strong that night that we had to keep the door and all the windows on the north side of the house shut and the steady moaning kept me awake for a long time.

Next morning I set out to survey some rice lands for Victor Sugrim Singh in the second depth of Pln Bloomfield, which bounds Letter Kenny on the west. The second depths of these two estates had been subdivided into lots many years ago and licensed out to proprietors of the first depth in proportion to their respective holdings. Unfortunately, when an original proprietor died, his heirs naturally wanted the lands divided so that some or other of these second-depth lots were always under survey.

It was while carrying out these surveys that I had my first view of the hoatzins, Canje pheasants, or as they are locally termed, 'stinking hannahs'. They were the shape and size of an ordinary pheasant but with a handsome crest of plumes on the top of the head. These birds are of exceptional interest as being the only survivors of the link between reptiles and birds. Their habitat does not appear to extend westward of the Mahaicony but down the Courantyne they were very common.

As I walked back to camp, a car blew its horn repeatedly behind me and then pulled up as it drew level. It was Long, the District Commissioner, who was on his way back to New Amsterdam from his fortnightly visit to Skeldon. We had a short yarn in the course of which he told me he wanted to return to his old post of Commissioner of the North West District because his job as Commissioner of Berbice was hopeless due to the lack of staff. We then got to discussing the eastern boundary of the colony dividing it from Surinam, which I always thought was the low water mark on the left bank of the Courantyne River. To my surprise Long assured me that it was the high water mark. A former Attorney General, Sir Joseph Nunan, had ruled it to be the low water mark but the Law Officers in London had overruled him and declared it to be the high water mark. Thus the stellings at Springlands and Skeldon are in Dutch territory.

At camp I was just in time to wash and change when Ralph Rice turned up in a little Austin car in which he ran Walter and I back to his quarters for high tea. The estate staff was well provided for with a golf course and racecourse, the latter being run by the Port Mourant Club, which

Ralph proudly claimed to be the only one in the colony free from debt. I rather upset Ralph when I mistook the clubhouse for the mortuary!

After tea Ralph took us over the factory which was in the process of grinding. It was an immense place, producing some hundred tons of sugar a day. In addition to the Krajewski that broke and split the canes as they came off the carrier, there were no fewer than four sets of crushing rollers. From the last of these, the bone dry megass was carried on an endless belt up to the boiler wall where it was automatically fed into the furnaces. The cane juice as it came from the rollers looked far from appetising, a dirty black-looking liquid. Two things in the factory emphasised the keen competition in the sugar-making industry at the time: one was the complicated arrangement of belts and archimedian screws, whereby any single piece of cane that accidentally escaped from the rollers was recovered and put back through the mill. The other was the process by which the second quality sugar was worked up with fresh juice and converted into first quality produce.

The centrifugal pans, revolving at untold revolutions per minute, were most interesting. The minder having stopped a pan and scooped the sugar out of it would pull a lever and let in a mass of black viscous molasses which had the appearance more of pine tar than anything else. He turned another lever and the pan began to spin. In a few seconds the black mass was, by centrifugal force, plastered against the meshwork sides, forming a brown wall which, as the molasses was forced out leaving the pure sugar crystals, gradually changed to a yellowish white colour.

We returned to the car and drove into New Amsterdam for dinner. Ralph let me drive and once I got used to the feel of the vehicle I managed to rattle along at over forty miles an hour; the only fault I could find was a rather unreliable foot brake with the result that I had to slow down every time we approached any cattle or donkeys on the road. We made our way to a private hotel in the Strand kept by an old Englishman, a retired planter, by the name of Lynch. Seventy-four years old, Lynch had been in the colony for fifty-four years, twenty-four of which he had spent at Port Mourant where he had finished up as manager.

At the dinner table we met Whittacker, the District Engineer and McCowan the Magistrate. We complimented the former on the excellent state of his roads and he told us that the wider the road was, the cheaper it was to maintain, as the traffic had more room to spread itself out and did not cause the same wear and tear as on a narrow road. In the case of the long seven mile stretch beyond the Grand Canal, he had deliberately left several sections of this stretch in bad order to try and reduce the speed of the traffic. He maintained that burnt earth was the cheapest method of metalling the roads in the colony. In Queensland, Whittacker told us, they were experimenting with a new form of earth road where raw earth was laid over the road surface and then burnt insitu by a special machine that calcined the surface with burning jets of gas as it passed over it.

On the subject of the Grand Canal, Whittacker told how the proprietors of the estates bordering it had petitioned the Government that it be cleaned. When the matter was referred to him he looked into the old Dutch titles under which the estates were held and discovered that the tenants had the duty to maintain the stretch of canal running past their lands. Naturally, the Government passed the information back to the proprietors.

After dinner Ralph, Walter and I retired to the Gaiety Theatre where we saw the film *Stamboul*. The audience barely totalled a dozen.

After completing my work in a couple of days, we again boarded the Shanghai Express and proceeded eastwards. Passing Hogstye, I saw the fine big house where Phil had convalesced in 1932. At Kilmarnock we put up at the house of one Drepaul, whose younger brother had been indicted a few years before, with two other men, for the murder of a Corporal Mitchell, and later acquitted.

The survey I had to do for Drepaul was one of the worst I had ever tackled. The bush was so thick that the men got badly scratched and the further we went, the deeper became the water through which we had to wade until, in the end, I decided it was impossible to continue. When I returned to camp, much to the joy of the men, Drepaul then informed me that he had wanted to suggest that the water would be too deep before I began the survey, but thought I would not like it. His bashfulness had made me throw away three days' work.

Next morning found us standing on the roadside waiting for the Shanghai Express. Presently another bus came along, owned and driven by an East Indian named Sattaur who informed us that our bus had broken down. However, he offered to take us to Springlands for $4, which offer I immediately accepted, it being cheaper than the Shanghai Express. On our way we passed Tarlogie Police Station, a solitary building set in a pasture at a bend in the road. It was in charge of this station that Corporal Mitchell was murdered. Some distance further, just past Brighton Village, we came to the actual scene of the murder, marked by a black cross on a telegraph post. It was here that the corporal was shot dead whilst cycling back to his station one night.

We crossed over the Little Devil Creek, the original boundary between the colonies of Berbice and Surinam. It would appear that owing to the great width of the Courantyne River (at its mouth about twenty miles), the Surinam authorities had difficulty in controlling the coast westwards of the river. One day, around 1780, the Governors of the two colonies met and it was decided to move the boundary eastwards to the left bank of the Courantyne. This gave Berbice all the land between that river and Devil Creek; the Governor of Surinam retained control of the river itself and all its islands. This gentleman's agreement was subsequently ratified by their principals in Europe and holds valid to this present day.

We had not gone very far beyond Anamoramise, or No.63, when a figure was seen cycling behind us and waving frantically for us to stop. This we did and when the cyclist caught us up he turned out to be a Negro policeman clad in non-uniform trousers, a pyjama jacket and felt cap. He was very angry and could barely talk on account of his exertions. At length he demanded of Sattaur why he had not stopped when signalled to do so. Sattaur replied that he did not recognise him for a policeman, but mistook him for a passenger and, as he did not have any room, he did not stop. The policeman glared into the bus and, pointing to Parrett, asked, 'Who is dat?' The driver pointed to me instead and said, 'That is Mr Roth.' The policeman looked at me and, breaking into sudden smiles, all his anger gone, exclaimed, 'Mr Rat, eh, eh. How you do, Sah? You remember me at Kamakusa? That's alright, Sattaur, go ahead!' He had, of course, spotted the baggage and gear on the roof of the bus and the passengers inside and thought he had a case. When I explained that we were a government expedition, he was most profuse with his apologies for detaining us.

Soon the square brick chimney of Pln Springlands came into view and we stopped at the office of the district administrator where I collected my mail. Ulric Mapp, the sub-controller of Customs, was away at Skeldon so I was thrown on my own resources to find accommodation. Sattaur fetched Frank Mattias, the local manager of Lopes and Fernandes, an immaculately dressed Portuguese youth. He, on being asked if he knew of any suitable lodgings, looked up and down the road for two or three minutes, his mouth mumbling some soundless words. After an interminable wait, he said the only place he knew was at No.63. Pointing out that it was at Springlands we wished to stay and not Sixty Three, I politely thanked him for his assistance and told Sattaur to drive on.

After passing through the village known as No.78, or Eliza and Mary, we stopped at a shop owned by a man called Chan, who said he had met me once in town. He put the upper flat of the building at our disposal as he and his wife only occupied a ground floor room at the back of the shop. It was after I had concluded these arrangements that I realised that Chan had been indicted for the murder of one Fernandes some years ago, but had subsequently been acquitted. I seemed to have made quite a point on this trip of putting up at the houses of alleged murderers!

In the evening I went up to dinner with Clarence King, Manager of Skeldon. He invited me to put up at the estate but I had by then already fixed up with Chan. The manager's house, a tall building, stood close by the factory, and it was from its upstairs window that my old friend Parson Duffus had fallen to his death. Here I was met by Morris King, the younger brother of Edward H. King, the former Commissioner of the North West District. He reminded me that we had met once before in Morawhanna many years ago. He introduced me to his wife, the former Whanna Quick of Mora and Whanna fame. The elder sister, Mora, was the wife of Edward King, thus being sister-in-law to her own sister. Shortly afterwards we were joined by F.C. Chinn, the deputy manager, who had been a great friend of Dad's. Before going into dinner we discussed the piece of land I was to survey for the estate.

Next morning, as arranged, I sent the men on ahead and waited for the estate car to take me to Skeldon factory. There King and Chinn were waiting for me. Having declined to ride aback with them on a mule, they provided me with a small corial. An East Indian lad steered it whilst another towed it from the dam by means of a long rope. We went along the main navigation trench of the estate and overtook a string of empty cane punts being towed up the waterway by a mule.

Presently we approached a small group of East Indian women who, to my horror, were in the act of removing their skirts preparatory to crossing the trench. Fortunately they saw me in time to stop their disrobing until I had passed. Glancing back a minute later I saw them waist deep in the middle of the trench heading for the opposite bank. Soon I saw the white jackets and helmeted figures of King and Chinn standing on one of the high bridges built to allow the passage of loaded cane punts as they turned north along the crossdam. When we passed under the bridge I was towed into a cross trench that ran parallel to the dam along which King and Chinn had come. We were soon at the piece of land that I was to survey and, after clearing a few points of detail, King and Chinn rode off and left me to get on with the work.

The boundary dam along which we had to work was covered with dense bush and twelve foot high mocca-moccas rose from the stagnant water that covered the land. Away from the breeze the mosquitoes were very troublesome so I was glad when the work was done. Just as we were packing away the instruments, Chinn arrived on his mule. He took me back in the corial by a different route, as he wanted to show me an old Indian kitchen midden he had found on the estate. There was an all but imperceptible rise in the ground about two acres in extent and on going up to it I saw the unmistakable signs, countless pieces of broken pottery with the occasional broken bone. The soil was much darker than in the surrounding area and Chinn assured me that the sugar cane grown on this spot was always much more prolific than elsewhere. He had found several curious things here, including stone axes and mortars.

We picked up one piece of pottery that appeared to have been baked from a mixture of clay and crushed shell. Particles of the latter adhered to the outer surfaces but it could also be seen in the body of the clay at the broken edge of the fragment.

We passed a gang of black Barbadians and Chinn told me that they were part of a group of about eighty men and seventy women who had been on the estate for about fifteen years. Being what he called a hand-picked lot, they were very satisfactory labourers, doing much more work than the East Indians at a not very great increase in price. When they first came to the estate they tended to live by themselves but now were gradually integrating with the Creole Negroes.

Next day found us loading our gear aboard Sattaur's bus, bidding Chinn farewell and setting off for Crabwood Creek. We ran through rice fields which were being ploughed in preparation for the next crop. Houses were scattered all along the road, most, to my surprise, being of board with zinc-sheet roofs, mud houses with thatch being by no means as plentiful as I had been led to believe. This was because of the extraordinary cheap price of crabwood timber, $17 per 1000 feet. There were already three sawmills in the district and a fourth under construction.

On leaving Springlands, I pushed open the windscreen to let in some breeze. Sattaur did not object but merely remarked that he usually travelled with it closed and I soon learnt why. A marabunta flew in and stung me above the left eye. In my haste to brush off the insect I flicked my glasses right to the back of the bus and it was with great relief that I found both lenses were still intact. At length we arrived at our destination, Choong's Rum shop, a large two-storeyed building lying to the west of the road, the upper storey of which I had engaged.

The next day being Sunday I gave the men a break and caught up on my correspondence. After writing to Mother and Phil I wrote to the Commissioner of Lands and Mines seeking the Governor's permission to leave the colony, as required under Colonial Regulations, as I would have to do to carry out surveys beyond the termination of the road.

During the afternoon, Andrew Choong, the proprietor of my present lodgings, paid me a visit and I was surprised and pleased to recognise in him an old Mazaruni acquaintance of 1930, he had been one of the principals of the diamond trading firm of Choong and Lam.

Beyond the southernmost section of Pln Skeldon, the crown land along the Courantyne had been sold mostly to East Indians and the locality became know as Crabwood Creek after a small stream that flows into the river about three miles beyond Skeldon. The land was so popular amongst the rice growers that it was now my task to check some of the boundaries between the lots which had changed hands or been subdivided, and also lay out some new lots further back. The southernmost and last section of Pln Skeldon was the most easterly sugar growing land in the colony and known as New Calcutta. This was because it used to be common practice for indentured East Indian immigrants, escaping from the estates, to head eastwards down the coast under the belief that if they walked far enough they would return to Calcutta. Hence the last estate came to be called New Calcutta.

The work proved very difficult because the recent floods had cut the dams along which we had to travel in many places. At times we were waist deep in water and most days I finished up soaked through from head to foot. At several places on the dams we found carpets of snail shells several inches thick which crunched and crackled under our feet. These, I was told, were the feeding places of the curraow, a large bird that feeds almost exclusively on these snails.

Back at our quarters I found Mapp waiting for me. He wanted me to accompany him to Jumbi Creek to verify that a certain man, whom he was prosecuting, had cut timber on crown land and then give the necessary evidence in Court. This I said I was quite willing to do provided I got the District Commissioner's instructions on the subject and the Governor's permission to leave the Colony. This permission I received.

On the day of our visit to Jumbi Creek, Mapp picked up Walter and I in his little two-seater car and returned to Springlands where the Customs launch awaited us at the end of the stelling. At the landward end of the long wharf was a newly erected rice bond, packed with hundreds of bags of rice awaiting shipment to Trinidad and other West Indian Islands. There was also a sort of pen on the wharf where a dozen or so passengers who had just arrived from Nickerie were being examined by the police. They were mostly East Indians, although I saw one or two black people, including a dear old Dutch nanny wearing a tremendous head cloth. Mapp told me the launch came over three times a week bringing about thirty people at a time. At the end of the stelling was an open lattice work iron standard some thirty feet high on top of which was an automatic flashing gas light. As soon as dusk fell the light began emitting a flash every fifteen seconds until daylight returned when it switched itself off. It was one of Mapp's duties to check the gas pressure in the cylinders and to notify the harbour authorities when they needed replenishing. At the other end of the wharf was a short flagstaff from which fluttered half a Union Jack. Mapp remarked that it would have to last for at least another month or so as the authorities 'were not too free with their flags'. This I well knew, because for months at Kamakusa I had to fly a dirty piece of cloth that had once been a Union Jack. It was a noticeable fact that the flying of the national flag was not a popular local pastime in the colony. Requisition a government department for a Union Jack and ten to one the answer would be 'none in stock'. Once I received the reply, even when stationed near the frontier, 'There is no necessity for a Union Jack at your station.'

On our return from Jumbi Creek we went to Mapp's quarters on the upper floor of the District Administration building. It was a mansion, the main sitting room having walls close on twenty feet high before the tower-like roof started. There were two tiers of windows in the room, so that from the outside the building gave the impression of having three storeys. The grand effect was, however, spoilt by the wretched colour with which the walls were painted, a brilliant yellow but now stained with mould. From this central apartment two wings branched off containing rooms almost equally large but of more normal height. These rooms gave onto narrow balconies that ran along the front of the building. I expressed surprise at government building such a magnificent residence for any district officer and learnt that this was originally a famous manager's house, built by De Montpellier in the early 20s when he founded the township of Bonsall up the Courantyne River.

If ever money was wickedly thrown away it was done in the name of Bonsall, an American timber man with more money than sense. Irwin De Montpellier, his local representative and the man who spent the money, was a stout, bull-headed Italian, pugilistic in appearance, whom rumour alleged had spent time in Cayenne. But he was a plausible scamp, lavish with money and lionised in the Colony. He had a timber grant just above the mouth of the Arobayo Creek near Dalgin on the Demerara River. Here thousands of logs of lightwood, purchased at fabulous prices, were stored within a large boom consisting of logs chained end to end. One night this boom broke and hundreds of logs floated adrift. Montpellier offered $100 for every log returned. As soon as news of the reward got about the boom broke regularly but the money was still paid. When he wanted to travel he would hire a steam launch from Sprostons on which, clothed in silk pyjamas, he was accompanied by a couple of ladies of easy virtue, similarly garbed. I saw this with my own eyes. Once his hat blew off at Springlands and to the man who picked it up he gave $5. Then to crown it all he built Bonsall as his business headquarters – everything there being of the most costly design. When it was all completed he hired the *S.S.Mazaruni* together with a whole militia band and brought the then Governor up on a visit. The crash came shortly after and De Montpellier vanished. The buildings at Bonsall were bought by various people and moved to different parts of the Colony. A house in High Street, Kingston, is one, the office of Pln Skeldon is another and the administration building at Springlands, a third. This last one was bought and rebuilt on its present site by J.C. Fernandes who subsequently sold it to government.

Mapp invited us to go along with him to Pln Skeldon where he had, in his capacity as distillery officer, to seal some rum vats. I asked if I could drive his car and was very sorry that I did. I realised that the steering wheel had some five inches play, though when it engaged it was so stiff as to require real physical effort to have any effect on the wheels. The result was a violent form of zig-zag down the road, missing people and the roadside trenches by inches, so that by the time we arrived at the factory I was bathed in perspiration.

Accompanied by the distillery manager we went to the rum store, double-padlocked with a great iron bar across the door. In a large whitewashed barn-like structure, five great vats, holding a total of some 1500 gallons of rum, were ranged on stands round two walls, the tops connected by pipes. The remainder of the floor space was occupied by empty puncheons awaiting filling. The windows were criss-crossed with stout iron bars let into the window frames, whilst to obviate the chance of any unauthorised entry through the wooden walls of the building, the wall boards were criss-crossed with strips of iron. Altogether the place gave the impression of being an impregnable fortress. Mapp's job was to seal and lock two of the vats into which rum was to be run from the still during the night. This was done by placing metal covers over all the faucets in such a manner that the handles opening them could not be turned. These metal covers were locked with padlocks of a most ingenious design. Made of brass in the shape of an outsize matchbox the padlock had a hinged flap across its face with a keyhole fitting exactly over the keyhole in the body of the lock. The padlock having been fitted to the eyelets in the faucet cover, the hinged flap was opened and the padlock locked. In the recess in which the flap fitted, the distillery officer then placed a piece of paper, numbered, signed and dated, and torn from a counterfoil book in which its duplicate remained. This paper fitted exactly in the slot, thus covering the keyhole as well. The hinged flap was now closed and snapped shut by a spring. The whole secret of the padlock was that although the flap could be shut down over the lock after the latter had been locked, it was impossible to raise the flap without unlocking the lock and punching the paper beneath it with the key. Very simple, but each lock nevertheless cost about £7. Mapp explained that the reason why Government took such precautions to prevent the theft of rum on which duty had not been paid was because of the tremendous duty payable – $4.50 per proof gallon. In this particular case, the rum here being sixty degrees over proof, every gallon in the vats represented about $8.00 in revenue.

The next day I caught up with old man La Rose, whose back boundary I had just finished checking, and who was on his way back to No.78. As we walked along the road together we discussed various topics until we got onto the subject of race. La Rose told me how worried he was that Negroes were slowly being ousted from the district by East Indians. 'But what can you expect, Sir,' he added, 'when the black girls prefer East Indian men to those of their own race.' The imminence of Good Friday compelled the old man to remark, 'Tomorrow is the Passion of our Lord.' I told him that I intended to respect the day from consideration of my men's feelings rather than from any personal sanctity, as my beliefs inclined more towards Judaism than Christianity. The old man nearly dropped the sack he was carrying and looked at me with horror as though I were some unclean thing. 'What!' he exclaimed at last, 'You are a pagan, Sir.' I said that a man could be sincere and God-fearing without being a Christian, to which doctrine I got him to subscribe by the time we had reached my quarters. I even persuaded him to join me in a bottle of beer in the rum shop below them, though he kept an eye on me over the rim of his glass as though he was not certain whether he was sipping with Satan or not.

On the Saturday afternoon, I saw a little Austin car stop a few hundred yards up the road. The driver had a few words with a small East Indian boy then turned the car round and headed back down the road and slowed down as it approached the house. I realised that it was Ralph Rice and Bill Cooper, the latter apparently having come down from Georgetown to spend the holiday weekend with Ralph. After tea I took Ralph and Bill over to Skeldon and persuaded Ralph to let me drive. The going was not too bad until we reached the entrance to the estate where the locals were holding their weekly market. Donkey carts lined both side of the road displaying the various wares, whilst the roadway was blocked by the milling throng. Never before have I seen people so scornful of a motor car. Despite the continuous blowing of the horn and shouting they would not move and only when they felt the pressure of the bumper did they condescend to clear a path for us.

Chinn came out to meet us, invited us into his house for swizzles and insisted we stayed to dinner with the rest of the staff. It was served in the large dining room of the manager's house, some fifteen overseers seated at one long table, Chinn occupying the head of the table and Wheeler, the head overseer, the foot. The dinner, served by three or four East Indian manservants, was quite good and, to my surprise, included roast beef and Yorkshire pudding, although the latter did not come up to the standard of my own. The meal over we trooped outside and stood yarning in the moonlight until Chinn suggested we went to the local cinema in the village which was not two hundred yards from the estate gates.

In the foyer a burly Negro met us with a fistful of large red tickets. When he demanded our money, Chinn coolly informed him that we were only going upstairs for a drink. At that the ticket seller nodded to a diminutive East Indian youth who was attempting to bar our way up the stairs, and he stood aside. I naturally thought we would find a bar at the top but all that greeted my eyes was a flat-floored gallery containing several rows of folding chairs, the front ones of which were occupied by a few East Indian women and children waiting for the show to begin. Our party took some unoccupied chairs and placed them in a convivial circle so that some had their backs to the screen to give the impression that we were only there for a drink and not to see the show. Presently a waiter appeared with a tray full of immense soda tumblers brimming over with shandy gaff. Whilst we were imbibing this the show began and I remarked to Chinn that this was a novel way of gaining admission to the cinema. He explained that if we remained unduly long the cost of admission was added to the price of the drinks and thereby the management stood to lose nothing.

The holidays over, I set about organising my trip to Orealla. I hired a thirty-foot sloop whose forward section was decked, its centreboard fitted through this decked section. This was made up of greenheart planks and, when raised, held in position by an iron pin resting on the deck. On the morning of our departure we were astir by six o'clock and loading the sloop which, with the Blue Ensign flying, looked very business-like. We started at half past seven and were soon gliding silently up the muddy waters of the Courantyne. I took the tiller myself. We had not been sailing ten minutes when the dorsal fin of a porpoise showed nearby and, a moment later, the creature rose almost alongside the sloop. It lifted its body for quite half its length perpendicularly out of the water and seemed to look at us with a most comical expression in its great round black eye set near the base of its beak-like snout. It repeated this performance twice and then, as if to show us what it really could do, leapt right out of the water in a slow graceful curve. The animal must have been at least seven to eight feet long, its back and sides a handsome bluish grey and its belly a pale salmon pink.

We passed Parrot Island and came to the upper end of Long Island with little Napoleon Island sheltering close alongside its north-western shore. We took the wide channel between Long and Queriman Islands, thus having Dutch territory on both sides of us. We had a cold breakfast on board and as soon as we had finished a squall came on. It soon passed, however, and then we got the wind so dead against us that we had to come about and tack. Then another rainstorm hid the land so I steered by the pressure of the wind on the sail with the result that when the rain held up and I got my bearings I found we had run back down the river close on a mile. Fortunately, at this juncture a slight sea breeze set in and, letting the sail full out, we were able to run before it until it dropped. We had now been in the reach above Queriman Island for quite two hours and did not seem to be able to get round the next point, round which lay our day's destination, Kasi Creek.

As the wind dropped altogether we began to drift back with the ebb tide, so we ran for the bank and tied up alongside another sloop similarly situated. In it was a burly, round-faced Negro who had balata bleeder written all over him. We got into conversation about the river and he complained bitterly about the manner in which the Indians were ruining the accessible crabwood forests above the falls. 'An Indian will get a permit to cut fifty logs. He cuts a hundred, hauls out ten and leaves the other ninety to rot. There are millions of logs rotting all along the river.'

A light breeze sprang up again so we made another attempt to proceed but as soon as we got into the stream the wind dropped and a torrential downpour set in. We managed to drop back to a landing by a small pasture and tied up there. When the rain at length held up I went ashore and arranged for lodgings in the house of a Dutch Negro named Samuels for whom, as it happened, I had to inspect a wood-cutting grant above Orealla. There also I met an East Indian youth, Ranjawan, for whom I was to inspect another wood-cutting grant at Kasi Creek on the following day. He coolly informed me that his boundary lines were not yet cut and wondered whether I could inspect the place on my downward journey.

Samuel's house was a floored logie with walls and roof of manicole thatch laid perpendicularly in the manner of troolie thatch. Two or three East Indian youths and another elderly Negro occupied the house and the former sat on their haunches looking at me stolidly whilst I changed into my pyjamas. When my camp furniture had been set up I sat down and proceeded to write up my journal. The mosquitoes were so bad that I had to put up my net, the first time for the trip. My writing completed, I retired to my hammock and read *Algernon Knox, Detective* by Oppenheim.

I woke up at half past four next morning and turned everybody out with the bugle. During the night several more people had come in and the house was now full of hammock nets. One unfortunate black man had no net so he had swathed himself in rice bags as a protection against the mosquitoes. Stuck in the roof of the house I noticed half a dozen immense white feathers which, I learnt, were those of the Negro-cop, the local giant stork.

We managed to get away by a quarter to seven and, running up river before a gentle sea breeze, cleared Long Island and arrived at the three islands known as Three Sisters. Here the wind changed and we had to tack past them. Just as a nice breeze set in we arrived at our destination, the camp of an East Indian by the name of Jaimal, for whom I had to do a survey. We found Jaimal and his family and his Negro partner, an old Dutchman named Francois Brown, eleven all told, occupying a little tumble-down shed, in front of a new clearing of about an acre. Since there was no other accommodation, there was nothing left to do but build a camp on the muddy clay that formed the terrain there. The men started work at eleven o'clock and it was not until after one that the camp was in a state where we could prepare breakfast.

I had not been ashore long before I was called to look at Jaimal's two year old daughter who had crushed her finger between our boat and a corial. Her two sisters, Maimhood and Hahmud, were real nuisances and would not leave us alone for a moment as, sitting on a log, they watched us build camp, eat breakfast and change our clothes. The rain continued all afternoon and after supper, having written up my journal, I was driven into my hammock by the mosquitoes.

Accompanied by Jaimal's wife, eldest son and old Brown – Jaimal having gone down to Skeldon the previous afternoon – we set off in their boat to look for the paals of the abandoned tract below their lot. Having found them I laid out a connecting line down river and, leaving the men to carry on, returned to camp in a corial that had accompanied us. As the water by now was rather choppy, the short trip was not without excitement and by the time I got back to camp I was thoroughly drenched.

Parrett told me that the two girls were still being a nuisance. The young monkeys had been begging cigarettes that they were smoking by his fireside, hidden from their mother's sight by the palm-leaf windbreak forming our kitchen. Being anxious to get away from this damp, muddy and uncomfortable camp, I made the men work on through Sunday.

Soon after we left on Monday, a gentle wind sprang up and we sailed past McLennans Island and the British shore where some old stelling piles indicated all that was left of Warleigh where Geoffrey Phillips first saw the light of day. The breeze now dropped for a while and we drifted slowly back on the falling tide. However, by dint of much whistling, we persuaded the wind to return, which it did with a vengeance, right astern. With the mainsail full out we went spanking up past Little and Big Baboon Islands and the little Mocco Mocco island. As we swung round the head of the reach by the little Jumbi Island, a heavy rain squall sprang up astern with amazing suddenness. The mast bent as the heavy sail bellied with the strong wind and the sloop heeled over almost to her beam ends and the crew began to get frightened.

Poor Austin, who had never been in a small boat before, held onto the gunwale like grim death. His black skin turned a sickly grey as he yelled, 'Put um ashore, put um ashore'. Ramdeo began shouting excitedly, 'Loose um sail, loose um sail', which last exhortation I thought advisable and gave the necessary order, though before we got the sheet down we were all but over. We now ran with just the jib but at an amazing speed before the squall. We were rushing through an opaque white mist and only by the set of the waves did I know I was still heading up the river. The squall at last died down as suddenly as it had sprung up and as the mist cleared we could see the pinkish white cliffs of Orealla ahead.

The breeze dropped entirely and the rays of the setting sun warmed and dried us as we took down the sail and got out the paddles. As we approached the cliffs of almost pure white kaolin clay, I saw they were between sixty and seventy feet high, the forest on top giving place to scrub savannah. Bushes covered the face of the cliffs except for patches of exposed clay too steep for the growth of vegetation. We recognised the mission of Orealla by the wooden cross topping the thatched roof of the church that stood on a narrow shelf below the cliff.

At the landing a raft of crabwood logs was moored as well as several corials and a small bateau or two. A crowd of curious Indians, mainly women, the majority having babies in their arms, gathered to see the visitors. Indeed, we saw very few men during our stay, the majority being away hauling crabwood logs. Although the tide was nearly high, the river bank rose sheer for about ten feet and access ashore was by a stoutly built stepladder five to six feet wide. Besides the church and the rest house, also built of thatch with walls of split manicole, was a substantially built frame house of boards and shingles, the residence of the Catechist. He was a tall, middle-aged, quietly spoken Negro by the name of Tucker who, at the moment of my visit, was engaged either making or repairing a khaki coat on a sewing machine. He kindly put the rest house at my disposal. I enquired about the possibility of hiring a bateau and Indians for my journey up to the falls, and he sent for Captain Crawford, a little white haired Boviander who had been on the river for fourteen years, though originally hailing from Fort Island in the Essequibo. With him I arranged for the hire of a small bateau, himself and three Indians who were to meet me at Potoko Creek on the following Wednesday. The three men I proposed hiring I saw personally. Two were pure Indians and the third a burly man of mixed race named Sertima.

I was struck by the number of people of mixed race here, their proportion being much greater than I had seen on other missions. I noticed, too, that all the paddles were of a different type to those used in other parts of the colony, having blades shaped in the form of narrow pointed ellipses. I learnt from Tucker that the population of the mission, not including the children, was about two hundred adults. They were mainly Arawaks though there were also quite a number of Warraus amongst them.

Having plenty of room to sling my hammock I woke after a cool refreshing sleep. After coffee I had a look at the church. In the chancel I was surprised to see a window of real stained glass, with the design picked out in lead. It contrasted strangely with the rest of the building which was mainly palm thatch.

As the tide would be falling all morning I decided to delay our departure until after breakfast. From my table in the rest house, my attention was drawn to a little Indian boy, just off the landing stage, paddling the slightest apology for a craft I had ever seen. It was actually the sawn off end of a corial, not six feet in length. With the boy's weight it sat so low in the water that even if he only leaned his head to one side it would take in water. Yet he handled it as comfortably as if it was a woodskin with three inches of freeboard.

Walter, who had climbed up the cliff, spoke so enthusiastically of the scene up there that I decided to go and look for myself. The path climbed the cliff on a slant and I was surprised to notice that the surface here and also on top consisted of loose white sand that evidently overlay the kaolin. The ascent was so steep that I stopped several times to admire the view that, from the actual top, was certainly worthy of admiration. Immediately below, the roofs of the mission building and the houses of the Indians peeped up from between the groves of fruit trees and clumps of bamboos. In the middle distance, the wide bow of the broad river swept away to either side, apparently encircling the high forested peninsular on the Dutch shore. Far down to the left Mapenna Island hugged the nearer bank, whilst in the distant east the forests of Surinam disappeared over the horizon.

At the top of the cliff, the path ran in both directions along the edge, and I followed the one running down river. At intervals, branch paths lead off into the forest of thorn palms and cotton trees and most of these paths revealed more houses only a short distance from the edge of the cliff. Presently the main path came to several houses in which women were busily engaged in the preparation of paiwarri. They, as was their custom, said nothing to a stranger beyond replying in like manner to the usual greeting, 'Howdee'.

At length I found a house in which a solitary man sat making baskets. I asked the way to the savannah and he directed me back along the cliff top until I reached a wide road leading to the burial ground. This I followed for a couple of hundred yards through a forest of awara palms until I came out on the savannah. It was part of the same savannah I had seen the previous afternoon from the river, consisting of gently undulating parkland with patches of low scrub and small islands of forest set amidst the expanse of coarse grass. Where the path emerged from the forest was the burial ground – a clean, weeded patch of some two acres where rows of unpainted weather-beaten crosses of uniform size projected from the brown clay soil. Few of the crosses had any inscriptions on them and their uniformity reminded me strongly of a war cemetery. Returning to the cliff, I descended it in a less dignified but much faster manner than I ascended and, it being close on one o'clock and the tide almost dead low, I had the sloop loaded and we tried to make a start.

Of course, the moment we left the landing the wind blew in all directions but the right one and twice we were blown onto the sand beach that was exposed in front of the steep river bank. To add to the confusion, a heavy rain squall came on and, as we were pushing off from the land for the third time, someone shouted, 'Look, steamer!' Sure enough, I saw a steamer looming up through the mist that was too thick to allow us to recognise the vessel. We dropped back to the shore to await the arrival of the boat which, in a few minutes, we could see was one of the white-painted, short-funnelled government steamers. As we watched, she suddenly came to a standstill as she ran onto a sand bank in the middle of the river. Going astern, she got off, and once more approached, this time hugging the British shore. I rightly guessed that she was carrying part of the British Boundary Commission that was preparing to delineate that portion of the British Guiana–Brazil boundary lying between the sources of the Essequibo and Courantyne Rivers. As her two anchors were dropped, we saw she was the *S.S. Arapaima*. A lifeboat was lowered into the water, several people got in and she put off for the shore. As she got alongside us I recognised William Cunningham, the Chief British Commissioner and with him, to my surprise, Captain Piquero of Bartica.

Cunningham offered to take me up as far as the steamer was going, so, sending the sloop out to the steamer, I transhipped into the lifeboat. We rowed out to the steamer where I found two priests, Fathers Keary and Mather, who were on their way back to their missions in the interior, and were taking the opportunity of travelling up the Courantyne with Cunningham. In charge of the *Arapaima* was Captain Douglas, the commodore of the fleet of government steamers. Pinned down on a table near the wheel he had a fine Dutch chart of the river showing the soundings in metres, and it was by this that he was navigating. Presently a large Dutch steam launch rounded the point ahead of us on its way down river. As it drew abreast it saluted us with a blast on its whistle, to which we replied in a similar manner. Presently we sighted the giant silk cotton tree towering above the riverside forest that marked the old balata depot at Tarakuli, the ship's destination. There the anchors were dropped and the four Boundary Commission boats were hoisted off the well deck, where they had been stowed during the trip, and lowered into the river by means of the steam derrick. Whilst the men went ashore to have a meal, I had tea with Cunningham and the two priests in the saloon. The tea was much better than I ever could have hoped for on the Courantyne

River and included iced cake. Cunningham tried to persuade me to spend the night on board and even had a cabin prepared, but as I anticipated contrary winds ahead, and being due at Lana Creek on the Saturday, I decided to go on at once.

After a stirrup with my hosts, I boarded my sloop and, the wind and tide being in my favour, soon left the steamer a mere speck against the bush. Ahead of us the river swung eastwards to the left. Here the British bank consisted of high clay cliffs similar to those at Orealla. This place is called Second Hill and from here a path just four miles long runs to Piruru Village which is some twenty one miles higher up the river, which makes a big loop to the east. We saw a solitary Indian house high on the cliff but the ascent was too steep for our baggage to be taken up, so as Ramdeo said he remembered another house in a bay just north from the cliffs, we went in search of it.

Just below Puruni Creek we came to the house, an exceptionally large building on level land. It was located in a small field that together with the house had apparently been abandoned for a couple of months, though certain of the *lares* and *penates* were stored in a chamber of thatched walls. Here we camped for the night. I saw a wooden mortar of a type new to me, which I discovered was commonly used in this district. The bowl was wine-glass shaped and stood on a truncated cone with an octagonal base. It was rather a striking piece of kitchen furniture and stood about three feet high with a diameter of some fifteen inches.

Dusk had fallen by the time we were settled down so Walter had to bathe on the landing by lamplight. As he took off his shirt he felt something on his bare back and, holding up the lamp, saw a labaria snake hanging from a bamboo over his head. He called Fraser who was nearby and the latter severed the snake in half with one slash of his cutlass.

In order to catch what little of the flood tide was left, we were away by a quarter past six the next morning. Our course now lay for a couple of miles to the north and, as a light sea breeze was blowing, we had to progress by short tacks from one bank to the other. By nine o'clock the tide began to fall strongly and the wind dropped, so we lowered the sails and paddled up the Dutch shore in search of a landing. The bank here rose precipitously from the water in a clay wall ten to twelve feet high. Festooned along the riverside forest were numerous vines of the wild simatoo bearing hundreds of yellow fruit. We crossed over to the British side where a high mora forest grew on land that did not rise so steeply from the river as that on the opposite bank.

Our progress was not more than half a mile an hour, but eventually we sighted a large group of buildings some three miles ahead on the Dutch side of the river. This was Tropica, the headquarters of a large timber outfit. Shortly after four o'clock we were opposite the place.

A few hundred feet above the settlement a large stelling appeared to be under construction whilst on the land in the rear lay a great pile of what looked like iron rails. As no camp was in sight on our side of the river I decided to go over to Tropica and ask for lodging, especially on hearing from Fraser that, on his trip up here last year, Kaufman had spent a night here both on his up and down trips. As we approached the stelling, a crowd of black labourers began to assemble on it, including one who from his floury white apron was apparently a baker. Aback from the stelling were magnificent magenta coloured bougainvillaea and on a bench beside one of these sat a blonde white woman and two little children.

I sent Fraser ashore to enquire about accommodation. There was only a foreman on the landing; he said he was sure we could have a lodging but as all the authorities were aback we would have to await their return which might not be until seven. As we were all tired from our long day's paddling, the prospect of sitting in the sloop for another two hours did not appeal to me, so now seeing two thatched houses about a quarter of a mile ahead, on the British side of the river, I decided to go over there and camp. We found two tiny abandoned huts, very small and congested with partitions and cabans, or rough bedsteads. However, as rain came on, we made the best of things and packed ourselves away in the narrow quarters. We were almost exactly opposite the old Dutch police station at Kapseri Creek. When darkness fell we saw the settlement at Tropica break out into numerous bright points of electric light.

On board by a quarter to seven we slid gently up the river assisted by the paddles and an occasional light puff of wind. We passed the houses of numerous Indians on both banks of the river, a couple of islands by Jumbi Creek, and then Lana Islands. As the tide was falling I would not stop for breakfast so long as the wind continued to push us up against it and it was after one o'clock when it finally dropped. Seeing a couple of Indians at a landing, we went over to enquire the whereabouts of Lana Creek, above which I had to inspect a wood cutting grant for Sankor and Jaggernath. They told us it lay about half a mile ahead, that there was no camp there and that Jaggernath himself was at Piruru Village about three miles higher up where we also would find camping accommodation.

Heavy rain now set in making it inconvenient to do any cooking, so we ate some cassava bread bought in Orealla and continued up river. Parrett remarked to me gratefully, 'Well I'll never despise cassava bread again.' As we rounded the river to the west the rain was accompanied by a stiff wind which permitted sailing once more. Walter was at the tiller and the prolonged cold wind and rain made his teeth chatter as though he had ague, but he insisted on remaining at his post. As we reached the lower end of Piruru Island the wind and rain ceased and once more we had to resort to the paddles. Now, not far ahead a high bank was visible on the British shore, with low bush on top.

This was the landing of Piruru Village. A small bateau or two and half a dozen corials were moored at the foot of a stout step ladder. Going ashore with Fraser I followed a well beaten track that led to undulating savannah on whose eastern edge, half hidden by their surrounding fruit trees, stood a group of houses. In the largest of these I found a tall old black man who made me welcome. His name was Emanuel Morris. As a boy of twelve, fifty-eight years ago, he had accompanied the first schoolmaster to be stationed at Epira Mission and had remained until the mission was abandoned some years ago when he moved down here and established this settlement. He had been married twice, on each occasion to an Indian; and the remainder of the Epira Indians, mostly his relations by marriage, had accompanied him and built their homes around his at Piruru. He introduced me to his family; his wife, a stout staid-looking Indian woman of about fifty, his two sons, strapping big Boylanders, and a host of daughters-in-law, brothers and sisters-in-law, the latter mostly pure Indians, and a whole host of little children ranging in colour from almost black, the coppery-black of the Boviander, to the pure Indian red.

In his household was an amusing character, a very Anglicised Indian with toothless gums and a long outjutting underlip. His name was William James and he claimed that the late H.P.C. Melville's wife was his niece, he being a Wapisiani. He had lived here with old Morris for about twenty years. Without being asked, he cut wood, fetched water, assisted to lay table and helped bring the food to it. Morris made us sling our hammocks in the body of his house, a large building with earthen floor, three sides being without walls and the fourth occupied by a chamber of split manicole with a board floor raised a couple of feet off the ground. Next to the other end of the house stood a large kitchen, entirely enclosed with walls of split manicole.

Just before dark, a huntsman came in and I was surprised to recognise him as Sertima, one of the men I had engaged at Orealla to take me on up river. It appeared his home was here, he also being a relative of old Morris. On his back he had a large quake heavy with the cleaned quarters of a peccari, a powis, and many fine fish, cartabac, averaging three to four pounds in weight each.

After dinner Morris showed me a magnificent large pegall he had made himself, showing that with his half a century's residence amongst the Indians he had acquired much of their arts and crafts. He told me that in his younger days he made a living piloting the balata boats up and down the falls on the Courantyne. In view of his long and undisturbed residence in the district, Government in 1931 granted him a free permission to occupy five acres here at Piruru for the remainder of his life.

At the upper end of the savannah, near the river, was a house occupied by Jaggernath, the East Indian for whom I was to inspect the wood cutting grant at Lana Creek the following day, and another right up at Huma Creek, above Governor Falls. This man now came and told me he was withdrawing the latter application as he had just been up there to discover that there was not sufficient crabwood at the spot to warrant the expense of taking out a wood cutting licence. This shortened my river journey by at least a week, there now being no necessity to cross the falls. Next day I wrote to Tucker, the catechist at Orealla, asking him to cancel my arrangements with Captain Crawford for the trip up the falls. I arranged with Sertima to take this letter, together with my other mail, across the trail from here to Second Hill whence he would proceed down to Orealla in a corial he had hidden in Piruru Creek.

Having occasion to get up an hour or so before dawn, I was privileged to witness a magnificent sight. There was no moon but the stars were shining very brightly and steadily. Over the savannah it appeared that some of these stars had descended from the sky and were holding a dance. Never had I seen such a gorgeous display of fireflies. Their brightness equalled that of the stars and that of the two or three lights that shone from the houses in the savannah. Indeed, it was only from their incessant motion and occasional flickering that the fireflies could be distinguished from these. I was so enthralled that I stood watching the wonderful sight for quite a while until the chilliness of the pre-dawn drove me back to my hammock.

Over coffee, old man Morris complained bitterly about the havoc done to his field and the plants around his homestead by the oxen of Jaggernath and other East Indians in the neighbourhood who held wood cutting grants. When not at work, these animals were allowed to roam through the forest and savannah at their own sweet will. The house I had seen at Piruru had been abandoned for this reason, the Indian's farm having been destroyed by these wandering cattle. The matter was complicated by the fact that some of the Indians themselves had cattle, and when damage was done, the East Indians would lay the blame on the Indians' cattle, and vice versa.

When Morris had finished relating his problems I set out to inspect the wood-cutting tracts applied for by Jaggernath and Sankor. Unlike the lands applied for under agricultural titles, when the boundaries are actually cut by the surveyor, those of wood-cutting grants are cut by the applicants themselves in such a manner as to enclose the timber they desire. These lines are then roughly surveyed by chain and compass or inspected, as it is called, by a surveyor.

The bush, whilst containing a fair amount of crabwood, had a thick undergrowth of mucru, that peculiar, smooth and hard-stemmed plant from which the Indians make much of their basketwork. The cut stems, lying on the ground, were very slippery, and a fall could mean impalement on the cut points left upstanding in the ground. Consequently we had to proceed with great care. From what I saw there appeared to be a great deal of illicit wood cutting taking place on crown land and with no forest ranger in the district there was very little that could be done about it.

Presently our nostrils were assailed by the scent of hubudi plums and soon we came to where the forest floor was carpeted with the small, yellow, sweetly-acid fruit. A small green snake glided away at our approach. One of the men remarked that this snake ate plums. I was rather inclined to believe that what attracted it there were the small rodents that, from the evidence of gnawed fruit, came to eat the luscious plums. On the back of a small tree beside the line we saw some stick insects quite a foot in length.

Returning to camp I found a modest jollification in progress. That morning the Indians had formed a *massiri manni*, that is a gathering of the male community to assist old Morris clear one of his fields. They had finished the work by breakfast time and had returned to the house where they were now partaking of the old man's hospitality in the liquid form of paiwarri and taparau. The former, buck stout, as it is sometimes called, was of course well known to me and I have described its manufacture elsewhere in these pages. Taparau on the other hand, though I had heard of it occasionally, I now saw and tasted for the first time. Made from a small red cherry-like fruit, it tasted not unlike sparkling burgundy and certainly was the finest of all the Indian drinks I yet had come across.

The proceedings were unusually quiet, evidently on account of my presence. Two men strummed a fiddle and a small guitar whilst four others sat around a game of bishka whilst an old Indian with spectacles sat in a hammock making a matapee, while his daughter brought him a cup of paiwarri every ten minutes. Parrett assured me the old man had been drinking like this since mid morning but it did not appear to make much difference to him.

After a few samples of paiwarri and taparau I got into my hammock where I was continually being knocked by the voluptuous posterior of a young Indian girl who was carrying the drinks around. As the fumes of the liquor warmed their blood the women and girls became a little less modest in the manner in which they tucked their skirts beneath them when they sat down on the stools and low benches. The result was that I was disconcerted by several glimpses of soft round limbs, paler than those portions exposed daily to the light. To distract my thoughts I got up, wrote up my journal, did some official correspondence and, this done, then went for a short stroll along one of the savannah trails.

It was now that I realised what a really pretty spot this was. Looking back I could see Morris' house and those surrounding it huddled together at the edge of the bush forming the eastern wall of the savannah. They were partially hidden by the mango, lime, cotton, coconut and plantain trees that surrounded them. In the savannah itself were scattered three or four houses at varying elevations according to the contours of the grass-covered land, which was criss-crossed by well-beaten paths connecting the houses. The newer houses had walls of palm thatch on their weathersides. I returned to camp and sat down to a fine roast fowl provided by my host. About nine o'clock Sertima returned from Orealla, having walked alone through the night forest. He brought a large parcel of mail for me that Mapp had forwarded there by some Indians and as a result I stayed up to a late hour going through it.

Having heard about numerous sand banks and rocks in the river above Potoko Creek, I decided it would not be advisable to take the sloop above this point. Accordingly, I arranged with Sertima and one of Morris' sons to meet me at that point the following afternoon with a small bateau. This done, we loaded the sloop and continued our journey up river. A little way beyond Piruru we saw a large boat coming up behind us, propelled by a single oar and a couple of paddles. We assumed it contained Samuels who was to meet me the following day to point out the boundaries of Beresford's wood cutting grant at Potoko Creek, but with the good wind we soon left this boat far behind before it had a chance of overtaking us.

Soon we were passing the site of the old Epira Mission. According to Morris the Indians left the mission because the then schoolmaster or catechist, a Negro, was interfering with their womenfolk. One consequence was pointed out to me at Piruru in the shape of a little Boviander boy. The Catechist stuck to his post for some three months after the last family of Indians left, and then he also departed.

With the good following wind we soon made Potoko Creek. Many large blue and yellow macaws flew about overhead screaming their raucous objections. A few hundred yards up the creek we came to an old clearing on the left bank which, from the description I had, was probably Beresford's old camp. It appeared he had worked the tract some two years ago and then abandoned it. Going ashore, I found the place knee high under grass, whilst numerous pumpkin vines were strung out over some eight or nine huts. We chose the three largest of these and, clearing up their immediate surroundings and a path from the landing, we made them waterproof with tarpaulins and settled down. After breakfast I set fire to a few of the more dilapidated huts which, being damp from the rain and protected by the foliage of the creepers, gave out dense rolling billows of dirty yellow smoke that rose high in the air, dimming the sunlight. We found numerous pepper bushes, all laden with their fiery red and yellow fruit, of which we picked a large quantity. Walter pickled his with salt but I ordered mine to be sun dried with the idea of making some cayenne pepper. We also found several small ripe pumpkins that were a welcome addition to the larder.

The night being delightfully cool, I awoke after a refreshing sleep. The boat we had seen on our way up did not show up so I dropped down to the mouth of the creek in the expectation of seeing it by a landing there. But when we got out into the river there was no sign of it so we returned to camp where I spent a quiet day at Mr Beresford's expense, as he would have to pay for another visit of inspection since, through his own neglect, this one had proved abortive.

About noon, Sertima and Morris' son arrived in their small bateau. I noticed in two of the old camps here a peculiar type of oven used for bread baking purposes. Built on wooden frames, out of clay, they were shaped like beehives with a square base and the top ending in a blunt point. A rectangular door was at one side and a small hole at the opposite side acted as a vent for the fire that was built inside the oven. When the clay container had been heated sufficiently, the fire was raked out and the bread put in and the vent and door were closed. My men baked some bread during the evening but preferred using kerosene tins to these extraordinary ovens.

As I put on one of my socks next morning I experienced a violent stinging sensation on the instep. Examining the sock, I found what is colloquially termed a hairy worm, a hairy caterpillar with stinging spines. The creature looked like a piece of rust coloured fluff. The pain of the sting lasted for nearly half an hour.

The expedition now split up. Walter, Fraser, my Indian, the two men from Piruru and I went on up the river; the others took the sloop, in charge of Parrett, back to Piruru to await our return. The little bateau just held the six of us, our camp gear and a week's rations nicely. A favourable light breeze sprung up so we put up the little mast with its square sail consisting of two sugar bags sewn together. Because of the course we were on, we landed on the right bank to cook breakfast and so I put my first foot on shore in Surinam.

In the afternoon I lay on top of the tarpaulin and had a nap from which I was awakened by the noise of young Morris playing and landing a large cartabac he had hooked. Whenever we passed a likely fishing ground he would make a couple of casts with his rod, his hook being baited with a yellow fruit the size of a cherry, called kakurin. The cartabac were very fond of this fruit and once they took the bait they were firmly caught, it being only a matter of playing the fish until it was exhausted. Some of them ran up to five pounds in weight. They were known locally as kuriyuri. At four o'clock we stopped and built camp on the English side of the river, at a spot just one hundred miles above Springlands. Whilst Walter, who was acting as cook during Parrett's absence, prepared dinner, I fished from the boat but instead of catching anything I lost two hooks to the perai, so I gave up in disgust.

We had not proceeded half a mile up the river when we saw a large bateau coming towards us from upstream. It had a palm thatch tent and contained three black men. Their leader gave me a letter from Samuels in which he explained that he could not come up river but had sent the bearer, the eldest of the three men, to show me the line of the wood cutting tracts. This man then told me that he had seen me ahead of him three days previously below Potoko Creek, but when he got to the mouth he did not see my boat anymore so, thinking I had gone straight up river, he had followed on without going into the Potoko. On being pressed, he admitted he was not particular about being involved in the inspection of Beresford's tract and, as a matter of fact, did not know the boundaries with regard to the other tracts near Cow Falls for Mahazarali and Samuels. He had been up there and found that the boundaries had not even been cut. As there was thus no point in going further up the river I promptly turned round and started my hundred mile return journey.

Returning homeward next day we saw a small sloop at the last East Indian house on the Courantyne, a little below Epira, but as we were close to the Dutch shore we did not recognise it. At Piruru, looking at what I thought was my sloop, I had to rub my eyes. I had left it painted a bright green, now there was not a scrap of paint on the craft. I looked harder; it appeared to have grown. At last it dawned that it was not my sloop at all. But where was my boat? Going ashore I learnt from Parrett that old Morris had borrowed it to go on a massiri mani up the river and also to cut a new boom, the old one having cracked when the sloop was returning to Piruru. Parrett had apparently had quite an exciting trip down because, in addition to breaking the boom, the craft ran onto a sand bank and all but smashed the centreboard.

When Morris returned the following day with the sloop and its new bamboo boom, he was most disappointed to learn that I was departing so soon as they were preparing some paiwarri for a farewell feast. He even suggested that I sent the sloop and crew round to Second Hill to which point I could walk overland. 'Them girl will carry you baggage for you,' he added, but I was not going to be tempted. When we made our final departure from Piruru, the whole village, headed by old Morris, came down to the landing to wave their farewells.

Just after we set off I noted a low mud bank with a few high bushes on it projecting from the water. As we approached, a flock of muscovy duck arose and flew off up the river. I now saw a hide constructed of palm leaves on the mud bank, in which the Indians secreted themselves to await the approach of the ducks to their feeding ground on the bank.

As we slowly tacked down river on the last of the tide, we saw ahead what turned out to be a large balata expedition on its way up to the Kabalebo district. Two large corials in the rear section of the convoy put ashore for breakfast and we followed suit. The men were all Dutch Negroes and it was interesting to listen to the 'talkie-talkie' in which they conversed, a bastard dialect of Creole Dutch, English and African.

The morning had been fine, but we had not been long under way before a thick blanket of cloud sprang up astern heralding a squall. We managed to run before it for a couple of miles and by the time the wind dropped and the rain ceased we could just see the buildings of Tropica. The tide was now running up too powerfully to permit us to make any headway so I decided to go ashore at one of the Indian houses on the Dutch shore. Just as we were putting into a landing, Walter pointed to a Canadian canoe ahead. It was crossing over towards the British side and looked very quaint to eyes accustomed to the sharp pointed bows of the local canoes.

We climbed a staircase cut in the high clay bank and came to a pretty little settlement consisting of three or four houses, walled and floored, nestling amongst fruit trees and flowering bushes. Some children of mixed race were playing about and in a large kitchen four women were cooking portions of a tapir, or kama, as they called it. With the exception of one woman who was suckling a child, the others were half-Indian, two young ones, slim and comely, the fourth stout and sloppy looking. They all spoke English, though with some difficulty. They told me the whole settlement was known as Washiaba and that, not two minutes walk further down the bank, was the Mission where I could find the schoolmaster.

We followed a well trodden path and came out to a large opening in which several buildings were set amidst crotons and flowers and weeded paths. Outside one of the houses stood a short, stout coloured man in singlet and trousers who introduced himself as the schoolmaster and catechist. He too spoke English and told me his name was Halfhide. He gave me a chair in his house, a comfortable little residence. In the sitting room were several pictures, including a large one of the Queen of Holland and her Consort. Over the door leading to an inner room was a small shrine, a statuette of the Madonna with two unlighted candles before it, the Mission being Roman Catholic. In the gallery, an Indian was cleaning a large revolver whilst an assortment of rifles and guns leaned against a wall. Halfhide told me they belonged to a German who was staying there, who had just gone across the river to bathe. His was the Canadian canoe we had seen.

Discussing the timber activities at Tropica, Halfhide threw up his hands in the air and gave me to understand that they were throwing money away. They were building a light railway fifty-four kilometres long which passed close behind the mission. We went out to see it. About 300 yards behind the houses we came to a straight swathe cut through the forest, about fifteen feet wide. The rails had not yet been laid as they were awaiting the completion of a bridge across the Washiaba Creek.

Back at the catechist's house, I saw a tall, blonde-bearded, blue-eyed man reclining in a deck chair in the gallery. He introduced himself as Dr. O von Sickingen of the University of Pennsylvania. Speaking with a slight German accent, he told me he had been on the Courantyne for six months, as well as the Trombetas in Brazil. His partner was, at the time, back in the States collecting a new outfit, the first having been lost on the Courantyne when they first arrived. He was due back anytime with an amphibian plane. He said that his main interests were bacteriology and climatology. However, it struck me that the upper Courantyne was an extraordinary place to study these subjects and von Sickingen showed an extraordinary interest in the doings of the Boundary Commission. He expressed scepticism as to the possibility of reaching a successful conclusion in the territory between the sources of the Essequibo and Courantyne. He was evidently a great hunter and showed me his weapons with pride. These consisted of a fine Mannlicher rifle and a beautiful little .22 which fired express cartridges and was fitted with both ring and telescopic sights. His double-barrelled hammerless 20 bore gun was like mine, an L.C. Smith. All the weapons were in spotless condition. An Indian boy was cleaning and oiling them the whole time I was there. As we were talking, some women arrived from the fields, stooping under the weight of the great quakes of cassava they carried on their backs. One was a pure Indian but the other, a very tall girl with very pleasant features, was a light-skinned woman of mixed race. She was Halfhide's wife and when, half an hour later, she was washed and dressed, her figure and carriage, was most impressive.

Von Sickingen insisted on Walter, Parrett and I having some coffee. Whilst we were enjoying it, a young yellow-haired Dutchman arrived from aback. He was hatless and clothed in a green khaki shirt and breeches in leather leggings. Von Sickingen introduced him as Mr Rodenhuis, the engineer in charge of the railway project. He offered to take me down to Tropica in his launch which was down at the landing. So, sending the others down to the sloop and bidding farewell to von Sickingen and Halfhide, I boarded the little open launch with Rodenhuis. He told me more about von Sickingen. Apparently, his real object was the discovery of radium. He and his partner had obtained indications of a deposit of pitch blende in the neighbourhood of the head of the Courantyne, but whether it was in Brazil, Dutch or British Guiana, they were not sure. Anyway he had spent considerable time searching for it from the Trowbetas side and was now about to investigate it from the Courantyne. I learnt too, with regard to the timber business at Tropica, that these were conducted by a Belgian company, the successor of four or five companies that had operated under the present manager, although some of them had lasted only a matter of months. A great deal of mora had been shipped to Europe for use as railway sleepers. Steamers came right up to Tropica and loaded there direct. The present scheme was to extract greenheart from the Marataka River area, bring it to Tropica by the light railway and ship it from there. Rodenhuis was a little doubtful as to the financial success of the project. Changing the subject, he confirmed the impression I had that the peculiar wineglass-shaped mortars here were of African origin, the Indians having copied those used by the bush Negroes.

We went ashore at Tropica and were met by the blonde-haired lady and the two children I had seen on my way up. These Rodenhuis introduced as his wife and daughters, Edith and Mary. Mrs Rodenhuis, though by no means pretty, was a very nice homely little woman who wore smoked glasses. They took me up to their quarters, two rooms and an attached kitchen in a large wooden building, the river end of which served as a shop. Sitting in comfortable wicker chairs on the verandah, we were given tea by Mrs Rodenhuis. Whilst Rodenhuis, who had been five years in the colony, was a Dutchman from Holland, his wife was a white Surinam Creole.

Rodenhuis then took me to see the wharf and the railway terminus he was constructing. The rail appeared to be very slight for the purpose for which it was intended and I am sure it did not weigh more than 25lb to the yard. It was laid in rail lengths screwed on flat iron sleepers, the whole thing being simply laid flat on the ground without any ballasting. There was a funny little steam locomotive named *Louise*, much smaller than Sill's engine at Sandhills on the Demerara River. The whole outfit struck me as being more like a toy miniature railway than a serious undertaking for the transportation of timber weighing 75 pounds to the cubic foot.

Rodenhuis next took me to the shop to see 'the policeman', the official who, in the absence of the manager in Nickerie, was virtually in charge of the place. He, in addition to being the general administrative and police officer of the district, was also the agent for the timber company and for one of the balata companies operating higher up the river. He was a little coloured man with a distinctly Semitic caste of features, though his name was Donaghue and he said he was born in Barcelona. When it was explained to him that I sought a night's lodging for myself and my men, he readily agreed to let me occupy the quarters that Kaufman had used the previous year.

After a splendid dinner, which included fresh beef, I retired to my quarters.

These consisted of three interconnecting rooms in a long range with wooden floors, split manicole walls and, strange to say, glass windows, and a thatched roof. A gallery ran along the whole front of the building whilst at the back a kitchen was provided for every two rooms. Rodenhuis told me this was the type of range used in the rubber estates of Java.

At a quarter to six next morning I said good-bye to Mrs Rodenhuis (her husband had already left an hour earlier) and Donaghue and proceeded down river. With a strong falling tide and a favourable wind we made good progress reaching Second Hill in two hours. It was near here that we saw the broad black back of a manatee slowly emerge from the water.

Just below Hepziba, near Tarakuli Creek, we saw banks of heavy grey cloud gradually rolling up behind us, and soon after a wall of white mist appeared, shutting out the white cliffs of Second Hill. The clouds released the wind-driven rain that, where it struck the river, made a black streak on the water. We battened down everything securely and awaited the coming of the squall, which was on us with alarming suddenness. Fortunately it was dead astern so we were able to run before it in the desired direction. The mainsail, let out at almost right angles to the boat, bellied with the weight of the drenched canvas, whilst the force of the wind kept the boom jumping up and down until eventually it swung back onto the opposite bow. I was not quick enough in getting clear of the mainsheet which caught my elbow and gave it a painful wrench. However, I had no time to think about it as all my attention was taken in keeping the sloop from turning over. To prevent the boom swinging again I had a man stand on it near the mast. Still the wind blew and the rain came down like hail whilst the bow cut the water with a constant hissing sound. Now and again an extra strong puff would bring the boat almost onto her beam end and the new bamboo boom gave an ominous crack or two. This decided me to lower the mainsail and run on the jib alone. Even so we were doing a good twelve miles an hour.

After about half an hour the wind dropped sufficiently to permit the raising of the mainsail again. The thick mist was now ahead and we had to watch carefully for the cliff denoting Orealla. It was just on noon as we ran into the landing at the very moment that the children were rushing out of school for their midday recess. As I was about to get out of the sloop, Basil called, 'Look your ring, Chief.' Hastily glancing at my little finger, I saw the white band of unsunburnt skin where the ring should have been. It lay on the stern deck, not an inch from the edge. It must have been pulled off without my knowing it when my arm got entangled with the mainsheet at the beginning of the squall. Ashore, I found Tucker still in school attending to some defaulters and he again put the rest house at my disposal, where I had a hot bath and a change of clothes.

In the afternoon I went for a stroll along the riverside path of the mission and saw the neatest and most modest manner of a woman bathing that could be imagined. As I approached one of the landings, a middle-aged Indian woman of no apparent beauty passed down a cross path to the landing in front of me, loosening her skirt as she passed. On my way back, as I passed the same spot, I was arrested by what I saw and was unmannerly enough to stand and look. The woman's skirt and bodice lay on the beach whilst she squatted with her back to the land in about fourteen inches of water, naked as she was born. Her white shift was folded up and balanced on top of her head while she splashed water over her breasts and that part of her body out of the water. I was surprised at the graceful lines of her body that had by no means been evident when I saw her clothed. I was about to move on when, in a twinkling of an eye, she raised her arms, unfolded her shift and let it fall over her head and body as she rose from the water, modestly covered.

We were away by seven o'clock next morning with a falling tide but against a strong headwind that necessitated constant tacking. Off Jumbi Island we encountered another squall. I took no chances this time and lowered the mainsail until the worst had blown over. Our breakfast, of cold tapir pepperpot and cassava bread, was eaten as soon as the storm had passed. Then the tide turned and with a headwind against us we could make no further progress so we made for the shore near Palm Island and set up camp.

The following day the weather was much the same and when the tide turned and the water began to race up the river like a mill sluice, I could see that we would make little headway, so we made for a nearby landing where an East Indian named Pooran put a small but clean and weatherproof house at our disposal. I learnt that the whole of this district was known as Frankville, after some white man of that name, a retired planter, who had settled here with his East Indian mistress.

We left early on the following day as I hoped to make Crabwood Creek without further stops. We made good progress until about one o'clock when the tide turned against us some three miles above Crabwood Creek. We were compelled to go ashore at the grant of an East Indian called Kamta, and there have breakfast. One thing that interested me on this trip were the quaint clay stoves I saw in every East Indian house. Built generally on the ground, (though I did see some on raised platforms) they were shaped like a roughly oblong box with a hole in front through which the fire was fed and two holes on top on which the pots were placed. These upper holes had, round their circumference, three clay knobs that held the pot an inch or so above the stove, thus leaving a vent for the fire to draw.

About four o'clock the householder and some East Indians returned from aback and proceeded to prepare their evening meal. The former poured a handful of masala out of a bottle and ground it on a square stone plate with a roller of the same material. Then he crushed four figs of garlic into the mess and, finally, four immense hot green peppers the size of small tomatoes. When he had ground this fiery mess into a smooth paste he dumped it with his rice into an iron karahee, as the shallow round cooking utensil is called. I was glad I did not have to share in that meal!

By five o'clock the tide had turned sufficiently to allow us to proceed but as the wind was blowing strongly and steadily in from the sea we again had to progress by a series of long tacks. Dusk had already fallen when we sighted Wajidalli's sawmill, the only landmark in the endless fringe of riverside bush and, a few minutes later, we took down the sails for the last time and paddled up the trench to the road. I admit to uttering a prayer of thankfulness at our safe return from our river journey that, to me at least, had not been without occasions of distinct danger. I had not handled a sailing boat since I left Brisbane in 1905 and, at the beginning of the trip, I had had to learn all over again. By seven thirty we were established once more in our old quarters above Choong's rum shop.

Next morning I sent Fraser aback to see if the water had dropped sufficiently so that I could complete the surveys that I had been unable to do on the outward journey. Meantime, I wrote up my journal, a letter to Chinn at Skeldon informing him of my return and one to Commander Rushbrooke, forwarding what I had learnt of von Sickingen's activities for the Governor's information. When Fraser returned he said there was only one section where the water was low enough for us to work so I arranged that we would do it on the following day.

Several changes had taken place in Crabwood Creek during our absence. No fewer than five houses were in the course of construction as well as a pavilion on the cricket field near the temple, the red flags of which were now washed to a pale pink. The rice fields were all harrowed and only awaited the coming of the rains for the paddy planting to begin.

Our work at last completed, we were ready to return home. Sattaur arrived with his bus at eight o'clock. We loaded up the vehicle, climbed aboard and said farewell to Crabwood Creek. Near Tarlogie I saw Long talking to H.O. Durham, the surveyor, so I called to Sattaur to stop so that I could inform him of the completion of my work. He told me he was going to Kamakusa as Deputy Commissioner of Lands and Mines and Magistrate and that Macnie was succeeding him as District Commissioner of Berbice.

We ran into New Amsterdam at ten thirty and, after closing the special account opened for the purposes of the trip at Barclays Bank and collecting some railway passes from Nurse at Colony House, I repaired to the Strand Hotel where I found Walter and Parrett. We had a couple of swizzles with

Stumps Evelyn who was also there after a busy morning selling Ford cars to some East Indians. We had breakfast, the service of which was so frightfully slow one forgot what the last course was by the time the next one arrived.

The steamer left at half past two and, reaching Rosignol, we boarded the train where I had a first class compartment to myself. It was a wearisome journey and once past Mahaicony we seemed to stop at every other side line as well as at the regular stations. I was glad I had stopped by at the Berbice Gazette Store and bought a book to read. Between Buxton and Beterverwagting we could see the long breach in the concrete sea wall at Nog Eens where the waves were being tossed twenty feet into the air. It was close on seven o'clock when we finally pulled into Georgetown station. There I discovered that the luggage put in at Rosignol was buried under a ton or so of other luggage put in at the intervening stations. I left Fraser and Walter to sort things out and went home on a bicycle Ronnie had brought to the station.

Mother seemed fairly well but poor Phil was very thin and still confined to her room after seven weeks of illness.

CHAPTER XXIV

KAIETEUR
1934

One evening shortly after my return, I had just got into bed when Phil said she suspected that Henry had clandestinely gone out with the car. I went downstairs and, seeing that the garage key was in its usual place, I was just about to go upstairs again when something told me to take the key and check the garage. The car was not there. I got dressed and went round to Wong's garage and found Wong himself sitting in one of his small cars. I explained the position to him and, getting into the car, we went round to Mrs Juister's in Regent Road. She told us that Henry had been there to dinner but had come on his bicycle and that, after the meal, he and Martin had gone out. She suggested that I tried Walter's place at Ogle. I knocked up Walter, but he said he had not seen his brother at all that evening. Returning back along the Sea Wall we were overtaken by another car, mine. It was going at a fair speed so, telling Wong to 'step on it', we pursued. Realising this, the people in the car began to twist and turn in all directions through Kingston and Cummingsburg until at length, in Urquhart Street, the car came to a halt and we drew up alongside. Martin Juister was driving, whilst a young Portuguese fellow, a stranger to me, sat beside him. Packed in the rear seat was Master Henry and three girls. I bundled everybody out into the street and ordered Henry to drive the car home. Then, on second thoughts, I called the girls into the car and, leaving the two boys on the road, drove them to their homes.

My contretemps with Mullin finally resolved itself. He called me into his office with Christiani and admitted that he had been mistaken in thinking that I held the Department to ridicule. I admitted that I was wrong in thinking he was biased with regard to me. We shook hands and all was peace.

I was still finding it hard to make ends meet so I decided to look around to see if I could raise a loan. After a long chat with the manager of Barclay's bank I arranged an overdraft of $240 repayable in sixteen monthly instalments.

Phil still continued to be poorly, which was a constant source of worry to me, and Dr Nichols was now prescribing for the eruptions she had on her skin. Then, to add to everything, Mother had an accident. I was brushing my hair in my room when I heard a bump and a cry of 'Oh, my God!' from Phil. Rushing to the head of the stairs, I saw Phil standing half-way down and Mother in a sitting position on the bottom stair, holding her left wrist. She was moaning with pain and said she had broken her wrist. All the servants rushed up; there was a wild scamper for smelling salts and eau-de-cologne, whilst I tried to get a doctor on the telephone.

I tried Edmonds, but he was out, so I rang Columna House and got Romiti. He was, however, such a long time coming that I had to ring a second time, and then stood impatiently at the gate. A goods train about half a mile long was trundling its slow way across the end of the street and this, I rightly guessed, was blocking the doctor's way at the level crossing in Parade Street. A couple of seconds after the last truck had disappeared, a large car come tearing down the road. Out of it jumped Dr Romiti. He had Mother taken upstairs and put to bed where he examined her arm and found both bones broken just above the wrist. He rushed back to Columna House and returned with splints and bandages to tie up the injured limb and then departed after arranging for me to take Mother up to the hospital to have it set. By the time Mother and I arrived there, Romiti had everything ready in his X-ray room. He quickly took two photographs and retired to a little cupboard under the staircase to develop them.

Whilst he was in there, I stood outside with Dr Coia who was repraising the wonderful X-ray apparatus they had installed, adding that it was of German manufacture. The words were barely out when the darkroom door burst open and Romiti, a dripping print in his hand, jumped out and excitedly exclaimed, 'What you say, German? It is Italiano, Milano. I go especially to Milan to buy it and I have not charged the hospital with the cost of the trip, and you say it is German!' He showed me how the X-ray photos clearly indicated the fractures in both bones of Mother's arm, though fortunately the displacement was slight. Mother was taken upstairs to a private room and a mobile operating table brought in, on which she was made to lie. Then little Coia administered ether to her and as soon as she went under its effects, the whole contraption was trundled along to the operating theatre at the back of the building where Romiti, now clad only in trousers and singlet, awaited to set the broken bones. In five minutes, Mother was back in her room where, after a burst of hysterics, she regained entire consciousness and calm. We took her home the following day and her arm mended quite quickly considering she had just celebrated her sixty-ninth birthday.

During the evenings I continued to transcribe my journals and, finishing the draft of my book, 'Mission to Moruca', I started another 'Memoirs of Mazaruni'. I was still working on a large scale map of the colony for the *Daily Chronicle*. Most afternoons, after arriving home from work, I would take Mother out in the car for a spin, usually going up the East Coast road to Ogle or Beterverwagting and when Phil was feeling well enough she came along too. Then at the beginning of August, some three months after my return from the Courantyne, I was told by Mullin that I was to be appointed as Warden of No.2 Mining District, stationed at Garraway Stream on the Potaro. However, just before I went up there I had to appear in Court at Suddie to give evidence on behalf of the Crown.

On the train to Parika, Cyrus the lawyer, introduced himself and we yarned throughout the trip. He told me the inside story of the trial of a man accused of murder. He was convicted and condemned to death, but Cyrus, his lawyer, had appealed to the Privy Council on the grounds that the Judge had misdirected the jury. He had no doubt that the murder was done by another man who had been acquitted. This man was the nephew of a very influential obeah man who was so feared that none of the witnesses would speak as to the true facts.

At Parika we went aboard the *Hassar* where we were supplied with a jolly good breakfast. We reached Aurora on the Essequibo coast shortly after twelve thirty and were met by a car sent by David Foo, the party summoning me. We raced along to Suddie where I found Togo Low waiting for me. Court being opened, I went into the witness box to be questioned by Souza, the lawyer. I gave my evidence and then made a hair-raising car trip back to Aurora where the *Hassar* was ready to leave, the captain having waited for me fifteen minutes beyond the scheduled time of departure.

A few days later I was again on the train to Parika, this time on my way to Potaro. My fellow passengers included the geologists, Grantham and Smith Bracewell, Sub-Inspector Bell and little Miss Wilkie. At the stelling we were disappointed to find that we were to travel up the Essequibo in the little steamer *Arapaima*, the more roomy *Basra* being in dock for overhaul. On board I met my old friend C.O. Carter, who presented me with a nice new pipe. When I was introduced to Sub-Inspector Bell, he enquired if the 'young lady', meaning Miss Wilkie, was my daughter!

The journey up river in the tiny crowded boat was very uncomfortable as I could not get a chair but had to sit in one of the dining chairs in the saloon. Bracewell devoted himself to entertaining Miss Wilkie until she left us at Ithaca, her home. Shortly afterwards, big H.H. Griffiths came on board, leaving us at the Settlement, bound for Kalacoon, where he was planning to open a quarry. It was thinking of Kalacoon that reminded me of a story C.J. Maggs had told me about old Michael McTurk. Amongst his other official positions, McTurk was Protector of Indians, and when he retired the Indians could not understand what had become of him. One day a cargo boat was wrecked on its way up river and its contents drifted downstream. A party of Indians salvaged some of the goods, including a case of tinned soups. The old chief of the party, who had a smattering of education, picked up a tin of mock turtle, gazed at the label and slowly deciphered the inscription: 'Mac, Mac, MacTurk,' he exclaimed. 'Ah, that why we no see McTurk – he inside here!'

We got to Bartica about five o'clock and adjourned to the Hotel Moderne. After dinner we went over to the theatre where Miss Peggy Daniels and two gentlemen were giving a variety entertainment. The whole troupe was black, the show consisting of rather rough jokes by the gentlemen and a series of dances *a ventre* by the lady.

By six thirty next morning I was down in the bond checking up on my baggage which was to follow me in one of the lorries, whilst we travelled ahead in the station wagon, a little seven seater omnibus. We left Bartica at a quarter to eight and had barely begun to climb the hill when I realised what fine springs the vehicle had. At Seven Miles we stopped at the camp of Claude Craig, the road overseer, with whom we had a minute or two's chat before resuming our journey. At three o'clock we ran into Garraway Stream and I saw the completed bridge for the first time. The scene was very different to when I last visited close on two years ago. The tarpaulin-covered camp of the construction gang was gone and its place taken by a single board and thatched building, the newly erected rest house of the Transport and Harbours Department. The Office of Works still remained and there I decided to establish the warden's office.

I then went down to my new quarters, the house built and occupied by Aldie when he was building the bridge, and christened Chateau Aldie by Sir Crawford Douglas Jones. It was a roughly constructed wooden building with a shingle roof containing four bedrooms and open-fronted sitting room. There was a water closet and bathroom with shower but the tank feeding these had to be filled by hand with buckets, the pump at the riverside being out of commission. Bracewell and I went back to the rest house on the road and put up there. I then visited Pires & Silva's where I met the general manager, my old friend Alfred Clark, and arranged for an account there. I had dinner with Bracewell who had been provident enough to bring a small amount of rations in the station wagon with him. The baggage lorry not yet having arrived, we borrowed some of the rest house cots and tried to settle down for the night. This was rather difficult as just outside the house a lorry with a broken chassis was being repaired by some mechanics who had come up from Bartica with us to do the work. They talked and drilled and hammered throughout the night. Anyhow, I eventually dropped off to sleep to be awakened at ten o'clock by a noise outside and the light of a Tilley lamp. I found the big Thorneycroft lorry outside, its crew unloading our luggage and some furniture sent up by the Public Works Department for my quarters. As this great vehicle was not fitted with headlights, she had travelled throughout the night aided only by a single electric torch. On one occasion she left the road and finished up against a tree, very fortunately damaging only one of the bumpers. Having seen all my gear unloaded, I returned to bed where, despite the noise, I soon fell asleep.

Two days after my arrival, Sam Taylor and Art Williams arrived up in a lorry. I had met Art Williams and his associate Earl Knight at Sam Taylor's house just before I left town, when I learnt that they had flown in from Miami with a view to opening up an air service in the colony. Now they were on their way to Kaieteur to inspect conditions with regard to its suitability for landing a seaplane there. They insisted that I accompanied them as their guest, which I accepted without hesitation, and by ten o'clock we were on our way, Taylor driving.

The mile and a half of new road between the bridge and the old Potaro-Konawaruk Road was pretty stiff going, the way lying up and down numerous small hills whilst the road was metalled with great chunks of broken granite. As the broad tyres of the lorry rolled over this surface, it made a persistent clashing noise which, until one became accustomed to it, was very disconcerting. We branched off along the road to Kangaruma. At one place the lorry stuck in the sand and we had to get out and place pieces of brushwood under the wheels to enable them to take hold. Kangaruma consisted of a small group of somewhat ramshackle buildings, the neatest of which was McTurk's shop, before which we came to a stop.

Whilst the boat was got ready, I strolled over to Pires & Silva's shop to buy some rations. This shop was housed in the bottom flat of a big two-storeyed shingle building originally erected by John Fernandes but now in a somewhat dilapidated condition. The manager, Charles Alves, insisted on taking me upstairs and showing me how the upper flat had been divided off into cubicles for the accommodation of tourists when Pires & Silva's shop ran a service to Kaieteur. A little below this shop was a smaller building occupied by Lamport and Watson, the representatives of Botsford & Co., who had applied for large mining concessions in the district. The house was originally Sproston's rest house, where Dad used to hold his Courts when he was magistrate in the district.

By noon we were on board the boat, but the Archimedes motor took close on half an hour to get started. We had a crew of six and besides the three of us there was a Patamona Indian with his wife and child who were returning to their home in the upper Potaro. Our breakfast was a rough and ready meal consisting of a couple of tins of pork and beans and tomatoes with a bottle of beer, finished off with some dates. We had no plates, cups or cutlery – only a single spoon.

We had barely left the landing when we sighted the mountains ahead and passed the mouth of the Mahdia River that was discharging its dredge-stained muddy waters into the black stream of the Potaro. On the left bank we passed the mouth of the Uewang River and two or three solitary camps of gold diggers. We rounded a bend to see the great white cataract of Amatuk Fall tumbling down forty or fifty feet in majestic grandeur. Going ashore on the left bank, we quickly portaged our baggage and the engine across to the upper landing where we found a large ballahoo to which the engine was attached and we proceeded on up the river.

The scenery now began to be very grand, the thousand feet high mountains gradually closing in on the river which, however, still wound about a great deal so that a high bluff or precipitous wall of rock which at one moment was on our left hand, appeared a few minutes later on our right, so that the scenery was constantly changing.

About five o'clock we reached Waratuk Fall, much smaller and far less imposing than Amatuk. Here the portage was on the right bank. Whilst the baggage was being transported we made a light meal of bread and cucumber and getting into another ballahoo proceeded on once more. The setting sun now increased the beauty of the scene by showing up the rocky walls or the precipices in all shades of red and brown. We passed a large kibiki or coatamundi that was climbing down a branch projecting into the water to have its evening drink. It took no notice of our approach until we shouted at it when it turned round and clambered hastily back up the branch with evident signs of annoyance.

Just before dusk we got our first glimpse of Kaieteur. Looking straight up the gorge we could see a portion of the upper part of the great fall, the rest hidden by a shoulder of the mountains. In the distance it looked like a motionless white streak against a dark cliff, but then, further up the river, it was hidden by the nearer forest. Shortly before seven we reached the foot of the gorge where the Potaro River emerges over the Tukeit Fall. There, on the left bank of the river, stood the government rest house recently erected by the Transport and Harbours Department.

In charge of it was Captain Johnson, an old Potaro river captain who had spent the greater part of his life on the upper river. As soon as we got ashore, Taylor began to question him as to the possibility of walking to the top of the fall that night and sleeping at the rest house up there. I promptly declined to accompany him and Williams agreed with me so we got one of the men to cook up a big stew of ochroes and corned beef and after we had disposed of this we retired to the cots which the rest house provided.

We were up again at five o'clock and set off along the trail leading to the top of the plateau. For the first few hundred yards the trail was wide, clear and more or less level. Then just as dawn broke, we began to climb the mountain. At first the slope was fairly gradual, but after crossing a rustic bridge over a forty foot wide boulder-strewn stream, the path began to ascend and then turned sharply uphill.

Following the main trail we began to climb a sort of staircase, the lower part of which was cut out of the red clay and built up with sticks. As the slope got steeper we climbed from rock to rock. The ascent now began to tell on Taylor and me and after every twenty yards or so we had to sit down to regain our breath. Looking through the trees we could see the top of the further side of the gorge and judged ourselves to be still some hundred feet from the top. At one point we glimpsed a fine cascade that tumbled down the cliff on the further side of the gorge. By this time Williams had left us and Sam and I continued our toiling climb, resting repeatedly. I discovered that my new canvas boots were too small, with the result that the backs of my heels got chafed.

At last we reached what appeared to be the top of the plateau and, expecting to see the fall within the next few minutes, were very disappointed when Sam, pointing to the south west, told us the fall lay about a mile off in that direction. Still, the terribly stiff climb was over, and the path now undulated along the top of the ridge dividing the main gorge from another smaller and narrower one to the north.

The forest now began to thin out and give place to a low scrub growth. At length we emerged into a wide open space of almost solid rock, in whose crevices stunted bushes strove for existence. The surface for the most part was covered with a sparse moss whilst in some places it lay under an inch-thick film of water, the result of the nightly mists that, unable to percolate through the hard surface, waited to be evaporated by the sun.

We passed the broken-down remains of what used to be Sprostons' rest house and then saw, looming up through the mist the new government rest house, similar in design to that at Tukeit. Taylor and I were both dying of thirst and eagerly made for the iron gasoline drums that served as water vats, but were warned by the men who had arrived before us not to drink the water as it was sour.

Suddenly a voice hailed us and, looking through the mist, I saw Williams standing a couple of hundred feet away near the edge of what looked like the end of the world. It looked like that because, some six feet beyond him, the rock floor suddenly stopped and gave way to mist-filled space. From somewhere below a soft hissing sound came up, but no roar from the fall. 'Where's the fall?' I asked, somewhat disappointed. Gripping my arm, Williams pointed into the mist and exclaimed, 'Mr Roth. Look there and keep looking.'

Obeying his instructions, I kept on looking 'right there'. Presently, for a space of a few seconds, the mist thinned slightly and, through a glass darkly, I got my first glimpse of Kaieteur Fall.

It was much like its photographs, only it moved. That was my first impression and, before I could form another, the curtain of mist closed down and hid it from sight. Lying on my stomach I now peeped carefully over the edge of the world. An incredible distance below me I could just distinguish the tops of the forest trees. Retracing our steps through the mist, which gradually thinned out as we moved away from the edge of the gorge, we followed the trail to the upper landing.

Away to our left, a strip of forest indicated the course of the Potaro above the fall, whilst far away in front of us, towards the west, a chain of distant mountains rose blue on the horizon. But the wonderful mountain scenery of the lower river was gone; we were now on top of the Kaieteur plateau. Presently the scrub got thicker and higher, the rock surface broke up into pebbly gravel that supported coarse grass and larger trees and soon after, a little over a mile's walk, we entered forest again and suddenly stood once more on the banks of the Potaro that, but for being slightly narrower, looked much the same as it had away down the hills.

The men then hauled from beneath the water a large ballahoo, kept there by Mrs Violet McTurk, and in this we all embarked and paddled off up river in search of a suitable place for a seaplane to land. Some six miles above the landing, we at length found a reach long and straight enough for that purpose. Turning round, we ate a light breakfast as we paddled back downstream. Near the landing we saw a large alligator swimming with the whole of its head, about a foot long, out of the water. As we approached, it slowed down, then stopped, turned round and began to swim away a few feet when, with a sudden characteristic flick of its powerful tail that cast a shower of spray over us, it disappeared beneath the surface. It confirmed the scarcity of boats and visitors in this part of the Potaro that the alligator immediately reappeared scarce ten feet away, eyeing us balefully for a few moments, before setting off at top speed for the further shore, its blunt head forming a wake like a miniature speedboat.

We put one of the men ashore at the landing to cook breakfast, and the rest of us went down the river about three quarters of a mile towards the fall in search of a landing site nearer than the upper one and found it in the reach immediately below the landing which, owing to the curve of the river, was at least two miles above the fall. We left the men to their breakfast and set out on our return journey to the fall which we reckoned would now be free of mist.

The heat on the rock-covered flat was very intense and the air shimmered all around. The surface water had long since evaporated and the heat burnt through the rubber soles of my canvas boots, which by this time had thoroughly blistered the backs of my heels so that I walked like the famous cat on hot bricks. As I got in sight of the rest house I saw that the mist had cleared away entirely and the forest on the further side of the gorge was now visible. I approached the rock ledge that earlier in the morning had seemed like the edge of the world. With each step my anticipation increased until, some six to eight feet from the actual edge, Kaieteur burst full upon my vision.

My first sense was one of stupefaction, followed by one of aesthetic ecstasy. Despite the numerous photographs, drawings and paintings I had seen of the fall, the dozen of written descriptions I had read, the actual spectacle was beyond anything I had conceived. Some rare artist endowed with a God-given genius might be able to catch a true idea of the wonderful scene, but the dead blacks and whites of the photographic plate could not do so, nor is our language sufficiently pliable to truly describe this most glorious sight in a manner worthy of its colossal grandeur and vivid beauty. Naturally, it is Kaieteur itself, the actual fall, the eight hundred foot high living curtain of falling, falling, falling water that forms the focus of attention, but this alone does not produce the thrill of beauty experienced by the beholder. There is the background of precipice, the vast amphitheatre of cracked and seamed rock ranging in hue from warm salmon red through the russet browns and greys to the dark gloom of the vast cavern behind the fall. Then above the brilliant greens of the forest, and higher yet, is the azure canopy of the cloudless tropic sky.

Below, one sees the emerald green of the forest at the bottom of the gorge, looking in the distance like wet moss, whilst the Potaro, a mere dark ribbon, cuts its way in almost a straight line down the four-mile length of gorge, broken at frequent intervals by patches of white wool as it churned and boiled down the cataracts. Above the fall, the forest-covered country undulated in gentle swells to where distant mountains rear their bluish-grey slopes. In the middle distance the sinuous course of the upper Potaro appeared from amidst the forest, flowing placidly onto the very brink of the half-mile wide amphitheatre with slow stateliness, to fall down into the hissing white cauldron below. As the dark amber coloured water rolled slowly over the ledge, it transformed into a snow-white curtain of foam glinting in the sunlight. The water formed into a series of ropes, like a mighty fringe, and these as they descend transformed themselves into strings of superimposed loops, each one of which could easily be followed by the eye. Thus it was possible to time the drop from the moment one of these loops formed to the moment it disappeared into the clouds of watery vapour that ceaselessly boiled and churned at the bottom. The average time was twelve seconds.

This vapour was one of the peculiarities of the scene. Although consisting of minute globules of water, it looked like an angry cloud of steam rising from an immense geyser. Also strange was the absence of the deep roar one expects to hear from such a colossal cataract. Instead there was a deep-toned hissing sound. As I lay flat on my stomach looking over the edge of the precipice, I was alarmed, at first, by the would-be attacks of the famous Kaieteur swallows, a small party of which were perched on a bush that projected from a cranny in the face of the rock some feet below me. These pugnacious little birds seemed to resent the intrusion of strangers and every now and then one of them would fly towards us as if to attack, only swerving off when within a few feet of our heads. These birds had a smoky plumage with breasts of a dirty orange colour.

Williams, who sat beside me rapt in awed contemplation, remarked seriously, 'Mr Roth, this is one of the wonders of the world. If people up in the States and Canada could but realise it, you would have them coming down here in steamer loads to see it.'

It was now close on three o'clock, so we began reluctantly saying farewell to Old Man Kaieteur. The descent I found more painful than the ascent, for in addition to the weariness of my limbs, the wretched tight boots gave me excruciating pains as the descending slope caused the full weight of my body to come on my toes. I had to rest even oftener than I did on the ascent. My slow progress caused me to lag far behind the others. We finally reached Tukeit at five o'clock when I went straight to my cot and slept soundly until seven, when Taylor woke me up for dinner.

By seven o'clock next morning we were embarked in our ballahoo and making good progress down the river. Most of the riverside mountains were clothed in mist and it was not until we reached Amatuk that the clouds lifted and we had a glimpse of them. As we approached Kangaruma we passed a small engine-driven ballahoo going upstream, with two people in it, a boy driving the engine and steering and a huge white man sitting forward. This was H.H. Watson of Botsford & Co., a mining engineer who was making a survey of the colony. When he saw the Blue Ensign flying at our stern he turned round and followed us back to Kangaruma, where we arrived exactly at noon, forty-eight hours after leaving.

When Watson arrived and introduced himself, he invited us up to his house where he handed me a radio from the Commissioner instructing me to proceed at once to the construction camp on the Tiboko Road and investigate and do what I could to relieve conditions of unemployment there. It was reported that over one hundred and twenty unemployed and starving men were hanging about the camp. At McTurk's shop I found another radio urging me to proceed at once to the Tiboko Road, the congestion there being of 'paramount importance'.

Returning to say good-bye to Watson, I found that Lamport had turned up and, after a short yarn, Taylor, Williams and I got on board McTurk's lorry and set off for Garraway Stream. The lorry was very ramshackle and we had to stop several times to fix the bonnet which kept rocking itself loose. At length we took it off and put it in the back of the truck. Going down the last hill before the bridge we met Pires & Silva's lorry with Alfred Clark on the way to Kangaruma. We stopped and, as Clark assured me he would be back in the afternoon, I arranged to hire the lorry to take me to the Tiboko Road. I also learnt from Clark that Shorey would be glad to take on some of the unemployed men as he was thinking of sending to Georgetown for labour. At Garraway Stream I borrowed a ballahoo and went down to Shorey's claim. I found Shorey at home and he assured me that he would be willing to take twenty-four men if I would bring them down.

Returning across the river, I found Clark had returned from Kangaruma and was waiting to take me to the Tiboko Road. Just as we were about to start, one of the Transport and Harbour Department lorries arrived from Bartica with Frank Spencer, my old Kamakusa cook, on board. I made him tranship into my lorry and we set off just after five o'clock whilst Taylor and Williams went on to Twelve Miles in the lorry that had just come in.

The lorry being empty, we made good progress, reaching Ninety One Miles, where the road to Tumatumari branches off, well before dusk. Presently the headlights were put on and we went rushing through the dark aisles of the forest. At Seventy Five Miles we came to the Geological Survey camp, much to the surprise of Grantham and Phillips who were just about to sit down to dinner which they insisted I shared.

We resumed our journey on the Tiboko Road, which now I travelled for the first time since I had laid it out some eighteen months ago, but in the dark I was not able to recognise very much of it. A group of small unfinished buildings flashed by and the driver told me this was a prison that was being built for a gang of convicts who were being brought up to work in the quarry nearby to provide road metal. About nine o'clock we began to roll gently down to the Blackwater River and presently numerous lights twinkling between the trees indicated the construction camp.

We came to a halt behind a large six-wheeled lorry that was loaded with rations ready to start for the road ahead at Twenty Five Miles early next morning. A guide took me up the hill between various stores and camps to Aldie's camp, a huge tent composed of three or four tarpaulins, a board floor and a couple of tarpaulin walls. Here, by the light of a powerful Tilley lamp, I found Aldie and old Daddy Davenport sitting down discussing the day's doings. Aldie's first remark was, 'Christ man, what the hell's brought you here?' When I showed him the Commissioner's radios he roared out laughing, apparently considering the whole matter a huge joke. He had not done so at first, however. It appeared that when he knocked off work for the August Bank holiday and went to town with his three hundred odd men, he warned the Transport and Harbours Department that he would require sufficient lorries to bring in this number when he returned to resume work. He reckoned that the Transport people, instead of complying with his request, shipped up a couple of hundred other men who had bought through tickets to Potaro, but switched off to Tiboko in search of employment on the road.

When Aldie got back he found about sixty strange men waiting to get work. As he had his own regular gangs he had no work to give them and sent a radio to Bartica telling them not to send any more men. But still they continued to come by the daily lorries, so he sent another radio requesting 'for heavens sake' that no more men be sent. Yet they continued to arrive so he sent a third radio: 'For God's sake stop sending men.' Soon there were over two hundred unemployed men hanging around his camp and then, seeing that his appeals were in vain, he sent a final message that there was a likelihood of his ration store being raided, in which case he proposed to climb a tree and look on. Fortunately, the numbers began to diminish as the men gradually drifted away, some to Honey Camp and Okuwa, some to Potaro and others to Bartica, an eighty-odd mile walk away. When I arrived there were barely sixty of them left and these for the most part were being fed by their friends in the construction gangs. When I told Aldie that I would take a couple of dozen with me to work on Shorey's claim, he doubted whether any would go with me as Shorey had a bad name amongst the labourers. Aldie and I yarned until close on midnight, no doubt much to the annoyance of those trying to sleep within a hundred yards because, owing to our mutual deafness, we carried on a friendly conversation at the tops of our voices.

Next morning I called in at the police station and they confirmed that things in the camp had more or less returned to normal. I also questioned about fifty of the unemployed men. They all swore they wanted work but when I offered to take two dozen of them down to Garraway Stream and give them positions as porkknockers on Shorey's claim, barely a dozen came forward and when I was finally ready to leave only eight put in an appearance.

Back at Garraway Stream I spent the rest of the day catching up with office work and letter writing. As there was no Post Office Savings Bank up there I sent some money down to Belmonte at Bartica to put in the bank for me

Next day Taylor and Williams called in for breakfast on their way back from Twelve Miles. Clark invited us all over to dinner at Flavio da Silva's house on Claim Bridge View which he was temporarily occupying. We could not stay long as Williams and Taylor wanted to travel on to Bartica that same night. As the night was yet young, Basil Parrett, Solomon and I accompanied them for the first half mile to Van Vield's Hall where the 'Oriental Circus Company', a local Negro vaudeville troupe, was giving a performance.

The main attractions were two shapely young Negro women, Madame Sally and Dinah May who, in a minimum of clothing, gave several exhibitions of tap dancing that invariably ended up with a violent oscillation of the hips. It was very vulgar but not a little thrilling. The leader of the troupe, Grey, was a good saxophonist whilst another male member unconcernedly ate a glass tumbler, danced barefoot on a pile of broken rum bottles, on which he also lay whilst another man stood on his chest. The show came to an end sometime after midnight and then the dancing began. I clicked with Madame Sally, who was quite a good dancer, and we danced until close on four in the morning when we started for home.

At Pires & Silva's we stopped to discuss another bottle of whisky and finally got home at half past four. I was up again at seven and worked in the office until ten when Lamport arrived and I decided to leave the work for the rest of the day. Adjourning to the house we were joined by Mesdames Sally and Dinah May, who had been invited to breakfast. The party gradually warmed up and continued well into the night.

Claude Craig dropped in the next day saying he proposed to make his headquarters in Garraway Stream whilst he reconditioned this section of the road. After closing the office, Craig and I went up to the shop and discussed a bottle of whisky with Eton Wilson. Parrett and Solomon subsequently joined us and we had a supper of sardines and bread. Towards eight o'clock we heard a loud cry on the hill where there were numerous cottages of the women of the fields.

Thinking that someone was being beaten, we rushed up to the source of the noise and there we saw a most weird sight. The little Negro girl known as Koba, who was about sixteen and said to be a bush Negro from Surinam, was throwing a cumfu fit. She would roll, head over heels on the hard rock or roll sideways with incredible speed until she would fetch up violently against a prone tacouba or tree stump which she would proceed to batter with her head until the wood resounded with a deep boom. How she did not crack her skull was a mystery and the sight of the girl brutalising herself gave me a feeling of nausea. All the time she kept singing, first in English, then Dutch and then some unintelligible gibberish. In the course of throwing herself about, the girl came up against a washtub which apparently she mistook for a drum and which she began to knock with a rhythmic throb. Someone suggested that she be given an egg as a soother and presently a woman brought one and placed it on her head. At this the girl went on with her rolling and somersaulting, holding the egg undamaged in her hand, until finally she broke it over her head and resumed her head banging on a tree stump. A man then brought a bucket of water with which he doused the poor girl, but even this had no effect in stopping her ecstatic fit. She then got up and ran down towards the road where a lorry had just arrived and in the glare of its headlights she continued with her head-knocking and rolling on the hard and sharp-edged lumps of granite road metal. Leaving the girl to her gyrations we returned home.

I borrowed Craig's lorry next day and I set off with five men for Mahdia. My first call was at the headquarters of the Minnehaha Development Company, where I was met by E.H. Humphrey, the manager, and C.H. Parsley, the surveyor. I stayed at Humphrey's house for several days whilst I did my work in the district. On the first evening of my stay I had a most luxurious hot bath in a long enamel bathtub. At dinner that night I met young Dyrth and Harold Humphrey, one of V.B. Humphrey's sons, who were managers on their uncle's claims at Prosperity Hill and Kongo Heart-Burn respectively.

An evening or so later, Parsley, Harold Humphrey and I went down to see the Oriental Circus Company which had moved up to the school hall. The hall was so full that we had to send up to the house for chairs and these were placed right up against a platform that consisted of two long tables placed side by side. So close were we that we had to duck our heads when the high kicking events came on. Poor Harold blushed and looked very uncomfortable when the girls began their hip contortions. The glass eater varied his act by eating an electric light bulb instead of a tumbler.

My next area of inspection were the claims on Look and Weep Mountain, which I did with Parsley. As the company lorry was taking some goods up to Fifteen Miles we got a lift on it. Passing the branch road leading to the machine shop we passed what Parsley termed the French Quarter of the village where the St. Lucian labourers dwelt. In addition to the large logies for the men with their tiers of sugar-bag bunks, or cabans, there were numerous cottages of the gentler, if not, fairer sex. Many of these had names painted on little boards over their doorways. The most conspicuous of these was 'Mon Nid'.

Leaving the houses, the road skirted a large underbushed section of forest through which could be seen the paddock, at the far end of which squatted the dredge, its endless chain of buckets slowly turning. We passed several old-time gold workings, now covered with second growth forest, until we came to and crossed the Kettledrum Creek and approached the head of the Mahdia Valley. Here as the road twisted and turned it reminded me of the mountain roads in Dominica. Presently, as we swung round a sharp corner, we came in sight of some half dozen houses nestling almost on the crest of the divide. This was the Fifteen Mile settlement, of which the largest building was H.F. Galliene's shop. Here we left the lorry and spent the rest of the day inspecting various claims in the vicinity on foot.

After several days at Mahdia House I returned to Garraway Stream in De Groote's lorry. He was driving, as he was about the only person who could handle this wonderful contraption. He told me it was variously known as The Pork knocker and Puffing Billy. To me it was more like an Emett-designed machine than anything else. It had no body, just a few boards fixed over the chassis and a box for the driver and a passenger to sit on. The driver was held in position by the steering wheel, the lower rim of which revolved against his groin, whilst the passenger held on as best he could to an upright lath nailed to the side of the box. The engine was held on to the chassis more by wire and bits of rope than by bolts. The radiator leaked so much that one had to stop at every creek crossed and fill it up with water. Looking down under the engine I saw a great half pound bolt swinging wild at the end of a piece of wire. I drew De Groote's attention to it, and he explained that it was the carburettor spring. The manifold leaked so badly that I had to spread my legs wide apart to keep them clear of the exhaust. Finally, there were no brakes, the desired effect being obtained by putting the engine in reverse. And yet, strange as it may seem, apart from the difficulty of hanging on to the precarious seat, this extraordinary agglomeration of motive junk gave an easier ride over the coarse road metal than did the big Ford V 8s and other lorries.

Next day in the office I was so hot that I took off all my clothes and worked in my bathing costume, much to the amusement of Reggie Humphrey and the Reverend Bryant who called in to see me on their way to Minnehaha. I don't know whether it was this action that gave me a fever, because a couple of days later I was laid low with a high temperature which forced me to stay in bed for several days.

When I recovered, I set off on a trip to Tumatumari and Konawaruk. I made the two hour journey down river in McTurk's little boat, disembarking at the upper landing. I set off along the road to the lower landing and on the way met Gravesande, manager of Pires & Silva's shop there, who had come to meet me. Passing below Sprostons' Hotel, now rented to the Eagle Mountain Holding Company, I saw a neatly clad, slim, blue figure waving to me from the gallery and recognised my old friend, Sylvia Henriques, who was housekeeper there. Going down to Pires & Silva's shop which was housed in Sprostons' old bond at the lower landing I had a couple of drinks and a yarn with Gravesande and then climbed the steep hill up to the hotel where Lamport had told me to make myself at home. Sylvia was alone up there and showed me over the house, a smaller model of the old Rockstone Hotel and now very comfortably furnished.

I spent the next morning issuing mining privileges and then went down river in a corial to inspect a large farm just above Tiger River. On the way back I went ashore at Johnsons Village, which lies at the foot of the falls opposite the lower landing. Here I saw a concrete tombstone, all but hidden by bush, covering the body of a white man, one of twenty or thirty victims of a terrible disaster here some thirty years ago when Sprostons' launch missed the upper landing and was swept down the falls. I believe there was only one survivor. The drowned included two or three white miners and this tomb was erected over one of them by his friends.

We set off for the Konawaruk River next morning at half past seven. In addition to my own three men, I engaged two Patamona Indians as droghers. They had come down from the upper Potaro and could not speak a word of English. The trail had not been maintained by the government for a number of years, but showed signs of having been a very fine bridle path. It was carried across various creeks on the remains of what had been very substantial bridges. Mules had been used here by the Guiana Gold Company that had once operated dredges in the Konarwaruk. My father used to walk this trail regularly on his periodic visits to hold Courts in the district.

The trail followed along a high ridge until we came to a couple of logies forming the camp of Fraser and Eversley's gold claim. Here we overtook Eric Pile, the manager of McTurk's Konawaruk shop, and we continued our journey together. We were now proceeding along the right bank of the Tiger River. Presently a roaring sound was heard ahead and soon we came to the Washerwoman Falls. With a drop of some eighty feet, it was very picturesque. Beyond the fall, the level of the land rose and the trail crossed numerous old gold workings and canals across which it went on very rotten bridges. In most cases only the stout beams remained and in a few instances even the beams themselves had fallen down at one end so that one had to pick one's way along them very carefully between the great spike nails that formerly held on the boards.

After a while we came to a fork in the trail, a signpost indicating that the branch track to the west led to Ten Miles on the Potaro-Konawaruk Road, by the Mahdia River. Keeping to the main trail, we crossed the Tiger River for the last time and then climbed the highest hill met, known as Majuba, which is situated on the Potaro-Konawaruk watershed. The descent into the valley of the Konawaruk appeared longer than the ascent on the northern slope. Reaching flat undulating country once more we made better progress as the trail was wide and comparatively clear and it was not long before we reached the Konawaruk River itself.

From this point the trail ran up the left bank of the river, crossing numerous tributaries on bridges and their remains. Crossing one in particular gave me severe qualms. All that was left of the structure were the two twelve inch wide timbers forming the beams, all the planking having gone. These beams were quite sixty feet long and some twenty feet above the water of the creek which they spanned. I started off along one of these beams until I reached the middle where I was struck with vertigo, being unable either to go forward or back. After standing stock still for a moment and still looking straight ahead I got down on my hands and knees and crawled to the further end.

A mile or so further on we stood on the banks of the Chinese River, the largest tributary of the Konawaruk we had yet met, over fifty feet wide and from which all traces of a bridge had vanished. We managed to wade across although the water was waist deep. The land at the side of the creek was now fairly flat and in places the trail ran on a made-up causeway. We passed several old workings and the occasional piece of rusted iron alongside the trail until we came to St. Mary's, where, amidst a thick grove of giant bamboo, the skeleton frame of the manager's house rose gaunt and grim beside the trail. Not a sheet of zinc nor a single board remained on the structure, even the staircase had gone. Near the house, great numbers of dredge buckets and much machinery lay about, all overgrown with bush.

By this time I was getting very tired indeed and the inside of my thighs were badly chafed, but Pile assured me that his shop was only 'a mile or so away' so I pushed on. Suddenly, some sixteen miles from Tumatumari, we came to a signboard with the arrow pointing across the river and the legend, 'To McTurk's shop and the highest prices for gold.' Across the river I saw a square, wattle-walled flat-topped building sitting in a two acre grass-covered clearing at the foot of a gentle slope. A large ballahoo was moored at the landing on the opposite bank. At first glance the place looked quite deserted, the shop door was shut and no smoke rose from the rear quarters though it was close on five o'clock. However, after Pile shouted a couple of times, a black boy appeared from behind the building and brought the ballahoo across the river, over which he then ferried us. The whole place had a most desolate and lonely appearance. Pile told me that the trail continued up the left bank of the Konawaruk River for several miles to Glendor, the original southern terminus of the Potaro-Konawaruk Road.

I settled down with Pile in the shop whilst my men occupied the thatched logie nearby. The stock in the shop was very low – a half bag of flour and a couple dozen boxes of matches or so. The whisky or other liquor, to a schnapps of which I had been eagerly looking forward, was noticeable by its absence. The business done by the shop was with just half a dozen gold diggers operating on Good Hope Creek, a tributary of the Mowassi. After a cup of cocoa and some bully beef I climbed into my hammock. So tired was I that I slept through and missed the arrival and departure of the droghers from Good Hope who slept on tarpaulins on the floor below my hammock.

As the river had risen I was not anxious to start the return journey but, bearing in mind that we had to wade across Chinese Creek, I completed the checking of the shop's books, which did not take very long, and as soon as breakfast was over, I got Pile to ferry us back across the river. We had no sooner started on the sixteen miles walk to Tumatumari when a heavy rain began to fall, soaking us to the skin. We got safely across Chinese Creek, by which time the rain had ceased, but I still had the high bridge to cross on my hands and knees. Yet, when I came to it, I walked straight across without, on this occasion, experiencing any vertigo. My wet trousers were chafing my legs so I took them off and continued in my shirt tails. As we walked, I noticed that the mileage on this trail was marked by the numerals cut out of tins like stencil plates, instead of the numbers being painted on the tin plates – a much more economical method as no periodical repainting was necessary. During the afternoon I climbed Majuba Hill whence I once more had a look at the mountains to the south. They did not appear to be of such a nature as to present much difficulty for the extension of the road to Siuruni. Reaching the Tiger River once more, I came to Gilgeous' claim, where I decided to break my journey.

He put a zinc logie at my disposal and when my droghers arrived I sent them up to it. When I finally went myself I found it to be leaning at a crazy angle and very shaky, so not wishing to run the risk of being crushed under the roof during the night, I had my hammock moved to another large abandoned palm-thatched camp lying some distance back on the trail. Gilgeous warned me that this leaked badly, which was self evident from the number of stars I could see through the thatch. However, I preferred to take the chance of getting soaked through rather than that of being injured or killed in the night so I stayed where I was.

Fortunately there was no rain during the night. The remainder of the journey back next day was uneventful and by eleven o'clock I was back in Pires & Silva's shop having a drink and yarn with Gravesande, who gave me an amusing account of McTurk's lorry that transported their goods from the lower to upper landing here. It was in a worse condition than De Groote's Puffing Billy. Like the latter it had no brakes, but as often as not, when the engine was put in reverse to act as a brake, some pin or other gave way and the only method of stopping the lorry's downhill rush was to run into the bank of the cutting through which the road ran to the landing. Sometimes it would prevent itself from running into the river by using the shop as a buffer. Gravesande said that when he first came up here he was having breakfast when he thought an earthquake had hit the building. It was McTurk's lorry 'putting on its brakes'.

Two days after my arrival back at Garraway Stream I took to my bed with a high fever. After about four days in bed and feeling no better, I began to suspect that I was getting another attack of blackwater fever, as I felt just like I did when I got my first attack at Kamakusa in 1927. Consequently

I watched my urine very carefully. Sure enough, the next day the expected blackwater came on with a flow of urine black as ink. A nice position to be in – no medical attention and impossible to risk the hundred mile shaking-up in a lorry to Bartica, so I drafted a wireless message to the Commissioner of Lands and Mines informing him of my condition and one to the Government Medical Officer at Bartica asking for his advice. As all this happened on a Sunday there was no chance of the messages getting through before the following day, so Craig went to Twelve Miles and brought out the Government Dispenser, Dash, a big burly Negro, who told me what I already knew, to keep quite still and drink plenty of liquid.

My messages were sent out first thing on the following morning and at noon I received one back from the doctor at Bartica, saying that he was on his way up to see me. Shortly after this I received a second message from Georgetown saying that a plane was leaving at one thirty and bringing Dr Coia and that on no circumstances was I to be moved. I could not make out from whom this message came. It was a coincidence that it was Dr Coia who, at Kamakusa, gave me first aid on the occasion of my first attack. I later learnt that I had Mother to thank for chartering the plane and arranging with Dr Romiti for Dr Coia to come up.

The plane did not, in fact, leave until some two hours later than planned. The delays were due to several causes; firstly no flying licence had yet been issued to Art Williams by the local Air Board and special permission had to be obtained from the Governor for the plane to make the trip. Then, before the plane could leave La Penitence, the big police launch had to be hauled out of its way, and this took some thirty policemen and two inspectors a couple of hours.

Shortly before five we could hear the plane high in the sky. It was very cloudy and from where I lay in my bed, I got a glimpse of it for a second as she passed between a gap in the clouds about two thousand feet up. Then we heard her no more for a few minutes until Craig, running back from the landing, told me she was taxiing up the river. It appeared that because of the clouds Williams was having difficulty in making a landing until, watching for a gap in them, he waited until they were over the river when he immediately put the plane into a side-slip and dropped like a plummet for fifteen hundred feet until he got through the clouds. This put the wind up poor Coia who, never having flown before, thought his last moment had come.

Presently the plane came in view, tied up at the landing and from it emerged Sam Taylor and Dr Coia. The latter's first words were, 'Well, I sent you down last time and I've come to bring you down now. We'll just have time to get you down to town before dark.' After he made a quick examination of me and of the urine that stood in a row of lemonade bottles on the table, he had me put in a Berbice chair which half a dozen men then carried down to the landing. It was a ticklish job lowering it down the steep bank and I breathed a sigh of relief when we reached the sand beach.

The next ticklish job was to get me into the plane, as the only means of entry was through a small hatch in the roof. But, after considerable manoeuvring, they got me in and placed me in a leaning position on two mattresses so that my back was against one of the rear seats and my legs more or less across the knees of poor Coia who sat beside me. Taylor got in the co-pilot's seat beside Williams and while Coia gave me an injection, the plane moved off from the landing, taxied under the bridge, which by now was lined with spectators, and then Williams swung her back downstream and, with a shouted question of 'All right?' opened up the engine. With a deep roar the plane jumped forward and, shooting under the bridge at almost fifty miles an hour, was in the air by the time it passed my quarters.

The cabin was arranged very similarly to that of a five seater car, the sides, front and top consisting of panels of Triplex glass. The bullet shaped nose of the great nine-cylinder engine could just be seen above our heads. By the time I had settled down comfortably on my mattress and could devote my attention to the scenery below, we were already over Tumatumari, which looked like a pretty little toy village beside the river a thousand feet below. We flew diagonally across the forest to the Essequibo which appeared to be very swollen and muddy. I don't remember seeing much of interest for the next quarter of an hour as the country was more or less covered with wisps of low-flying cloud, but I was able to recognise Arisaru Mountain rising like a great wall between the Essequibo and Demerara Rivers. Then Williams brought the plane down close to river level and rushed along at a hundred miles an hour only twenty feet or so above the water. The sight of the forest trees flashing past gave me a good idea of what this speed meant. Near Parawika we passed Kalamadeen's boat upward bound for Tumatumari, its passengers waving wildly to us as we flashed past just over their heads.

I next recognised the southern end of Gluck Island, along the eastern side of which we flew to Rockstone. As we were gradually rising again because of our imminent approach to the falls, we passed it at about a thousand feet and I was only able to make out the old railway station. For the past several miles we had been flying down a single channel over a mile in width that, up to Gluck Island, comprised the entire Essequibo, but now immediately below Rockstone the scene changed considerably. Instead of the great wide river, all we could see were numerous narrow channels that criss-crossed each other and here and there showed the white water of rapids and falls. The outermost channels must have been some three miles apart. I had the impression of a vast swampy forest rather than of a great island-studded river. This impression was enhanced by the tufts of mist that rose everywhere out of the vast forest beneath us.

Then in the distance we could see where the numerous channels gradually united again into a single stream that was constricted by the narrow gut at Monkey Jump. Beyond this the vast tidal estuary of the Essequibo could be seen in the gathering dusk. Next Bartica came into sight, but as we were flying at about five hundred feet along the eastern bank of the river I could not see it very clearly. When opposite the centre of the Mazaruni mouth, Williams suddenly turned the plane inland over the forest in a north-easterly direction and I realised that owing to the lateness of the hour he was cutting across to the Demerara.

We flew barely a couple of hundred feet above the forest. Williams remarked afterwards that should the engine give out we were bound to crash into the tree tops, and it was better to do so from a height of a hundred rather than a thousand feet! We passed over a narrow forest stream that flowed almost due north in a narrow ribbon-like savannah. This apparently was the upper course of the Boerasirie River. The forest now began to thin out and give place to a vast ite savannah in which the great palms grew singly here and there. Presently, I recognised the tortuous windings of the upper Kamuni River. We flew right over its junction with a large canal that had recently been dug to connect this stream with Pln Wales.

Suddenly a blinding pin-point of light flashed in our eyes from the north east, the million candle-power light of the beacon at the bar of the Demerara. The river itself then appeared, its placid reaches showing up like dull silver streaks against the darkening ground. We flew right over the buildings of Pln.Wales where numerous lights twinkled up at us. Over the river, Williams headed the plane northwards once more and then, with the engine shut off, the plane dipped into a downward glide. After the incessant roar of the past hour and a half, the ensuing silence was very marked. I could barely sense when the seaplane touched the water and as soon as it did the engine roared into life again as we taxied across the water to the Pan-American Airways barge, anchored off Poudroyen. Here waiting for me was Walter, and with him a couple of policemen with St. John's Ambulance brassards on their arms. After considerable difficulty they managed to get me onto the barge where they placed me on a stretcher which was then carried on board the PAA launch that was moored alongside.

A few minutes run across the river and we landed at the Customs wharf where Dr Romiti met me. As they were taking me up the steps of the wharf, I all but rolled off the stretcher. At the wharf gate I was placed in a motor ambulance. It was just striking seven as we passed the Stabroek Market.

I was taken to Columna House Nursing Home where the two ambulance men carried me, still on the stretcher, up the wide stairs, and again nearly tipped me off. The hospital was so full that I was placed in a nurses' breakfast room which had been converted temporarily into a bedroom. Romiti then very kindly went and fetched Mother and Phil as he said they would only worry until they saw me. They only stayed a few minutes after which he ran them back home in his car.

I was then in a semi-conscious condition, being just aware that two people were in the room with me, standing one on each side of the bed, but who they were I neither knew or cared. Presently, I saw that one was Walter and the other Percy King, the acting Colonial Secretary. His wife was also a patient in the hospital and he was visiting her when I was brought in and he had dropped in to see how I was. It appeared that they thought that I was dying. After they had left, some nurses came in and began to arrange a contraption of basins, jugs and rubber tubes on a high stand. This they brought alongside the bed and gave me a saline enema. The tube was so constricted as to allow the liquid to pass through only a drop at a time. During the night an attack of ague came on and several more blankets were piled on me, after which I passed into a fitful doze.

Next morning I was lifted onto a wheeled stretcher and rolled into another room where a fan was kept going night and day to make it just bearable. Here I remained for a full week during which time a great many people came to see me until I got too tired to see anyone else, so a placard was put on the door to the effect that no visitors were allowed. The only exception to this was the Commissioner, to whom I sent a message saying that I particularly wanted to see him and he came the same evening.

I said I was sorry to let him down in this way, to which he replied that these things happened in the best regulated families. He asked whether this was not my second attack of blackwater fever and on my replying in the affirmative he replied, 'No more bush for you.' I then explained how I had left official matters at Garraway Stream and asked that my successor, when appointed, be sent to me so that I could fill him in on the details before he went up there.

I felt pretty rotten during the first week in hospital, during which time the saline enemas were continued daily. During this period my hours of sleep were not necessarily governed by those of darkness. When I was not asleep I spent most of my time reading. All this time I was sustained solely on liquids – coconut water, orange juice, milk and soda. As time passed, my urine gradually turned from black to blood-red. Percy King paid me a second visit during the week and told me that he was recommending that the cost of the seaplane, some $356, which had been paid by Mother, should be a charge on the Government.

At the end of the week I was moved into another room on the south side of the building. The room was very bright and cheerful having windows on three sides and a balcony on the south side. I had a very pleasant view from my bed and gradually began to take an interest in life again. At the end of the second week I was moved to a bigger room, though the view from the window was confined to Parade Street and the Eve Leary Parade Ground. Here I spent the balance of October.

By the end of October I was well on the road to recovery and had every hope of being quite my old self by the end of November when, one day, the nurse changed my urine bottle, bringing in place of the small one I had been using, a large greasy looking utensil with a glass handle. I did not like the look of it but the thought never entered my head that it might not be clean. Suffice to say that I had not used it two days when I began to feel an itching in the groin area which, in the next day or so became so bad that when I showed it to the doctor, he gave me a lotion with which to bathe it.

On the 9th November, I came out of hospital and went home where I was comfortably installed in my own bedroom. It was during the next day or so that I bought for $35 a Morris Cowley 1924 model car. Walter and Henry brought it to the gate so that I could have a look at it from my bedroom window. However, my trouble grew worse with the result that I had to send for Dr Coia who arranged for me to return to the hospital for a minor operation.

The following day found me on the operating table where Romiti suggested doing the operation under local anaesthetic. I appealed for ether, not having forgotten my experience on the last occasion I had a local anaesthetic for haemorrhoids. 'I'm not afraid of ether,' I said. 'No, but I'm afraid to give it to you,' replied Romiti. His fear was because of the weak condition of my heart consequent on the blackwater fever. However, he had a consultation with Coia who sounded me and the next thing I knew was that he had the rubber anaesthetising mask clasped to my face. The ether was much less unpleasant than chloroform, but it seemed to excite me the same way and I began talking rapidly to Coia, telling him all that I knew about him which, fortunately, was little and good.

The next thing I knew was a voice in the distance yelling at me to keep still – then I heard some bad language and recognised Romiti rushing out of the theatre in a passion. Then Coia's voice came to me, 'Do keep still a moment Roth.' It appears that owing to the weak state of my heart they had been afraid to give me a full dose of ether and I had come out just as the cutting was being completed but the stitching not yet done. Romiti then returned and put in four stitches. When it was all over I learnt that I had struggled terribly under the anaesthetic and it had taken the efforts of two powerful nurses to keep me sufficiently quiet to permit the operation to be performed. I was trundled into the dispensary and left there for half an hour, after which I was allowed to go home, which I promptly did and went straight to bed. In the early afternoon I had another of those terrible attacks of stomach cramps that succeed blackwater fever.

Coia called twice a week for two weeks to change my dressings, which was a very painful operation and then after that I went to the hospital every day in the car to be dressed. The healing was an exceedingly slow and painful process and the end of the year found me still in bandages, though I was able to hobble about and occasionally drive the car. Christmas we all spent quietly at home, listening to the radio in the evening. On New Year's Eve, Walter married Ivy Pile at the Brickdam Cathedral, Henry being the only member of the family present, the marriage having taken place without my or Mother's approval. The pair went up to live at the chicken ranch at Ogle.

Early in the New Year I went to the *Daily Chronicle* where I saw Delph who gave me a pleasant surprise. He said that in future I would receive the paper free and my debt to the firm, a matter of some $40, was to be considered as paid. This I took to be in view of my articles for which, up to the present, I had only been paid 72c per column as against $2 I used to receive from the *Argosy* in Lupton's time.

In mid February, Thomas Kelman, the announcer for the Radio Station VP3BG, came to borrow some records which I had offered to lend him and whilst we were talking he asked me to broadcast a talk over the station on the following Monday night. This I agreed to do and on the Monday evening went to the Radio Station at Crystal's Photo Studio and gave my broadcast talk on Kaieteur. I understood this to be a one-off engagement but in the end I found myself doing it every Wednesday evening for several weeks after that.

At the end of March, my sick leave having expired, I returned to the office. Mullin told me he had asked Government to put me before a Medical Board for a report as to my fitness to return to the bush and, in the event of the report being unfavourable, he was recommending that, unless there was a possibility of my transfer to another department in the immediate future, I be pensioned off on the grounds of ill health. He assured me that this was not a personal matter but for my own good, and that of the Department, as he would be bound to send me in the bush eventually, and a third attack of blackwater fever would undoubtedly be the end of me. He would do all in his power to assist my application for transfer to another branch of the Service and failing this would recommend the addition of three years to my service for the purpose of accounting my pension. That evening I discussed with Mother and Walter the pros and cons of my building a house next to Walter's at Ogle in the event of my being retired.

In May I went before a Medical Board consisting of Drs Mearns and Gomes who, after a verbal and physical examination, decided that it would be inadvisable for me to return to the bush. I continued working in the office and in June Mullin sent for me and told me that Messervey was being temporarily seconded to the Colonial Secretariat and he wanted me to take his place as Superintendent of Lands, which I was happy to do.

EPILOGUE

Compiled by Michael Bennett

Vincent Roth finally retired from Government Service in 1936 on full pension and with the end of his work in the interior his journals end. But he was not idle for long and for the rest of his life he regularly wrote journalistic pieces describing events around him. In 1935, he suffered a tragic loss in the death of his beloved wife, Philomena.

Then on 22nd February 1936 he married a long time family friend, Alma Forde. On his marriage his mother, Edith Roth, decided to spend some time on the Courantyne Coast and the lease on the house in Waterloo Street was terminated. Mrs Roth lived on until her 89th year when she died in March 1951. After her return from the Courantyne she set up home in Church Street where she lived until her demise. For the last ten years of her life she was virtually bedridden, following a fall downstairs. After a well attended service at St George's Cathedral she was laid to rest beside her husband.

In 1937, he was engaged to organise and lead the Booker Bros. Puruni gold prospecting expedition. On completion of this he returned to Georgetown and joined the *Daily Chronicle* as Librarian and Second Editor. In the same year the couple were blessed with a daughter, Elizabeth, and in the following year a second daughter, Audrey was born.

In 1939, at the outbreak of the Second World War, the Government of British Guiana paid tribute to his knowledge and experience by appointing him to act as District Commissioner and Magistrate in the North West District. In the following year he was appointed manager of the Aruka Estates (rubber and coffee) after having been turned down for military service. Later on he returned to the *Daily Chronicle*.

A new phase of his life began when on 7th April 1943, His Excellency the Governor directed the publication of the following telegram from the Secretary of State for the Colonies:– 'His Majesty has been pleased to give instructions for the appointment of Critchlow, Edun, and Roth to be nominated members of the Legislative Council.' Of his co-members, Mr Critchlow was the General Secretary of the British Guiana Labour Union and Mr Edun, a jeweller, journalist and trade union organiser. Vincent Roth represented Mining and Interior interests and, in 1947, when re-elected for a second term, Interior, Forestry and Mines.

Roth evidently took his position as a nominated legislator seriously. A newspaper used to publish a table giving the loquacity of the members of the Legislative Council. Taking a typical period, December 1948 to March 1950, it is seen that Vincent had a pretty good attendance record, 49 out of 53, and spoke an average of 289 words per attendance. At the head of the list was the Hon. Dr. Cheddi Jagan with 2,252 words per attendance and at the bottom of the list was W.A. Phang with an average of 35 words per attendance.

By the time Vincent was elected to the Legislative Council he had acquired a hearing aid and it was said that, on occasions, when the discussion became somewhat mundane, he would switch off this aid. This is hard to believe and is probably a joke of Vincent's own making. His time in the legislative council coincided with the beginnings of the long political service of the late Dr. Cheddi Jagan, who used his position as an elected member to challenge colonialism with every breath. It was a known fact that the political views of Dr. Jagan and those of Vincent were diametrically opposed and one day when both gentlemen met each other outside the Chamber Dr. Jagan said, 'Mr.Roth, you don't like me do you?' to which Vincent replied, 'I like you, Cheddi, it's your politics I don't like.'

But if Vincent Roth was, by comparison to Dr. Jagan, a political conservative, he was by no means a defender of the status quo. Hardly a week passed without a letter to the press on some topical subject from Vincent. When he learnt that a medical store had been set up under one of the surgical wards at the Public Hospital, Georgetown, he wrote a strong letter pointing out the potential fire hazard this created. This particular issue continued for a year or more as the authorities were so slow to do anything about it. Vincent had a very pragmatic approach to resolving problems. Feeling that the service offered by the hospital was not what it should be, he went up to the hospital and pretended to be drunk. He sat on a bench and waited to see how and when he would be attended to, which was not much. He did a similar thing to check on the police. He went up to Vlissengen Road and started to stagger about on the roadside and then collapsed in feigned unconsciousness. One policeman tried to arrest him whilst another attempted to relieve him of his wallet!

As a legislator, Vincent Roth evidently pursued his interests in Guyana's history and the development of the interior with great vigour. Of the former interest the *Daily Chronicle* of 7th July 1943 reported:

His Excellency the Governor, Sir Gordon Lethem, ended his stay in Berbice on Thursday, when he left New Amsterdam by plane for Fort Nassau, Berbice River to declare open the Luther Memorial Park. For fifteen minutes the Hon. Vincent Roth kept his audience spellbound while he gave a historical account of Fort Nassau including the story of a jug of English ale which started a row between the wives of the parson and another gentleman, which subsequently developed into a fight among these same gentlemen. Concluding, Mr Roth said: 'May I express the hope that the personal interest evinced by your Excellency's presence here today is but a harbinger of Government's intention to continue that interest by taking steps for the preservation and protection not only of this, but also of the numerous other sites of historical, archaeological and anthropological interest scattered throughout the length and breadth of the Colony.'

And the *Daily Chronicle* of Sunday 17th October 1943 gave considerable emphasis to Roth's vision for the development of the interior:

'The development of the hinterland may possibly take a form unexpected by the majority at the present moment. Air transport has been developed to such a remarkable extent since September 1939, that it is quite a reasonable possibility that our interior development may be based on a system of air transport with feeder roads – in which case the old ideas of a trunk road will be scrapped. For this reason, I do not think that Government, at this time, will consider spending a large sum of money over and above that required to maintain the existing trunk roads.'

The foregoing statement by the Hon. Vincent Roth, J.P., at a meeting on Monday night last at Brigoldo Hall, 108 Miles, Potaro may be regarded as an indication of plans for the development of the hinterland. Mr Roth visited the district recently at the invitation of his constituents. He left the city on Saturday, October 2. At Bartica he was met by Mr John Aldie, P.W.D officer. They left on Sunday morning reaching as far as 70 Mile Potaro. On Monday morning they inspected the four mile branch road to Tumatumari recently opened, and afterwards went to the headquarters of the B.G. Consolidated Goldfields at 108 Miles Potaro, where they were the guests of the General Manager, Mr Geo. S. Harris. The party, on arriving at 108 Miles Potaro, saw the trial run of the new motor locomotive, *King George VI* built by Mr Cyril Shotton, and was constructed to run on wooden greenheart rails, the first of its kind in B.G. Mr Shotton is the Chief engineer, and those who enjoyed the trial run included officials and their wives, labourers and visitors.

Mr Roth, during his stay at the Consolidated Goldfields, was taken over the plant and there he saw the dredge, *E.J.Waddington*, while it was being moved to another stretch of the river.

At 8 o'clock on Monday night, a largely attended public meeting was held when Mr Roth gave his constituents an account of his stewardship. The following is the address:–

'Ladies, Gentlemen, Temporary and Permanent residents of Potaro: I must preface my remarks with expression of my thanks to those hundred odd of you who extended to me the invitation to make this visit and of my special thanks to Mr Harris for the very warm hospitality he has shown me.

When, exactly nine years and six days ago I was flown away from Garraway Stream with blackwater fever, after a short sojourn among you as your Warden, I had little idea that the next time I should come beneath the shadow of Look and Weep it would be as your accredited representative in the legislature.

As the Nominated Representative of Mining and Interior interests it is especially gratifying to me that my first visit to my scattered constituents should be to that district in which I last served as a Government Officer. Now I must tell you that I am no public speaker, most of my speeches in days gone by having been as perhaps some of you may remember – something short and sweet like this: '$10 or a month!'

However, I will do my best and should my flights of oratory not reach those heights you expect from a legislator, I pray your forgiveness on the grounds that in this respect I am young and inexperienced. Furthermore, I am sure that you did not invite me up here to listen to pleasant platitudes – but to hear an unvarnished account of my acts of Commission and omission in regard to your interests in this particular district.

Your main grievance in recent times has been, I gather, the curtailment of transport. You have written to me on more than one occasion and I have passed on your wishes to Government along with my recommendations, based on personal knowledge. I have sent you copies of written replies I have received from Government. Since the last one I had personal interviews with the Chairman and the Transport and Harbours Board and with the General Manager of the Department. At that meeting the Chairman gave me the impression of being sympathetic. I cannot say the same of the General Manager. A few hours before I left town I received a letter from the Acting General manager.

Since my arrival here this afternoon I learnt that the lorry position is not so bad – two coming once a week. My own impression is that little more can be done as there is no doubt as to the difficulty of the tyre situation. I would suggest that as long as the situation gets no worse that you try and put up with it until the return of better times.

Other matters on which you wrote to me were those concerning a school, Agricultural Instructor's visits, and improvement of the road now that the traffic is diminished. With regard to the first two items I have asked you for further information. Perhaps this can be provided this evening. Improving the road is another and a very big one. In the first place Government has tremendous commitments at present – one being a twenty year scheme involving millions of dollars. By mentioning this I don't want to suggest that interior interests should or are to be neglected – but – the development of the hinterland of this country may quite possibly take a form unexpected by the majority of us at the present moment.

Our transport has been developed to such a remarkable extent since September 1939 that it is quite a reasonable possibility that our interior development may be based on a system of air transport with feeder roads – in which case the old ideas of a trunk road will be scrapped. For this reason I do not think that Government at the present time will consider spending a large amount of money over and above that required to maintain existing trunk roads in the interior. Therefore I suggest that the fourth request contained in your last letter be left in abeyance for the time. Now, in conclusion I would like to assure you how happy I am at having been able to come and visit you and to give you my promise that I shall always be at your service.'

After this address, Mr Roth was requested to make representation to Government for the following:– New trails wanted; urgent need for a school in the district where on the B.G.Consolidated Goldfields plant there were twenty three children. Fifty children from the district were sent to city schools, but parents would be glad to get them educated locally, the cost of upkeep in the city being fairly high. There is also a need for a teacher. Hardship in getting nails to build sluices was also stressed. Milk, pickled meats and fish, be included in the preferential freight rates as is done in the case of sugar and rice.'

In May 1944 Vincent went on a flight to the interior and this was probably the first such journey he made that was without medical connotations. Of it he wrote:–

'Dwellers on the dear old mud-flat which many of us visualise as comprising the whole of British Guiana may find it difficult to realise that little over two hours direct flying will bring them to the magnificent upland country of the Pakaraima area where the land ranges from great forest-covered flats and rolling savannahs two thousand feet above sea level to precipitous mountains towering a mile high in the clouds. Yet so it is, and this is the story of a flight I made there.

The 15th May, 1944 was a dull, cloudy day when, at 11.10 am. in company with Mr G.O. Case, the Consulting Engineer, and Mr B.A. Barker, one of his surveyors, I took off from the Demerara River in one of the small but high powered planes of the B.G. Airways Ltd., piloted by my taciturn old friend, Harry Wendt. Flying at about 800 feet, wisps of smoke-like cloud already floated below us as we skimmed over the West Coast, the two sugar plantations looking like miniature museum models beneath us. As we turned up the Essequibo River the clouds thickened and we had to descend to some three or four hundred feet to keep the edge of the river in sight as our guide. Suddenly the clouds closed in all around us and the river edge disappeared from view. I wrote on my pad – 'Now I know what blind flying is', and passed it to Harry. He returned it with a written comment – 'Not blind yet', the truth of which I was to realise an hour or so later.

Then the country ahead was hidden by a mass of opaque white cloud. We could almost feel the plane hitting the solid wall of rain that emerged from it. The pilot swung the craft sharply to the left, or south, in an effort to get round the storm. Now I remembered that some ten miles from the river was a four thousand foot wall of mountain. We were travelling at well over a mile a minute only a thousand feet above the forest plain which could just be discerned through the clouds. Did I have the wind up? Yes, I certainly did, until, watching the compass, I saw we were gradually veering round to the west. Then the mountain wall came into sight not two minutes flight away. As we continued I recognised beneath us the extraordinary meanderings of the Merume River and, as we crossed it, we got clear of the storm and at 1.10 pm, we were flying over Kamakusa, where I had lived for five years. From the air it looked but little changed since I had seen it fourteen years previously.

We now flew almost due north for six minutes, cutting off the loops of the river till we reached it again at Oranapai, easily recognisable from its island. Going on above the river I looked carefully for places I knew. Twice I looked before recognising, on the left bank, the strip of bright green 'second growth' forest where, twenty years ago, had stood the thriving mining centre of Buck Cannister Sands with its twelve shops. Two minutes later the Government Station and extensive diamond workings of Enachu came into sight and, at 1.25 pm, two and a quarter hours after leaving Georgetown, we alighted on the river at Tumareng, the low hill opposite the mouth of the Eping River.

Going ashore, I met several quondam acquaintances who poured into my ears their tales of woe concerning the alleged sins of commission and omission of the Transport Department. The rain fell heavily as we had a picnic lunch in Mr A.A. Cooper's country cottage where he stays on his monthly diamond buying visits. For some time there were doubts as to the advisability of our continuing the flight over the mountains that day and, whilst waiting for the weather to clear, we examined several parcels of diamonds in the shops there.

Eventually Harry Wendt decided we could go on, so, after filling up the petrol tanks, we started off once more at 3.10 pm. and headed south towards the Merume Mountains which we hoped to cross through the Eping pass. When we were only a thousand feet above the forest, the cottonwool-like clouds closed in below us and we were flying in the middle of a dense white mist – at ninety miles an hour – towards a wall of mountain that reared itself at least three thousand feet above us. As I never had flown before under such conditions I am not ashamed to say that I was distinctly nervous. I really began to get the wind up, and on at least two occasions had to bring myself forcibly to remember that the pilot's life was as sweet to him as mine to me and that, therefore, he was taking no risks, despite appearances which, to a novice, were very much to the contrary.

Some minutes later I happened to look down and there, through a hole in the cloud carpet, I got a faint glimpse of what looked like green pastures, but which actually were the savannahs of the upper Mazaruni. Then we were over the mountains. Swiftly we dropped, the clouds disappeared and there beneath us was the winding rock-filled course of the Partang River with, just below its confluence with the Mazaruni, a neat little doll house-looking building with, near it, a long, white landing strip clearly marked on the savannah. This was Imbaimadai, or Sawarri Nut Savannah, the headquarters of Mr P. Storer Peberdy, the Field Officer for Amerindian Affairs. Making a wide circle, we swooped down on the long black reach of the upper Mazaruni where we alighted at 4.20 p.m., one hour and one minute after leaving Tumareng. We taxied up to a small steep sand bank at which was moored a large brightly painted canoe and on which stood the lean, brown bearded figure of Mr Peberdy, surrounded by half a dozen Akawoio Indians.

After mutual greetings we climbed on board the big canoe in which we were ferried across the river to the further bank, a steep declivity covered with dense bush. Climbing up through this we came out on an undulating savannah, where, a couple of hundred yards away, stood the temporary headquarters, a large and comfortable thatched house with wattled walls, a kitchen of similar material and an Indian round house, constructed round one of the aerials of the station's radio telephone. Mrs Peberdy here greeted us and we spent the balance of the afternoon and evening sitting in home-made easy chairs and yarning.

Next morning, we all walked across the savannah a quarter of a mile for Pilot Wendt to examine the aeroplane landing strip that Mr Peberdy had had made. It had been our intention to fly south west over Mt. Ayanganna from here, and then strike the head of the Potaro and follow that stream down to the Essequibo, and so home. But the summit of Ayanganna was still wrapped in cloud. The pilot shook his head but said he would not decide before eleven o'clock whether to take that course or not. As it turned out the decision did not have to be made as a message came over the radio-phone from the Government Geologist, asking us to pick up an injured employee at Tumareng and take him down to hospital.

Just below Piameh, the Mazaruni swings suddenly from its northerly course to the south east and this bend forms its nearest approach to the Cuyuni River, the intervening distance being only some twenty-two miles. Mr. Case had the idea that this might be a suitable place for a road joining the two rivers and we decided to go and have a look-see. Judging from the map one would have surmised the existence of a range of mountains that caused this sharp deflection in the course of the Mazaruni, but, to our surprise, as we flew north north west over gently undulating country, we found that the mountains stopped abruptly to our left, there being a clear unobstructed view ahead straight to the Cuyuni valley. Less than ten minutes' flying brought us in view of the Ekereku River, a large tributary of the Cuyuni and from this point we returned to the Mazaruni which we followed down to Tumareng, arriving there at 2.50 pm.

Having refuelled and taken the injured man on board, we resumed our journey down river at 3.34 pm. The weather was now fine and we got a splendid view of the great stream. Little over an hour's flying brought us to Kaburi where I was most interested in getting a bird's eye view of the numerous cataracts I had so arduously examined by boat some twenty-two years before. Now I saw I was correct in two surmises I made at that time, that the Mazaruni at this point is at least two miles wide from bank to bank, and that by far the greater volume of the river flows not over Paiarimap, Warra-Warra and Kaburi Falls themselves, but over the Looking Glass Fall adjacent to the left or north bank. Compared with this maelstrom of seething, tortured water, the former three falls, fearful enough when viewed at close quarters from a boat, appeared as mere ripples.

We reached Cuyuni Mouth at 5.04 pm. and, flying to the north of the Penal Settlement, struck the Essequibo at Tiger Creek. Flying down this local Father of Waters we left it a little below Bonasika when we flew to the junction of the Boerasirie Canal with the creek of that name. As we followed the canal eastward I was greatly struck by the wonderful extent of the cultivation on the West Coast and Canals Polder and realised, as never before, that, so far as the coastlines are concerned, British Guiana is indeed an agricultural country.

It was just forty-five minutes after five when we dropped gently down on to the Demerara River after one of the most interesting flying trips I yet had made.'

By this stage in his life, Vincent Roth was evidently something of a local celebrity. In February 1944 a journalist, Herbert Haines, wrote a profile on Vincent and reported an interview with him in which adds a little more to what is known of his family origins. Haines had remarked that all the people he had ever known by the name of Roth were Jews and asked Vincent about his ancestry. 'Roth', Vincent had answered, 'is not an Hebraic name. It is from the German word *rote* meaning red. Many Central European Jews commonly transposed their Hebraic names – or their family or personal description, if they lacked a name – to the European equivalent. But my grandfather, Mathias Roth, was a Polish Jew. Mathias fought with Kossuth for the freedom of Austria back in 1848. When Kossuth's effort failed, his lieutenants were taken prisoners. Mathias, being a surgeon, was put to work in a hospital instead of a prison camp. After a few months he managed to escape from the Continent and get to England where he subsequently married my grandmother.'

The article, after outlining Vincent's achievements, concluded as follows:–

'If I have dwelt on Vincent's varied activities and his broad talents, I do not mean to give the impression he is a universal genius. There are some things he cannot do. When he joined the B.G. Militia in 1914 they made him a cook, presuming that anyone who had spent as much time as he had in the bush must know something about rustling up a bite to eat. As a symbol of his monumental ignorance of the finer points in the culinary art, the amount of rice he chose to use the first day expanded in the pot until it just about filled the room. And the taste was worse. There was mutiny in the ranks – or rather a firm resolve to execute a little mayhem on a certain cook. Vincent managed to save his neck by passing word around that any molestation of cooks would result in a heavy dosing of the soup with glauber salts!'

In February 1945, at a time when he was a legislator, librarian and second editor at the *Chronicle* and an officer of the Royal Agricultural and Commercial Society, Vincent Roth was well placed to decribe the disaster which struck the heart of Georgetown. As he described so vividly:–

Around half past three in the afternoon of Friday, 23rd February 1945, I was sitting in the Director's Room of the Royal Agricultural and

Commercial Society going through some correspondence with Miss Martins, the Librarian. It was a bright sunny afternoon. Suddenly the usual street noises were disturbed by a terrific short sharp explosion, like a large motor tyre bursting, but many times louder. With an exclamation of, 'Hell! That was no tyre', I rushed to the window looking out on Church Street but, for a few moments, observed nothing out of the ordinary – no smoke visible anywhere, the traffic continuing as usual but for one or two pedestrians stopping and looking about them to ascertain the cause of the explosive noise.

After about, I should say, half a minute, I saw two men clamber up the posts supporting the pavement canopy in front of Bookers' Home of Limacol, a tall four-storeyed wooden building immediately opposite us. Reaching the corrugated iron roof of the canopy they hastily ripped open the wire netting over one of the first floor windows, through which they helped a man out. Up to this moment there was still no external sign of any fire, but as soon as the three men reached the pavement, there was a sudden burst of almost invisible blue flame of burning alcohol from the very window through which the two rescuers had pulled the man, and also from the one immediately above it on the next floor.

From now on things began to move fast. Within a couple of minutes brilliant flame was spouting out of all the windows facing Church Street, the while a deep and ominous roaring sound, to which nothing is comparable, began to come from the doomed building. Now as the structure as well as its very inflammable contents caught fire, showers of sparks began to rise and be blown across the street. Although at this stage I never for one moment dreamt that the fire would cross the fairly wide street and the grass lawn that separated the Museum and Library from the street, I realised the danger of these live sparks and ordered all the windows shut.

While I was superintending this, the fire spread with unbelievable rapidity. When I next looked out, Bookers Drug Store to the east and the garage to the west were both on fire. Having seen that everybody was out of the Museum and Library, I went out into the street where I encountered Mr. Alfonso, the Head Mechanic at Bookers Garage. He looked more than worried and intimated to me reason for his alarm and the certain result of what would happen when the underground gasoline tank went up, which in his opinion it was bound to do.

Luckily his prognostication proved wrong, as most fortunately the ventilating pipe remained undamaged and took off all the excess gas, which, long after the fire was under control several hours later, kept spouting a flame, and thus relieved the pressure in the reservoir. An interesting sequel to this boiling of the gasoline was the fact that when subsequently the remainder was sold, it was found by those car users who were lucky enough to get any of it that it gave a vastly increased mileage.

The heat in the vicinity of Water Street and Church Street was becoming unbearable. The roof of the Georgetown Club now caught and within fifteen minutes the whole structure was a mass of ruins. Incidentally there is a story told of two of the oldest members rushing into the burning building and insisting on the barman making a last swizzle for them before escaping.

The fire now jumped across Hincks and North Streets and, in a few minutes, the Museum and Royal Agricultural Society and the General Post Office were masses of flames. Even in the midst of the worst tragedy there is invariably a touch of humour for those who can see it. Thus the story of the office boy who, at about 3.30 p.m., had been sent to post his firm's letters. Arrived at the Post Office he stood up and gazed in wonder at Bookers' Drug Store hidden in flames and smoke. Then he saw the Georgetown Club catch alight. He remained watching the terrible scene in silent wonder till a noise over his head caused him to look up and see the tower of the post office on fire – 'Ow, me Gad,' he exclaimed. 'Post Office a fire – Let me post these letters one time before it burn down.' And he did so!

I now bethought myself of my office at the *Daily Chronicle* where I kept all my Legislative Council and other correspondence. Despite its immediate contiguity to the outbreak of the fire, the *Chronicle* building was not yet actually on fire though some of the wooden jalousies were blistered and smoking. To reach the building I had to go through Robb and King Streets across the Cathedral Oval and down Church Street where I saw Sir (then Mr.) Frank McDavid supervising the playing of a garden hose on the wooden doors of the Public Library. I arrived at Chronicle House to find a scene of confusion. Mr Charles Noel Delph, the Manager, who was suffering from a heart attack had been removed to a friend's house higher up Main Street. Meanwhile the staff strove valiantly to save the building. Some took spells at the semi-rotary pump supplying water to the bath cisterns at the top of the house, where others used this water to dash on the walls and roof. I found my way through the printery, which was almost at burning temperature and where Big Bill Shankland and a couple of firemen played a hose on to the walls and roof. Reaching my own office above the bindery in the next building, I managed to remove my papers and take them across the street to the Hotel Tower. On my return I found a fire hose lying across my desk whilst a little Anglican curate, clad only in pants, singlet, and clerical collar was vociferously superintending the use of the hoses with most unclerical language. I later learnt that he had been a member of the National Fire Brigade during the London blitz.

Now one of the Chief Reporters seemed to have lost his head and began to shout excitedly, 'All out of the building! Police order everybody out. It can't be saved.' Fortunately the others took no notice but redoubled their efforts in keeping the walls from catching alight, despite the fact that it was encompassed on two sides by a regular fiery inferno. It was evident it would not last much longer. Then the miracle happened. The easterly breeze, which hitherto had been very light, suddenly freshened and by six o'clock it was apparent that the danger to that building at least was over.

I staggered across the street to the Tower Hotel in search of a drink but the bar was closed and locked. However, my friend Major Lewes, who was a guest there, took me to his room where he poured a half tumbler of neat whisky down my throat.

And then was heard the dull boom of explosions as the authorities, having at last found a professional blaster, were dynamiting some of the buildings on the waterfront.

By seven o'clock the fire was under control and, with a friend, I climbed up to the top flat of Chronicle House whence a terrible sight met one's eyes. Where a few hours ago had stood the business heart of the city, now spread several acres of black and smoking debris, picked out by numerous flashing points of light where the flames still flickered and occasionally shot up several feet in the air. The room in which we stood was several inches deep in water and it spoke well for the solid construction of the floor that it had not yet leaked through. By midnight the ruins were cool enough to permit passage through the streets intersecting the devastated area. We went inside the Barclays Bank building which only seven hours earlier had been an incandescent inferno and even now was too hot for us to remain longer than a few minutes. Although all the interior woodwork had been consumed, the concrete walls, galleries and roof apparently had withstood the fire so well that within a week business was resumed at temporary counters. Across the street the Royal Bank was a blackened heap of smoking ruins, from one corner of which the solid concrete vaults stood solitary out of the debris. In the vast open space between Robb Street and Chronicle House, the flickering light of the sporadic flames showed up various white urinals in obscene nakedness against the surrounding ruins.

Whilst the fire was still raging in the late afternoon I had met the Postmaster General looking for quarters in which to carry on postal business. Fortunately we met the Moderator of the Scots Kirk who kindly put at his disposal St. Andrews School Hall.

Next morning, in conjunction with Mr. W.A. Walker, the then President of the Royal Agricultural Society, I was able to obtain the lease of Freemasons

Hall on Company Path in which to re-establish the Society's Library, where it remained until the opening of the present building in 1951.

The value of the buildings destroyed by this fire was estimated at over eighteen million dollars, excluding the value of material and stock, not to mention the valuable library and exhibits of the Natural History Museum of the Royal Agricultural and Commercial society.

Mr. S.L. Van B. Stafford, Q.C., the Commissioner appointed to enquire into the origin of the fire, placed the blame impartially between Messrs. Bookers, the Town Council and Government, for neglect and non-enforcement of the Regulations. But, as no cloud is without a silver lining, the four acres of blackened debris blossomed within ten years into the present business and cultural centre, the most imposing in the British Caribbean territories.

But little more than two years after this, in the early evening of 19th May, 1947, a fire broke out in Hincks Street on the site of the original Central Garage. Before it was got under control it had wiped out almost the whole of the two blocks bounded by Water Street and High Street and Regent Street and South Street. Only the all but superhuman efforts of the Fire Brigade, assisted in the later stages by the American Army apparatus from Atkinson Field, saved Bookers' large building in Water Street. Had this caught, there is little doubt that, owing to the narrowness of that part of Water Street, the destruction would have equalled that of 1945.

The General Post Office, which was temporarily in occupation of the wide spreading Regent Hotel, was destroyed for the second time in little over two years. Two hotels in High Street also went up in flames.

About the same hour of the evening of 30th November, 1951 occurred yet another great fire. It broke out in the rear of the premises of Resaul Maraj Ltd., and almost immediately engulfed the adjoining Bookers' Drug Store, which itself stood alongside the new Ferreira & Gomes Building which succeeded the one destroyed in 1945. Although the Fire brigade did its best, assisted by the fire floats in the river, the whole of the central portion of the block between Church and Holmes Streets on both sides of Water Street were destroyed before the fire was got under control.

Amongst the buildings burnt were those of the Demerara Meat Company, Fogarty's Wholesale, Garnett & Co., and those on the east side of Water Street. The iron building of the Stone Depot and Ferreira & Gomes concrete building stopped the fire to the south, though the latter building sustained damage in the vicinity of forty thousand dollars. To the north, the Brigade managed to control the fire at the buildings facing on Holmes Street. In this fire vast quantities of edible oil, hundreds of barrels, were destroyed as well as a large number of motor vehicles just landed and not yet removed from the wharves. At the Meat Company's abattoir, though the draught horses were saved, it was impossible to remove some oxen, which were destroyed.

Shortly after the great fire of 1945, when the Second World War came to an end, Vincent decided to celebrate the fact in style. He hired a jackass cart and, dressed in his pyjamas, drove around the city with his family and friends on board, much to the delight and amusement of the inhabitants of the streets along which they passed.

With the end of the war, during the next few years many visitors came to the Colony. These were mainly zoologists and anthropologists, including Michael Swan, David Attenborough, Gerald Durrell, Audrey Butt and Evans and Meggers from the Smithsonian Institute. All would call on Vincent for his advice and knowledge of the area and even the Government Information Officer would at times telephone for help on some local problem.

It was in the area of developing the knowledge of Guyanese in their own past that Vincent Roth perhaps made his greatest contribution to his country's life since his retirement. Since coming to Guiana, Vincent had always taken an interest in the country's history and was surprised how little the Guianese knew of the extraordinary patchwork of events, tragic and comic, which go to make up the history and tradition of the country. When, one day, he heard a well known and promising young lawyer coolly assert that 'British Guiana had no history' he really got off the mark and, going straight to his friend Delph at the Chronicle, explained the position and suggested to him that he print and publish a cheap edition of all the books dealing with the country, its history, condition, contents and peoples – an edition cheap enough to make it available to everyone, and that he would be pleased to edit it. Delph, somewhat to Vincent's surprise, swallowed the idea hook, line and sinker, and told him to go ahead. As Vincent was still in the Government Service he had to get official permission to act as editor of the forthcoming publications. So was born the *Chronicle*'s *Guiana Edition of reprints and original Works* dealing with all phases of life in British Guiana. Before his retirement Vincent had compiled a *Who's Who in British Guiana* for the *Daily Chronicle* and in the next few years this was updated and replaced by the *Who's Who and Business Directory*, again for the *Daily Chronicle*. He also wrote the 'Olla Podrida' column in the *Sport and General Magazine* and continued as Second Editor of the *Guiana Edition* of reprints and original works dealing with all phases of life in British Guiana and contributed many stories and articles to the *Chronicle Christmas Annual*.

He also began writing about his own life. One topic he dealt with concerned his supernatural experiences. In his youth Vincent claimed he had no belief in ghosts and when someone told him a jumbi story he would listen with the condescending smile of a sceptic. But after a couple of adventures, related below, he ever after kept an open mind on the subject:

'One of my best chums was a brother surveyor, Jim Sykes, who whilst I was in barracks in 1914, was sent to act in my place as Land Officer at Christianburg. One afternoon at parade I was surprised to see R.O.H. Spence, the Assistant Commissioner of Lands and Mines come rushing up and hold an earnest conversation with our Commanding Officer, Captain Pollard. I was even more surprised when I was called up and given temporary and immediate leave from military service and given orders to proceed next morning back to Christianburg to relieve Sykes who had been taken seriously and dangerously ill.

The transfer was made and in due course Sykes recovered his health and went to England on leave. At that time the Land Officer had a beautiful little launch, only twenty feet long, but fitted with all conveniences including a little brass steering wheel at the bow. As I did a lot of night travelling, it was my custom on such occasions to steer the craft myself in the narrow waters of the upper Demerara, so that in the event of an accident there would be no question as to where lay the blame.

One very dark night I was taking the launch down river towards Malali. I sat on a small camp stool immediately behind the wheel, with, on either side of me, narrow lockers which could also be used as seats. It was so dark that I could only see my way by watching the dim line formed by the edge of the jet black forest against the only slightly less black sky. Behind me the crew sat nodding half asleep. The steady throbbing and clicking of the little engine, an old fashioned 'Hot-ball' Seal, had a soporific effect but that I at least wasn't asleep was amply evidenced by the fact that the craft kept following the winding course of the river without crashing into the forest on either side.

Suddenly, out of the corner of my eye, I saw Sykes sitting beside me on the port locker. I did not realise it at the time, but I felt no sense of fear or surprise. When I turned my head to look, the apparition had disappeared. 'Peculiar,' I thought. Resuming my watch into the gloom ahead, I realised that my friend had returned and was again sitting beside me. This time I swung my head sharply to look at him directly, but again he disappeared. 'Stranger and stranger', I thought, still without any sense of trepidation. When for the third time he appeared at my elbow I waited a few seconds realising his presence but, not turning my head this time, I suddenly and swiftly shot out my left hand with the intention of grabbing him. But as my hand was all but broken against the gunwale I realised that the physical cannot grasp the astral. By this time I realised that I really had seen a spirit, ghost or apparition, and had no doubt as to who it was. I also realised that I must be getting sleepy, so, calling the captain, I gave him my place at the wheel and lay down to sleep on the locker, having deliberately refrained from telling the men about my experience.

Next morning, at Malali, I casually asked the captain where Mr Sykes usually sat when travelling in the launch. 'On the port locker, next the wheel', was the reply, the very spot where he had appeared thrice the previous night. Some days after my return to Christianburg I learnt of Sykes' unexpected death in England. As a matter of curiosity I made it my business to find out as nearly as possible the actual date and hour of his death. Allowing for the three and three quarter hour's difference in time his death occurred approximately at the time he had appeared to me in the launch in the upper Demerara River.

Many years later I had a second somewhat similar experience. Round about 1920 I was very friendly with Philbert C. Pierre, the manager of the Aruka Estate Ltd., a thousand acre rubber and coffee plantation on the Aruka River, within which is now situated the Government centre of Mabaruma. Pierre was a man of vision who not only believed in the future prosperity of the North West District but did all in his power to further it. Along the central ridge of hills running through the estate he laid a road and planted rubber trees on the slopes on either side. This road is now incorporated in the public highway running from Morawhanna to Wanaina at which latter place he established a large orchard of his own.

In 1939, some years after Pierre had died, I returned to the district as Acting Commissioner and occupied the palatial residency at Mabaruma where he and I used to ramble and dream of the future of the country. One afternoon I went for a walk along the road about half a mile east of the compound. I was striding along the highway, on each side of which rose Pierre's rubber trees, now hefty timbers, that still struggled amidst the re-growing forest. Thinking of nothing in particular, I suddenly realised that Philbert Pierre was walking beside me, just as he had done previously. And he spoke. He said, 'Yes, Vincent, it's just as I imagined it, only there's too much bush.'

Again, as in the case of Sykes' appearance on the launch, I experienced no sensation of fear or surprise, but at the time took the incident as a matter of course. It was only afterwards when I told Pierre's sister-in-law of my adventures, that the extraordinariness of the adventure occurred to me, that for the second time I had seen a ghost and that on this occasion it had spoken to me. So it is understandable that since then I should have an open mind on the subject of ghosts, jumbies, apparitions and the like.'

As well as his writing, Vincent Roth was heavily involved in practical work following the fire of 1945. By 1951 the rebuilding of the Royal Agricultural and Commercial Society building, together with that of the Museum, was completed and duly opened by the Governor. Vincent was then able to set about the re-equipping of the museum, to which he gave his full attention. Once this was in train he secured a grant from Government to form a zoo in the Botanical Gardens and this he considered one of his greatest achievements. He once remarked, 'If the people cannot get out to see the fauna of their country then we must bring the animals to the people.' In order to devote as much time as possible to the work which he so much enjoyed, he resigned from numerous committees of which he was a member. The zoo was a success thanks to the efforts of Vincent, Stanley Lee, the Superintendent, and his brother George, the Head Keeper. Vincent produced the quarterly journal of the British Guiana Museum and Zoo which was read in over fifty States and Territories. He was also the Hon. Secretary of the Royal Agricultural and Commercial Society and Editor of the Society's journal *Timehri*.

In June 1951, his services to British Guiana were recognised when the press carried the news that His Excellency the Officer Administering the Government had much pleasure in announcing that His Majesty the King had been graciously pleased to bestow the following honours on the occasion of His Birthday :– Officer of the Most Excellent Order of the British Empire, The Hon. Vincent Roth and Mr. Hubert Nathaniel Critchlow.

In December 1956 his elder daughter, Elizabeth, was married to Hugh Tilley, who was on the staff of Barclays Bank, D.C.O.. In 1959, their younger daughter, Audrey, married Michael Bennett, a civil engineer with the Public Works Department, based at Triumph, East Coast Demerara.

In 1958 *The Daily Chronicle* published *Roth's Pepperpot* a book full of information not only about the country but the world at large, followed two years later by *Tales of the Trails*, being extracts from his journals covering the period from 1918 to 1921.

Vincent continued to spend all his time at the Museum and in the early 1960s set about creating panels of parquetry wainscoting in the Hall of Anthropology. Each panel consisted of over two thousand four hundred pieces of wood donated by the Forestry Department from the species brown silverballi, manni, purpleheart and white cedar. The designs depicted such items as canine genitalia in the centre with periwinkle shell at the ends and a Wapisiani circular basket. Most of these panels can still be seen in the National Museum, as it is now known.

In 1964 Vincent and Alma decided to leave Guyana and moved to Barbados. It was while he was here that he started to write his memoirs.

After a year or so in Barbados, they joined their daughter, Audrey, her husband and three children in Hythe, Hampshire.

Vincent's son, Walter, by then a divorceé, helped his father with the move to Barbados. When Vincent and Alma moved to England, Walter decided to remain in Barbados and it is understood he remarried. Vincent's other son, Henry, married Cecilia Jovance, by whom he had several children. They settled in the Rupununi.

Vincent passed away in October 1967 and was buried in Dibden churchyard close to Southampton Water, down which he had sailed with his father to the then British Guiana almost exactly sixty years before.

INDEX